DATE DUE

~~DE 1 8 98~~		
~~DE 18 98~~		

October Cities

October Cities

The Redevelopment of Urban Literature

Carlo Rotella

University of California Press

Berkeley / Los Angeles / London

University of California Press
Berkeley and Los Angeles, California

University of California Press, Ltd.
London, England

© 1998 by
The Regents of the University of California

Library of Congress Cataloging-in-Publication Data

Rotella, Carlo, 1964–
    October cities : the redevelopment of urban
    literature / Carlo Rotella
        p.   cm.
    Includes bibliographic references (p.   ) and index
    ISBN 0–520-20763-7 (cloth : alk. paper).
    ISBN 0–520-21144-8 (pbk. : alk. paper)
      1. American literature—20th century—History
and criticism.   2. City and town life in literature.
3. Cities and towns in literature.   I. Title.
PS228.C54R68   1998
    810.9'321732—dc21   97–27980
                                                  CIP

Printed in the United States of America
9 8 7 6   5 4 3 2 1

Cover photo of Nelson Algren © 1949 by Art Shay,
"Snapshots of Nelson Algren"

The paper used in this publication meets the minimum
requirements of American National Standards for
Information Sciences—Permanence of Paper for
Printed Library Materials, ANSI Z39.48-1984.

0

For my parents

Contents

Illustrations

Acknowledgments

This book was first written as a dissertation, which was blessed with exemplary advisers. Robert Stepto helped me find my way to my subject, encouraged me to pursue it far afield (and back home to Chicago), and pushed me to define a job of work and get it done. Michael Denning, from whom I learned a great deal about how to do the job, did me the honor of disagreeing cheerfully with almost everything I wrote or said between 1988 and 1994. In his freestyle written commentaries and on long haranguing walks to New Haven's industrial waterfront, Jim Fisher helped me see what was moving beneath the surface of my arguments. The three of them have been enthusiastic co-conspirators, as well as teachers by example.

Tom Sugrue, Eric Lott, and Richard Slotkin read the manuscript in its entirety, were generous with their insights and their encouragement, and offered valuable suggestions for revision. Tom Sugrue also helped me explore Philadelphia, and I owe him special thanks for facilitating my conversion to the subtlest of great cities. For the University of California Press, William Murphy, Naomi Schneider, David Severtson, and especially Juliane Brand were gracious and astute editors.

Among many more than I can mention here, Jean-Christophe Agnew, Robert Beauregard, Carla Cappetti, William Cronon, Philip Deloria, Chris Erikson, Benjamin Filene, Dolores Hayden, Carol Johnson, Brian Light, Suzanne Smith, David Stowe, Glenn Wallach, and students in courses I taught on urbanism at Yale University, Wesleyan University, and Lafayette College shared their wisdom, directed me to useful sources, or otherwise changed the way I thought about this project. David Bradley, Claude Brown, Denise Scott

Brown, Stuart Dybek, and Diane McKinney-Whetstone were especially generous with their time and ideas in interviews. Steve Hastalis of the Chicago
Transit Authority, Kimberly Everett of the Philadelphia Housing Authority, and
David Baldinger and David Knapton of Philadelphia's City Planning office
helped me find unpublished materials and answered my questions. The good
people at Yale University's libraries and Lafayette College's Skillman Library,
especially Janemarie Berry and Kandyce Fisher at the latter, provided invalu-
able help in gathering published sources. The Cartographic Laboratory at the
University of Wisconsin, under the direction of Onno Brouwer, prepared the
maps; a research grant from Lafayette College paid for the maps and some of
the other illustrations.

My parents, Salvatore and Pilar, and my brothers, Sebastian and Sal Jr., have
contributed readings of drafts, inspiration, incitement, and useful skepticism
regarding my opinions. This project probably took germinal form during conversations around the kitchen table on the South Side of Chicago long before I
left home. Writing in New Haven, Easton, and Cambridge, I have had that mar-
ble-topped table in mind, and their voices and faces around it, even though the
table itself has been moved to New York and the family has moved all over the
place.

Tina Klein has given freely of her clarity-inducing criticism, discussed long-
forgotten scenes from near-extinct novels at odd hours and in a curious assort-
ment of places, and tempered patience with pointed references to Ben Franklin's work habits. In the fitful internal monologue that the routines of research
and writing tend to encourage, I often find myself paraphrasing Boxer the cart-
horse in *Animal Farm*: Tina is always right; I will work harder.

Introduction: The City of Feeling and the City of Fact

Lucy carried in her mind a very individual map of
Chicago: a blur of smoke and wind and noise, with
flashes of blue water, and certain clear outlines rising
from the confusion. . . . This city of feeling rose out
of the city of fact like a definite composition,—
beautiful because the rest was blotted out.

Willa Cather, *Lucy Gayheart*

"There's a steam hammer half a mile from where I live," Nelson Algren wrote
to fellow Chicago novelist Richard Wright in 1941, "which pounds steel rivets
all night, putting buttons on the subway. Every so often it makes a sound as
though ripping up all the steel it's been sewing down, and all the neighborhood
dogs howl for half an hour after, as if something had torn inside them."[1]
Recently established in a cheap apartment on Evergreen Street in Chicago's
Polish Triangle, Algren ate stew every night from a never-emptied and never-
cleaned pot, reread his favorite Russian novels, and wrote. He kept his eyes and
ears open for material, visiting police lineups and brothels, mixing with hoods
and gamblers, hanging out at the fights. Even when he was home, working in
his austere apartment, dogs and steam hammers in the night reminded him that
the processes of exchanging old urban orders for new proceeded with mechanical, brutal regularity.

Claude Brown was seeing off some friends at a Trailways bus terminal in
Washington, D.C., when he spotted a paperback copy of Wright's *Eight Men*.
Brown was surprised to find a book by Wright, his literary idol, that he had not
read. He bought it, went home, and read it straight through. Late that night, he
put a sheet of clean paper in the typewriter and started work on his Harlem
memoir, *Manchild in the Promised Land*. It was the early 1960s, people were

1

speaking of an incipient urban crisis centered on the black inner city, and a large audience was eager to read what a reformed but not overreformed black delinquent had to say about Harlem. Brown had a compelling story to tell about the aftermath of the great migration of Southern blacks to the urban North, years in the street life had endowed him with a store of good material, and he had a big advance for the book from Macmillan, but he had not been able to write anything since signing the contract six months before. Reading Wright got him started.

Pete Dexter had been working on a novel, his first, when he was not writing columns for the *Philadelphia Daily News* and *Esquire*, drinking in bars, or working out at a boxing gym. Perhaps that full schedule kept him from dedicating himself to the novel, but in 1981 some strong misreaders who had taken issue with one of his newspaper columns administered a terrific beating to him outside a bar in Devil's Pocket, a neighborhood in South Philadelphia. His broken bones and mangled scalp healed, but blows to the head with baseball bats had permanently deprived him of the pleasures of drink. Now that alcohol tasted like battery acid to him, he had another thirty hours or so per week to devote to writing. He finished the book, called it *God's Pocket*, and settled into a career as a novelist.

Diane McKinney-Whetstone had a full schedule, too, and a career as a public affairs officer for a government agency, but the fiction writing she had done in workshops at the University of Pennsylvania and with the Rittenhouse Writers Group had convinced her to try a novel. She had in mind a story of "contemporary relationships" in the 1990s, perhaps something on the order of Terry McMillan's *Waiting to Exhale*, but instead she found herself writing a novel about family, community, and redevelopment set in black South Philadelphia in the 1950s. Evocative period details—Billie Holiday's singing, Murray's hair pomade, the arrival of Jackie Robinson in town with the Dodgers —and her parents' stories of the days before the urban crisis drew her back to the world of her childhood. The family had left South Philadelphia in the 1950s, persuaded to get out by news that the city planned to build a highway through the area, but the old neighborhood persisted in their memories and in her writing.

These writers, and others I will discuss in the following pages, were city people and wrote books about city life. Each of them was engaged with the social world in which he or she was situated, and the material conditions of city life in a particular time and place—becoming the "material" from which a writer made literature—exerted shaping pressures on their work. Each writer was also a reader engaged with the world of words on the page, and their writing also traces a lineage to other writers' and readers' notions of how to write about cities, how to think about cities, what matters about cities.

Responding to the material and textual worlds in which they moved, these writers have explored the literary possibilities afforded by American urbanism since 1945. Together they tell a composite story of the postwar transformation of American cities: the breakup and contraction of industrial urbanism, the emergence and maturing of postindustrial urbanism, and all the shocks and opportunities afforded by those vast movements of people, capital, and ideas. Reading these authors within the resonant urban and literary history of the 1940s, 1950s, 1960s, and after, we can make out the contours of change happening in both material cities and traditions of writing about them: the balance of persistence and succession that characterizes the layering of urban orders, the redevelopment of real and imagined terrains, the ways in which transformation becomes crisis and vice versa.

This is a book about the relationship of urban literature to the cities it draws upon for inspiration. It is about the work of some writers who, like other people in the cities they lived in and wrote about, practiced their trade using the materials at hand. Like political operatives, developers, journalists, academics, and neighbors and strangers in conversation, literary writers are in the business of imagining cities. They build textual places traversed by the minds of their readers. These "cities of feeling" (to use Cather's phrase), which are not imagined from scratch, tend to descend from two sources. One is other texts, since writers read one another and swim in the greater sea of culture, assemble repertoires and influences, repeat, and revise. The other source is "cities of fact," material places assembled from brick and steel and stone, inhabited by people of flesh and blood—places where, however sophisticated we might become about undermining the solidity of constructed terms like "real" and "actual" and "fact," it is unwise to play in traffic. ("Traffic" may be nothing more than a constructed set of ideas about the circulation of people and goods, a fact invented by social agreement, but there is something powerfully unconstructed about being flattened by a speeding car.) Cities of feeling, then, are shaped by the flow of language, images, and ideas; cities of fact by the flow of capital, materials, and people. And each, of course, is shaped by the other. On the one hand, cities of fact are everywhere shaped by acts of imagination: redevelopment plans, speeches, newspaper stories, conversations, movies, music, novels, and poems create cities of feeling that help guide people in their encounters with the city of fact. These texts affect material life. On the other hand, and here is where this book finds it principal subject, cities of feeling emulate and manipulate the models offered not only by other texts but also by the overwhelming material presence of cities of fact.

In the decades after World War II, dramatically transformed American cities of fact presented a new set of formal and social problems to the people who considered it their business to write about urbanism. In the 1950s and 1960s, especially, these urban intellectuals set out in various ways, and often at cross purposes, to explore the literary possibilities and social consequences of a world that was changing under their feet and over their heads in exciting, confusing ways. High-rise public housing projects casting long shadows over bungalows, row houses, or walk-up tenements; expressways cut through the fabric of the prewar city's neighborhoods; office and apartment towers clustered in densely redeveloped downtowns; the industrial infrastructure of loft buildings, workers' housing, rail and port facilities falling into "blighted" ruin—these were the most obvious physical signs of a transformed urbanism in the inner city. They were elements of a great sea change: the passing of the nineteenth-century industrial city of downtown and neighborhoods, and the visible, speedy emergence of the late twentieth-century, postindustrial metropolis of suburbs and inner city.[2] That change, almost invisible to many at midcentury, would develop into a full-blown "urban crisis" by the mid-1960s.

We can trace the imprints and meanings of a vast, general process like postindustrial transformation in the forms of particular neighborhoods and particular texts. I will trace those imprints in bodies of writing that converge on three neighborhoods: Chicago's Polish Triangle, around Milwaukee Avenue and Division Street; Philadelphia's South Street, where Center City meets the old neighborhoods of South Philly; and New York's Harlem, a so-called capital of black America. The written representation of these neighborhoods and cities follows the contours of postindustrial transformation: the midcentury culmination and exhaustion of prewar traditions, like Chicago realism, fitted to representing the industrial city, and the refitting of those traditions to tell the story of the industrial city's decline (the subject of part 1); the development of representational habits to engage with the emergence of a postindustrial social landscape (exemplified in part 2 by a series of Philadelphia novels); the ascendance of new orders of inner-city writing, exemplified by the work of Harlem writers in the 1960s, as postindustrial transformation developed into an urban crisis (the subject of part 3).

This is a story of persistence as much as it is of succession. In the city of fact, elements of the industrial city can still be discerned, underlying and poking through the fabric of the postindustrial landscape. Factory loft buildings have been converted to new uses or left to decay, immigrant-ethnic urban villages have been incompletely transformed by ghettoization or gentrification, somewhere near a new waterfront esplanade one can usually find the old docks. In the city of feeling, the reader finds that, despite the advent of new genres of writing and new cohorts of urban intellectuals, there are recurring character types (e.g., violent young men, writers in crisis), narrative strategies (family sagas, stories of decline), and thematic concerns (racial conflict, the pervasive threat posed by urban transformation to a familiar way of life) that join the postindustrial literature to the industrial. This study, then, tells a story of literary change over time driven by a mix of persistences and transformations discernible in both the city of fact and the city of feeling.

American urbanism entered into a time of particularly massive transformation in the postwar period. If deindustrialization and suburbanization had been working subtle changes on American cities since at least 1920, those changes had been masked by the effects of the Great Depression and World War II. The dislocations of the war followed by public and private investment in redevelopment and suburbanization made for a dramatic wave of urban change in the postwar period, characterized above all by movements of population and capital. The great folk migrations to midcentury America's two promised lands interlocked to initiate a massive demographic shift: as black and white Southerners came north to settle in the inner cities, and black Americans became a predominantly urban people, waves of white city dwellers (and some middle-class blacks) moved outward from those inner cities to the growing suburban periphery. At the same time, industrial jobs and capital of all kinds moved to the suburbs and the Sunbelt (and, in some cases, to other countries), departing the old Northeastern and Midwestern manufacturing cities that were still the leading models of American urbanism. Both public and private investment in the inner city began to shift toward service industries rather than manufacturing, and wealth and resources reconcentrated in the redeveloped downtown cores, where developers produced masses of steel-and-glass skyscrapers in the matrix of ramifying highway systems built by the state.[3]

These movements, and the efforts of governments and private interests (large and small) to manage and respond to them, shaped a transformed social landscape—a term embracing the physical order of a city and the social, economic, political, and cultural orders housed in it. The industrial city's distinctive arrangements of space and ways of life began to break up and recede beneath the surface of new orders: "white-ethnic" enclaves (the landscape mapped in part 1) persisting from the industrial city's neighborhood order, which had been dominated by European immigrants and their descendants; high-rise developments, renovated districts, and a massive downtown core where the growing service-professional classes lived and worked (part 2); high-rise projects and other urban renewal schemes sited to lock the black "second ghetto" into place even as it grew beyond its traditional limits (part 3). This process proceeded by fits and starts, at some times and in some places impressively visible and in others all but imperceptible, and the industrial and postindustrial social landscapes overlapped significantly—as they do to this day, producing a significant proportion of our urban culture out of the overlap. However, if in the late 1940s a perceptive observer might see the emergent order showing here and there in the urban fabric, by the mid-1960s many observers had come to regard survivals of prewar urbanism as persistent atavisms.

Efforts to understand and address the emergence of the postwar inner city's social landscape gave rise in the 1950s and 1960s to a spreading, deepening conviction that America's cities were in crisis. The crisis mentality proceeded not just from the actual changes in the city of fact but also from a sense that existing habits of thinking about cities—embodied in the generic cities of feeling that circulated most widely in the culture—were no longer adequate to describe the transformed metropolis. The last great wave of national attention to the city as a matter of pressing social concern in its own right had subsided in the 1920s. The national, rather than specifically urban, crises of depression and war had dominated discussions of even such traditionally urban subjects as poverty and violence. Consideration of the city in its own right, a conversation that had thrived in the Progressive Era, when the problems of ethnic immigration and acculturation were plotted on the industrial city's landscape, was pushed into the margins of national discourse until after the war. The complementary postwar waves of ghettoization and suburbanization had deep roots extending into the nineteenth century, but the postwar reassessment of the American scene tended to regard the emergence of the postindustrial metropolis as a relatively sudden—even a violently sudden—phenomenon. Since the war, it seemed, the American city had been made over in ways that inspired description and demanded explanation.

If the notion of urban crisis addressed the whole social landscape as it embraced a complex of issues—racial and ethnic succession, deindustrialization, criminal violence and social disorder, the problem of youth in the city, urban planning and redevelopment, competition with the suburbs, slum clearance, poverty, housing, public education—the crisis eventually achieved mature form as it coalesced around the problem of the black ghetto. The extended postwar transformation of cities and of thinking about cities was conventionally collapsed (and continues to be so in popular and scholarly memory) into the phase that marked its climax, when the postwar second ghetto moved to cultural center stage during the violent social upheavals of the mid- and late 1960s known as "*the* urban crisis." Like the word "ghetto" itself and like most of the subjects listed above, racial and ethnic difference had a long history in American thinking and writing about the city: cities of feeling have served as stages on which a great variety of social and cultural issues can be dramatized. However, the scale and pace of postwar change in the social landscape seemed to demand new ways of thinking and writing about even the most traditional city material.

I want to extend the concept of urban crisis in two ways: in time, to cover a period stretching from the late 1940s through the 1960s; and as a term describing the problem of creating the city of feeling as much as it describes events in cities of fact. What seemed to be an apocalyptic crisis in the 1960s, with rioting in the streets as the conventional sign of urban order in collapse, looks in retrospect to be the painful coming to maturity of postindustrial urbanism as we still know it. That process took place as much in the urban imaginations of Americans as it did in the streets of American cities. The term "urban crisis" describes events and processes that added up to a social emergency, but the term also describes an urgent need to understand and respond to those transformations that led to widespread revision of cultural conventions. That cultural impulse to tear down and rebuild the city of feeling guided novelists as well as politicians, journalists as well as homeowners, policy intellectuals as well as the young black men who commanded so much of their attention. The constantly shifting and increasingly vehement national conversation about cities in the 1950s and 1960s called into question every form of urban order—not only the political, social, or architectural but also the representational. As urban intellectuals struggled to recognize and engage with the emergent postindustrial city, they engaged as well with the problem of representing it.

Urban intellectuals are experts, professionals, and artists of all kinds whose cultural work it is to produce cities of feeling that circulate through the channels of culture. As it did to neighborhoods in the path of urban renewal and expressway projects, the emergence of the postindustrial metropolis threw the community of urban intellectuals into disarray. As the new social landscape took recognizable form, the standard representational habits and divisions of intellectual labor shaped to the task of representing the industrial city increasingly seemed inadequate to represent the transformed metropolis— especially its suddenly unfamiliar inner city. Urban intellectuals confronted new and different opportunities to map the city and pursue the imaginative possibilities it presented. I will discuss in depth the work of a dozen or so mostly literary writers—Nelson Algren, Gwendolyn Brooks, Mike Royko, Stuart Dybek (the Chicago writers); Jack Dunphy, William Gardner Smith, David Bradley, Pete Dexter, Diane McKinney-Whetstone (Philadelphia); Warren Miller and Claude Brown (New York)—but I will also assemble a large supporting cast of urban intellectuals, a various group that includes the critically revered novelist Ralph Ellison and the purveyors of a paperback delinquent literature usually dismissed as junk fiction; the editors of *Newsweek* and the *New York Herald-Tribune;* the archetypal machine politician Richard J. Daley and the leftist intellectuals grouped around the journal *Dissent;* city planners like Philadelphia's Edmund Bacon and critics of city planning like Jane Jacobs. The supporting cast includes, as well, a number of journalists—prominent among them A. J. Liebling, Harrison Salisbury, and Tom Wolfe—and social scientists: Robert

Park and his associates of the Chicago School, who in the early twentieth century dominated sociological study of the modern city; Albert Cohen, Lloyd Ohlin, Richard Cloward, and other students of juvenile delinquency; Daniel Patrick Moynihan, Harlem social psychologist Kenneth Clark, and other students of the second ghetto. Together these urban intellectuals and many more like them responded to the social and formal problems presented to them by urbanism in transition.

Placed end to end and intertwined as they are in this study, the texts produced by these urban intellectuals offer a composite story that renders postindustrial transformation as a kind of urban mythos. The breakup of the industrial neighborhood order, the transfer of "black America" to the inner city and its development there, the promises and social costs of efforts to reconfigure the inner city for a postindustrial era, the coming of urban crisis and its apocalyptic temperament—these are the historical themes of urban literature in the 1950s and 1960s (and, of course, after), and these texts explore them in explicit and implicit ways that command our critical attention. The texts—and especially the literary works—enter into conversation with the postwar transformation of the city to the extent that they make imaginative use of the period's urban themes and problems, develop coherent understandings of urban orders or pull apart those understandings, presciently anticipate events and ideas, or turn a selectively blind eye to the material they engage with.

Set in specific neighborhoods in specific cities, representing the urban dramas of the day, even the most narrowly "literary" works I analyze were received at the time as *socially* weighty protests or warnings. Reviews of these books typically explored the fit between social reality and the literary imagination: "I hope the Mayor and the Governor read this book," concluded one enthusiastically shocked review of Warren Miller's j.d. crime saga *The Cool World*, a novel that its author expressly intended as "an *Uncle Tom's Cabin*" that would generate in its readers the political will required to redress the postwar inner city's defining problems.[4] However, even though almost all the literary writing I analyze was widely read at the time of publication, there is not much point in arguing that urban literature itself played a leading role in shaping the thinking of many Americans, let alone mayors and governors, about cities. Rather, the value of a historical reading of these texts lies in the tendency of literature— especially the kind of socially observant, engaged literature treated here—to gather together, dramatize, and exploit aesthetically the materials made available by a historical moment. The novels and Brown's novelistic autobiography offer sustained considerations, codifications, and imaginative extrapolations of important and city-shaping ways of thinking we encounter all over the culture, from newspaper readers' letters to the editor to the assumptions behind governance. Literary works also show us how the language, landscape, and habits of mind made available by the postwar inner city provided materials that writers put to use in crafting works of art.

Although my first duty in this book is to account for the city of feeling, it is important to remember that imaginative work done by all manner of players on the urban stage—developers, mayors, migrants to and from the inner cities, even literary artists—exerts a shaping influence on the city of fact. A housing project or an expressway makes concrete certain ways of understanding the city; they are moraines left by the passage through the cityscape of narratives and ideas. Like a mayor giving a speech or a developer preparing a brochure, neighbors stopping in the hallway to talk about a "wave" of violent street crime in the news, their "declining" neighborhood, high property taxes, and the virtues of suburban life are mapping a city of feeling in a way that may soon initiate an incremental change in the tax base and demography of the city of fact. There are studies of urban form, culture, and governance that draw arrows of causation from the city of feeling to the city of fact—and many more such studies yet to be done, especially of the postwar period.[5]

The present study, however, draws those arrows the other way, although they take the fantastically meandering paths of symbolic and artistic practice, never running straight from the material city to a mirrorlike textual city. Reading works of imagination in relation to material cities and other textual cities helps to account for precisely those formal qualities that make interesting or difficult literary artifacts. The extremeness of language and sense of ultimacy pervading the El-enclosed world of Algren's *The Man with the Golden Arm;* the repetition throughout the South Street novels of family narratives, expressive landscapes, and passages in which characters are borne against their will through the landscape of South Philadelphia; the progressively divided cityscapes and the progressively contrived dialect narrations of Warren Miller's *The Cool World* and *The Siege of Harlem;* the wandering narrative, analytical diffuseness, and spatial precision of Claude Brown's *Manchild in the Promised Land*—all these qualities make more sense when read against the formal problems offered to authors by their material and when read with an eye to each author's engagement with traditions of thinking and writing about the city.

In deciding what language to use, what stories to tell, what landscapes to imagine, what underlying structures to lay bare, the texts treated here respond to the problem of how to write about cities. In telling stories about the emergence of new urbanisms, about the formation of new kinds of urban intellectuals fitted to represent the postwar city, the texts also respond explicitly to the problem of who writes about cities. My account of the emergence of a postindustrial urban literature therefore pursues a second, subsidiary track of argument in which the literature plots the formation of urban intellectuals variously equipped or unequipped to write it. We can read in the narrative and spatial plots of the cities in these texts, and in the language with which those plots are executed, a series of meditations on the changing accreditation and authority of those whose cultural work it was to create cities of feeling.

Writer-characters move through the literature, speaking for different genres of urban intellectuals as they work out their relation to the city they live in and the task of writing about it. *Golden Arm*'s crazed mythographer of decline, Sophie Majcinek, who collects evidence of coming apocalypse in a scrapbook, finds herself trapped in the collapse of the urban village, just as Nelson Algren understood himself to be the last of the old-style Chicago realists trapped in the collapse of the industrial city's literary order. Formative, frustrated, and desperate writers pervade the literature of South Street, struggling violently to determine what and how to write about the place as the old neighborhoods give way to downtown redevelopment and the postindustrial neighborhood order. Warren Miller's and Claude Brown's narrating black protagonists confront new barriers around the ghetto, erected by the canonical logic of urban crisis, that condition the movement of what were read as white (Miller's) and black (Brown's) authorial personas through the city of feeling in crisis.

Especially when we are examining works of fiction for signs of their relationship to historical period and place, it is important to recognize that the author moves through the pages of his or her writing without being a character in the fictional world imagined by the text (the diegesis). Within the text, but not within the diegesis, the *author's* presence is tangible as a persona that creates and reveals the diegetic world. Throughout the urban literature I will examine, one finds that *characters* are writing, narrating, producing representations of the city around them in the text, interpreting that world, and otherwise behaving in ways that parallel the work of urban intellectuals like the author. In these cases, I am encouraged by the parallel between author's and characters' work to treat the diegetic language and action of the characters as encoding the author's nondiegetic presence or as otherwise addressing problems of the intellectual's relation to the city faced by the author. Once that parallel is established, we can look for meaningful connections of the text to time and place by reading the author's presence in a text against that of his or her characters, against his or her historical presence in a city of fact, and against his or her encounter with other intellectuals in reviews and other texts.

An awareness of authorial persona in the text, then, helps us to trace the terms and consequences of urban transformation for the community of urban intellectuals, who were galvanized into a variety of responses by urban transformation in the postwar period. One important facet of this collective response was a struggle, building toward a climax in the mid-1960s as the urban crisis gathered momentum, to determine who was equipped to write about the postindustrial city and how to judge their work. In reviews, criticism, and the routine of imitation and revision that makes up their system of exchanges, urban intellectuals evaluate one another's writing, treating it as credentials for the cultural work of representing urbanism. Think of them as a group that inhabits and maps a composite city of feeling, and then one can seen them struggling to decide whose maps are authoritative, who gets to live in a particular literary neighborhood, who can pass through the generic and critical gates that separate those neighborhoods from one another. The stakes in these exercises get higher in times of urban crisis, such as that of the 1960s, when a significant role in the urban conversation can lead to professional and financial rewards, positions of advantage in the world of intellectual exchange and policy making, and opportunities to help determine the nation's social and cultural arrangements. One can see those rising stakes, and the struggles they inspired, not only in reviews and cultural manifestos of the 1950s and 1960s but also in the ways that authors inhabit their novels and poems of the period. In these texts, one can see signs of artistic inspiration or despair; struggles with other intellectuals to determine their responsibilities and standards for good, useful, or authoritative writing; and the constant pressure of new possibilities raised by the emergence of the postindustrial city. In the literature, the signs—both coded and explicit—of writers in crisis express the sense, widely felt in the two decades after World War II, that urban intellectuals needed to re-equip themselves to do the work of rewriting the transformed American city.

The writers I will analyze, both those who wrote in the period 1945–65 and those who provide epilogues to it, are players in the extended postwar urban crisis. They all made their mark to some degree on the literary world, earning the urgent, confused, knowing reviews that inner-city "problem" writing tends to get. Some of them enjoyed relatively great success. Nelson Algren appeared at or near the top of almost every midcentury list of contemporary realists or latter-day naturalists, and various critics proposed David Bradley, Pete Dexter, Warren Miller, and Claude Brown as successors to Algren in that distinction; there are winners of National Book Awards (Algren, Dexter), Pulitzer Prizes (Gwendolyn Brooks, Mike Royko), and many other honors among my cast of writers, attesting to the enduring place of urban literature in the canons of twentieth-century writing. Some of the writers I discuss also played extraliterary roles: for example, Claude Brown's wildly successful ghetto autobiography attracted a wealth of excited commentary, his opinions were much in demand in the aftermath of urban riots in the summer of 1965, and he was urged to run for public office and invited to speak on ghetto life to a subcommittee of the United States Senate. In the cases of older texts, traces remain of the original marks they made: for example, Algren's *The Man with the Golden Arm* and Brown's *Manchild in the Promised Land* are in print, have attracted the attention of critics over the years, and have influenced several generations of urban intellectuals—from white-ethnic newspaper icon Mike Royko to the black writers and directors who helped guide Hollywood into the inner city in the

1980s and 1990s. Some of the other writers and texts, though, have disappeared with barely a ripple: three of the South Street novels and both of Warren Miller's Harlem novels have long been out of print. They are "dated," which means that these books are freighted with period associations, and part of my objective is to show how these books illuminate the moments in which they first appeared and were widely read. Together, these variously persistent and almost-forgotten writers and their prose contribute pieces to a story greater than the sum of its parts, and the texts have been chosen as much for the intertextualities binding them together as for their individual merits.

What the writers I will discuss have in common is participation in a tradition of writing about the city that developed along with the industrial city of the nineteenth century and took some strange and satisfying forms in engaging with the emergence of the late twentieth-century metropolis. If the canonical American and European realists and naturalists of the late nineteenth century and early twentieth century initiated an important literary engagement with the modern industrial city, the writers treated in this study engaged with the gradual eclipse of that city and the coalescence of its successor. Zola's characters watching the advance of Baron Haussmann's boulevards in industrial Paris rhyme with David Bradley's characters watching the advance of Edmund Bacon's urban renewal as the old buildings come down and the high rises go up around South Street in postindustrial Philadelphia: in a literary sense, they live in the same neighborhood. Both are watching the machinery of urban process exchanging old orders for new. If a kind of naturalist decline seems to be a dominant story line in the postwar urban literature discussed here, it may be because those who work in the broad tradition of Zola, looking to the city of fact around them as inspiration for the work of mapping the city of feeling, find it easier to see and describe the order that exists and erodes than to recognize the next phase of order as it emerges piecemeal.

I concentrate most of this study's analytical energies on the years between 1949 and 1965, a so-far nameless period between the war's end and general acceptance of the advent of urban crisis, in which the overlap of old and new urban orders threw urban literature into a period of "redevelopment" to match that occurring in the cities themselves. Nelson Algren's epic of the industrial neighborhood order's decline, *The Man with the Golden Arm*, was published in 1949; also in 1949, federal legislation made available important funding streams that would enable urban renewal and redevelopment projects that reshaped the inner city for a postindustrial future. Claude Brown's ground-breaking account of life in the postwar ghetto, *Manchild in the Promised Land*, was published in 1965 (as were Kenneth Clark's *Dark Ghetto* and *The Autobiography of Malcolm X*); by 1965, also, the first rounds of ghetto riots and a growing body of analysis had begun to convince a variety of observers that urban renewal and redevelopment on the model enabled by the 1949 legislation were not going to solve the postwar city's problems.

In a sense, the postwar crisis of representation began to end in the 1960s when enough people, urban intellectuals leading and guiding them, began to agree on some coherence-building oversimplifications: that there was an urban crisis that threatened the destruction of previously accepted urban orders; that the crisis conditions derived from the growth and continuing immiseration of black ghettos and the suburbanization of the white middle classes and capital; that the crisis was taking place in a social landscape violently divided into expanding black ghettos, white enclaves, and monumental downtowns; and, finally, that this was the way things were going to be from now on, the War on Poverty notwithstanding. What comes before and after, a span represented in this study by satellite texts ranging from Theodore Dreiser's *Sister Carrie* (1900) to Sapphire's *Push* (1996), is prologue and epilogue to the period of transition and confusion from the late 1940s through the mid-1960s, in which urban intellectuals redeveloped the city of feeling.

The analogy between the rewriting of cities of feeling and the redevelopment of cities of fact rests on a definition of "redevelopment" that involves both reconfiguring a city and exploiting the opportunities presented by that process. Like developers and speculators in the city of fact, urban intellectuals stake out tracts in the city of feeling and build something—new representations—on them. Sometimes they are repeating, incorporating, or adding to what is already there (an established genre, narrative strategy, character type, vocabulary), but they also tear down existing structures by revising, criticizing, or ignoring (in effect, building right over) them. "Building, breaking, rebuilding," as Carl Sandburg once described the makers of Chicago, urban intellectuals remake and revalue the landscape of our collective city of feeling. The "profit" in that process, for literary intellectuals anyway, is measured by the range and depth of meanings that we find in their work, by the kinds of cultural authority we respect or demand, by the kinds of representations that acquire cultural and social substance.

The authors I discuss, professional artists doing a job of work, were not concerned with producing a unified body of literature so scholars could write about it. They were trying to construct good novels they could sell to publishers and readers. As I build my interpretive readings and my understanding of period and place on their writing, I too am engaged in an act of redevelopment. In the pages that follow, I make my argument on the ground of their works, combining and refitting the parts they provide in order to construct a greater whole—a composite story at once familiar and (I hope) enlighteningly strange. If at times I have bulldozed a nuance or built up a subsidiary motif in a text in order to make the parts fit into the whole, I have also sought to respect—and often to recover from obscurity—the relation of each text to the world in which it was made. I have also sought to treat the authors as people (not just vehicles of period ideologies) caught up in the close-grained textures of particular times, places, and professional situations.

"The city," that abstract generalization, is made up of many cities and by many representational strategies. The writing of cities is, to paraphrase a piece of mantric political wisdom, in that sense always local. It is painful but necessary in analyzing the writing of cities to rule out most of the good stuff—towering piles of unjustly underread texts as well as many of the most frequently read ones, long lists of cities and neighborhoods with powerful stories to offer—so that one can condense the chaotically expansive subject at hand enough to say something both coherent and original about it. A series of choices, worth noting briefly, led to the three relatively local case studies that follow, which aim not only to do justice to the texts and neighborhoods I have included but also to provide arguments that can extend to other texts and places that might have been included but were not. (I hope the analyses that follow do suggest additional texts and cities to the reader and that the reader extends my arguments to them.)

First, I have confined myself to the literature of large Rust Belt inner cities, although the postwar period offers vast complementary literatures dealing with the suburbs, the Sunbelt, and smaller cities. I have chosen to follow the developing logic of urban crisis into the inner cities, where the palimpsest of the older city could be discerned in and among the emerging orders and where the crisis took most urgent and represented form. I have concentrated on the manufacturing cities of the Midwest and Northeast because these were still in the postwar period the leading models of American urbanism and thus the leading templates for the city of feeling, even though Los Angeles, Houston, Miami, and other Sunbelt cities were then developing to the point of challenging that primacy.[6] I have, for similar reasons, chosen neighborhoods in large literary capitals rather than in small cities. The neighborhoods I discuss in Chicago, Philadelphia, and New York (as opposed to neighborhoods in, say, Youngstown, Bethlehem, and Fall River with equally powerful and instructive stories to offer) attracted large and various bodies of writing that got published and nationally circulated.

Second, I have intentionally followed conventional habits of representation and the canonical logic of urban crisis in rendering one of my principal plot lines in black and white, brutally simplifying the historical moment's demographic and cultural complexity. Even if one accepts the utility of "black" and "white" as artificial constructs that sort enormously varied groups of people into social categories, by the mid-1960s observers could see (if they wished to) that the so-called third-wave migrations of Hispanic and Asian people to the cities would soon challenge the efficacy of "black" and "white" in organizing an understanding of American urbanism's ethnic dimensions. This study examines the black-and-white palette that urban literature developed to represent the world made by previous waves of migration from Europe and the American South, but one must recognize that palette's declining utility in figuring and explaining the post-1965 urban world. That said, it remains true that representations of the inner city in the 1950s and especially in the 1960s tended to depict a crisis in black and white, one of the many simplifying condensations practiced by those who struggled to make sense of a prodigiously involved, hard-to-figure transformation. The characters who inhabit the books I will examine, and the writers who created those characters, are almost without exception descended from the two most important sets of migrants to the inner city from the late nineteenth century through the mid-twentieth: Southern blacks and the Irish, Italian, Eastern European, Jewish, and other once-"new" European immigrants whose latter-day descendants are now often lumped together as "white ethnics." The engagement of blacks and white ethnics, a running complex of transactions invested with the resonances of both marriage and war carried by the word "engagement," has been of fundamental and only intermittently acknowledged importance in shaping American urbanism and literature.[7]

Third, it bears mentioning that the literature examined in this study is dominated by men, and at times it can be buffoonishly male. There are important female characters at work in the cities of feeling I have chosen to study, but, more often than not, violent young men and family patriarchs in various stages of ascent and decline are those who do the work of moving through the cityscape, standing for urban peoples and orders, and dramatizing the situations of urban intellectuals. Even more than today, if possible, American culture in the 1950s and 1960s was obsessed with the conjunction of violent men and cities, a conjunction codified in the 1930s and 1940s by the Chicago neighborhood novel (think of protagonists Studs Lonigan, Bigger Thomas, Bruno Bicek) and Chicago sociology (the jackroller, the gang member) and given further expression in the 1950s and 1960s through the stock figures of the juvenile delinquent, mugger, predatory drug addict, rioter, revolutionary, and backlash neighborhood racist. Especially before 1965 and the establishment front and center of the "female-headed household" as part of the city of feeling's generic population, the kinds of books received by the overwhelmingly male gatekeepers of urban literature as urgent protests and warnings from the inner city tended to be about men and were usually written by men.

Finally, I have followed one of the literature's principal formal strategies in choosing a set of spatial metaphors—mapping, landscape, movement through

space—to describe the cultural work of urban intellectuals. Because the texts
and the characters in them tend to read the city's biography in its physical
forms, I devote important attention to reading the content and argument condensed in the bits and pieces of landscape presented by postwar cities of feeling: the skyline of massed office towers, the high-rise housing project set in an
artificial moonscape, the aging enclave of modest brick buildings bounded by
old railroad tracks and new expressways. These spatial bits and pieces resonate
with those found in cities of fact *and* in other cities of feeling. Therefore, to
trace the provenance of the bits and pieces of landscape in the text, and elucidate the meanings they make available, is to trace the two principal sources of
influence shaping change over time in urban literature: the shifting models provided by material cities and the generic examples provided by textual cities. I
will, then, use particular swatches of terrain—the Division Street El structure,
the rowhouse blocks of South Philadelphia, the intersection of 125th Street and
7th Avenue in Harlem—to map the generic urban landscapes through which
Americans and their fictional avatars have for almost half a century imagined
themselves to move.

Part 1

The Decline and Fall of the Old Neighborhood

1

Exposition:
The Story of Decline

Whon Nelson Algren got back to the Near Northwest Side of Chicago in 1945 after two years of military service, he got back to work. He was a writer, and his job as he understood it was to write about Chicago. If the city seemed to have changed in his absence—"The last of Chicago's gaslamps had gone out," and "Fluorescent neon lit brands of beer never named before"[1]—he still could pick up where he had left off before the war. After making a name for himself with a first novel, *Somebody in Boots* (1935), and short stories in the 1930s, he had begun to win significant acclaim for his novel *Never Come Morning* (1942). In 1945, he was poised to make his mark on the literary world. Working from observation of postwar Chicago, his wartime experience, and a base of stories and poetry he had written in the 1930s and 1940s, Algren produced three Chicago books in relatively short order: a collection of short stories entitled *The Neon Wilderness* (1947) set the stage for two longer works, the novel *The Man with the Golden Arm* (1949) and the book-length prose poem *Chicago: City on the Make* (1951). *Golden Arm*, which was awarded the first National Book Award for fiction in 1950, was Algren's best and best-received work. It sold well, and influential writers and critics like Richard Wright, Ernest Hemingway, and Malcolm Cowley identified Algren as a major postwar novelist on the rise. They, and the publicists at Doubleday whose ad copy for *Golden Arm* urged readers to "add the name NELSON ALGREN to the honor roll of Chicago authors . . . who have entertained you and inspired you with novels that have made American literary history," agreed that Algren was the next big Chicago writer: one in a line that extended back through Wright and James T. Farrell to

Carl Sandburg, Theodore Dreiser, and other masters who had explored the literary implications of industrial urbanism as exemplified by Chicago.[2]

In retrospect, though, the fanfare accompanying Algren's arrival as a Chicago writer marks the end of his most productive period, and he never wrote another sustained, original treatment of the city with which he was so closely identified. *Golden Arm* and *City on the Make* were his last Chicago books, and together they drew a portrait of midcentury Chicago as a city in steep decline—if not in ruins—about which Algren would not have much else to say. The two books are a literary epitaph for the city Algren knew and the city he wrote.

The October City

Algren was identified as a Chicago writer, but he had never been a civic booster. From the very beginning of his writing career, he marked out the sphere of the desperately dispossessed as his literary territory, and his body of work advanced a critique of the arrangements of power and meaning in the industrial city. The workers and drifters who populate his books always play hopeless hands against a house that stacks the political, economic, and cultural deck against them. Like the Chicago novels of Farrell and Wright, who shared with Algren the project of representing the industrial city's neighborhoods, Algren's Chicago novels and stories are overhung with a sense of the inevitable: people without access to wealth and power will be ground up by urban business as usual—the production and consumption of goods, services, and the status quo.

If Algren's postwar writing sustained the terms of critique he had developed before the war, it put them to a new purpose. *Golden Arm* and *City on the Make*, refitting the language and imagery of his earlier work and of the Chicago tradition in which he placed himself, move from the urgent contemporaneity of social critique toward the retrospective, elegiac mood of the decline narrative. Midcentury Chicago was in many ways a boom town, beginning to flower into new, postindustrial shape under pressure from suburbanization on the periphery and redevelopment in the center, but for Algren it was an aging industrial city that was rapidly exhausting both its productive vigor and its cultural importance. At midcentury, Algren looked back upon high-industrial Chicago, which had been the subject of his starkest renderings of urban modernity, as the capital of a golden age populated by outsize heroic figures: not just the working men and women who made the industrial city in the late nineteenth and early twentieth centuries but also great reformers like Jane Addams, literary icons like Carl Sandburg, larger-than-life victims like Shoeless Joe Jackson, and even the fantastically villainous industrialists, owners, and politicians who exploited and opposed them. *Golden Arm* and *City on the Make* narrate a decline from this golden age to a debased, reduced present. They do not so much advance a critique of industrial urbanism as imagine — and nostalgically mourn — its passing.

In *Golden Arm*, something has gone obscurely and finally wrong in mid-century Chicago. The novel's characters, operating within the tightly circumscribed limits of neighborhood life in the Polish urban village around Division Street and Milwaukee Avenue (see figs. 1 and 2 for locations referred to in part 1), can sense the local effects of massive change without being able to specify its dimensions or causes. The invalid Sophie Majcinek, sitting at her window in a wheelchair late at night, reads intimations of apocalypse in the crowded, low-rise landscape of walk-up apartment buildings, rooming houses, factories, churches, and elevated train tracks:

> Moonlight that had once revealed so many stars now showed her only how the city was bound, from southeast to the unknown west, steel upon steel upon steel; how all its rails held the city too tightly to the thousand-girdered El.
>
> Some nights she could barely breathe for seeing the flat and unerring line of cable and crosslight and lever, of signal tower and switch. For the endless humming of telephone wires murmuring insanely from street to street without ever really saying a single word above a whisper that a really sensible person might understand.
>
> For the city too was somehow crippled of late. The city too seemed a little insane. Crippled and caught and done for with everyone in it. No one else was really any better off than herself, she reflected with a child's satisfaction, they had all been twisted about whether they sat in a wheelchair or not.
>
> She grew tense to see how the nameless people were bound, as they went, to the streets as the streets seemed bound to the night and the night to the nameless day. And all the days to a nameless remorse.[3]

The news is bad but incompletely articulated: the vista murmurs to Sophie of nameless remorse and an imminent but unspecified disaster. All she knows for certain is that things were better in the old days, when "some happier, some might-have-been, some used-to-be or never-was Sophie" lived in a world that had not yet "gone wrong, all wrong." If that receding golden age of the 1920s and 1930s was like spring, then at midcentury Chicago has reached October, when the year begins its steep decline into Chicago's famously brutal winter:

> sultry September had come and gone and the wind was blowing the flies away.
> "God has forgotten us all," Sophie told herself quietly. . . .
> The wind was blowing the flies away. God was forgetting His own. (99)

The year's decline and fall seem to resonate with a larger, parallel decline and fall of the world she knows.

The world she knows is the industrial city, and more precisely the industrial neighborhood order, that flourished between the Chicago fire of 1871 and

World War II. Chicago was the paradigmatic American city of that period, the model of industrial modernity and the kinds of urbanism associated with it. Migrations from Chicago's various hinterlands—not only the small-town and rural Midwest and South but also Germany and Ireland, Scandinavia, Eastern Europe, Southern Europe, Mexico, the Philippines—brought people of modest means to Chicago to work in its factories and the service industries they engendered. For foreign immigrants, the urban villages that grew around factory workplaces, streetcar lines, and local institutions were staging grounds in which they came to terms with the transition between the Old Country and America. European immigrants and their descendants dominated the urban villages of industrial Chicago, which ringed the downtown core in a vast patchwork. The urban villages, and the ways of life they housed, were the heartland of the industrial city's social landscape, formed on an armature of rail lines, port facilities, factories, and other infrastructure dedicated to circulating raw materials, manufactured goods, and the people who processed and bought them. Sophie sees this world from her window—the old neighborhood bound to the rail lines, "steel upon steel upon steel"—and obscurely mourns its passing as she reviews her own hard luck and the intimations of personal disaster still to come.

Golden Arm tells the decline as neighborhood tragedy, so claustrophobically local in scope that the decline seems ungraspable, mysterious, inchoate; Algren's prose poem *City on the Make*, published two years after *Golden Arm*, extends the decline into new registers—poetry, history, cultural criticism, sociology—and to a metropolitan scale. *City on the Make* surveys the landscape from a more omniscient and informed remove; it commands spatial and temporal perspectives beyond the imaginative reach of *Golden Arm* and its characters, like Sophie, who are hemmed in by the near horizon of the El and the limits of the urban village. In *City on the Make*, the decline plays out on a grand scale:

> Wheeling around the loop of the lake, coming at Chicago from east and south, the land by night lies under a battle-colored sky. Above the half-muffled beat of the monstrous forges between Gary and East Chicago, the ceaseless signal-fires of the great refineries wave an all-night alarm.
>
> Until, moving with the breaking light, we touch the green pennant of the morning boulevards running the dark-blue boundary of the lake. Where the fortress-like towers of The Loop guard the welter of industrial towns that were once a prairie portage.[4]

City on the Make reads in the metropolitan landscape a myth of creation in which factories make the city of Chicago and the way of life housed in its neighborhood order. The first paragraph is all color and sound in the darkness: the monstrous forges beating like artillery or a gigantic heart, signal fires against the night sky. The stuff of the city is being forged, refined, destroyed, remade in bursts of heroic activity. The second paragraph maps the results, a landscape coalescing like a newly forged creation at daybreak: parks and skyscrapers along the lake, neighborhoods like "industrial towns" clustering around the Loop and stretching away across the flat prairie. The creation myth informs a familiar historical narrative in which the people who live in the industrial towns and work in the factories have, while fighting a constant battle against the people who own the factories, produced a mature industrial metropolis from the kernel of a frontier outpost in barely a century's time. This is the generic Chicago of the period between the Great Fire and the mid–twentieth century: a capital of industrial modernity, shaped by manufacturing and peopled by urban villagers.

The moment of creation passes, and the momentum built up by the initial swing from the southeast carries the reader onward in space and time, north up the lakefront as the day begins. The point of view drops down to a motorist's perspective from Lake Shore Drive as we pass Lincoln Park and eventually into the suburbs beyond, where the narrator launches into a standard, uninspired version of the midcentury critique of suburbia: "the people are stuffed with kapok," "the homes so complacent, and the churches so smug, leave an airlessness like a microscopic dust over the immaculate pews and the self-important bookshelves," and so on. This suburban landscape is a "spiritual Sahara": "the beat of the city's enormous heart, at the forge in the forest behind the towers" (26–27), cannot be heard at this remove.

The narrator finds himself, at the end of this journey up the lakefront, deeply out of place. The story of the industrial city seems to have ended in the suburbs, about which he has nothing of interest to say, and his grand aerial perspective on the cityscape seems to have collapsed into that of a cultural hobgoblin of the postwar period, the suburban commuter tooling along Lake Shore Drive. Deposited in what he regards as alien territory, the narrator ends up far from the industrial neighborhoods that form the city's heart and his principal inspiration. It is an apt figure for the historical moment *City on the Make* addresses: the poem's great project is to show how and why the narrator's Chicago is disappearing, to bring to a close the generic narrative of prairie portage grown into manufacturing capital. The industrial city of downtown and neighborhoods gives way to the postindustrial metropolis of inner city and suburbs, and the old neighborhood order shows signs of breaking up. The narrator finds himself growing estranged from Chicago itself, increasingly adrift even when he is within the once-familiar landscape of the neighborhood order. These changes come slowly—the monstrous forges still beat all night, and from the air the old neighborhoods look just as they did a generation before—but a final transformation appears inevitable. At midcentury, industrial Chicago has entered the late autumn of its years.

City on the Make's autumnal mood derives in part from the poem's abrupt telescoping of time: "An October sort of city even in spring. With somebody's washing always whipping, in smoky October colors off the third-floor rear by that same wind that drives the yellowing comic strips down all the gutters that lead away from home" (72). The comic strips yellow with age even as they blow down the gutters; spring collapses into October; the newly forged city of day-break ages to a grim seediness by nightfall, when emerge "the pavement-col-ored thousands of the great city's nighttime streets, a separate race with no place to go and the whole night to kill" (60). In the course of the narrator's life-time (he was still a boy in 1919), Chicago has fallen vertiginously from youth-ful promise to early dotage, spring prospects turning to October regrets. The martial imagery of industrial creation—the "battle-colored sky" and "signal-flares"—takes on new meaning when the reader enters the streets of the pris-tine city seen from on high at daybreak: the narrowed, annihilating landscape of midcentury Chicago resembles a battlefield after a great defeat. In the working-class neighborhoods, where in Algren's account all the casualties fall, laundry whips from the line off the third-floor rear like off-white flags of surrender.

That surrender indicates the end of the battle and thus the end of the myth of creation. At midcentury, industrial Chicago has reached full maturity in the final transformation of prairie into metropolis: "The pig-wallows are paved, great Diesels stroke noiselessly past the clamorous tenements of home. The Constellations move, silently and all unseen, through blowing seas above the roofs. Only the measured clatter of the empty cars, where pass the northbound and the southbound Els, comes curving down the constant boundaries of the night" (75). The "clamorous tenements" of the industrial neighborhood order frame the heartlike engines that shape the city and power its commerce. A series of limits—the iron perimeter of the El, the asphalt underfoot, and the sealike sky above the roofs, with jets moving in it like Melville's sea creatures swimming beneath the pillows of sleeping Nantucketers—define the city's form and contain the way of life lived in it. The paragraph begins with the strokes of life-giving engines and ends by arriving at a limit in both space and time: the El forms "the constant boundaries of the night" as well as of the land-scape. *City on the Make* wants to show that the industrial city has likewise reached some limit in its development.

In the next paragraph, a ghost-haunted survey of the high-industrial era identifies midcentury Chicago's landscape as the industrial city's terminal form:

The cemetery that yet keeps the Confederate dead is bounded by the same tracks that run past Stephen A. Douglas' remains. The jail where Parsons hung is gone, and the building from which Bonfield marched is no more. Nobody remembers the Globe on Desplaines, and only a lonely shaft remembers the four who died, no one ever fully understood why. And those who went down with the proud steamer *Chicora* are one with those who went down on the *Eastland*. And those who sang "My God, How the Money Rolls In" are one with those who sang "Brother, Can You Spare a Dime?" (75–76)

Like the aerial rush up the lakefront, a movement in space, this swift pass through seventy years of history spanning the Civil War and the Great Depression makes a portrait of the city in time. The train tracks provide a spine connecting the October city to echoes of its past: two great wars of the last century, one between North and South and one between labor and capital (the "four who died" were hanged after the Haymarket Square riot; Inspector Bonfield led police against them); long-ago ship disasters on Lake Michigan; echoes of songs associated with the prosperity of the 1920s and the hard times of the depression. Midcentury Chicago seems to have passed a dividing line. Even the 1920s and 1930s, easily within the lifetimes of relatively young adults at midcentury, seem to have fallen far astern: the people who sang songs of the 1920s and 1930s merge "as one" into hindsight in the same way that people drowned in different ship disasters are "as one" at the bottom of the lake.

The foundering ships reinforce the Atlantean image of the people of Chicago going down with their city. At the end of the slope of decline, still in the future but within sight (like the dead of winter from the perspective of October), lies a final collapse described in *City on the Make*'s closing lines: "We shall leave, for remembrance, one rusty iron heart. . . . For keeps and a single day" (77). At the end of its history, industrial Chicago—the El, the monstrous forges and the diesel engines, the neighborhoods like villages and the towers of the Loop like fortresses—will stand in ruins like Atlantis or Troy.

This decline provides the main theme of *City on the Make* and the principal subtext of *Golden Arm*. Sophie Majcinek, penned within the close horizons of industrial urbanism as it is lived in the old neighborhood, senses only the vague outlines of this decline in the "rumors of evening" that filter down to her in murmurous, coded fragments. Nelson Algren, whose own windows looked out on a similar vista in the 1940s and early 1950s, could feel the change coming, too. He could not have known then that *Golden Arm* and *City on the Make* would be his last Chicago books, but one can feel his unease, like Sophie's, with the intimations of change he felt moving through the familiar landscape of the neighborhoods he lived in and wrote about. Algren's literary subject was industrial urbanism; his literary project was to represent the industrial city and infuse it with meanings, as had a number of celebrated Chicago writers before him. He understood the decline of industrial Chicago to mean the end not only of the neighborhood order he knew but also of the literary tradition in which he worked.

The Logic of Decline

Any city at any time is going to hell in one sense or another. Narratives of decline seem to spring from the overlap of orders in time and space: the overlap of established residents and newcomers; of pieces of social landscape arranged to serve different sets of people and functions; of different institutional arrangements for making money, exercising power, making life meaningful, living poorly or well. However, specific arguments for decline have historical and generic provenance that can be traced to period and place, to particular structures of thought and traditions of representation. Nelson Algren's version of Chicago's decline was part of a larger literature of urban decline that thrived at midcentury and has since become a staple of postwar urbanism. That literature embraces a variety of fictional and nonfictional accounts, written by a range of variously accredited and influential urban intellectuals, many of whom agreed on little else.

"In the years just after the Second World War," observes Robert Beauregard, "the trauma of the country's large central cities could hardly be avoided." That "trauma" was most evident in the great industrial cities of the Midwest and Northeast, and it was, most immediately, the result of "15 years of depression, war, and inflation"[5] in which specifically urban problems had been pushed to the back burner: factories, civic buildings, and especially overcrowded neighborhoods were physically deteriorating; cities' economies, especially factory production and downtown retailing, were showing signs of long-term erosion; pollution was increased and traffic congestion exacerbated by the proliferation of cars in streets originally designed for the horse and wagon; city governments were denounced as weak and corrupt, while federal government was potently committed to suburbanizing the nation; many cities' tax bases shrank as poor in-migrants, especially Southern blacks, settled in the inner city while middle-class whites and businesses dispersed into the suburbs. The trauma was also, however, part of a larger change in the form and function of cities. The industrial cities that had for generations been the leading models of American urbanism were undergoing a profound transformation. The gradual shift of primary economic function from manufacturing to services, the prodigious rise of the suburbs as places to live and work, the expansion of the black inner city, and the erosion of the industrial village—these were the big groundswells, just beginning to shake the foundations of industrial urbanism, that would make urban history in the second half of the century. One can perceive their effects, as well, in the way urban intellectuals wrote and thought about cities. There had always been a vigorous literature of antiurbanism in American culture, and there was a long tradition of equating cities with specifically moral decline, but we can make out a particular genre of decline narrative—promulgated especially by people who loved cities—that appeared after World War II and has descended to us as one of our fundamental ways to think about and represent inner cities. In many different versions, and pursuing an enormous range of particular subjects that range from traffic to class conflict, the postwar narrative of decline considers the causes, effects, and meaning of the endlessly complex set of changes that add up to postindustrial transformation.

Chicago, the paragon of industrial urbanism, provided an especially resonant setting for the postwar decline. "There is an opinion," observed A. J. Liebling in 1952,

> advanced by some men who worked in Chicago transiently during the twenties, as well as by many native Chicagoans, that the city did approximate the great howling, hurrying, hog-butchering, hog-mannered challenger for the empire of the world specified in the legend, but that at some time around 1930 it stopped as suddenly as a front-running horse at the head of the stretch with a poor man's last two dollars on its nose. What stopped it is a mystery, like what happened to Angkor Vat.[6]

Jack Lait and Lee Mortimer, New York newspapermen who had worked more than transiently in Chicago before World War II, made a similar claim in their hard-boiled insider's guide, *Chicago Confidential* (1950): "In 1910 Chicago breezily and confidently expected to surpass New York by 1950; in 1950 it no longer talks of growing bigger than New York—it wonders when it will be smaller than Los Angeles."[7] Liebling, Lait, and Mortimer, reporters all, did not claim to have formulated the story of Chicago's decline; rather, they claimed to have collected it as it circulated ready to hand in the culture around them. Having gone to Chicago to do what amounted to follow-up pieces on the well-known story of its remarkable growth into a world city in the half-century before the Great Depression, they had returned with stories of decline.

The reporters' claims to having found the next chapter of the Chicago story in the narrative of decline found support from Carl Sandburg, whose literary persona continued to enjoy a close identification with the story of industrial Chicago in the ascendant, a story he had definitively told in the early twentieth century. Sandburg was not a "native Chicagoan," but he was poet laureate of Illinois and author of the city's semiofficial poem, "Chicago" (1914). That poem had been quoted and referred to so consistently (even by people who had not read it or any other poems) that over time what Liebling simply calls "the legend" of Chicago had become condensed into a few of its richly freighted phrases: "Hog Butcher," "Big Shoulders," and so forth. Sandburg wrote in *Holiday* magazine's special issue on Chicago in 1951, "There is a question that occurs: Is Chicago less vivid and strident than in former generations? That could be, might be, I'm not sure."[8] Like Liebling, Sandburg employed a passive construction—"There is an opinion . . ."; "There is a question that occurs . . ." —that imputed to the decline the status of received wisdom. The hesitant tone of Sandburg's answer to the "question that occurs" at midcentury makes a striking contrast to the belligerently assertive language of his celebrated poem. In 1914, he had imagined industrial Chicago issuing a challenge:

> Come and show me another city with lifted head singing so proud to be alive and
> 	coarse and strong and cunning
> Flinging magnetic curses amid the toil of piling job upon job, here is
> 	a tall bold slugger set vivid against the little soft cities.[9]

At midcentury, Sandburg's drastically changed tone seemed to concede the loss of the youthful vigor and prospects with which his earlier poetry had infused its portrait of the industrial city. The *Holiday* article repeats the poem's language, like the word "vivid" (which seems to be associated with productivity), but drains the words of their original stridency. Writing about midcentury Chicago, Sandburg seemed to be unsure of what to say about it.

If midcentury Chicago as a literary subject was still importantly defined by themes and language evolved in the late nineteenth and early twentieth centuries in response to the shocks of industrial modernity, then the passing of industrial urbanism suggested a decline and demanded a revision of the Chicago story. If Sandburg was not prepared to write it, others—like Liebling, Lait, Mortimer, and Algren—were. The story of decline, literary and journalistic, told of Chicago's passage from a bygone moment of limitless promise to a reduced and dispirited present day. Variants of the decline appearing in the late 1940s and 1950s told of Chicago's fall from aspiring world city to the humbler estate of one regional capital among many, from industrial dynamo to rusting postindustrial dinosaur (anticipating by decades the Rust Belt elegies that accompanied the city's great period of deindustrialization in the 1970s), from literary capital to cultural wasteland, from vigorous city of neighborhoods to blighted inner city eclipsed by prosperous suburbs, from a vital congeries of white-ethnic villages and Black Metropolis to an archipelago of white enclaves surrounded by pathologized black ghetto. The story of decline argued for the passing of a moment when Chicago had been the right place at the right time. It had once been the way station between metropolitan America and its resource-rich frontier, the destination of immigrant laborers drawn to the industrial city, the cultural capital of the Middle Border during the maturing of urban America and the revolt against Main Street. Now it was at best like everywhere else and at worst a ruin.

Especially because the decline tends to treat the city like a single individual—who is getting old and fat, who once aspired to better things, and so on—it tends to reduce complexity to simplicity or mysticism. The imputation of general decline tends toward analytical vagueness, always prompting the question "in what sense?" Because a city, like a nation, is complex enough to be simultaneously rising and falling by any number of measures, the story of decline acquires coherence and authority by both specifying and mystifying its terms to evolve a kind of symbolic shorthand. On the one hand, the story tends to range in great leaps across the spectrum of historical information, unifying disparate but evocative details into a grand impressionistic whole. For instance, the failure of Chicago to become a center for the manufacture of automobiles, the departure of important literary figures in the 1920s, and the passing of its great criminal entrepreneurs hang together thematically in Liebling's account in ways that suggest an across-the-board failure of the city's creative energies. On the other hand, the decline tends to condense drastically in order to make sense, identifying a particular Chicago in time and space and making it stand for the whole. Thus, the decline formula can be adapted to recount the transformation or disappearance of many different or overlapping golden-age Chicagos: the Middle Border capital raised by hard work and entrepreneurial inspiration from the swamps and the ashes of the Great Fire; the city of European immigrants negotiating through hard work and solidarity the passage from horse-and-wagon days to American modernity; the Midwestern literary capital that produced stark realists, prairie modernists, muckraking reporters, and dialect humorists and was in turn produced discursively by them.

Although they infused the formula with different sets of meanings, most of the versions of Chicago's decline agreed upon the general contours of the story. All assumed that the city had enjoyed a golden age of promise more than a generation before. Lait and Mortimer only specify that in 1910 the golden age had not yet elapsed. Liebling dates the city's moment of ascendance from around 1890, when the census employed by Frederick Jackson Turner to argue for the closing of the frontier also showed that Chicago had passed Philadelphia to become the nation's second city, to about 1930, when Chicago mysteriously collapsed in the stretch of its run at First City status. He notes that in the 1920s Colonel Robert McCormick's incorrigibly boosterish *Tribune* was still printing daily on its editorial page a "Program for Chicagoland" that featured as Article 1 an injunction to "Make Chicago the First City of the World." By midcentury, the *Tribune* had dropped this grandiose program, which Liebling takes as tacit acquiescence to the notion of decline. The novelist James T. Farrell, a leftist who otherwise had little in common with the famously right-wing and anti-union McCormick, provides a similar periodization of the golden age. He remembered that he "grew up inside of the city of Chicago, and after the city had passed its period of greatest hope," which he defined as a stretch from 1880 to 1910 in which Chicago's bankers and industrialists had created a world capital and its progressive liberals had given the city intellectual life and conscience.[10] Farrell saw the city as somehow broken by its failure to deliver on its golden-age promise of high productivity tempered by social justice.

Like Farrell, Nelson Algren understood himself to have been born during the city's age of promise (Farrell in 1904; Algren in 1909) and come to maturity as the city declined toward eventual ruin. In the autobiographical *City on the Make*, Algren presents the end of the golden age as coinciding with his first disillusionments: the Black Sox scandal of 1919 marks in retrospect the end of "the silver-colored yesterday" dominated by "giants." The humiliations endured in preadolescence by the poem's autobiographical narrator for believing in his baseball heroes feed into a citywide sense of loss that has grown through the present day. Algren's account of the fall or departure of giants—Shoeless Joe Jackson, Theodore Dreiser, Eugene Debs, Jane Addams, even self-serving "clowns" like the politician Big Bill Thompson and the traction magnate Samuel Insull—nicely illustrates Liebling's observation that, at midcentury, "Chicagoans are left in the plight of the Greeks at the beginning of history, when the gods commenced ceasing to manifest themselves."[11] The present, then, constitutes a postheroic age extending from the 1920s to the distant but foreseeable end of history.[12]

What happened? How to account for postheroic Chicago's collapse into history? Each story of decline offers its own understanding of the engines driving it, but the various explanation systems tend to fall into two categories: those organized around material changes in the city of fact and those organized around discursive changes in the city of feeling. The former impulse, dominant in Lait and Mortimer's *Chicago Confidential*, produces a story that explains how and why *the city* and its people have changed; the latter impulse, dominant in Liebling's essays (collectively entitled *Chicago: The Second City*), leads to explanations of how and why *the story* of Chicago has changed. Algren's *City on the Make*, to which I will turn after discussing the other two examples, offers a synthesis of the two approaches, a grand unifying theory of decline.

Lait and Mortimer identify two intertwined historical processes as the motors of change: the city's development from frontier outpost to industrial center to suburbanized metropolis, and the ethnic-racial successions that have accompanied the stages of development. They "can fix Chicago's decline at about the time its founding fathers went to their Valhalla." The race of giants who built the city—"titans of the nineteenth century," "dynamic, hairy individualists who hewed and wrested a new world out of the woods and the mud"—dissipated their energies in reacquiring Eastern ways, losing their hirsute frontier virility when corrupted by the civilization they had enabled. The founding fathers' descent into history encapsulates the city's descent from heroic prehistory toward an exotically degraded, unproductive new order in the inner city. In *Chicago Confidential*'s conventionally gendered account, neither the productivity of male entrepreneurs nor the civilizing influence of female reformers like Jane Addams has proven able to forestall or contain the barbarous new order's emergence. The creeping "physical decadence" of the city once "rebuilt fresh and new [by the titans] after the big fire of 1871," combined with "the overflow of foreign immigrants" and the succeeding "influx of Negroes," leads to the concomitant flight of "good families," followed by the "middle classes and the respectable lower classes," from "the smoke and the grime and the daily conflict to pleasant suburbs."[13]

This is a précis of the rise and fall of the industrial city, but Lait and Mortimer are less interested in economics than they are in the sensational appeal and explanatory force of race. Like so many other narratives of decline, theirs treats folk migrations not as the highly visible tip of a larger iceberg of urban transformations but as the engine of history. *Chicago Confidential*'s account of struggles among ethnic and racial types makes the turnover of neighborhood populations the change that causes all others, bending this particular story of decline toward a familiar simplifying formula: "there goes the neighborhood."

"Hundreds of thousands of whites still live in Chicago slums," report Lait and Mortimer, the "still" suggesting the eventual departure of these whites,

and lebensraum problems are as drastic throughout as they are anywhere. But Negroes, with full right to do so and virtually with none to hold otherwise, are entrenched as far south as 90th Street and are approaching Hyde Park, along the south shore of the lake, not too long ago a seat of white society. . . . In truth, an amazing American anti-climax emerges: instead of being hemmed in by whites, the Negroes are hemming in the whites.[14]

Hyde Park, dominated by the University of Chicago and since the late nineteenth century a preserve of white professionals, is on the South Side, near the old Bronzeville ghetto that was expanding under pressure from an influx of black Southerners at midcentury. On the city's West Side, *Chicago Confidential*'s account of change over time in the area around Halsted Street shows that white-ethnic urban villages are also about to be engulfed. Settled in waves by the Irish, Russian and Eastern European Jews, Poles, Bohemians, and Italians, this definitively immigrant neighborhood—where Jane Addams established Hull House—gradually lost these populations as "the older people died, the younger ones grew and many prospered, honestly or notoriously, and moved to more happy abodes. As the Europeans left, the new Negroes came." Lait and Mortimer paint a highly stylized picture of the neighborhood in its present state of racially heterogeneous decline:

Negroes live in hovels without roofs, caved in on the sides, steps missing, tilted like miniature towers of Pisa. As many as a hundred live in a shack meant for two families. . . . Filth overflows to the walks and weedy lots and everywhere junk is piled. At night, Halsted Street thereabouts is a fantastic riot of smells and colors, a jammed jamboree of Negroes, Mexicans, skull-capped Jews, Filipinos and Levantines. . . . You can buy anything on the street from a girl, price $5, to a stiletto, price $2.50. Street-hawkers sell guns openly at $20, knives, Spanish fly, contraceptives and obscene pictures and other crude pornography.[15]

In these images of enclaved white professionals (Hyde Park) and urban villagers (Halsted Street) hemmed in and displaced by blacks and other nonwhites living in extravagantly impoverished physical, social, and moral conditions, *Chicago Confidential* offers an early version of one of the most important stories of decline told by Americans about the postwar inner city: the breakup of the industrial neighborhood order and the emergence of a new social landscape dominated by the racial ghetto.

Ethnic succession and the city's physical and economic transformations mean little to Liebling, however, who does not believe that material changes account for the proliferation of narratives of decline. The decline formula, not the material city, is his true object of study. Although he touches upon the kinds of historical processes discussed in *Chicago Confidential*—the suburbanization of the middle class, the postwar housing shortage, the violent tension between expanding black neighborhoods and the established structure of white-ethnic blocs—he explains the "disparity between the Chicago of the rhapsodists and the Chicago of today" as largely a matter of perception. No city could live up to the rhapsodic story of Chicago's limitless ascent told in the early decades of the century. Dismissing suggestions that the city's economy has changed as "too materialistic to satisfy me," Liebling places more value in a second line of explanations suggesting that the narrative of decline proceeds from a discursive adjustment: deflated by the city's failure to live up to its boosters' impossible "first-or-nothing" aspirations and by the predictable exodus in the 1920s and 1930s of local heroes to the first-line cultural capitals of New York and Los Angeles, the overblown narrative of Chicago's incipient greatness has collapsed into the exaggeratedly grim decline.[16]

Seen in this light, the notion of a golden age was a cultural "St. Vitus's Dance" whipped up through "mutual suggestion." The exit of major characters like Addams and Dreiser broke the spell, and each departure also provided a roadmark on the downward path traced by the narratives of decline that naturally appeared in the ensuing period of despondency among the city's house intellectuals. Liebling quotes in this regard a correspondent who admits that she saw the city "through the eyes of the Dell-Anderson-Masters-Sandburg-Monroe coterie," all writers prominent in the 1910s and 1920s. It is no surprise that as these figures recede into history and obscurity her "Chicago Dream has faded slowly but steadily," a kind of dreamwork that can proceed almost independently of any material change in the social landscape.[17]

Liebling's "rhapsodist" label fits Chicago's business boosters well enough and embraces as well some of the critical boosters of its literary golden age, but the label fits badly with important elements of Chicago's literary tradition. Even Sandburg's canonical "big shoulders" poem, relentlessly quoted and misquoted by civic boosters, devotes itself as much to considering the industrial city's endemic brutality as it does to valorizing its heroic productivity. Algren and the other neighborhood novelists who dominated Chicago writing in the 1930s and 1940s—Farrell and Wright chief among them—were in no sense rhapsodists: social and cultural critics might be a more accurate label. But Algren did see himself as the last figure in a line of Chicago writers that extended back to Sandburg, Dreiser, and other writers of a clearly defined golden age. When Algren discussed Chicago, he did not mean the Chicago of boosters who "talked of growing bigger than New York"; but he did mean, at least in part, the composite Chicago assembled by a set of writers who aspired to literary significance in representing the city that exemplified industrial urbanism. One important chapter of the narrative of decline recounted the fading from prominence of a literary tradition that drew imaginatively upon the rich materials of Chicago to assemble a Chicago of feeling—a "Chicago Dream" built by writers.

Stories of Chicago's decline treat literary history as a significant case study, an important way in which the city has been diminished since the golden age.[18] The story of decline's investment in literary decline proposes a two-way traffic between the city and its literature. During the golden age, great writers and great books moved Chicago stories to cultural center stage; conversely, the city's dramatically compressed experience of urbanization, immigration, and industrialization moved its writers to center stage by providing them with the most compelling social matter America had to offer in the late nineteenth and early twentieth centuries. Stories of Chicago's decline account in widely varying ways for the linked fortunes of the city and its canonical literary tradition, but they almost unanimously tend to assume the linkage itself.

Noting that the "shift from the cream to the skim-milk is reflected in every artery of the city's life," Lait and Mortimer observe that "Chicago forty years ago was the hub of a virile, vigorous circle of literature, art and, strangely, a center of poetry," as well as a publishing capital. Now, they claim, "Chicagoans no longer write books about their city, because it has few citizens left who can write and of those even fewer are brave enough to tell the real story."[19] Although tossed off by Lait and Mortimer with their characteristic flippancy, the startling assertion that Chicagoans do not write about their city, or do so timidly and falsely, seems expressly designed to explode the notion of Chicago as a literary capital. Lait and Mortimer propose a city of illiterates who cannot write—given form in the horde of Negroes, swarthy foreigners, and the less-than-respectable lower classes thronging Halsted—and of cowards who, in an age without entrepreneurial "hairy individualists," great reformers, or great reporters, lack the resources to practice either the kind of muckraking social criticism or the forthright boosterism popularized by their predecessors. "For a city where, I am credibly informed, you couldn't throw an egg in 1925 without braining a great poet," agrees Liebling, "Chicago is hard up for writers."[20] For Liebling, who argues that Chicago partisans are nostalgic for a golden age that took place largely in the imagination of its writers, the end of Chicago's literary renaissance constitutes the essence of Chicago's decline. Deprived of its most able proponents by the departure of first-class writers in the 1920s and 1930s, the myth of Chicago's importance as both literary center and literary subject cannot sustain itself.

The claim that there were no "Chicago writers" left, or that there was only one (Algren), is startling enough to merit further investigation. What did this self-consciously hyperbolic assertion mean? First, it meant that notable writers associated with the city tended to leave it. For writers, Chicago had not lasted as a central place of the first rank commanding its own cultural hinterland; it was, rather, a subsidiary way station, helping to funnel talent out of the vast mid-American plain east to the nation's literary and journalistic centers or west to the movie industry. Second, the notion of a city without writers provided a forceful way to figure the end of a particular tradition or traditions. The story of decline reported by Lait and Mortimer and Liebling had in mind a canon of novelists, poets, and journalists who had lived and worked in Chicago or had produced representations of Chicago, a group that typically included Theodore Dreiser, Frank Norris, Robert Herrick, Edgar Lee Masters, Floyd Dell, Finley Peter Dunne, George Ade, Carl Sandburg, Harriet Monroe, Vachel Lindsay, Sherwood Anderson, Upton Sinclair, Ben Hecht, Willa Cather, James T. Farrell, and Richard Wright.[21] These writers—gone from midcentury Chicago, no longer writing, or dead—had together in the first half of the twentieth century imagined a composite textual Chicago that had a significant place in American literature.

If Algren was the last of the Chicago writers, a label applied to him by more than one narrator of decline, it meant that he was the last well-known writer in Chicago with generally acknowledged ties running all the way through that tradition. Liebling presents Algren, who was in 1949–51 enjoying his greatest popular success following the publication of *The Man with the Golden Arm*, as the last of the Chicago writers who "had stuck by his West Side Poles after all the rest of the stark Chicago realists had fled to Hollywood." In Liebling's account, Algren becomes a 1930s writer adrift in midcentury Chicago. "Still wearing steel-rimmed spectacles and a turtle-neck sweater"—which Liebling apparently regarded as an outdated proletarian-intellectual uniform—a forlorn Algren makes the rounds of dull literary parties at which he eats the free turkey, Virginia ham, and cocktail shrimp while besieged by "patrons of the arts and the faculty of the University of Chicago."[22] Liebling casts him as an embarrassed dinosaur whose nostalgia-inducing presence earns him treats.

Algren may not have been so self-deflating, but he proceeded from a similar assumption about Chicago's literary history: as late as the 1920s, he argues in *City on the Make*, Chicago was "the homeland and heartland of an American renaissance. . . . Thirty years later we stand on the rim of a cultural Sahara with not a camel in sight" (54). Algren's story of Chicago's literary decline arrives at a midcentury scene of cultural desolation strikingly similar to that found in *Chicago Confidential*'s account of the degrading of the city's gene pool. One should remember that Algren's narrative of Chicago's decline differed violently in most particulars from Lait and Mortimer's. He did not, for instance, share their understanding of "good families," "foreigners," the meaning of race, and the political left. (*Chicago Confidential* knowingly explains that communists, who made up important parts of Algren's literary and social circle in the 1930s, habitually compel white female party members to have sex with black men.) But Algren's version of Chicago's decline dovetails with *Chicago Confidential*'s and Liebling's versions on the subject of literature: at midcentury, *City on the Make* argues, Chicago has become a cultural desert because its artists have abandoned their mission. In Algren's view, that mission is to stand up for "neighborhood" people against the power wielded by political and economic bosses; the writers have given up that fight in an age of suburbanization and consensus. More generally, the mission of Chicago realists, at least as it was grasped by narrators of the city's decline, was to write about industrial urbanism, and that appeared to be a dying subject. "It used to be a writer's town" (62), argues *City on the Make:* "It has had its big chance and fluffed it" (55). For Algren, good dreamwork, like good steady factory work in the changing inner city, was getting harder to find.

The Unmaking of Industrial Urbanism

The story of decline thus embraces the social landscape of urban villages and Chicago's literary tradition as two orders rooted in industrial urbanism and threatened by the city's postwar transformation. The pall hanging over the urban village in Algren's midcentury writing figures both the material prospect of urban change and the textual prospect of a literary tradition's exhaustion.

City on the Make, therefore, presents the decline of industrial urbanism as the defeat of an imagined alliance between factory workers and writers of the industrial city. Chicago is "a poet's town for the same reason it's a working stiff's town, both poet and working stiff being boys out to get even for funny cards dealt by an overpaid houseman weary long years ago" (63). The poets are allied with the working stiffs (i.e., "neighborhood" people) because, in Algren's belligerently narrow definition of literature as social critique pure and simple, "literature is made upon any occasion that a challenge is put to the legal apparatus by conscience in touch with humanity."[23] The writers of Algren's Chicago tradition thus form a kind of collective social conscience as well as an aesthetic order, allied with the city's wage-earning and marginal classes against those who own the industrial and political machines. This latter group and their cronies make Chicago "also an American Legionnaire's town, real Chamber of Commerce territory, the big banker-and-broker's burg, where a softclothes dick with a paunch and no brain at all . . . decides what movies and plays we ought to see and what we mustn't" (63). The two factions have fought a war for Chicago, with battles contested in the streets and on the printed page, and the poets and working stiffs have lost, the game being fixed in favor of big business and its antiliterature of boosterism. Algren the neighborhood novelist runs up white flags flapping from laundry lines in the urban village.

This is not a dramatic reversal or surprise defeat but rather the playing out of a logic readable throughout the city's development: "An October sort of city even in spring" suggests that the seeds of decline can be found even in the city's rise. Chicago was founded by "marked-down derelicts with dollar signs for eyes" (10), and their more pious and respectable inheritors have defeated all challenges from City on the Make's honor roll of radical leftists, labor leaders, Lincolnian liberals, Progressives, and genuine Christians. When Algren refers to Colonel McCormick as "the inventor of modern warfare, our very own dimestore Napoleon, Colonel McGooseneck" (65), he both pokes fun at McCormick's empty military posturing and puts the McCormicks—an industrialist clan but also relentlessly boosterish newspaper publishers—at the center of the winning side in the "modern warfare" over Chicago. The naked exercise of stockyard logic has always been Chicago's social trademark—"Wise up, Jim: it's a joint where the bulls and the foxes live well and the lambs wind up head-down from the hook" (56)—and McCormick's faction of industrialists and allied politicians, cultural arbiters, and civic boosters has grown fat in victory. In City on the Make, Chicago's golden age was a time when one could believe that this inevitable victory was as yet in doubt, that reformist "giants" could sway the industrial city onto another, less brutal course. But, in this most fixable city, the fix was in: "its poets pull the town one way while its tycoons' wives pull it another, its gunmen making it the world's crime capital while its educators beat the bushes for saints. Any old saints. And every time a Robert Hutchins or Robert Morss Lovett pulls it half an inch out of the mud, a Hearst or an Insull or a McCormick shoves it down again by sheer weight of wealth and venality" (57).

The city that staggers into middle age—"Up, down and lurching sidewise. . . . Small wonder we've had trouble growing up"—remains a capital for hustlers, operators, and thieves living by stockyard rules. In City on the Make's

account, the poets and the working stiffs disappear from the stage, hounded by cries of "'Hit him again, he don't own a dime'" (57). The "city that works" tends to disappear from *City on the Make* as the industrial city declines toward the present day. Urban villages and factory jobs increasingly belong to the bygone "silver-colored yesterday." The city of poets and writers disappears in a parallel movement, having been eclipsed by the city of American Legionnaires, the Chamber of Commerce, and a critical establishment captive to the McCormick faction and its successors, the progrowth and redevelopment ideologues. Only two classes remain in Algren's October city—big-time operators, who enjoy official authority, and the small-time losers they victimize. The nightly battle fought in postwar Chicago now pits a legion of anonymous scufflers against the annihilating city itself:

> As evening comes taxiing in and the jungle hiders come softly forth: geeks and gargoyles, old blown winoes, sour stewbums and grinning ginsoaks, young dingbats who went ashore on D Plus One or D Plus Two and have been trying to find some arc-lit shore ever since. Strolling with ancient boxcar perverts who fought all their wars on the Santa Fe. . . .
> Every day is D-day under the El. (59)

Algren, who saw himself as a lone survivor who made literature in the Chica? tradition, understood his job at midcentury to be to explore the imaginative p(sibilities afforded by these grim players in industrial Chicago's endgame.

City on the Make offers a version of decline in which militant capital def(workers and their literary supporters, but, as Lait and Mortimer's accoun entrepreneurial capital defeated by racial heterogeny should remind us, decline genre allows great variation in representing the rise of the postindus city. There is, of course, a story of the 1930s and the 1950s in Algren's po of poets and workers defeated by the expansive postwar bourgeoisie and tion against the political left. Algren was a Popular Front leftist, celeb before the war as a proletarian writer, who saw fewer and fewer allies sphere of cultural politics as postwar America became Cold War Americ that familiar story, which Algren retold in *City on the Make* and often aft(does not do justice to Algren as a writer of cities: he was one of the gre; ary formulators of the postwar decline narrative, a genre contributed t(manner of urban intellectuals across the political spectrum. The equa poets and workers in *City on the Make* does gesture back to the Popula but it also reminds us that industrial urbanism was a many-faceted art which Algren's brand of literary realism and the industrial villagers' w; formed only two facets. The cultures of cities may have significantly the Popular Front but only as one among many cultural and social for

Besides thinking of himself as a social critic and a leftist, Algren, t ceived of himself as falling within a specific genre of urban intell(

Chicago novelist and poet on the prewar model. In this sense, he placed himself within a larger set of Chicago realists: a complex of urban intellectuals encompassing not only literary figures but also journalists (including cartoonish anticommunists Lait and Mortimer) and social scientists (especially the Chicago School of sociology associated with Robert Park), who had before the war produced a body of closely observed urban writing that responded to the formal, social, and political problems raised by the industrial city. At midcentury, Algren perceived an imminent crisis in the passing of the industrial urbanism that had provided Chicago realism with its defining subject. His identity as an urban intellectual was rooted in the industrial villages he wrote about, neighborhoods that had been since the 1930s the Chicago novel's home terrain. The suddenly foreseeable breakup of those neighborhoods, part of postindustrial transformation, formed an important part of the story of decline. Algren therefore saw himself in danger of being cast adrift from the materials he drew upon in doing his cultural work.

Algren's postwar writing bears the marks of its historical moment: the sense of literary-historical desperation, the flows of capital and population already transforming postwar Chicago's social landscape. Chapter 2 describes Chicago's midcentury transformation from an industrial city of downtown and neighborhoods into a postindustrial metropolis of inner city and suburbs, a transformation that shapes the story of decline and the reading of it that follows. The argument therefore plants one foot in the city of fact. It plants the other foot in the city of feeling: the story of decline also embodies and considers the postwar exhaustion of what Algren understood as his tradition of Chicago realism, which forms the second subject of chapter 2. These two structural supports undergird a reading in chapter 3 of Algren's *The Man with the Golden Arm*, the definitive, if often obscure and deflected, story of decline in novel form and a culminative masterpiece of Algren's Chicago tradition. Chapter 4 begins where Algren imagines an apocalyptic end: it concludes part 1 by assembling the pieces of a post-Algren Chicago tradition, which revises (redevelops) the city of feeling he constructed as it maps the postindustrial inner city. Algren's postwar writing, which tends to give the impression that after he is done there will be nothing left to say about Chicago, thus introduces and underlies new generations of Chicago stories, landscapes, and urban intellectuals.

Chapters 2, 3, and 4 follow Algren's lead in emphasizing landscape. Like Sandburg's personification of Chicago and various updatings of it, the landscapes constructed in texts embody the complex and diffuse idea of Chicago in a concrete form that can be infused with meanings. To the extent that the texts discussed here are about Chicago, their landscapes enter into conversation with

one another and with the city's changing social landscape. The landscapes we find in Chicago literature afford us ways to consider a historical moment suspended between the industrial and postindustrial eras, between a prewar urban literature and the genres that would rework and replace it. In particular, the pervasiveness of the El in the landscapes of *Golden Arm* and *City on the Make* affords a way to consider the relationship between Chicago and the city constructed by its literary tradition: both the city of fact and the city of feeling grew around their railroads, which thereby acquired a powerful symbolic charge that survives well into the age of the expressway that began around midcentury. The El's great rusting trestles, many of prewar vintage, continue to this day to serve as a resonant shorthand for Chicago: they still carry loads of meaning, just as they still bear trains filled with flesh-and-blood passengers. The El reminds us that with all the midcentury talk of decline, apocalypse, and the "disappearance" of Chicago, the prewar city did not fall overnight into ruin but instead became absorbed into a new landscape. The first act of that drama—the passing of industrial Chicago, with its habits of life and literature—is the subject of part I.

The Old Neighborhood: Industrial Chicago and Its Literatures

Sandburg's Chicago, Dreiser's Chicago, Farrell's and
Wright's and my own Chicago, that was somebody
else's Chicago. That was a play with a different plot.
    Nelson Algren, *Who Lost an American?*

In *Nelson Algren's Chicago*, the photographer Arthur Shay makes a gorgeous record of the relation Algren cultivated to the city he knew. Pictures of Algren idling in bars and walking in the low-rise streetscape of his neighborhood, pictures of drunks on West Madison Street and petty criminals in court, pictures of resonant characters eager to tell their stories to the writer—these are dramatizations of the link between authorial persona and urban orders. In his introduction to the book, Shay folds the story of Algren's relation to the Chicago he knew—and the Chicago that supplanted it—into a narrative of decline.

Driving south toward downtown Chicago on the Kennedy Expressway in the late 1980s, Shay feels a professional appreciation for the skyline vista rearing up before him, for the aesthetic self-presentation of "a city that stretches from the John Hancock Building and the Gold Coast on the left all the way across the vaunted Loop to the world's tallest building, the Sears Tower, just about dead ahead."[1] Shay accords to Chicago's densely redeveloped Loop and Near North Side lakefront the status of being "a city" unto itself, well defined and separate from the spreading low-rise metropolis of inner city and suburbs that stretches south, west, and north of this core for many miles. The expressway, connecting core and suburbs, passes above and through the inner city, carrying commuters like Shay toward the steel-and-glass towers ahead—"all of them," the novelist Saul Bellow has written, "armored like Eisenstein's Teutonic Knights and staring over the ice of no-man's-land at Alexander Nevsky."[2]

Moving south among the inbound commuters, Shay encounters an old friend's ghost, which rises disembodied from the inner-city neighborhoods below to impinge on the closed system of downtown, expressway, and suburban periphery:

> The moment I cross Fullerton I glide over to the left lane and in a few seconds cross what was once the short stretch of Wabansia Avenue that intersected North Bosworth. Rolling over that sector of long-gone Wabansia, the part that was eminent-domained by Mayor Daley's myrmidons and turned from mangy gray two-flats into mangier gray roadway to hurry us Loop-ward, I think of Chicago novelist Nelson Algren and French novelist-philosopher Simone de Beauvoir, who occupied that precise space more than a third of a century ago, sharing Algren's squeaky bed on the second floor of 1523 Wabansia. An air space vacated so long ago that a billion cars have long since occupied it momentarily, hurrying toward the city with which Algren had a lifelong love-hate affair.[3]

Nelson Algren, "long-gone" novelist of the industrial inner city, offers Shay passage into a lost Chicago.

In Chicago, as in many American cities after World War II, a "progrowth" coalition of political and business leaders used governmental authority, federal funds, and the money and expertise of the private sector to help reconfigure the city for a suburbanizing, deindustrializing age. Slum clearance, housing projects, highway construction, and downtown redevelopment helped change the city's landscape, giving new form not only to the core but also to the neighborhoods that had since the late nineteenth century encouraged resident and visiting observers (Algren among the former and de Beauvoir among the latter) to characterize Chicago as a loose confederation of industrial villages. Some places, like 1523 Wabansia, ceased to exist; others were allowed to decay; others were made over by new infusions of capital.

These physical transformations intertwined with concurrent demographic change. The old neighborhood order was also an ethnic order, dominated by European immigrant groups that came to work in industrial Chicago in great numbers in the late nineteenth and early twentieth centuries — Poles, Bohemians, Czechs, Lithuanians, Italians, Greeks, Eastern European Jews — and by the earlier-established Irish, Germans, and Scandinavians. Describing the passing of Algren's Chicago, Shay sketches an ethnic succession that carries forward in a parenthesis from the 1950s to the 1980s:

> [Algren's] neighborhoods and haunts changed. The Poles and Slavs he knew either had died or moved to the suburbs, and the language of the people who replaced them was alien to him. (After his death, when an admiring alderman

managed to get part of Evergreen Street [a nearby street on which Algren had also lived] renamed Algren Street, another alderman, following his Hispanic constituents' howls that they had never heard of Algren, got it changed back.)[4]

Beginning during World War I, when a half-century of prolific European immigration came to a close, new waves of migration brought black and white Southerners to Chicago—a movement that peaked in the 1950s and 1960s—as well as Mexicans, Puerto Ricans, and, especially after 1965, immigrants from South and Central America, Asia, and the Caribbean. During those decades, many whites were moving out of Chicago proper to the nation's fastest-growing suburban area, pursuing opportunities for jobs, affordable homes, better schools, a restricted choice of neighbors. For many white ethnics, the move to the suburbs meant moving from the hyphenated immigrant-ethnic sphere into the larger community of the American middle classes; especially during the prosperous 1950s and early 1960s, they could imagine themselves securing a stake in a perfectible America. As the city's segregated black sections expanded and the mid-1960s round of violent inner-city upheavals got under way, more whites also saw themselves as moving away from street crime, racial conflict, or black (and Hispanic) people period.

The most important demographic change during the post–World War II period took place in the city's balance of black and white populations. By 1950, there were almost 500,000 blacks in Chicago, constituting 13.6% of the city's population, and by 1980 there were almost 2 million (39.8%). Hispanics formed another fast-growing ethnic bloc, increasing from 3% to 17% of Chicago's population between 1960 and 1983.[5] Blacks and Hispanics took up residence in the postwar inner city, often in South Side or West Side neighborhoods that had once been occupied by white ethnics. At the same time, an expanded class of professionals, managers, and office workers employed in the service industries that supplanted Chicago's waning manufacturing sector took up residence in the band of redeveloped neighborhoods clustering on the North Side lakefront and around the Loop.

Contrary to the impression one might derive from Shay's expressway reminiscence and other narratives of white-ethnic decline, the industrial neighborhood order did not "fall" overnight like Troy (sacked by Myrmidons) or some decadent empire overrun by barbarian hordes (pathology-bearing "minorities" streaming over one border, gentrifying "yuppies" over the other), but Chicago's urban villages were drastically reduced and broken up by postindustrial transformation. Sociologists of the Chicago School had used the term "inner city" in the 1920s and 1930s to describe the industrial neighborhood order, but "inner city" has since the urban crisis of the 1960s become shorthand for a very different and distinctively postindustrial arrangement. The term now conventionally calls to mind for many Americans, as it already did for Lait and Mortimer at midcentury, a social landscape of black and Hispanic ghettos surrounding the city's redeveloped core, surviving enclaves of white ethnics, and expanding colonies of preponderantly white but ethnically neutral urban professionals; the whole surrounded in turn by an inner ring of older industrial suburbs (housing white ethnics and some blacks and often reabsorbed into the inner city) and beyond by a largely white suburban expanse. In the 1950s and 1960s, the suburbs and exurbs of "Chicagoland" expanded with unrivaled speed around Chicago's emerging postwar inner city, marching away to Indiana in the south, into the farm country of northern Illinois in the west, and toward Wisconsin in the north.

Algren's ghost, charged as it is with resonances of industrial urbanism and its decline, reminds Shay of the old Chicago—a city of fact, half-remembered—layered under the new. The quintessentially postindustrial Kennedy Expressway, literally built on the ruins of Algren's Chicago, carries Shay through the eerily persistent industrial city as he passes through the ghost of the building at 1523 Wabansia. Similarly, the encounter with Algren's ghost, charged with resonances of a tradition of Chicago writing *about* industrial urbanism, brings Shay into contact with another old Chicago—the city of feeling created by its writers. His approach by expressway echoes a long sequence of such scenes that extends back to late nineteenth-century scenes of entry into Chicago by train, a staple of industrial-era Chicago writing exemplified by the paradigmatic opening of *Sister Carrie* (discussed in chapter 3), with its long lines of telegraph poles, railroad tracks, and outlying houses telling a story of speculative desire as they lead Carrie's eye across the prairie into the big city.[6]

The arriving motorist's view from the expressway is to postindustrial Chicago what the arriving passenger's view from the train was to industrial Chicago: a representational strategy that opens up a landscape for infusion with meanings. In *Nelson Algren's Chicago*, Shay enters from the northwest, passing through layers of social and literary history as he approaches the Loop. In the passage from Algren's *City on the Make* discussed in chapter 1, the reader soars up the lake shore and through the city's industrial history from the southeast but descends to Lake Shore Drive and suburbanization soon enough. In *Chicago: Race, Class, and the Response to Urban Decline*, an economic and social study of postwar Chicago, a section entitled "The Rise and Fall of Smokestack Chicago" begins with an approach from the southeast, retracing the swoop along the lakefront in *City on the Make*, through "a gauntlet of industrial development that rivals any heavy industrial concentration in the United States." Passing first through the lakefront belt of steel mills and other heavy industry in the Northwest Indiana towns of Gary, East Chicago, and Hammond, the imagined driver enters the city proper via the Chicago Skyway, from which you get a bird's eye view of Chicago's industrial backyard. You pass over the entrance to Calumet Harbor, which is relatively quiet compared to earlier years when Great Lakes ships carrying everything from grain to iron ore could be seen entering and leaving. The modest bungalows and two-flats in the surrounding blue-collar neighborhoods are framed by industry. USX's South Works dominates the lakefront and a few smaller factories dot the grid of streets.[7]

The ships and factories establish the industrial frame that gives shape to the kind of neighborhood urbanism suggested by bungalows and two-flats. But the expressway, connecting suburbs to city and embodying priorities more characteristic of a metropolitan region organized by the demands of a service economy, places a postindustrial frame around the scene below. Like the dwindling ship traffic—more remembered than observed—the industrial vista is becoming a ghostly echo of the high-industrial moment, still perceptible but already tinged with the quality of anachronism that Shay ascribes to Nelson Algren's old neighborhood beneath the Kennedy. The entry by expressway, like the entry by railroad, is bewildering and enlightening because it creates a portrait of the city by peeling back the layers of urban order.

Passing through vestiges of the urban village as he navigates through the postindustrial social landscape, retrofitting the railroad scenes of industrial literature to do the work of representing that postindustrial landscape, Art Shay steers his car and his consciousness through an encounter with both of Nelson Algren's "old neighborhoods." One old neighborhood is the Polish urban village around 1523 Wabansia; the other is that section of the genre map of American letters occupied by Chicago realism, the tradition of writing that evolved around the project of representing the industrial city. Algren made literature from recognizing that both old neighborhoods faced the end of an era as Chicago entered into a period of postindustrial transformation at midcentury.

The Industrial City

The phrase "postindustrial Chicago" takes some getting used to: the word "Chicago" has built-in industrial connotations dating back to the late nineteenth century. Chicago was the right place at the right time, a city visibly produced at near-miraculous speed by the industrial transformations, population movements, and rapid urbanization shaping the terrain of America in the late nineteenth and early twentieth centuries.[8] The central place of a vast region stretching from the Rockies to the Cumberland Gap and from the Mississippi Delta to the north woods, commanding the rail and water routes along which passed extracted resources and manufactured goods, a center of heavy industry as well as a center of commercial and financial activity, Chicago was early twentieth-century America's "national economic city"[9] —the prototypical modern industrial metropolis. As "the classical center of American materialism,"[10] Chicago came to be understood as a place where the structuring economic forces of American life manifested themselves with unique clarity and vigor.

Chicago's relatively late start (in 1850 the fledgling city still had fewer than 30,000 inhabitants; in 1900 it had almost 2 million)[11] and the wholesale rebuilding of large sections of the city after the Great Fire of 1871 made for a city uniquely responsive to the shaping forces of a factory-based industrial order. "Chicago epitomized a major shift to industrial capitalism in the institutional base of U.S. cities," argues Sidney Bremer. "Postfire Chicago was designed—much of it literally from the ground up—to accommodate the expansion and consolidation of modern economic ventures."[12] Large manufacturing and processing plants clustered around the urban core, lined the river and the rail lines converging on downtown, and expanded south and east along the lakefront into Indiana, seeking locations with access to coal and other raw resources, to "good intra-regional transportation and commercial linkages," and to "a large factory labor force" who walked and in time rode mass transit to work.[13] Railroads criss-crossed the city, many of them running at grade level through residential streets, linking up at union stations and interchanges. Warehouses and department stores made the downtown core a commercial center; centralized stock and commodity exchanges and banks made it a financial center; an iconic cluster of ostentatiously "cultural" institutions—library, art museum, opera house—made it a cultural center. Many of these various functions were housed in skyscrapers, state-of-the-art factories, and distinguished municipal buildings that made Chicago an architectural exemplar. In the early twentieth century, Chicago had the look of the foreseeable urban future.

The city's neighborhood order took shape around the frame of industry. Professionals, managers, and the wealthy (especially white Protestants) gravitated over time toward the lakefront and to increasingly distant suburban removes, away from the industrial interior's clamor, dirt, and heterogeneous crowding, while a vast patchwork of neighborhoods housing the city's laboring wage earners spread inland from the core. These neighborhoods of apartment walk-ups and Chicago's characteristic blocks of close-packed bungalows developed in waves as established immigrants, pushed by new arrivals and the expansion of the factory belt, followed streetcar and elevated lines away from the Loop. This form of urban growth yielded a city of "industrial villages"— neighborhoods organized around workplaces and commuter lines and often dominated by a particular ethnic bloc—grouped concentrically around the downtown core and ringed by streetcar suburbs. A common reliance on manufacturing and the influence of ethnically ordered local political machines, which brokered among the various interests, stabilized this distinctively industrial form of urbanism.

Industrial Chicago was prototypically modern not only in the growth of its industries but also in its ethnic heterogeneity. Three-quarters of its population was listed in the 1890 census as foreign born or as children of foreign-born parents. Chicago's population streamed to its neighborhoods from a complex of hinterlands: Midwesterners and Westerners, many of them European immigrants, came to Chicago from small towns and farms in search of a new, urban set of opportunities; Easterners came west in search of business opportunities and new starts in an industrial boom town; peasants, craftspeople, and others of modest means from Europe, the American South, Mexico, the Middle East, and Asia found their way to industrial Chicago's crowded immigrant neighborhoods and factory jobs.

European immigrants dominated the city's working population and neighborhood order. They tended to settle initially near the concentration of industrial workplaces in the city's core, then to follow streetcar lines further away from the core over time.[14] The communities they established spread inland across the South Side and West Side, often solidifying into neighborhoods around institutions—not only workplaces but also national parish churches, banks, stores—and around property owning. The typical ethnic neighborhood was not solidly settled by one group; typically one or two ethnic blocs dominated a heterogeneous mix through weight of numbers or political influence. The increasingly segregated Black Belt forming in the early years of the twentieth century on the near South Side (which wealthy white residents had begun to abandon for the North Side lakefront before the turn of the century) constituted a signal exception to this mixed pattern. Especially after the first great migration of Southern blacks to Chicago during and after World War I, the Black Belt's population and institutions grew together into what came to be known as a Black Metropolis—a microcosmic city created by severe residential segregation—contained within the patchwork of villages but separate from them.

Describing early twentieth-century Chicago in *Boss* (1971), his study of Mayor Daley (the First), newspaper columnist Mike Royko definitively sketches the neighborhood order as remembered by the story of golden age and decline. Daley, the man most responsible for the shape of the transformed post–World War II city, "grew up a small-town boy, which used to be possible even in the big city. Not anymore, because of the car, the shifting society, and the suburban sprawl. But Chicago, until as late as the 1950s"—Royko's periodization conforms precisely with the appearance at midcentury of a body of decline narratives—"was a place where people stayed put for a while, creating tightly knit neighborhoods, as small-townish as any village in the wheat fields."[15] The villages formed "larger ethnic states," which Royko maps in a grand panorama:

> To the north of the Loop was Germany. To the northwest Poland. To the west were Italy and Israel. To the southwest were Bohemia and Lithuania. And to the south was Ireland.

It wasn't perfectly defined because the borders shifted as newcomers moved in on the old settlers, sending them fleeing in terror and disgust. Here and there were outlying colonies, with Poles also on the South Side, and Irish up north.

But you could always tell, even with your eyes closed, which state you were in by the odors of the food stores and the open kitchen windows, the sound of the foreign or familiar language, and by whether a stranger hit you in the head with a rock.[16]

The neighborhoods as Royko describes them were self-contained systems. Each had within it the institutional ingredients of a small town: a main shopping street, businesses (tavern, funeral parlor, vegetable store, butcher shop, drugstore, pool hall, clubs), locally famous characters (drunk, trollop, village idiot, war hero, sports star), a police station, a sports team, a ball field, churches. There were also factories: "Some people had to leave the neighborhood to work, but many didn't, because the houses were interlaced with industry." With characteristic nostalgia-deflating irony (to which I will return in chapter 4), Royko sums up his thumbnail portrait of the neighborhood order by emphasizing the tension between the security and the fragility of neighborhood in a typically urban climate of constant economic, demographic, and cultural change: "So, for a variety of reasons, ranging from convenience to fear to economics, people stayed in their own neighborhood, loving it, enjoying the closeness, the friendliness, the familiarity, and trying to save enough money to move out."[17]

All of Them Reek of Chicago

The Chicago of fact that flourished from the late nineteenth century to the mid–twentieth century was structured by a distinctive set of orders that expressed the industrial city's function and history: the pattern of urban villages that housed its heterogeneous workforce, the armature of railroads converging on the core, the complex of hinterlands with which the city exchanged resources, products, people, and capital. The Chicago of feeling that flourished in that same period was similarly ordered by a distinctive set of literary strategies that expressed the industrial city's effect on the American literary imagination. Representations of industrial Chicago accordingly developed a series of standard images and meanings associated with Chicago's signature forms: for example, the iron city of railroads, ordered by the pitiless processes of production and commerce, harder than human flesh or will; the rationalized bloodbath of business as usual in the stockyards; a landscape of large buildings and crowded neighborhoods that monumentalized class difference, the impulse to maximize return, and the wish to temper commerce with aesthetics or conscience; the shocks felt by hinterlanders (like Sister Carrie) and native sons and daughters (like Algren's characters) encountering urban modernity in the street.[18] Chicago's astounding growth "variously fed the imaginations and assaulted the sensibilities of observers the world over" from the aftermath of the fire of 1871 to the eve of World War II.[19] Within the writing of this larger group of observers, though, we can make out a distinctive Chicago realist tradition—by which I mean a tradition of writing that placed primary emphasis on the thematic and formal problems posed by industrial modernity—that took shape around the task of mapping and considering the meanings of industrial Chicago.

A loose but cohesive complex of novelists, poets, critics, social scientists, and reporters guided industrial Chicago's entry into American letters, fixing for posterity the terms commonly used to understand and represent Chicago.[20] Algren—a novelist who had set out as a young man to become a sociologist, trained and worked as a reporter, tried his hand at verse and prose poetry, and would eventually take to calling himself a journalist for the last two decades of his writing life—linked himself in a number of ways to the various networks of writers who had together created the canonical literary Chicago. When he chose to think of himself as the last Chicago writer, Algren placed himself at the terminus of a tradition rooted in the period identified by the story of decline as the city's golden age. He presented himself as the last remaining architect of a composite textual city fashioned by his literary ancestors and allies—writers he read, admired, took as models, and in many cases knew as professional colleagues.

In the past, the story goes, the city they imagined had aspired to the status of world capital, just as Chicago itself had seemed on the verge of becoming a world city of the first rank. The story of Chicago's decline, in its obligatory cultural chapter, usually makes reference to H. L. Mencken's repeated, unabashedly hyperbolic, and at least semi-serious contention that early twentieth-century Chicago was the emerging literary capital of America. Mencken wrote in the *Chicago Sunday Tribune* in 1917 that Chicago had produced "all literary movements that have youth in them, and a fresh point of view, and the authentic bounce and verve of the country and the true character and philosophy of its people." Nine times out of ten, the writer who "is indubitably American and who has something new and interesting to say, and who says it with an air . . . has some sort of connection with the abattoir by the lake," having been "bred there or got his start there, or passed through there during the days when he was tender." The writers he had in mind—he named Fuller, Norris, Dreiser, Anderson, Herrick, and Joseph Medill Patterson as exemplars—"reek of Chicago in every line they write."[21] In 1920, Mencken again made his case for Chicago as the "Literary Capitol of the United States," this time in the *Nation* (London), adding the poets Masters and Sandburg and the newspaperman Ade as auxiliaries to his list of novelists. For Mencken, Chicago's reputation rested principally on the work of novelists: "With two exceptions," he concluded, "there is not a single American novelist, a novelist deserving a civilized reader's notice—who has not sprung from the Middle Empire that has Chicago for its capital."[22]

The heroes of Mencken's scenario were authors whose work both figured and enacted principal social and cultural dramas of his time: the urbanization and industrialization of America, the arrival of new European immigrants, the emergence of literary traditions grounded in the speech and habits of the middle and lower classes rather than in the genteel tradition, the westering of the acknowledged wellsprings of American culture. Mencken's net thus sweeps up not only the authors producing representations of Chicago as the prototypical industrial city (e.g., Dreiser, Norris, Upton Sinclair, Sandburg) but also Midwesterners and Westerners looking back to the hinterland from the distinctly metropolitan perspective afforded by Chicago (e.g., Anderson, Masters, Herrick, Cather). The former strain dominated the Chicago literary scene at the turn of the century, while the latter strain formed the center of a second renaissance during the 1910s and early 1920s.

A third wave of fiction writers, the neighborhood novelists of the 1930s and 1940s, took up the representation of the industrial city at street level. They completed the movement of the Chicago realist tradition's primary focus from the urban core and the Midwestern hinterland to the inner-city landscape of the industrial villages. Mencken, reacting perhaps to the waning of the town-city conflict in Chicago writing, lost interest in the 1930s in his claim for the primacy of Chicago writing, but other critics came forward to lionize the neighborhood novelists as proletarian writers or latter-day naturalists.[23] Farrell was the most celebrated neighborhood novelist during the 1930s, while in the 1940s Wright and Algren came to be seen as his principal successors.[24] In mapping the world of the South Side Irish, Southern blacks in Bronzeville, and Poles in the Milwaukee Avenue corridor, these authors made a further move toward rendering as literature the language, habits, and daily routines of people largely excluded or exoticized by the genteel tradition. It was this movement away from the genteel that had originally attracted Mencken to what he called "the Chicago Palatinate." He was perhaps less sympathetic to the neighborhood novels' brand of social and cultural criticism, which considered the increasingly discouraging implications of industrial urbanism for a cast of characters drawn from the ranks of those transplanted hinterlanders who formed Chicago's working class.

Novels like Farrell's Studs Lonigan trilogy (1932–35), Wright's Native Son (1940), and Algren's Never Come Morning (1942) proposed a critique of industrial urbanism with a set of characters, landscapes, and urban processes grounded in close observation of neighborhood life. As a group, these novels ordered themselves around a line of inquiry that, at least in the literary world, enjoyed a charge of special urgency during the depression and its aftermath. As Wright put it in 1942 in his introduction to Algren's Never Come Morning, the neighborhood novels directed "microscopic attention upon that stratum of society that is historically footloose, unformed, malleable, restless, devoid of inner stability, unidentified by class allegiances, yet full of hot, honest, blind striving." Wright predicted that "there will come a time in our country when the middle class will gasp and say (as they now gasp over the present world situation): 'Why weren't we told this before? Why didn't our novelists depict the beginnings of this terrible thing that has come before us?' "[25] Algren, in mapping the neighborhood and the minds of its "boys on the street," was sounding a warning of future social crisis growing from the increasingly untenable condition of an economically and culturally impoverished urban proletariat. Wright's portentous tone and linkage of inner-city crisis to the rise of fascism ("the present world situation") typify a 1930s-vintage rhetoric of imminent crisis and class war, but they also anticipate future constructions of urban crisis (taken up in part 3 of this study) involving violent young men and the collapse of industrial urbanism: in the 1950s, juvenile delinquency; in the 1960s, urban riots and drug-related street crime.[26]

Farrell, Wright, and Algren, then, brought the Chicago novel definitively to the neighborhoods; they also solidified the links joining the Chicago novel to allied forms, especially sociology and journalism. The Chicago tradition that formed Algren's usable intellectual past was something much broader than a school or circle of writers but narrower than the totality of fiction, poetry, criticism, social science, and reportage produced in Chicago in the sixty years before World War II. Algren identified himself with a strain running through representations of Chicago that emphasized close attention to the material city in the form of research, observation, and precise description of urban types, language, terrains, and processes: "My kind of writing is just a form of reportage, you might call it emotionalized reportage, but . . . the data has to be there. Compassion has no use without a setting. I mean you have to know how do the law courts work. You have to know how many bars there are in a jail cell. You can't just say, 'The guy's in jail.' You have to *know*."[27] Applying to the Guggenheim Foundation for a grant to fund the writing of his novel *Never Come Morning*, Algren stated that his "ultimate purpose would be an accurate description of Chicago in his time," detailing "economic and political factors making toward juvenile criminality among some 300,000 Poles . . . on Chicago's Near Northwest side . . . through the methods of naturalism." He then listed a series of locations ("schoolyards, public playgrounds, churches, poolrooms, taverns") and authorities ("social workers, precinct captains, police lieutenants, and Mr. Frank Konkowski, an indicted alderman") that would provide "data."[28] He could have been proposing a study plotting the incidence and sources of delinquency on the Near Northwest Side—and, in fact, the eminent Chicago School sociologist Louis Wirth recommended him for the grant.

The neighborhood novelists' habits of observation brought the Chicago

novel close to the newspaper but closer still to the sociological study. Farrell
and Wright, and to a lesser extent Algren, had significant connections to the
University of Chicago's influential Department of Sociology, which in the first
half of the twentieth century set the pattern for urban sociology's encounter
with the industrial metropolis, from the "ecology" of its structural transformations to the daily round of its representative types: teenage gang members, taxi
dancers, the social register's Four Hundred, anonymous roomers, blacks in
Bronzeville, hobos, slum dwellers, immigrant laborers, single women, strong-
arm thieves, and so on.[29] These studies mapped the city metaphorically but also
in the most literal sense. Ernest Burgess's map of the industrial city (fig. 3) as
a set of concentric zones radiating out from the center served as one of the
Chicago School's most important theoretical frameworks. Specific studies of
particular areas and groups filled in the details of this master map at neighborhood level. The Chicago School's maps of the inner city literalized the overarching representational project of Chicago realism: to capture the city on paper
in ways that revealed its structuring logic.

The field observers of the Chicago School practiced a kind of theoretically
informed anecdotal reportage making for a markedly journalistic and even novelistic brand of social science. Robert Park, one of the Chicago School's central
figures, had trained as a reporter and acknowledged that "we are indebted
mainly to writers of fiction for our more intimate knowledge of contemporary
urban life," calling for sociologists to produce studies "more searching and dis-
interested than *even*" (italics added) Zola's Rougon-Macquart novels.[30] The
Chicago novel overlapped at many points with this sociological-journalistic
effort to map the city: Dreiser's mock-clinical asides on fashions and occupational types in *Sister Carrie*, Sinclair's heavily researched muckraking in *The
Jungle*, the neighborhood novels' careful depictions of daily life in the gang,
tavern, and slum.[31]

Algren's Chicago realist tradition, then, consisted of writing that turned the
spaces of the industrial city into places by mapping them in detail and investing them with human meanings, writing that found ways to represent the city's
structuring logics and its inner life. This definition puts in the foreground representations of Chicago and Chicago people; it therefore consigns to the background much of the writing of Midwestern regionalists like Anderson, Masters,
and Cather, as well as the institution building and criticism of Harriet Monroe,
Floyd Dell, and Francis Hackett, all of whom helped to give form to Chicago's
literary movements. However, the narrowed definition of Chicago realism as
the project of writing about industrial Chicago does, whatever its limitations,
identify a logic informing and connecting a vast body of representations produced in the first half of the twentieth century. If Algren read and wished to
emulate a wide range of writers from Dostoevsky to Céline, his conception of
himself as a Chicago writer took shape in a narrower forum: he placed himself

among the various realists of the Chicago tradition who "made American literary history"—as Doubleday's advertising copy for *The Man with the Golden Arm* claimed—in producing a composite set of landscapes, characters, narratives, and figures through which the industrial city could be known and understood.

Postindustrial Chicago

Between 1947 and 1982 Chicago lost 59% of its manufacturing jobs. The city's economic reliance on heavy industry made Chicago particularly vulnerable to a general decline of manufacturing in America's older industrial centers that accelerated in the years after World War II.[32] The suburbanizing of population and industry meant a spatial decentralization of capital—private investment, public funds, jobs, tax revenues—that redistributed resources outward from central cities into metropolitan regions. People who had power to direct the futures of central cities saw themselves entering into a crucial competition with one another and with the suburbs for remaining manufacturing jobs and the industries of the growing service sector. They responded by encouraging the reconcentration of capital in the urban core, not in the neighborhoods.

Chicago had taken form in relation to the flow of money, goods, and people typical of a manufacturing city embedded in regional, national, and international markets. As its position in those systems began to change, waves of change swept over the city: new political orders like the progrowth coalition eventually headed by Daley (who was not the simple "old shoe" political boss he appeared to be), new physical orders like clustered high-rise housing ("luxury" towers in some places, notoriously bad public housing in others) and the cutting of elevated freeways through the old neighborhoods, a new demographic order shaped by the outward movement of white ethnics toward the inner ring of suburbs and the southward and westward expansion of the city's so-called Black Belt. As John Mollenkopf puts it, postindustrial transformations "dismantled the mosaic of blue collar ethnic segmentation which developed within the occupational and residential order of the older industrial cities."[33] From the powerful influence on Chicago's Department of City Planning exercised by the business leaders of the Chicago Central Area Committee to the decisions of the most modest taxpayers, private initiative combined with governmental decision making—however one interprets the relationship between the two—to reshape the city, clearing the ground for a postindustrial order by demolishing elements of the gradually obsolescent industrial order. By transforming the landscape, the redevelopment process also revalued land, especially around the downtown core and on the North Side, in ways that guided both private investment and government activity.

The group Art Shay calls "Daley's myrmidons," a progrowth coalition uniting business leaders and city planners with political leaders organized into the Chicago Democratic machine headed by Richard J. Daley from 1955 to 1976, planned and executed the reconfiguration of post–World War II Chicago. Chicago's great age of urban renewal and redevelopment stretches from the first postwar projects of the late 1940s, through the federally funded redevelopment boom of the 1950s and 1960s, to the demise of urban renewal as a social program in the 1970s and Daley's death in 1976. In that period, Daley's progrowth coalition responded to (and helped to shape) two fundamental changes in the great industrial cities of the Midwest and Northeast: the contraction of the industrial manufacturing sector and complementary expansion of the service sector, and the interlocking folk migrations that brought black Southerners to the inner city and white urbanites to the suburbs in unprecedented numbers.

The movements of people in large numbers were dramatically apparent, especially to the racially sensitive American eye. The economic transition was harder to recognize, but "even as early as 1947," report Gregory Squires and his coauthors in their account of postwar Chicago's economic transformation, "one could see changes on the horizon."

These changes were in part geographical: "Chicago's manufacturing base was starting to move from the city to the suburbs," as well as to the South and West of the nation (and to other parts of the world), where operating costs were lower and labor more easily managed.[34] The post–World War II boom in construction, major appliances, and automobiles, all tied to the tremendous expansion of America's suburbs and the redevelopment of its urban cores, helped to obscure the decline of older heavy industries   railroads, steel, meatpacking— that had flourished in Chicago until the depression and again during wartime. Although the complex and long-term process of deindustrialization in the larger cities had begun as early as 1920, the depression and the subsequent manufacturing boom and prosperity associated with World War II had slowed and masked its effects. This made all the more dramatic a massive wave of postwar suburbanization assisted by the federal government's unprecedented investment in suburban industry, home ownership, and the highway system.[35] Soon after the war, factory employment in Chicago, which had increased steadily until the depression and then again during the war, began a gradual decline from "a twentieth century high of 688,000 [in 1947] to 277,000 factory jobs" in 1982. During the same period, manufacturing jobs increased 131% in suburban Cook County and 195% in the surrounding counties of the extended metropolitan area. "This employment shift," conclude Squires and his coauthors, "follows a pattern of disinvestment and plant relocation, marking Chicago as the loser and the suburbs as the winners."[36]

"The changes were also sectoral; Chicago's economy was starting to shift away from manufacturing toward the service sector."[37] As was the case with other Midwestern and Northeastern cities that came to be known collectively in the 1970s as the Rust Belt, Chicago's physical arrangements and cultural character derived from the industrial imperatives of transportation and manufacturing (in Chicago's case, especially railroads and heavy manufacturing done in large plants). But after World War II Chicago increasingly became a service city, a regional and national center for corporate headquarters, banking, legal and other ancillary business services, real estate, insurance, government, education, health care, conventions, tourism. These functions required office towers, hotels, and convention centers rather than factories; more expressways and airports to move people rather than more railroads and port facilities to move goods; new apartment buildings and the renovation of old buildings to house the professionals, managers, and office workers employed in the service sector rather than more cheap housing in the aging urban villages for incoming industrial workers. Construction also boomed, therefore, becoming one of the city's leading industries as the progrowth coalition built a new core and a new set of connections to the suburban periphery and the national transportation network.

The redevelopment of Chicago centered on the Loop, not the neighborhoods; most of the enormous expenditure of resources and expertise devoted to redevelopment in the inner city went into remaking the core and its connections to the region, nation, and world. After a decade of early slum clearance and redevelopment projects and preliminary planning, the Department of City Planning, working closely with business groups like the Chicago Central Area Committee, codified the thinking behind postwar redevelopment in its "Development Plan for the Central Area of Chicago" of 1958. Squires and his coauthors point out that the development plan was "strikingly post-industrial," making almost no provision for the production of goods in the urban core.[38] Declines in manufacturing and the railroad industry, which had been steeply undercut by the new interstate highway system and air travel, had left a belt of abandoned factory buildings, vacant lots going back to prairie, and disused rail facilities around the Loop, which were mixed to the south and west with rundown residential sections. At the same time, large retailers in the Loop were losing business, both relative to the suburbs and in absolute volume of sales.

The plan's principal objective, therefore, was to create a densely developed, attractive, efficient core in the Loop and Near North Side that provided the entire Chicago metropolitan region with a concentrated central place for office work, shopping, entertainment, tourism, and "cultural activities." The plan emphasized channeling service-sector workers, shoppers, and goods from the suburbs (and the national highway system beyond) via new expressways to the core, which would be densely built up with skyscrapers devoted to office and retail uses. New housing developments around the Loop and on the lakefront would accommodate professional and managerial workers in the service industries. Outdoor plazas, beautification of the river front and lakefront, a new civic center, a downtown subway system, and a new University of Illinois campus southwest of the Loop would clear away encroaching "blight" and support the city center's management, finance, retailing, and other service functions. The development plan of 1958 argued that the dense tangles of railroad lines that had been one of industrial Chicago's signature forms were now obsolete and were in fact a form of "blight" that retarded the city's present transformation by keeping property values low in adjacent areas.[39]

The railroad yards south and west of the Loop now provided likely locations, easily cleared, for new high-rises and townhouses to house well-paid office workers. These private developments, subsidized in part by public funds, would become part of a new middle- and upper-class landscape surrounding the Loop and reaching north and south along the lakefront. On the South Side, new development extended down from the Loop to the new Michael Reese Hospital complex, the new Illinois Institute of Technology campus, housing developments like Prairie Shores and Lake Meadows, and to Hyde Park, where the University of Chicago took steps to stabilize the borders and population of its neighborhood, which abutted largely black and lower-income neighborhoods on three sides. Southwest of the Loop, inland, a new facility for the University of Illinois's Chicago campus replaced a predominantly Italian neighborhood known as the Valley. On the North Side, intensive private development reached all the way up the lakefront from the Loop to Evanston, eventually producing a solid strip of luxury high-rises buffered inland by variously fashionable, bohemian, and transitional neighborhoods. This high-rise development rarely reached more than a few blocks from the lakefront, but the gentrification of older low-rise housing stock has extended irregularly inland.

Loop- and lakefront-centered redevelopment deepened the traditional division between the core and the neighborhoods. On his first visit to Chicago in 1938, riding in from the airport through the neighborhoods of the West Side in an age before expressways, A. J. Liebling prefigured Art Shay in observing two cities: in the neighborhoods, "the low buildings, the industrial plants, and the railroad crossings at grade produced less of a feeling of being in a great city than of riding through an endless succession of factory-town main streets"; arriving downtown, "the transition to the Loop and its tall buildings was abrupt, like entering a walled city. I found it beguilingly medieval."[40] As public and private resources poured into the Loop and lakefront, and the industrial order structuring the "factory-town" neighborhoods unraveled, the difference between walled city and surrounding villages became more pronounced. From the progrowth coalition's perspective in the 1950s, the decaying industrial landscape encroaching on the core posed a threat to Chicago's postindustrial future. The neighborhoods and the old plants harbored the disease of "blight," which could spread to infect the core and cripple the city's service sector.

The concept of blight provides one key to the postindustrial fate of the urban villages. Originally introduced into the lexicon by progressive housing reformers seeking to improve living conditions in the industrial city's immigrant slums, blight came to serve as a rationale for clearing away the industrial-era infrastructure to make way for a variety of redevelopment projects. Once an area was identified as blighted—and "blight" became a verb used by planners and city officials, as in "we blighted that neighborhood"—the apparatus of redevelopment could be brought to bear on it. The city could exercise its right to clear the land (as Shay puts it, Algren's block was "eminent-domained"), and government-funded housing or government-subsidized private redevelopment could go forward. Housing that was crowded or dilapidated or otherwise substandard, factories and warehouse blocks, railroad tracks, densely packed residential areas without green spaces or boulevards—in other words, foundational elements of the industrial city that by midcentury had reached advanced middle age—had to be torn down to make way for expressways, open spaces, university and hospital buildings ("urban renewal for MDs and PhDs," as one commentator termed it),[41] offices and municipal buildings, stores, and housing that people from the old neighborhoods could not or would not live in. The concept of blight became a powerful tool in clearing the crowded ground of the old industrial inner city for the new inner city emerging from it.

As early as 1949, the Chicago Plan Commission (a forerunner of the Department of City Planning) used criteria like age and condition of buildings and overcrowding to classify 22.6 square miles of Chicago as "blighted" or "near-blighted" (fig. 4). In *Politics, Planning, and the Public Interest* (1955), Martin Meyerson and Edward Banfield explain that this territory "lay in a half circle around the Loop . . . and around the wholesale and light manufacturing areas adjacent to the Loop. The half-circle of slum areas was irregular, but for the most part it extended about five miles from the Loop. About one-fourth of Chicago's population lived in these areas, although they comprised about 15 per cent of the land in Chicago devoted to residential use." Around the "blighted" and "near-blighted" areas was a ring of "conservation" areas which, in the commission's judgment, could be saved from encroaching blight by judicious investment of resources. Meyerson and Banfield note that "the validity of the criteria" for blighting and conservation "was doubtful" and "left a good deal to interpretation": the age of buildings alone was not a reliable measure of their value or condition; good and substandard units were often mixed together on the same block; and plaintiffs in a court case charged that "when in doubt the Plan Commission classified blocks blighted if they were occupied by Negroes."[42] The "conservation" areas were typically white-ethnic neighborhoods that showed signs of breaking up; planners considered racial heterogeneity a sign, or a form, of blight.

This last item touches upon a second key to change in the neighborhoods: "the slums of the northern cities," noted Meyerson and Banfield in 1955, "had become increasingly Negro."[43] The arrival of a new wave of Southern blacks (and, to a lesser extent, Mexicans and Puerto Ricans) in the inner city formed an interlocking migration with the departure of white ethnics toward the city's outer edges and the suburbs. The traditional borders of Chicago's old Black Belt on the South Side and smaller segregated black areas on the West Side could no longer hold a rapidly growing, overcrowded population. "Every week during the 1950s, three-and-a-half blocks changed from white to Negro," as one geographical history of the city somewhat breathlessly puts it, and these blocks were typically located where the growing black neighborhoods met white neighborhoods in rapid transition.[44] In this manner, Chicago's black population grew enormously, moving south and west into what had been the white-ethnic heartland, without becoming any less segregated. The new black Chicagoans entered the city—drawn by manufacturing, especially defense, jobs available during and just after World War II—at a time when the manufacturing sector was beginning its long-term decline. The economic, cultural, and spatial constraints on blacks helped to confine them to the inner city at a time when opportunity and capital were moving to the suburbs. If the coincident black and white migrations of the 1940s and 1950s, to city and suburb, respectively, were responses to the "pull" factors of opportunity, the maturing of the black and Hispanic inner city in the 1960s became a greater "push" factor for those whites who now saw themselves as being left behind in an increasingly alien landscape.

This expansion of the black inner city set the stage for the transformation of the industrial-era ghetto—the Black Metropolis that matured between the wars—into the second ghetto: the expanded ghetto produced in the 1940s and 1950s by South-North migration, governmental attempts to lock the black inner city in place with monumental housing projects and expressways, continuing deindustrialization of the inner city, and the departure of those members of the black middle class who could break through the barrier of residential segregation.[45] The second ghetto's signature form is the high-rise housing project, built in great numbers under the auspices of federal urban renewal programs during the 1950s and 1960s. These projects, concentrated in the older parts of the inner city within a few miles of the Loop, were built to house the inner city's black population and to contain its spatial expansion.

Projects, expressway construction, and the complex politics of housing and public education produced a kind of spatial stability by the mid-1960s—and produced as well a great deal of violent social instability in the form of racial conflict over succession, segregation, and their consequences. After the rapid neighborhood turnovers of the 1950s and early 1960s, the old immigrant-ethnic neighborhood patchwork now looked more like a series of white-ethnic enclaves isolated—or fortified—by postwar construction. Like the expressways cut through the old low-rise city to the Loop, the new high-rise public housing, concentrated in areas that were already considered part of the black inner city, helped to fix the new boundaries of neighborhood in place. Expressways and projects together express the postwar progrowth coalition's primary concerns—saving and remaking the urban core as a regional center, housing the postindustrial workforce, confining "blight" to the neighborhoods, and protecting the white-ethnic neighborhoods that remained.[46]

And Chicago, I Mean Really

At midcentury, then, the industrial neighborhood order was still robust—indeed, it appeared to be in full flower during a time of general prosperity—but a perceptive observer could already see signs of the contraction and dissolution to come. Algren's *The Man with the Golden Arm* and *City on the Make* imagine precisely this crisis. If industrial Chicago "fell," Chicago realism as Algren understood it would cease to be, because the literature took life from writers' close contact with the familiar landscape, processes, and problems of industrial urbanism. Even in 1949 and 1950, at the moment of his greatest success, when everybody who mattered agreed that Algren was the next big thing, reviewers compared him to Hugo, Dostoevsky, Gorki, and Dickens, and (perhaps best of all) *Golden Arm* was the best-selling book in Chicago, Algren argued that Chicago was entering a literary dark age.[47] In *City on the Make*, Algren imagined himself the last of his kind: Chicago realism, unappreciated in both civic and critical circles, and with no new generational influx of talent to revitalize it, had come to the end of the line with him.

Algren saw in this decline of Chicago's literary reputation a sign of a larger postwar reaction against the kind of social criticism, pursued across a center-to-left spectrum from progressive to radical, he believed to undergird his line of Chicago novelists and poets. This view fits neatly with a standard reading of American literary culture in the 1950s—pursued, for example, by Algren's biographer Bettina Drew—that identifies a new valuation of formal sophistication and a devaluation of realism. This formalist turn is often regarded as a kind of political centrism correcting for the perceived excesses and limitations of 1930s-style "social realism" and the conventionally "political" engagement (characterized by vital centrists in the 1950s as extremist politics) from which it was assumed to proceed. Both the ascendance of New Criticism, which was supposed to be less overtly "political," and the apparent decline of the big, well-researched realist novel's critical reputation were thus in keeping with the intellectual climate of liberal anticommunism and consensus.[48] The ascendance of a new complex of academically credentialed writers and the institutions that supported their hegemony also helped to shift to the margins of American letters Algren and his line, who had established authority by positioning themselves as imaginative observers within the industrial city's social fabric. As

Algren told it in 1960, the "new owners" of American literature "arrived directly from their respective campuses armed with blueprints to which the novel and short story would have to conform." These critics "formed a loose federation, between the literary quarterlies, publishers' offices and book review columns, presenting a view of American letters untouched by American life."[49]

Algren thus saw himself operating in a cultural climate in which, during the 1950s, influential critics turned against him as part of a centrist or right-wing reaction against prewar radicalism. At the more elite end of the critical spectrum, an increasingly university-based pack of critics and writers began to find Algren tiresome. Bettina Drew reports that by the mid-1950s Alfred Kazin and Orville Prescott had turned to panning Algren's work, that Norman Podhoretz "couldn't fathom why '[Algren] finds bums so much more interesting and stirring than other people,' " and that "Leslie Fiedler dubbed him 'the bard of the stumblebum,' and after a long tirade against [Algren's 1956 novel *A Walk on the Wild Side*] finally dismissed him as a 'museum piece — the last of the Proletarian writers.' "[50] Describing Algren's rapidly diminishing critical status in the 1960s, Conrad Knickerbocker paired the reputational declines of Chicago as a literary subject and of the social realism associated with the 1930s: "So by that time, who was Nelson Algren? The world's oldest living W.P.A. writer? The winner, for God's sake, of the first National Book Award? ... and Chicago, I mean really."[51] Knickerbocker, who admired Algren's work, captured the sneering tone of critics' conventional wisdom: in the 1950s, a significant number of influential critics seemed to regard the problems of industrial urbanism as no longer a fit subject for serious literature.

At the more popular end of the critical spectrum, boosterish newspaper reviewers, book clubs, and the ethnic press (led by *Dziennik Chicagoski* and *Zgoda*) rejected Algren as a troublemaker telling dated stories populated by depression types about whom nobody wanted to hear anymore. While literary critics applauded a new set of writers with a new set of credentials, the *Chicago Sun-Times* parroted the emergent progrowth coalition in expecting that slums were soon to be a thing of the past in postwar America: "we have a feeling . . . that squalor is going out of fashion in Chicago. Perhaps it's been largely due to our mayor's efforts in brightening up and tidying our streets, the popularity of cheering colors and the Schenley advertising display of modern masterpieces in the subway concourse."[52] It appeared that the "bard of the stumblebum" was indeed an odd man out in postwar culture: his very subject was "going out of fashion."

Algren, Drew, and Knickerbocker tell this standard story of social realism's decline, meshing it with the story of Chicago's decline. Algren wrote a letter to critic Maxwell Geismar in which he claimed (in Drew's paraphrase) "he could make a list longer than his arm, of writers who had given up as soon as the thirties were done, and were silent or trying to live in the suburbs as if the spiritual uneasiness of the fifties and the American disease of isolation did not exist."[53] Giving up, in this context, means refusing to serve as a literary social conscience, and Algren maps that defeat on the metropolitan landscape as a retreat from the inner city to the suburbs. Like the decline it partakes of, it is a good story, with heroes and villains moving across an expressive landscape, but there are other, less wounded, ways to tell it.

For instance, we might look to the intimate association of Algren's Chicago tradition with an industrial city that was at midcentury beginning to slide into the past. The post–World War II transformation of Chicago still has not authoritatively unfixed the terms bequeathed to posterity by the Chicago tradition, terms with which Chicago has been discussed for a century now. (Sandburg's big-shouldered young laborer is well past his eightieth birthday.) Because Algren's Chicago tradition originally evolved to describe a late nineteenth-century city, this persistence of representational habits led to a growing disjunction between a stock literary palette of industrial vintage and the transformed postindustrial subject to which it is applied. Even those representations that set out to go against the conventional grain still find it necessary to devote their energies to repeating the fixed terms in order to contest them—they must labor to show that Chicago is no longer, or never was, "the city that works" or "the city of neighborhoods."[54] The post–World War II decline of Chicago's literary reputation might also be explained as a process in which the generic stories, vocabulary, and subject matters evolved by Algren's Chicago tradition gradually lost their authority to articulate American dramas of pressing importance and national application as they lost their close fit to contemporary urbanism in transition. At midcentury, after depression and world war, the problem and promise of industrial urbanism and the literary complex that evolved by considering it no longer compelled the attention accorded to it in the first half of the twentieth century.

The post–World War II transformation of cities, and of thinking about them, helps to explain as well the Chicago School's decline from its prewar dominance in the field of urban sociology. The ecological model, with its natural successions and formalized competition among groups, seemed badly fitted to account for the postwar inner city's seemingly permanent black ghetto and the purposive city-shaping of agents like progrowth coalitions. The Chicago School, so closely associated with the industrial city, had begun to lose its uncontested preeminence in American sociology during the late 1930s and 1940s. After the war, the Chicago School's ecological model was revised and pursued by a number of sociologists, but the original ideas of its founders were increasingly supplanted by new theoretical apparatus. However, the Chicago School's pioneering studies of topics of postwar interest, like juvenile delinquency and the ghetto, remained current well into the 1960s, when a widely recognized urban crisis moved the American inner city back to a center-stage position it had not occupied since the Chicago School's heyday, the late Progressive Era.[55]

The period between the early twentieth-century fixation upon industrial urbanism and the next great surge of thinking about the American city, the urban crisis of the 1960s, forms a kind of limbo into which Algren felt his critical reputation falling. As parts 2 and 3 of this study will argue, in the decades after World War II various genres and emerging traditions elevated the postindustrial inner city—repopulated by migrations, destroyed and remade by renewal and redevelopment, racially divided, racked by new rounds of violence, increasingly cut off from the suburban periphery—to and perhaps beyond the eminence in national discourse once enjoyed by the Chicago tradition's industrial city. These developments helped to make Richard Wright enduringly canonical as one of the first "ghetto writers" but only helped to move Algren further into the margins—although more than one reader, seeking a historical or sociological rationale for rehabilitating Algren, has pointed out that his pioneering depictions of drug addiction and the homeless underclass of drifters become more timely every day.[56]

The historical and conceptual transformation of the city as a subject of inquiry, combined with Algren's (and others') notion of a critical turn away from his brand of social realism in the 1950s, help to explain how Algren managed to go from being the next great urban realist and a budding major writer —so anointed by Farrell, Wright, Hemingway, various critics, and the judges who awarded the first National Book Award for fiction in 1950—to being a colorful regionalist character. By the 1960s, he was the vaguely embarrassing has-been to whom critical darling Richard Brautigan patronizingly imagines mailing a drunk named Trout Fishing in America Shorty in *Trout Fishing in America*.[57] Algren's literary star, and to a lesser extent that of Farrell (who had been Chicago's "next big thing" in the 1930s), went down with that of industrial Chicago and its characteristic types and terrains.

Algren's and Farrell's critical declines are fancifully explained in Henry Louis Gates Jr.'s 1990 essay "Canon Confidential: A Sam Slade Caper," a private eye pastiche that considers the process and stakes of literary canon formation. At the end of his investigation, Slade finds his way to "a vast industrial atrium" where "thousands and thousands of books" judged unworthy of the canon are being ground into pulp.[58] Among the once-lionized books riding the conveyor belt to obscurity, Slade sees "fat novels by James Jones and Erskine Caldwell and Thomas Wolfe and James T. Farrell and Pearl Buck," as well as "thin novels by Nelson Algren and William Saroyan" and other "literary has-beens of our age." Both Farrell and Algren, apparently, fall into this doomed category; they will soon be as one, so to speak, with those who went down on the *Eastland* and the *Chicora*. Slade discovers that the canon is a fixed game, "the biggest scam since the 1919 World Series" (fittingly enough, given the iconic resonance of that disillusioning event for Algren), a massive conspiracy managed by a few well-placed critics who serve a shadowy conglomerate. Although he was less amused by the prospect than Gates, Algren anticipated by three decades this view of his critical fate. At midcentury he already felt the conveyor belt moving beneath him, and by the 1960s he considered himself a forgotten man of American literature.

The Milwaukee Avenue Corridor

This is the Nelson Algren—succeeded but persistent—who confronts Art Shay on the expressway, who made literature from the neighborhood beneath the wheels of Shay's car. The transformation of that neighborhood around 1523 Wabansia—actually a congeries of neighborhoods between Humboldt Park and the North Branch of the Chicago River, arranged in a rough triangle around the diagonal spine of lower Milwaukee Avenue—encapsulates the postwar transformation of the urban village.

The lower Milwaukee Avenue corridor, just northwest of the Loop and uncomfortably close to the Near North Side, lay within the giant half-circle of blight identified by city planners in the late 1940s and 1950s. To the redevelopment-minded eye, the Milwaukee Avenue corridor at midcentury fit the profile of the obsolescent industrial-era landscape. Many of the residential buildings in the area were old and overcrowded by conventional standards. Manufacturing plants and tanneries that lined the banks of the North Branch and Goose Island were part of the belt of industrial infrastructure that had to be cleared away from the service-oriented core. Blacks and Hispanics—regarded by planners as indicators and agents of blight—were beginning to move into the area's oldest and most decayed housing.

The Milwaukee Avenue corridor, then, provided a good example of the industrial neighborhood order in late middle age. After the Chicago fire, the area had developed rapidly around rail, streetcar, and elevated lines. It was settled in turn by waves of German, Scandinavian, Polish, Ukrainian, Slovak, Jewish, Italian, Mexican, and Puerto Rican immigrants. The various groups supplanted, jostled, and mixed with one another over the years as new immigrants took up residence in the older sections on lower Milwaukee and more-established groups moved northwest away from the Loop. Poles dominated the area by the turn of the century, and the Milwaukee Avenue corridor became the city's—and perhaps America's—leading Polish neighborhood. Not only were the local parishes, St. Stanislaus Kostka and Holy Trinity, the city's most distinguished Polish parishes, but the Polish Roman Catholic Union and its rival the Polish National Alliance established offices a few blocks apart near the three-way intersection of Milwaukee Avenue, Ashland Avenue, and Division Street. The concentration of Polish institutions and businesses near that intersection gave it the title of Polish Downtown. More generally, the area between Humboldt Park and the North Branch became known as the Polish, or Polonia, Triangle.

Nelson Algren moved to the area in 1940, living at various addresses (including 1523 Wabansia) until he left Chicago for good in 1975. His ancestry was Swedish and Jewish, not Polish, and although he had been raised in the ethnic neighborhoods of Chicago (around Seventy-first Street and Cottage Grove on the South Side and, later, on North Troy Street on the far Northwest Side), his presence in the urban village went against the grain of his class trajectory. His father was an industrial worker—a machinist for Otis Elevator, Packard, McCormick Reaper, and Yellow Cab—but Nelson Algren's degree from the University of Illinois and his access to G.I. Bill benefits after the war destined him for the middle class. Algren's presence among immigrant-ethnic workers in the Polish urban village, face to face with his literary material, was the result of a conscious effort on the writer's part, not some mystical or genetically encoded identity. He had expended considerable effort to establish himself in the urban village, but after the war it began to change around him.

In the early 1950s, when Algren had lived in the area for more than a decade and was enjoying his greatest acclaim as a Chicago novelist, a combination of ethnic succession, economic change, and physical redevelopment began to work a profound change on the neighborhood he had written about in *Never Come Morning*, *The Neon Wilderness*, and *The Man with the Golden Arm*. Puerto Ricans and blacks began moving into older and more run-down sections abandoned by Italians, Poles, and Ukrainians. Some of the Puerto Rican arrivals were part of the massive out-migration from Puerto Rico that began after World War II, but others were Chicagoans who had been displaced by urban renewal on the North Side and by the growth of the black ghetto on the South Side.[59] The departure of white ethnics accelerated when construction began on the Northwest Expressway, later renamed the Kennedy, in the late 1950s. This highway cut a path through the stretch of neighborhood between Milwaukee Avenue and the North Branch, further separating the "blighted" Near Northwest Side from the opulent Near North Side as it connected the Loop to the northwest suburbs and to the new O'Hare Airport. The parishioners of St. Stanislaus managed to divert the expressway around their church and school, which were to have been demolished, the first of several fights over urban renewal projects in the area that carried well into the 1970s. These struggles were typical of the urban crisis of the 1960s, as were other, more violent conflicts: "the first major urban Puerto Rican riot in the history of the United States" took place on Division Street in the summer of 1966.[60]

Since the 1950s, the Milwaukee Avenue corridor has taken on the conventional aspect of the new inner city's social landscape, with the old inner city half-submerged beneath. Postwar construction—especially government projects like the Kennedy Expressway, the Noble Street housing projects, new community centers and schools—has been grafted onto older landscapes of industrial-era vintage: the residential mix of low brick apartment houses and bungalows; the older homes and graystones around Wicker Park and Humboldt Park; the institutional infrastructure of churches, commercial buildings, older schools. Buildings along the North Branch and on Goose Island that once housed industrial plants have fallen into disrepair, but others house new uses: a brewery and restaurant, loft spaces, even a small high-tech steel plant (a return of heavy industry, much changed, to the inner city).

A similar mix of persistence and succession characterizes the area's population. In parts of the Milwaukee Avenue corridor, Hispanic and black neighborhood orders have both replaced and layered onto the old white-ethnic order. People of Eastern European descent still live in the area, more immigrants from the Old Country have arrived since the end of the Cold War, Polish and Ukrainian businesses remain on the principal shopping strips, and descendants of the old parishioners still worship, among variegated congregations, at the old churches. The existence of white-ethnic enclaves has provided, as it so often does, a kind of social and institutional scaffold (composed of good food, an infrastructure of neighborhood services, and the reassuring presence of white faces) for an influx of artists and service professionals. A sizable stretch of neighborhoods in the corridor, especially in Wicker Park and Bucktown, were in the 1980s and early 1990s the city's "hottest" area for "artists initially attracted by cheap rents and professionals who fled the crowded lakefront"— people who might once have insisted on a lakefront location but who went inland in search of good, affordable housing stock and satisfying urban texture.[61] The *Chicago Tribune Magazine*'s account of their arrival in Algren's old neighborhood, accompanied by a photograph of "[t]uckpointing at 1958 W. Evergreen Ave., former home of the late Chicago author Nelson Algren," finds "an edgy quality here, a tension in the air, perhaps a product of the forced interaction of longtime white ethnic, Hispanic and black residents and the more-recent arrivals."[62]

On the one hand, then, Nelson Algren's neighborhood disappeared: in the decades after World War II it has been broken up and rebuilt (and tuckpointed) in significant ways and repopulated with a new cast of characters; the white ethnics of the old neighborhood have moved away in great numbers; the industrial plants have for the most part fallen into disuse or been demolished. What remains of the old order has been transformed and recontextualized by the new social landscape in which it persists. On the other hand, the old neighborhood remains, both in the interstices of the new order and as the bony substructure underlying layers of physical development and population typical of postindustrial Chicago. Art Shay, passing through the Milwaukee Avenue corridor as he heads downtown on the Kennedy, is driving parallel to the elevated train lines built by the Metropolitan Elevated Company at the turn of the century. The El trains run on this original structure between Division Street and Logan Square, next to Milwaukee Avenue and through the heart of the corridor, making connections to O'Hare Airport and the redeveloped Loop; they run everywhere through Algren's prose, as well, making connections to the trains that run through *Sister Carrie* and to the railroad city that confronted both Carrie and Dreiser.

3

Closing Time: *The Man with the Golden Arm*

Even as early as 1947 . . . one could see changes on
the horizon.

> Squires et al., *Chicago: Race, Class,
> and the Response to Urban Decline*

Some nights she could scarcely breathe for seeing
the flat unerring line of cable and crosslight and
lever, of signal tower and switch. For the endless
humming of telephone wires murmuring insanely
from street to street without ever saying a single
word above a whisper that a really sensible person
might understand.

For the city too was somehow crippled of late.
The city too seemed a little insane. Crippled and
caught and done for with everyone in it.

> Nelson Algren, *The Man with the Golden Arm*

Nelson Algren moved to the Near Northwest Side in 1940, at the end of the
Great Depression decade and just before the United States embarked on a war
effort that would help to drive the transformation of Chicago in the decades to
come. He set his best work in the Polish urban villages near the intersection of
Milwaukee and Division. That body of mature work culminated in *The Man
with the Golden Arm*, Algren's most virtuosic and best-received book.
Published in 1949, *Golden Arm* captures the delicately balanced feel of a tran-

sitional postwar moment, as dramatic movements of people and capital began to shape the long urban crisis associated with postindustrial transformation. That crisis was, as well, a literary-historical one: part of *Golden Arm*'s apocalyptic charge derives from its sense that Chicago realism had reached its terminus as the industrial city in which it thrived entered into a postwar decline.

Golden Arm simultaneously encourages and frustrates the impulse to trace its relation to its historical moment. The novel encourages that impulse because its characters move through the neighborhood under the threat that something large, terrible, and obscure is about to happen. I argue below that this sense of imminent, unspecified disaster gives expression to a set of anxieties about the transformation of both industrial Chicago and Chicago literature on the prewar model that Algren identified as "his" Chicago. As this chapter's epigraphs suggest, the novel "sees changes on the horizon," but much of *Golden Arm*'s power derives precisely from the novel's restricted representational range and its characters' restricted understanding. The impending catastrophe always seems to be taking shape just out of sight over the novel's horizons, even as those horizons close in until they have crushed the life out of the neighborhood types trapped by them.

The challenge of articulating *Golden Arm*'s engagement with its historical moment is that the novel does not have *City on the Make*'s historical imagination. *Golden Arm* assumes a pervasive exhaustion rather than identifying and figuring the engines driving this change. Algren does not pull back from the novel's action to fill us in on the deep background: there are no passages in *Golden Arm* that lay out in overview the situation of midcentury Chicago as does *City on the Make* or as Dreiser sketches nineteenth-century Chicago's "peculiar qualifications of growth" in chapter 2 of *Sister Carrie*.[1] *Golden Arm* does not offer representations of urban renewal, deindustrialization, or suburbanization. The novel does leave the Polish urban village to visit the Lake Street ghetto but does not devote its energies to bringing the reader up to speed on black migration, white flight, and other relevant aspects of the midcentury encounter between the white-ethnic neighborhood order and the black inner city. The novel does assess the situation of white-ethnic industrial workers during the postwar transformation, but it conducts the assessment without recourse to scene-setting historical argument.

These narratives and historical processes are not directly available within the diegesis as explanations for the sense of crisis enfolding the Division Street rooming house in which most of the novel's characters live. The "flat unerring line" of the vista outside Sophie Majcinek's window renders her breathless with fear and a sense of entrapment, but the messages the landscape sends to her remain below the threshold of understanding: the telephone wires' "endless humming" is an insane murmuring, never "saying a word above a whisper that a really sensible person might understand." The "city too was somehow crippled of late. . . . Crippled and caught and done for with everyone in it,"[2] but the logic ordering this turn for the worse operates at one remove from the novel's diegesis, maddeningly beyond Sophie's and the novel's range of perception. *Golden Arm*'s engagement with its historical moment takes place at a similar remove: the novel engages indirectly with the postwar transformations of Chicago as it imagines and enacts the exhaustion of industrial Chicago's characteristic genres of life and literature. These include Nelson Algren's two "old neighborhoods," the white-ethnic neighborhood order and the Chicago realist tradition.

Golden Arm takes place in an interim between the beginning of the end of "the old days and the old ways" and their final passing. This interim fits neatly with the situation of midcentury industrial urbanism. In the years just after the war, after more than fifty years of development and on the heels of a wartime boom in manufacturing, the industrial neighborhood order was still in full flower, but at the same time it showed signs of erosion, change, and eventual breakup under the action of suburbanization, long-term deindustrialization, inner-city redevelopment (in its early stages), expansion of the second ghetto, and the accelerating dispersal of immigrant-ethnic cultures into postwar America's expanding middle class. *Golden Arm* both makes a living portrait of the entrenched white-ethnic neighborhood order and imagines its final collapse —at a moment when observers were beginning to see that the way of life harbored in the vast system of ethnic preserves would be transformed as the postindustrial metropolis began to take shape.

On the one hand, then, *Golden Arm* grounds itself in a historical place and time. It maps the neighborhood landscape of the Milwaukee Avenue corridor, marks carefully the round of seasons from fall of 1946 to spring of 1948, and plots movements and figures that would become central to representation of the postwar inner city: the twilight of the white-ethnic neighborhood order; a visit to the expanding black ghetto; the life and times of a soon-to-be canonical street type, the criminal intravenous drug user.

On the other hand, *Golden Arm* takes place in an imagined place and time: a city beneath the El, lit by arc lamps and neon, gridded by the El's iron framework and criss-crossing wires; a city where it is always October, somewhere between the first chilly intimations of the year's decline and the dead of winter. This imagined city represents a final refinement and reduction of the composite Chicago of feeling mapped by Algren's Chicago tradition, completing several movements readable in the span of texts connecting Algren to Sandburg and Dreiser by way of Farrell and Wright: a gradual movement to the neighborhoods and the street, an increasing constriction of landscape and horizon, a shift from prospective to retrospective modes. *Golden Arm* thus also inhabits its historical moment as a culminative text that proposes and embodies the exhaustion of a literary tradition that Algren and others associated with industrial Chicago.

The following discussion of *Golden Arm* undertakes to account for the novel's extreme character: its portrait of neighborhood people in a condition of dire extremity, its self-conception as occupying the last extremity of the Chicago tradition, its extreme habits of language and metaphor. It will be impossible in this space to do exegetical justice to *Golden Arm*, which remains one of the most disciplined, sustained, and virtuosic pieces of overwriting in the urban literature—an extreme novel, deserving and rewarding extended critical treatments. I will confine myself, in the interests of this chapter's and this study's larger project, to exploring the sources and meanings of the sense of ultimacy running everywhere through the book. I will read *Golden Arm* as a sort of requiem for Nelson Algren's Chicago, a combination of historical and textual cities that have come at last to "closing time." To that end, I will begin with the novel's claustrophobic portrait of the old neighborhood in decline and then work outward along the textual connections that bind the novel to *City on the Make, Sister Carrie,* and the larger literature and history of Chicago.

The Narrowing Hours

Golden Arm recounts the decline of poker dealer Francis Majcinek, known to all as Frankie Machine, a son of Polish immigrants who lives on Division Street in the heart of the Milwaukee Avenue corridor. Although it devotes much of its energy to texturing subplots and explorations of the neighborhood order, *Golden Arm* takes dramatic shape around a story of crime and punishment. Frankie, a morphine addict, semi-unintentionally kills his supplier, Nifty Louie, in a desperate rage one winter night. Solly "Sparrow" Saltskin, Frankie's best friend, is a habitual criminal of the most petty sort—dog-stealer, shoplifter—but the police at the Saloon Street station pressure him with the threat of a long prison term into implicating Frankie in the murder. Frankie goes into hiding in the Lake Street ghetto, on the Near West Side, a short ride on the El to the south of Frankie's neighborhood. He is in the company of Molly Novotny, a young barfly, who supports them for a while by dancing in a black strip joint, but the combination of his weakness and the blackmailing scheme of Molly's ex-lover Drunkie John, who discovers their hiding place, forces him into the open. Finally, wounded by the police and unable to acquire the morphine he needs to carry on, Frankie hangs himself from the chicken-wire ceiling of a West Madison Street flophouse stall. Frankie's wife, Sophie, meanwhile, has been going irretrievably mad and is committed to an insane asylum, where she withdraws into near-catatonia, counting cards and reciting all the names of neighborhood characters she knows in the vague hope that completing these catalogues will somehow return her to the world she has lost. Molly and Sparrow survive, although both face jail terms.

This narrative plays out in the October city. In *Golden Arm*, industrial urbanism grinds on in the long moment between last call and closing time. The city's mechanisms continue like clockwork: "the music and the traffic passed, great freighters forced the river ice, the murmurous bridges strained slowly upward, paused and slowly fell. The clocks in all the railroad depots were synchronized to a second's fraction" (314). Except for Sophie's fear of "the spades" moving in (to which this discussion will return), *Golden Arm* does not figure the massive transformations already under way in the neighborhoods of the Near Northwest Side. There are no abandoned and razed industrial buildings, the "rusty iron heart" of *City on the Make*'s final image, on view in the Majcineks' neighborhood. (Such sights were beginning to appear in the Milwaukee Avenue corridor and catching the attention of city planners during the 1940s and 1950s.) Rather than imagining the moment of the rusty iron heart, in which the machines stop, *Golden Arm* imagines an extended winding-down in which the human orders that took form around the machines approach exhaustion at their logical extremes.

"That was the way things were because that was how things had always been. Which was why they could never be any different. Neither God, war, nor the ward super could work any deep change on West Division Street." The traditional mechanics of life on Division Street dictate that the ward super, the Democratic machine's local functionary, "puts in the fix for all right-thinking hustlers and the Lord, in turn, puts in the fix for the super" (7). Small-timers like Frankie Machine and Sparrow know their place in the process. The two friends are in the Saloon Street station lockup, as *Golden Arm* begins, because their boss, Zero Schwiefka, fell behind on his payoffs to the police. As low-ranking subalterns, they understand that they have to suffer for this failure to conduct business as usual. The ward machine—an arrangement among a local set of predominantly Polish politicians, criminals, and police—runs relentlessly, like the machines of the resonantly named Endless Belt and Leather works near Schwabatski's rooming house, at 1860 West Division Street, where Frankie lives. Frankie and Sparrow navigate among the moving parts of the industrial neighborhood order, imagined as a perpetual-motion machine that constantly expresses and manufactures its political arrangements as well as its factory products.

However, there are new things in the postwar world beyond the understanding of West Division Street's traditional gods. Neither "the super's God nor the super" knows about "the hypo Frankie kept, among other souvenirs, at the bottom of a faded duffel bag in another veteran's room" (8). On the one hand, the drug addiction and eventual suicide of the ironically nicknamed Frankie Machine do not interrupt the West Division Street machine's smooth working.

The Chicago of the neighborhood novelists has always ground up people like him. On the other hand, the narrowing and final collapse of Frankie's world, a deadly consummation accelerated by his morphine addiction, suggests a more general exhaustion. *Golden Arm* imagines the end of a way of life for a representative cast of characters whose Division Street rooming house suggests the urban village in microcosm. The winnowing of the weak and damaged who populate the novel's world leaves the aging machinery of the industrial neighborhood order to operate in a wasteland, like the ceaselessly passing empty El trains.

For all the massive, inhuman permanence of its perpetual-motion machines, *Golden Arm* is pervaded by a troubled sense of imminent, thoroughgoing, and ultimately unspecified change. "'We got all kinds of new ways to do things since you came back'" (15), Sparrow tells Frankie, the returned veteran, and Frankie explains their friendship by saying that Sparrow "'Knows the way it used to be 'n how it's gettin' now' "(10). " 'You fellows remember me?'" asks a lush in the lockup who " 'used to be a night watchman on the old Wabash'" and receives no reply because "those who remembered were gone with his strength, all down the drain with last year's rain; friends and family and foes together and the blood soon to follow the rains" (19–20). The detritus of an entire familiar world—friends, family, foes, the old Wabash railroad resonant of the industrial city's vigorous youth—washes down the drain, having been "ground slowly in the great city's grinder" (16). Characters move dreamily through familiar evolutions under this pall, each imprecisely aware that something has been lost, gone wrong, or slipped out of reach.

At Antek Witwicki's Tug and Maul, downstairs from Schwabatski's rooming house, the specter of the new Club Safari across the street unsettles the barflies. Antek's remains a bastion of "the old days and the old ways" reaching back well into the nineteenth century—no neon or fluorescent lights, "plenty of butcher-shop sawdust on the floor and an old-fashioned golden goboon for every four bar stools," and no TV. ("'I give it an honest chance,'" Antek says of television, "'and it don't work'" [44].) The Safari is all indirect lighting, mood music, and tablecloths; there are no drinks on the house, and customers gamble for drinks with a bar game called "twenty-six" (the ubiquity of which in Chicago's downtown night spots drove A. J. Liebling into a tavern purist's rage). Upstairs at the Safari, Nifty Louie Fomorowski reminisces about all the old neighborhood gangsters he has outlived and sells morphine to junkies, Frankie Machine among them. Frankie's youth and force having been spent on ceaseless petty hustling and in the war (he is in his late twenties when the novel begins and beginning to go soft under the strain), he goes to Louie to buy a respite that Antek's traditional alcohol can no longer provide. "'Fix me. Make it stop. Fix me'" (56), Frankie asks: sometimes he wants to be strong enough to be a working cog; sometimes he wants the machines to stop.

Frankie, like every one of the novel's characters, can specify local and personal sources of the regret and nostalgia for a better time that beset him. In particular, he regrets the drunken night at the war's end when, having had too many of Antek's A-Bomb Specials, he had insisted on going for a ride and crashed spectacularly on Ashland Avenue. The crash put his wife Sophie in a wheelchair, although nobody can tell if she was crippled by her injuries or by the need to bind the habitually negligent but now guilt-stricken Frankie to her once and for all. Dealing the cards in Zero Schwiefka's all-night every-night poker game, where the players' talk turns to nostalgia for long-dead hustlers and the Chicago of the 1920s and 1930s, Frankie misses "the old days, the old ways, before all the stoplights turned to red and there was still time between deals for a laugh or two over a nickel beer" (117). When he and Sophie lurched out of Antek's at closing time on the night of the accident, the jukebox was playing "one last sad bar of the final song of a world that had known neither A-bombs nor A-Bomb Specials," a song that lamented *There's nothing left for me/Of days that used to be*" (67).

Frankie's personal story of decline speaks to a general malaise. He universalizes his own regret—the stoplight he missed becomes "all the stoplights" in the world—and it speaks to similar feelings in the other players. The mood of the game, like the mood of the novel, takes on a desperate endgame quality: "Thus in the narrowing hours of the night the play became faster and steeper and an air of despair, like sickroom odor where one lies who can never be well again, moved across the light green baize, touched each player ever so lightly and settled down in a tiny whiff of cigar smoke about the dealer's hands" (119). Both space (the "sickroom") and time (the "narrowing hours of the night") seem to contract, and the whole process proceeds "faster and steeper." The narrowing world in which the players move has that "sickroom odor": that which has gone so obscurely wrong can never be put right again.

Sophie, wheelchair bound and confined to her apartment as if to a sickroom, also reads a more general disaster into their smash-up. "Ever since that night [of the accident]," she thinks, "everyone had become afraid of closing time everywhere, of having the lights go out in the middle of the dance while the chimes of all the churches mourned: a requiem for everyone trapped beneath the copper-colored sky of noon or the night-lit ties of the El" (97). *Golden Arm*, and all of Algren's postwar writing about Chicago, is pervaded by this unanimity and ubiquity—"everyone," "everywhere," "all the churches"—that generalize the travails of a few hard-luck nobodies into a citywide drama. Each mean reverse and failure multiplies itself endlessly through the novel's known world. That world's tightly circumscribed landscape, confined for the most part to a few blocks on Division Street west of Milwaukee Avenue, also extends by suggestion as far as the endlessly multiplied girders of the El and neon tavern signs reach: in a novel that imagines only "the neighborhoods," its landscape reaching almost but not quite to the Loop, Frankie's neighborhood serves as the type of everybody's neighborhood.

Church bells mark "closing time," the end of time that the neighborhood obscurely fears. Dozing at the window as the bells ring late one night, Sophie remembers her years of courtship with Frankie "like remembering an alien land." In that alien land—the same urban village they live in now, but remembered as a kind of Old Country—time passed in a seasonal round of Polish Catholic religious observances and the singing of "soft and wild ancestral songs." Together, "she and Frankie had carried Easter lamb to Old St. Stephen's for Father Simon's blessing." In Sophie's reconstruction of them, these were "years when everything was so well arranged. When people who did right were rewarded and those who did wrong were punished. When everyone, in the long run, got exactly what was coming to him, no more or no less. God weighed virtue and sin then to the fraction of the ounce, like Majurcek the Grocer weighing sugar" (62). In the hindsight afforded by the story of decline, the old neighborhood's landscape of churches, factories, and crowded walk-ups becomes an ethnic paradise ruled by that icon of neighborhood nostalgia, the corner grocer, as presiding deity.

Sophie is the novel's most sophisticated mythographer of decline. Haunted by echoes of prewar tunes drifting through the rooming house from the radio of "some old fool in pin curls" who "fancied it was 1917 again" (94), she tells herself a story of a better, larger, unbroken era receding into the past. Laboriously pasting newspaper articles and other raw materials into her "Scrapbook of Fatal Accidence," she constructs an account of the city's decline from order into chaos. The neighborhood landscape itself, not just the newspapers, speaks to Sophie in a coded language of apocalypse. Church bells and factory sounds, the girders and lights of the El structure marching away into the distance, the roar and spectacle of the trains, one of the city's countless cross-hatching wires tapping on the window, the thumping of ceiling fans from Antek's bar downstairs, kitchen noise and radio music drifting through the rooming house—she synthesizes these messages into grand visions of ruin. A passing fire engine suggests a second Chicago fire: she rouses the rooming house by shrieking, "'It's goin' up! Loop 'n all! It's all goin' up,'" and, when told it was merely a short-circuit down the street, laments that "'The whole fire was in my head'" (241). There is, indeed, in her head a disaster on a par with the fire of 1871, when the city did "go up," downtown and all. A secret destiny, almost revealed by certain cryptic signs but finally inscrutable, threatens the world she knows, the Chicago that took form in the Great Fire's aftermath.

Sophie, then, is a type of urban intellectual. She observes the novel's material city outside her window, traverses textual cities in what she reads, assembles her stories—and even a book—out of both evidence and fantasies. She ends up in a mental hospital because the stories she tells herself, the city of feeling she imagines, lose touch with the city of fact she inhabits. She retreats into delusions that alternate between paranoid fantasies of unseen oppressors and achingly sharp recall of treasured memories. If that makes her sound like Nelson Algren, soon to be alienated from both the city he knew and the critical consensus of the 1950s, it is because she inhabits his historical moment and does parallel work with a similar anxiety about what comes next.

Although the inner lives of people like the Majcineks were hidden from his view in the "juxtaposed dimnesses" of the neighborhoods, Liebling captured both Sophie's and Algren's turn of mind in his crack about Chicagoans "left in the plight of the Greeks at the beginning of history, when the gods commenced ceasing to manifest themselves."[3] Waking from a doze and looking out the window at the El, hearing church bells tolling midnight, Sophie feels her life and the history of her world condensed into one autumnal moment:

> And her whole life, from her careless girlhood until this crippled night, seemed caught within that fading chime. For now, as though no time had passed but the time it had taken to dream it, the leaves were stiff with age again, sultry September had come and gone and the wind was blowing the flies away.
>
> "God has forgotten us all," Sophie told herself quietly. (99)

Moving out of the Neighborhood

The hardscrabble losers who populate *Golden Arm* are not the kinds of people who need to worry about breaking up the neighborhood by moving to the suburbs. The novel does not, as so many identity-obsessed white ethnics of the 1970s did, lament the postwar attenuation of immigrant-ethnic cultures by upward social mobility and dispersal from the slum.[4] But the novel does offer a story of a neighborhood's dissolution, and, in a text that confines itself so rigorously to imagining the urban village as the vessel in which industrial urbanism is contained, that dissolution reads as a world-ending catastrophe in which the content of neighborhood life runs out of the broken vessel and down the drain. The novel does not imagine transformation as the overlap of orders: it imagines only half of that process, the end of what is, not the shape of what is to come. In that sense, *Golden Arm* develops the literary possibilities suggested by a familiar formula—"there goes the neighborhood"—so often applied by Americans to the shifting of neighborhood orders that characterizes ethnic succession, suburbanization, and other aspects of the dramatic urban transformations that were already under way at midcentury.

Golden Arm is the most extreme of neighborhood novels, representing a last step in the Chicago tradition's gradual move over time to the neighborhoods. It almost entirely eschews the metropolitan for the local, reducing Chicago in essence to the area around Division and Milwaukee and a handful of secondary locations bound together and contained by the El. Even Farrell's and Wright's characters occasionally leave the neighborhood, especially to go downtown; the Loop never appears in *Golden Arm*. Frankie's world conforms to the insular model of the neighborhood order drawn by Mike Royko in *Boss*, an order that Royko describes as beginning to disappear precisely at the moment of *Golden Arm*'s publication. Following Royko's model, the neighborhood in *Golden Arm* forms a self-contained system with its own main streets (Division, Milwaukee), church (St. Stephen's), taverns (Antek's, Widow Wieczorek's), factory workplaces (Endless Belt and Leather, an icehouse, the conveyor company), police station (the Saloon Street station), and local types: war hero (Frankie by default: he was wounded and no one else seems to have served), sports heroes (the hapless Endless Belt and Leather Invincibles), drunks (Drunkie John, Umbrellas Kvorka, many more), trollop (Molly Novotny), village idiot (Sparrow, Poor Peter Schwabatski, the simple-minded Umbrellas), and so on. This neighborhood order has arrived at the paradoxical state in which, although nothing changes in the internal mechanics of West Division Street, the end of time approaches.

In the fall of Frankie Machine and his associates can be read a prophecy of the fall of an urban people they represent, as the mechanical action of business as usual grinds up the way of life created by the Polish immigrants (the Majcineks' parents among them) who lived and labored in industrial Chicago's urban villages. The nameless apocalypse imagined by Sophie and the mundane downfall of a few Chicagoans recounted by *Golden Arm* express in fantastically melodramatic form the consequences of a then incipient historical process in which the biggest perpetual-motion machine of all, the city itself (guided by the progrowth coalition of business interests and Democratic machine, of which the West Division Street political machine forms a small piece), reconfigured itself for a postindustrial age. This reconfiguration transformed the urban world remembered by the narrating voice of *City on the Make*, by Sophie, by Royko, and by other purveyors of decline. The railroad had always been the Chicago literary tradition's particular figure of the city as a machine for making money, and the complete domination of *Golden Arm*'s terminal landscape by the El suggests that the industrial city is machining all its orders into ruins as it replaces them with new ones. The pieces will wash "down the drain with last year's rain," passing into history.

Frankie himself represents an aging version of Carl Sandburg's personified Chicago—the young, big-shouldered, productively laboring man. In his late twenties, Frankie has begun to go soft in the belly, his facade of toughness fools no one except the adoring Sparrow, and he has lost the will to stand up to the work of living in Chicago, relying on morphine to make his talented arm hold up. He is, in an updating of Sandburg's "young fighter who has never lost a battle," "tough and weak, like . . . a fighter who knows he's beat trying to convince everyone he can still take more" (316). Furthermore, like so many of the novel's characters (and like so many of the young male protagonists of the neighborhood novels), he differs from Sandburg's laboring man in that he cannot or will not do honest work. There are hard-working people in *Golden Arm*, but they form a nearly faceless minority. Sparrow, staggering drunkenly into the rooming house late at night, identifies some of its residents as such while he tries loudly not to disturb their sleep: "all the doors belonged to hard-working people. . . . All the people worked too hard, all the people deserved something nice in their declining years"(129). The keyword "declining," appearing in conjunction with "hard-working," reinforces the message sent by the echoes of Sandburg. Frankie, personifying "the city that works" and the urban village, shows every sign of having been used up by the city of machines.

Frankie and Sophie are relatively young—not yet thirty when Frankie hangs himself—and Molly Novotny younger, but the pattern of their lives has already been set. In each successive Chicago novel—*Somebody in Boots* (1935), *Never Come Morning* (1942), and *Golden Arm* (1949)—Algren's characters start out older, more defeated, more aware that their lives run on tracks according to a rigid pattern almost legible in the El-bounded landscape.[5] Frankie's industrial Chicago is similarly old before its time but not yet on its last legs, the contracting neighborhood order slowly destroying rather than reproducing itself. The novel's prematurely aging, childless, for the most part unemployed characters move through the once-familiar, once-sustaining neighborhood terrain with the regretful nostalgia of people twice their age.

The two families of Frankie's upstairs neighbor Violet frame this extended interim in a generational progression from decline to collapse. Her first husband, the doddering immigrant industrial worker Stash Koskozka, caricatures the older generation on its last legs. He only wishes to work at the icehouse, find bargains on cheap food, and live out his days in peace and quiet. He takes inordinate pleasure in rituals of resignation: reading the temperature on his thermometer, tearing the pages off the calendar. ("'I'm glad tearin' days off the calendar is all he wants to tear off'" (156), says Stash's younger rival Sparrow before Vi's sexual vigor wears him out as well.) Stash monitors the weather, a practice given added meaning by Sparrow, who proposes the notion of a changing climate as a metaphor for the largely unspecified changes coming to the old neighborhood. The Tug and Maul's dissolute beer-drinking dog Rumdum, Sparrow claims, has become a barroom regular because he can catch only one particular breed of squirrel, which is "'gettin' kind of rare over here account of the climate changin' so fast,'" leaving Rumdum "'nothin' to do but hang around taverns 'n wait for the climate to change back a little'" (53–54). Even the dogs, unfit to do a dog's work, hang around in bars and wait for the approaching end of time. The hard-working miser Stash, then, reads in his calendar and thermometer the elapsing of his time and his way of life, the passing of the orderly world as he was taught to conceive of it. Speaking a comic-opera version of immigrant English, and with the imprint of icehouse tongs permanently etched on his jacket (the mark of a job to be rendered obsolete by the postwar boom in household appliances), Stash embodies industrial Chicago's immigrant-ethnic past.

Vi's second family figures the breakup of the neighborhood order. After Stash's death (when he leans too far out the window to take a temperature reading), Vi takes up with her landlord, "Jailer" Schwabatski. The two of them go on the wagon, become Jehovah's Witnesses, and begin saving their money, immediately distancing themselves from the neighborhood's most fundamental institutional and situational bonds—bar, church, subsistence-level hustling—and making them likely candidates for an eventual move out of the neighborhood. (With luck, always in short supply in an Algren novel, they may even make good their escape to Cicero or Berwyn.) Unlike Vi and Stash, Vi and Jailer also form a full-blown family, the novel's only one, but the neighborhood order's inability to reproduce itself recurs in a new form. Jailer has a simple-minded adult son named Poor Peter, whose main activity has been to plant paper daisies on the rooming house's stairways while praying for an indoor rain. The novel's only family thus appears to be at a dead end in relation to the neighborhood, breaking its ties to the old order, offering no prospect of generational continuity, and proposing an embodiment of barrenness in the adult child Poor Peter. Despite his father's efforts to teach him a trade, Peter cannot even fix the rooming house's perpetually loose stair and wishes only to tend paper flowers that refuse to grow. The next generation, like Stash's generation of immigrants, is just waiting for the weather to change.

Vi, still young and vigorous but (like everyone else in the novel) unable to form a family that will reproduce the neighborhood order, takes desperate measures to save herself from a neighborhood order in collapse. Jailer's Division Street rooming house, in which she still remains at the novel's end, has been catastrophically depopulated by the departure of most of the novel's main characters. In a novel that represents the world beyond the neighborhood as a series of terminal institutions—police station, prison, mental hospital, skid row, potter's field—where weakness and entrapment give out into death, moving out of the neighborhood takes on an apocalyptic tenor: Frankie dies; Stash dies; Sophie is committed to the mental hospital; Sparrow, a regular visitor, goes to prison; Molly faces a prison term for helping Frankie avoid the police. The constriction of the novel's landscape gives special meaning to the notion of breaking with the neighborhood: *Golden Arm*, having completed the Chicago novel's move to the neighborhoods, cannot imagine a viable way of life other than the old neighborhood's.

Sophie, surprisingly, wants to move out of the neighborhood—because she fears that blacks are encroaching on it—but *Golden Arm* maps no tenable destination for such a move. Her increasing confinement, as the single furnished room in the shadow of the El gives way to the "cornerless room" of insanity in the mental hospital, illustrates the narrowness of the novel's landscape. When Frankie and Sparrow are arrested together for the last time, on a serious charge entailing a long jail term for Sparrow, Frankie tells him "'Looks like you're goin' to move out of this crummy neighborhood just like you always said you was goin' to'" (266). The continuity of prison and neighborhood compounds the joke. Prison figuratively falls within the boundaries of the El: the El-bounded city is "an open-roofed jail," and the jailhouse interiors double the El's form—from the bars endlessly repeating like the El's girders to the bulbs burning "in a single unwinking fury down the whitewashed tier" (15) like the signal lamps along the tracks. Early in the novel, when Frankie and Sparrow leave the police station after having been locked up overnight, they mount "the narrow steps toward a narrower freedom. On the street they waited for a northbound car" (25). They move seamlessly from prison to the track-bound streetcar and thus to Division Street and the El once more. The novel, like Sophie, cannot imagine anything outside the El's "flat unerring line."

The only alternative to the Polish urban village represented in *Golden Arm* is the Lake Street ghetto on the Near West Side—the degraded condition of which Lait and Mortimer describe so extravagantly, and not the place to which Sophie, who fears blacks, would move—and the Lake Street El runs, as well, by the door of Frankie and Molly's ghetto hideout. Frankie, an exemplar of white-ethnic Chicago, moves to the ghetto; Sophie worries about racial succession: the novel considers the encounter of the old and new inner cities in the form of an exchange between neighborhoods, one shrinking and one growing, under the shadow of the El. The railroad, condensing the inhumanly regular, irresistible action of urban money-making and power-ordering machines, also contains the inner city's transformation. Fittingly, when Frankie makes his final run from the police closing in on his Lake Street hideout, the El's iron stairs guide a policeman's misaimed bullet into his heel, hastening the final narrowing of his world to nothing.

The movement of blacks into the West Side that forms a key element in *Chicago Confidential*'s account of Chicago's decline becomes, like Frankie and Sophie's car crash, an element in Sophie's story of decline. Anticipating the reception he is sure to get from Sophie when he returns home from a night in the lockup for a minor offense, Frankie mimics Sophie's typical tirade: "'If she starts that screamin' about What was it for this time Why don't I get a broom in my tail 'n go to work on the legit Why don't we move out of the neighborhood the spades are movin' in it's gettin' smokier every day 'n if it wasn't for me she could be out dancin' . . .'" (26). In that last breathless phrase, the car crash and Sophie's paralysis run together with the encroachment of blacks from their domain farther south along the El tracks to suggest the breadth of provenance for Sophie's sense of a world in decline. Her personal encounter with the city's unyielding terrain—the crash occurred when Frankie had scraped a trolley (a close cousin of the El) and then plowed into a light standard and a billboard—conspires with a broad social transformation (the neighborhood's "gettin' smokier") to ring in closing time for the order she idealizes as a lost world of her youth, in which she was always dancing or singing or going to church.

Sophie's fear of racial succession, and her use of it to specify a larger anxiety about coming change, suggests that the notion of moving out of the neighborhood also derives a special apocalyptic charge from the novel's historical moment. Chicago at midcentury was a city in flux, with whites and blacks beginning to move in large numbers and coming into conflict at the boundaries of changing neighborhoods. *Golden Arm* does not imagine any blacks in the Polish urban village. As far as the reader knows, these rumored new arrivals in the old neighborhood, like the second Chicago fire, exist only in Sophie's head (as opposed to the blacks in the Lake Street ghetto, who exist outside her experience).[6] In Sophie's reasoning, racial succession is not so much a proximate cause as an effect of decline: her feverish logic suggests that the grocer-god's withdrawal broke the world, making it possible for Frankie to ruin her life and for "the dark people" to come. However, Sophie's conviction that, since the accident, everyone everywhere is afraid of closing time resonates with the kind of anxiety historically inspired in midcentury Chicago's white-ethnic neighborhoods by the prospect of racial succession.[7] In the narrowing world of *Golden Arm*, to think about incipient change and to think about moving out of the neighborhood means to conceive of a local apocalypse, either imminent or already in effect, that has pushed the "old days and the old ways" of the urban village almost out of sight into the past.

The Slope of the Years

Toward the end of *Golden Arm*, when the police are looking for Frankie because he has killed Nifty Louie and run off with Molly Novotny and what is left of the neighborhood is collapsing around her, Sophie Majcinek goes completely mad. Waking in the "low, sad light" of her room in the mental hospital "'at the end of the Irving Park [El] line'" (322), Sophie tries to work back along the path of her mental collapse to a sense of order. Figuratively, she tries to take the Irving Park El back to the old neighborhood. She tells herself that the "low animal moaning" from the next room is "that Drunkie John beating that poor hide of a Molly Novotny again" and draws a neighborhood moral: "'If he loves her, what are a few blows?' Sophie thought with a sudden clarity. 'If a man tells you you're his—what are a few slaps to *that?*'" (313). The superimposition of her rooming house neighbors on the mental hospital's terrain provides "sudden clarity." She further pursues clarity by telling the nurse "all the names she knew," running through the novel's main characters, supporting cast, and a few others we never meet. These last—Chester from Conveyor, Shudefski from Viaduct—suggest that the catalogue extends out into an entire industrial neighborhood order: a people living among conveyor belts and railroad viaducts. Last on the list comes "'Francis Majcinek. We got married in church'" (313), a church we know to be Old St. Stephen's. Closing her catalogue with Old St. Stephen's, the centerpiece of both her rhapsodic neighborhood nostalgia and the closing-time scenario in which church bells toll a requiem for her people, Sophie discovers with regretful clarity that even the neighborhood of feeling she constructs in her mind has arrived at the end of the line.

The same might be said of Algren's literary-historical situation as he understood it. Sophie's "neighbors" include not only the people of the changing Milwaukee Avenue corridor who provided Algren with material for his literary work but also Studs Lonigan, Bigger Thomas, Jurgis Rudkus, Carrie Meeber, and the other citizens of his Chicago tradition's composite city of feeling. This latter group of fictional characters forms a kind of shadow contingent continuous with the list of neighborhood characters Sophie recites in the madhouse, and their stories similarly form a shadow text continuous with her "Scrapbook of Fatal Accidence": *Native Son*'s grisly and titillating interracial murder, *The Jungle*'s horror stories about the meatpacking business, *Sister Carrie*'s tale of embezzlement, adultery, and suicide involving a well-known actress, and so on. Perhaps the most illuminating relation is between *Golden Arm* and *Sister Carrie:* these two texts form end points of the tradition that Algren and others had in mind when they wrote about "Chicago" writers and novels, and especially when they thought of Algren as the last of the Chicago writers. *Golden Arm* plays out to their conclusions a set of logics put in motion in *Sister Carrie*, suggesting that the Chicago tradition, like West Division Street, is reaching the terminus of its period with the aging and transformation of industrial Chicago.

Golden Arm shares a set of narrative contours with *Sister Carrie*. Their stories are by no means identical, but a rough common narrative bridges their differences, and in this sense they can be said to tell the "same" story. In this common narrative, a man (Hurstwood, Frankie) escapes an unsatisfying marriage to be with a younger woman (Carrie, Molly) temporarily allied to a weak paramour (Drouet, Drunkie John). The man spends most of his time in a particular bar (Fitzgerald and Moy's, Antek's), which provides an alternative to an increasingly suffocating and embattled domestic space (the Hurstwoods' stylish house near Lincoln Park on the North Side; the Majcineks' furnished room on the Near Northwest Side). The younger woman trades on her looks and sexual attractiveness to make a living (Carrie accepts lodging and money from Drouet; Molly hustles drinks and probably turns tricks). The crisis comes when the man semi-unintentionally commits a serious crime (Hurstwood steals from his employers; Frankie kills his dealer), precipitating a drastic break with his home life as he flees with his mistress. Once formed, the illicit couple moves to the limits of the novel's world (New York, the Lake Street ghetto) and sets up housekeeping. The woman goes onto the stage to make a living (Carrie rising in the theater; Molly eking out a living in a strip joint), while the man, at loose ends and increasingly exposed as brittle and unfitted for survival in the streets, wanders about and eventually drifts into more trouble. The man's suicide in a flophouse forms the story's dramatic climax, the arc of his descent into ruin contrasting with the stronger woman's survival.

The two novels place very different systems of emphasis on the narrative elements they do share, so that even the most strikingly similar elements have dissimilar contexts, but the existence of a common narrative serves as a jumping-off place in comparing two diegeses, two urban worlds. The common narrative schematized above provides a spine along which to begin arranging a reading of *Golden Arm* together with *Sister Carrie*. That reading could take many different forms and could indeed expand to great length in comparing the language, spatial and temporal plots, historical moments, and provenance of the two novels. Dreiser and Algren speak to one another in many different ways, from their interlocking plottings of naturalist decline to their shared tendency to mix journalistic-sociological reportage with the languages of melodrama and the urban surreal. The character systems of the two novels also suggest a wealth of comparisons, especially the matched sets of Carrie-Hurstwood-Mrs. Hurstwood and Molly-Frankie-Sophie. What follows, though, is a limited, preliminary comparison intended to establish the two novels as end points for Algren's Chicago tradition. This discussion centers on the novels' complementary landscapes, which, read together, tell a story of decline that plots on the grand scale the flat, unerring line of descent Dreiser calls "the slope of the years." The plotting of Carrie's rise and Hurstwood's fall tells the story in miniature; the plotting of Carrie's rise and Frankie's fall tells it against the backdrop of industrial Chicago's period, from golden age to the end of the line, as defined by midcentury stories of decline told by Algren and others.[8]

Arriving by train in the traditional manner in 1889, Carrie enters the prospective, expanding landscape of an industrial city on the make: "They were nearing Chicago. Signs were everywhere numerous. Trains flashed by them. Across wide stretches of flat, open prairie they could see lines of telegraph poles stalking across the fields toward the great city. . . . Frequently there were two-story frame houses standing out in the open fields, without fence or trees, lone outposts of the approaching army of homes."[9] That city is organized around its industrial infrastructure, indicated here by the converging rail lines that arrange the view. The processes of growth, exchange, and speculation shape the spokes of development radiating out from the region's central place. The city is organized, as well, around the promise of growing into its role as the model city of industrial modernity, in which all aspects of urban life derive from the city's central function of collecting resources for processing into finished products to be circulated and consumed. Among those raw materials flowing from the hinterland into the city is Carrie, whose small-town training has made her a kind of half-baked urbanite aspiring to bigger things. Philip Fisher has traced the parallels between Carrie's prospects and those of Chicago, which are readable from the train window in the landscape of the developing West Side that offers "a gigantic sketch of its own future":

> The Chicago that Dreiser describes is a mediating term. It is simultaneously a synecdoche for America, of which it is the most compact and representative part; and, on the other hand, it is a metonymy for Carrie whose small, future-oriented self with its plans and expectations extending out into reality like trolley tracks and strings of gas lamps, the surrounding city magnifies and gives expression to. . . . [T]he miniaturization of social and political fact is superimposed on the magnification of deeply interior psychological states.[10]

Reaching Chicago, Carrie enters the complex of social, economic, and cultural orders that characterize industrial urbanism. Having executed a kind of introductory pas de deux with the salesman Drouet during the train ride from Wisconsin to Chicago, during which the two establish the understanding that will underlie their affair, Carrie is crossing a boundary into ways of being that Dreiser presents as emblematic of industrial urbanism. She will learn to finesse the grinding processes of production and consumption as she moves from the "lean and narrow" constrictions of wage labor and neighborhood life to the "walled city" of privilege downtown, and she will do so by making both a more valuable commodity and a more efficient company of herself. She learns to bank on her unspoiled youth (a species of futures trading), to capitalize on the sentimental appeal of the "emotional greatness" she projects on the stage as an actress, to preserve her worth as she trades Drouet for Hurstwood and then drops Hurstwood when he runs out of money and desire. As Carrie and Drouet approach Chicago in the novel's opening chapter, they exchange addresses: that is, they place themselves in relation to the landscape through which they are passing, thus offering an account of relations between themselves and the circulation of resources and meaning in the city. They are "nearing Chicago" in the fullest sense of the phrase, a Chicago growing into its role as America's type of the modern industrial metropolis. The rail lines form the bones and arteries of a growing body, still awkward but still on the upslope of its development: "It was a city of over 500,000, with the ambition, the daring, the activity of a metropolis of a million" (13–14).

This is the opposite of *Golden Arm*'s Chicago, which is narrowing rather than expanding, aging rather than maturing, contained and exhausted by its rail lines rather than extended by them into a richly prospective future. If Carrie's story runs on deterministic tracks toward her entrance into the "walled city" of privilege and money, those tracks provide access to an expanding terrain: Chicago, Montreal, New York; department stores, the stage, Broadway. Frankie's story, like Hurstwood's, runs on tracks toward an ever-narrowing vanishing point. The second line of junkie's "tracks" running down Frankie's arm underscores the distance between the prematurely aged morphine addict and the "future-oriented" Carrie, two personifications of Chicago. Even the space momentarily opened up to Frankie by travel along the tracks made by the injection of morphine, which "hit[s] the heart like a runaway locomotive" (*Golden Arm*, 58), narrows into a "terrible pit" between "glacial walls" (57) as the euphoria of the high gives way to the addict's need for more. The train lines in *Sister Carrie* have, in *Golden Arm*, bent back upon themselves into an impassable boundary enclosing a narrow and airless terrain. Looking upon it from her window (one of Carrie's most characteristic positions), Sophie can "scarcely breathe."

Sophie's perception of an obscure threat of annihilation in the streetscape has roots in the earlier novel: *Sister Carrie* initiates and *Golden Arm* completes the Chicago tradition's movement to the street, parallel to but distinct from its movement to the neighborhoods. The move to the neighborhoods, linked to the emergence in American letters of the urban industrial order and especially of the white-ethnic immigrant groups who dominated its laboring classes in cities like Chicago, reaches an end point in the imagined disappearance of industrial workers and the world they made. The Chicago tradition's move to the *street* comes to fruition in *Golden Arm*'s variegated catalogues of hustlers, drifters, drunks, operators, hoods, and other types who collect at the lower margins of the neighborhood order where it verges on the street life. To be "out in the street"—a combined physical and experiential condition—is to encounter the city without buffers. In *Sister Carrie*, Hurstwood gradually moves from well-buffered interiors like Fitzgerald and Moy's and his home into the street, where he is utterly destroyed; but Carrie and most of the other characters maneuver to remain in or near the "walled city" of privilege, insulated by wealth, social placement, and mastery of urban technique. When she has no money and little familiarity with urban technique, the streets of Chicago become a place of menace where she fears she cannot mediate or influence the forces acting upon her, the concatenation of desires that make the city go. She experiences moments of vertiginous terror in the streets, feeling "a sense of helplessness amid so much evidence of power and force" (15) during her search for employment, the period when she begins to see that she might be consumed by the city—forced into the kind of hardscrabble existence pursued by her sister Minnie, menaced with the fate awaiting Hurstwood. In New York, insulated by money and position and a better grasp of urban technique, Carrie promenades on Broadway as if on a stage, protected even on the streets by invisible buffers of privilege.

In *Golden Arm*, conversely, everyone is always in the street. Some characters are better equipped to maneuver in and around the annihilating structure of the El, like the cats who pervade the novel, but the street extends everywhere. There is no walled city, and the unraveling of neighborhood orders breaks down even the modest buffers of community evolved by the industrial village. The "gutter-colored" light of the rooming house suggests a continuity between interior and exterior, and the constant intrusion of the El confirms that continuity. Passing Els rattle Frankie and Sophie's latch, as if city-structuring forces were demonstrating their access to the meanest furnished room. Upstairs at Vi's, the approaching Garfield Park Express sounds as if it "were running straight through the house" (130). The Loop-bound El roaring overhead makes Molly's curtain billow stiffly, "passionately and white" before it "slowly fell and went limp" (112), as Frankie and Molly sleep together, so that the El superimposes itself on their union and makes of it another show of the white flag of surrender to the city.

Golden Arm marks out as its key social terrain the line where the neighborhood order gives out onto the street life, something at once very old (like Hurstwood's Bowery) and very new—like the inner-city milieu of junkies that would become an object of fascination in the 1960s. In drifting below that line, as so many of the novel's characters are irrevocably doing, *Golden Arm* imagines as well a drift below the level of mass culture, which was introduced as a constitutive element of modern urbanism in *Sister Carrie* and vigorously critiqued as such by the neighborhood novels.

Carrie swims in a sea of urban mass culture as it takes form around her in the late nineteenth century, and her speedy acculturation opens the gate to the walled city. Clothes in the department store speak to her, helping her to finesse Drouet's attentions; the stage and its satellite world of newspaper coverage provide her with a model of behavior and a profession; she comes to understand the play of desires eddying around her as a young woman in the street, an actress, an urbanite. The department store's interior space expands infinitely in her subjective experience of it, presenting her with goods that represent the building blocks of a persona with access to an entire way of life and thus with access to a particular urban landscape—the residential hotels, Broadway promenades, and stage life of New York. Passing from the street to the store, she passes from anxiety to a sense of "relief from distress": "the whole fabric of doubt and impossibility had slipped from her mind" (*Sister Carrie*, 63–64).

The neighborhood novels of Farrell, Wright, and Algren (before *Golden Arm*) together launch a critique of exactly this numbing, easing effect of mass culture, arguing for the cultural impoverishment of the industrial proletariat

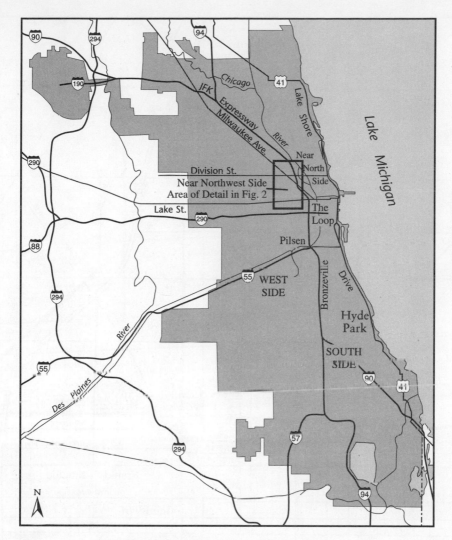

Figure 1. Chicago. University of Wisconsin Cartographic Laboratory.

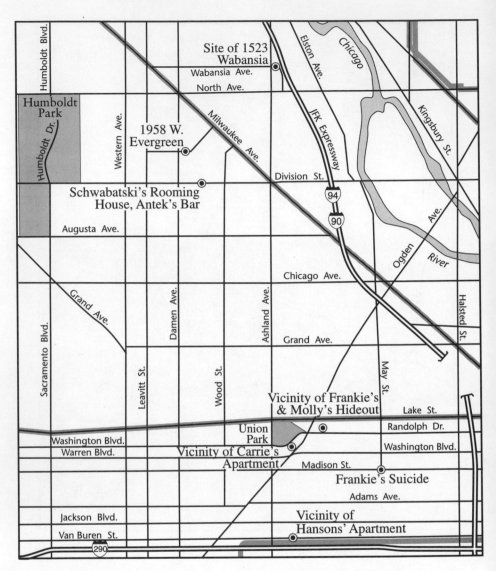

Figure 2. Detail map of Near Northwest Side and Near West Side, Chicago.
University of Wisconsin Cartographic Laboratory.

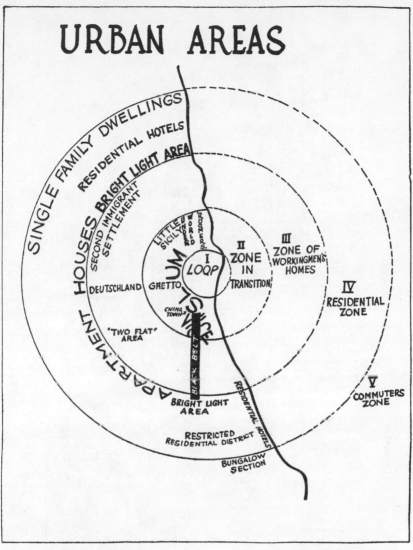

URBAN AREAS

SINGLE FAMILY DWELLINGS
RESIDENTIAL HOTELS
BRIGHT LIGHT AREA
APARTMENT HOUSES
SECOND IMMIGRANT SETTLEMENT
LITTLE SICILY
U-WORLD
ROOMERS
DEUTSCHLAND
GHETTO
SLUM
I LOOP
CHINA TOWN
"TWO FLAT" AREA
BLACK BELT
BRIGHT LIGHT AREA
II ZONE IN TRANSITION
III ZONE OF WORKINGMEN'S HOMES
IV RESIDENTIAL ZONE
V COMMUTERS ZONE
RESIDENTIAL HOTELS
RESTRICTED RESIDENTIAL DISTRICT
BUNGALOW SECTION

THE ANATOMY OF THE CITY.—The above chart discloses the gross anatomy of the city, the typical zones into which every city segregates as it expands. The chart shows, further, the segregation of typical cultural areas of Chicago within these zones (chart after Burgess).

Figure 3. Ernest Burgess's scheme of "urban areas," with caption, summarizes an "ecological" overview of the industrial city that the Chicago School's studies sought to flesh out in detail. Algren's Near Northwest Side would fall across zone II (rooming-house district and underworld) and zone III (workingmen's homes, second immigrant settlement). (From Harvey Warren, Zorbaugh, *The Gold Coast and the Slum*, p. 230.) Copyright 1929, 1976, by The University of Chicago Press. All rights reserved. Reprinted with permission.

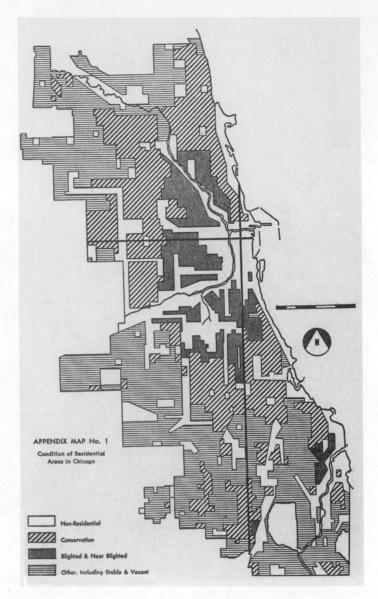

APPENDIX MAP No. 1

Condition of Residential
Areas in Chicago

☐ Non-Residential

▨ Conservation

■ Blighted & Near Blighted

▤ Other, Including Stable & Vacant

Figure 4. Chicago Plan Commission's overview of blight in Chicago, ca.1950. Note the concentration of blighted, near-blighted, and industrial areas around the core. The commission identified "conservation" areas as neighborhoods that could be saved from blight through government intervention. (From Martin Meyerson and Edward Banfield, *Politics, Planning, and the Public Interest*, p. 331.) Copyright © 1955 by The Free Press; copyright renewed 1983 by Martin D. Meyerson and Edward C, Banfield. Reprinted with permission of The Free Press, a Division of Simon and Schuster.

inhabiting the neighborhood order. They present department stores, movies, advertisements, radio, newspapers, and magazines as promising escape from a sense of one's immediate situation while reinforcing the circumscription of opportunity that ushers their young protagonists down narrowing paths to early destruction. "Most of us 20th century Americans are reluctant to admit the tragically low quality of experiences of the broad American masses," asserted Wright in his introduction to Algren's *Never Come Morning*.[11] Thus, the neighborhood novels typically contain extended descriptions of invented movies that illustrate the impoverishment of mass-cultural formulas; characters develop extravagantly circumscribed fantasies of power or fulfillment based on the repertoires made available to them by billboards, radio jingles, and movies.[12] The limits of mass culture double the tightly defined geographies of the neighborhoods, narrowing the neighborhood characters' sense of the world and what it has to offer, and those characters respond with ignorance to opinions and impulses external to their cultural repertoires. The constriction of cultural avenues available to people on the street and in the neighborhoods creates dissonance with the inchoate desires for more and different life fostered by mass culture. That dissonance motivates Carrie to upward mobility, which she accomplishes by exploiting the frustrated desire of urban theatergoers for more and different sentimental life, but in the neighborhood novels the dissonance makes for a violent and confused set of dispossessed young men—Bigger Thomas, Studs Lonigan, Cass McKay (*Somebody in Boots*), Bruno Bicek (*Never Come Morning*).

Golden Arm posits the exhaustion of this dissonance. Frankie has a dwindling and quickly expended supply of frustrated violence left in him. Describing Frankie's fellow inmates during a stretch in jail, *Golden Arm* describes the condition to which the inmates of the novel's "open-roofed jail" of a city are sinking. Not only are they "the ones who just wouldn't work" (as discussed earlier), but "they were the ones who had never learned to want. . . . They were secretly afraid of being alive and the less they desired the closer they came to death" (208). The engine of desire that drives Carrie's world, making its trains run and ordering its social strata, has wound down to a near-standstill. So has the neighborhood novel's cultural critique: three paragraphs later, the observation that these people without desire "didn't even read comic books" carries no particular charge. What can one say about the cultural impoverishment of people sliding below the threshold of culture as Algren and the neighborhood novel understood it? Similarly, Frankie and the others are sliding below the level of politics. Antek tells Frankie, who is being hotly pursued by the police for the murder of a universally despised drug dealer, that the police are acting on the orders of a machine politician who wants to appear tough on crime; Frankie tells Antek to "skip the politics" (321). Pressed so closely by the law, Frankie does not have the luxury to consider the reasons for his dire situation.

Preoccupied with their ceaseless subsistence-level hustling, then, Frankie and his associates are falling into a world below both politics and mass culture, which were two of Chicago realism's favored contexts for evaluating the situation of the industrial working classes. The characters in *Golden Arm* move behind and beneath the billboards that indicate how power and meaning are arranged in the inner city. Fleeing back to his hideout after visiting the old neighborhood to gather information, Frankie hurriedly passes a billboard that begs "shamelessly in five-foot letters: VOTE FOR UNCLE MIKE" (324), the man behind the manhunt. The barflies at Antek's drink beneath a row of liquor ads depicting alien beings in alien landscapes: "some usurer togged out in woodsman's gear . . . in a clean green land of night-blue lakes and birch trees so straight and tall they looked like ivory-tipped cues"; "a pink-cheeked, overstuffed illiterate" in a private library. "This freshly blooded race bred by the better advertising agencies looked down upon the barflies of the Tug & Maul, trying to understand how it was that these battered wrecks could look as though not one of them had ever seen a land of night-blue lakes with poolroom cues for trees. Nor any man's private library at all. They appeared not even to have discovered the public ones" (233). Like Hurstwood reading about Carrie in the papers, Sophie receives fragments of information from the world of mass culture and struggles to make sense of them by pasting them into her scrapbook. Sophie has yet some stirrings of desire—for a golden age receding into the past, for a real family with a real dog (as opposed to the flatulent Rumdum, given to her by Frankie), for order and clarity on the old neighborhood's model—which help to drive her mad. Many of the others are sinking toward the fate of Hurstwood, who loses access to any reserve of desire as he slides toward skid row and then suicide, asking, "'What's the use?'" (*Sister Carrie*, 458), a question that vitiates the impulse to consume on which mass culture depends. Frankie and Sparrow go to Gold's department store on Milwaukee Avenue to half-heartedly steal the period's novel consumer items (like "''lectric eye-rons'"), not to shop or to refine their consumer personae. Rather than opening up a vista of cultural repertoires, these expeditions deliver Frankie and Sparrow directly into the narrowest landscape of all: they are routinely caught and put in prison.

Drained of desire, Hurstwood and Frankie arrive at remarkably similar places in the final narrowing of their worlds to nothing. Moving within a "disgruntled mass" of Bowery characters "pouring in between bleak walls" into a flophouse, Hurstwood finds himself in a dingy cubicle—"wooden, dusty, hard" (*Sister Carrie*, 457). Wounded and dying for a fix, Frankie goes to ground in a flophouse on Madison Street, in a little alcove roofed with chicken wire. The two men take very different routes to arrive at this anonymous suicide hotel. *Sister Carrie* deflects the story of Hurstwood and its distinctly October-city conclusion away from Chicago in the springtime of its golden age to the "old world" of New York City. Hurstwood rides a series of trains across America to New York, then a series of streetcars through Brooklyn during his stint as a strikebreaker, before the tracks deliver him onto skid row. During that passage, he falls from the upper middle class into anonymous drifterhood, from the walled city into street life—in short, he falls into Nelson Algren's track-bound October city. Frankie never leaves it, riding the closed system of Els and street-cars back and forth, around and around the inner rim of the novel's "constant boundaries," until the final chase delivers him onto Chicago's most notorious skid row with no options left to him.

Frankie hangs himself in a hotel on Madison just east of Racine—within a few blocks of Carrie Meeber's first place in Chicago, the home of her sister Minnie. Minnie and her husband Hanson, a hard-working immigrant ethnic of Swedish parentage, lead a "clean, saving" life, paying "monthly instalments on two lots far out on the West Side" (*Sister Carrie*, 10). Like Vi and Jailer, they have little margin of error separating them from the street: if they both work hard, save, and do not weaken or suffer bad luck, they might eventually own a home in the developing neighborhoods of the West Side. Sickness, bad judg-ment, or a failure of thrift, on the other hand, will start them on the long down-ward slope toward the world of *The Jungle*'s Jurgis Rudkus or of Frankie and Sophie. Entering their home, Carrie instantly grasps this precarious situation: "She felt the drag of a lean and narrow life" (11). Minnie and Hanson, with a baby and a hope to own some property, are staving off the process of narrow-ing that has for the most part run its course in *Golden Arm*. Vi and Jailer con-stitute the heavily ironized exceptions to the rule: everyone else in the rooming house at 1860 West Division Street, childless and without prospects, exists far below the possibility of owning or even wanting anything, and in particular of owning a home. The bums in the lockup, the ones whose world has gone down the drain and who expect their own blood to follow, are privy to "the great, secret and special American guilt of owning nothing, nothing at all," a guilt that, fittingly, lies "crouched behind every billboard" (*Golden Arm*, 17).

When Carrie and Hurstwood flee to the edge of the world, they run to New York; when Frankie and Molly flee to the edge of the world, they go a few blocks down the El line to "where the dark people live, drinking cheaper beer" (127) in the Lake Street ghetto at the base of Milwaukee Avenue, where they take up residence in a tenement apartment on Maypole Street. The Lake Street ghetto resembles Polish Division Street, with its own bars, its own beer, its own Saturday night dancing and music, and its own domestic landscape of furnished rooms under the shadow of the Lake Street El. Even though *Golden Arm* does not understand the ghetto to present an explanation of decline—as opposed to Lait and Mortimer, who regard racial succession as a principal engine driving Chicago's decline—the ghetto serves to figure the terminal future of Frankie's world. Hurstwood and Carrie's flight to New York clarifies *Sister Carrie*'s composite urban landscape: there are two cities representing two ranges of possibility, the walled city and the Bowery. Fleeing from the white-ethnic inner city into the black inner city, Frankie and Molly discover that they have only narrowed their options a little further—only the faces and the music have changed.

Golden Arm imagines only one city, the October city under the El. It is almost springtime in *Golden Arm*'s expanding ghetto, but, as *City on the Make* declares, Chicago is "an October sort of city even in spring": "across the littered Negro yard next door . . . February's first touch of thaw was glinting along the rubbled earth. A wheelless, one-fendered chassis of something that might once have been a Chalmers or an Overland stood there with little puddles along its single fender. How many wheelless, one-fendered years it had rusted there no neighbor could have told" (*Golden Arm*, 315). The ruined machine—an avatar of *City on the Make*'s "rusty iron heart"—constitutes black Chicago's inheritance, what Frankie's people have left to turn over to their successors. Algren was taken with Carl Sandburg's reading of Chicago's race riots of 1919—"The slums take their revenge"—which he repeats in *City on the Make*.[13] Not only do the slums take their revenge on their inhabitants, but that revenge extends to cover all those living in Chicago's inner city after the industrial city has reached the end of time prophesied in *City on the Make*. Black Southerners poured into Chicago during the 1940s, 1950s, and 1960s, drawn in great part by precisely those industrial jobs that were leaving the inner city during this period (or would leave soon after). If *Golden Arm* does not speak directly to this linkage between industrial transformation and folk migration that helped to form the second ghetto, it does so indirectly by putting the ghetto in the shadow of the El and the "rusty iron heart" as the novel brings the October city down the course of "wheelless, one-fendered years" to a final winding-down.

Resonances between *Golden Arm* and *City on the Make*, like those between *Golden Arm* and *Sister Carrie*, suggest a larger story coded into *Golden Arm*'s claustrophobic landscape and narrative. In retrospect, *City on the Make* reads like a historical concordance to *Golden Arm*, providing precisely the big picture that Frankie and Sophie never quite grasp: the undefined doom hanging over their neighborhood is the decline of industrial urbanism that embraces both the urban village and Algren's literary tradition. *Golden Arm*, in turn, explores in rich and local detail the world of those people subsisting below the threshold of *City on the Make*'s historical imagination. Seen in one of *City on the Make*'s aerial passes, Chicago gives the viewer a "pang," a feeling that "something priceless is being left behind in the forest of furnished rooms, beneath the miles and miles of lights and lights" (76), but *City on the Make* cannot work down from the level of overview at which it operates (100 years of history and a large cast of famous Chicagoans in perhaps 20,000 words) to make a sustained examination of ordinary human figures moving at street level in the neighborhoods. *City on the Make*, outlining the story of decline, argues that the Chicago realist tradition must fall with industrial urbanism; *Golden Arm* aspires to be that tradition's culminative masterpiece, "the last of the Chicago novels" by "the last of the Chicago novelists."

City on the Make is a slim poetic survey, following the model of Sandburg's *Chicago Poems* and *The People, Yes* (and dedicated to Sandburg); *Golden Arm* is a thick realist novel, the Chicago realist tradition's principal literary form.[14] But the two books, both assembled in part from material Algren wrote in the 1930s, contain one another in shared figures and bits of language. Among other things, they share an autumnal mood and an El-enclosed landscape: they both map the October city. *City on the Make*'s landscape, extending much further in space (including the South Side, the Loop, and the suburbs) and in time (from early nineteenth-century prairie through the golden age to the rusting ruins of the future), contains the drastically narrowed midcentury neighborhood terrain of *Golden Arm*. One epithet for the El in particular, "the constant boundaries of the night," appears repeatedly in both texts, suggesting that the El runs between them, joining microcosm (the landscape of *Golden Arm*) to big picture (the landscape of *City on the Make*) as it joined past to present in *City on the Make*'s survey of industrial Chicago's history. The story of Chicago and the story of Frankie Machine take place in one composite landscape defined by the El, positioning the narrative of Frankie's decline and fall to double and condense that of Chicago.

The sense of regret pervading this landscape operates at both scales—primarily traced to a series of citywide failures and historical windings-down in *City on the Make*, traced to a series of intensely local and personal defeats in *Golden Arm*. *City on the Make* argues that there are "no more giants," by which it primarily means that a set of heroic historical figures—writers, reform intellectuals, political leaders, star athletes—active in shaping the city's golden age have no successors in the contemporary city. In *Golden Arm*, the corpses of anonymous drifters collect in a basement morgue until carpenters come to build coffins for them, "clean pine boxes" all in one size because "there were not many giants any more" (18). Appearing in *Golden Arm*, the notion of the giants' passing floats free of the frame of reference provided for it in *City on the Make*. Without sufficient reference to put the line in a suitably outsize narrative frame, this kind of mock-epic diction—"no more giants," "'God has forgotten us all,'" the tendency toward unanimity and ubiquity—grates against the inability of the characters to account for the Atlantean world in which they move. How could one car crash have made everyone everywhere afraid of closing time?

The events that form the history of *Golden Arm*'s world are intensely personal or essentially mythic—a car crash, the withdrawal of neighborhood gods—but these sub- or nonhistorical explanation systems gain much of their literary power precisely from their inadequacy. The pall over the neighborhood suggests an incomprehensible, annihilating process beyond the grasp of the novel's characters. The car crash, not deindustrialization and suburbanization, is therefore responsible for Sophie's highly developed apocalyptic sense. But the resonances between the city she sees from her window and the models on which it is based—the Chicago outside Nelson Algren's window and the Chicago tradition's Chicago as found in literary antecedents like *Sister Carrie* —allow a relatively concise, finite, discrete event like the car crash to figure the messy, complex, open-ended, and only intermittently visible transformations of urban life and literature under way in midcentury Chicago. The intertextualities binding *Golden Arm* to *City on the Make* and *Sister Carrie* encourage us in this project of extending Sophie's sense of ultimacy into a historical and literary realm beyond her horizons of understanding. If we read *City on the Make* together with *Golden Arm, City on the Make*'s sweeping decline seems to grow out of the story of Frankie Machine and his associates, who move through a world supercharged with ultimacy by the decline of industrial urbanism—a story too metropolitan and generational in scale to be articulated by such a relentlessly local-minded novel. Only Sophie can see the fall of industrial urbanism encoded in the world of *Golden Arm*, and that insight lands her in an asylum.

If Sophie Majcinek, neighborhood type and mythographer of decline, serves as a figure of urban intellectuals like Algren—living in the industrial city of fact and in a city of feeling that drew upon it for sustenance and order—then her conviction of imminent apocalypse begins to make sense. The entangling of neighborhood order and Algren's Chicago realist tradition begins to account for *Golden Arm*'s pervasive ultimacy and extremity. One of *Golden Arm*'s most jarring qualities is its willingness to imagine the industrial neighborhood order, still extensive and thriving in the late 1940s, on its last legs. Similarly, one of *City on the Make*'s most jarring qualities is its willingness to imagine the "monstrous forges" of heavy industry standing like a "rusty iron heart" in a landscape going back to prairie, a vista that did not become standard in depictions of Chicago until the 1970s, when the city's remaining heavy industry went through a highly visible latter phase of deindustrialization. Nelson Algren was not predicting the future, nor was he ready to believe that the phase of his most productive engagement with Chicago was at an end, but when we read *Golden Arm* as his last Chicago novel it becomes an elegy for industrial urbanism, the way of living in cities represented by both smokestacks and *Sister Carrie*.

After the End: The Story of Decline as Act One

Come and show me another city with lifted head
singing.

Carl Sandburg, "Chicago"

The dawn rises
Uuuhhh,
Like sick old men,
Oh, Lord,
Playing on the rooftops in their underwear,
Yeah. . . .

Stuart Dybek, "Blight"

In the 1950s, as Chicago changed around him, Nelson Algren worked intermittently on a Chicago novel about the drug scene entitled *Entrapment,* but he
gave up on it. From 1949 until his death in 1981, more than half of his professional writing life, Algren experimented with other styles and genres—nonfiction essays, prose poetry, cultural criticism, New Journalism, antic existen-
tialism. As we look back on *Golden Arm* from this perspective, the novel's
urgent sense of impending disaster proceeds not just from Algren's sense of
urbanism in transformation but also from a writer's panic: as Chicago changed
into something new and strange, he was running out of things to say about the
city he had staked out as his literary bailiwick. The Chicago sociologist Gerald
Suttles reports that during the mid-1960s he and Algren spent a drunken night
visiting Algren's old stomping grounds on the West Side. Suttles portrays

Algren as a writer out of touch with the landscape in which he moved, already receding into the half-remembered ghost city in which Art Shay encounters him: "Our ramble took the course of an homage to those places he had been before. He was so occupied with telling me what they were 'really like' that neither of us could notice what was going on. As he stood, absorbed, before an empty lot where his mother had run a boarding house, unmindful of the traffic around him, it came over me that he was trying to reink a dry pen."[1] Algren's pen was not dry in any absolute sense—it still had many essays and poems and one last novel (discussed in the conclusion of this study) in it—but he had nothing original left to say about the neighborhoods of Chicago. By the 1960s, Algren was writing himself out of the picture: "Sandburg's Chicago, Dreiser's Chicago, Farrell's and Wright's and my own Chicago, that was somebody else's Chicago. That was a play with a different plot."[2]

Having written his last Chicago novel, Algren observed and recorded the limitations of his engagement with Chicago. As the redeveloped core and suburban periphery grew and solidified in the late 1950s and early 1960s, Algren removed his authorial persona from the landscape of the postindustrial metropolis. In 1961, a decade after the publication of *Golden Arm* and *City on the Make*, he employed one of his favorite figurative strategies—an expressive landscape—to imagine his literary-historical situation: "On the day that the double-tiered causeway is merged with the expressway that merges with the coast-to-coast thruway making right-hand turns every mile into a hundred solid miles of mile-high skyscrapers, each rising a mile hope-high to the sky out of a mile dream-deep in the earth, my own name will not be brought up."[3] In other words, Algren understood his writing self to be so conjoined to the industrial city that to imagine a completed postindustrial transformation—its completeness indicated by the mile-high, mile-deep seamlessness of the landscape of skyscrapers and expressways—was to imagine his disappearance as a writer. This fantasy of literary obsolescence predicts that he and the people of this new city will have difficulty recognizing one another: he will not be equipped to tell their stories or map their city's social and psychic terrains, and his "name will not be brought up" by them (or attached to the landscape, as demonstrated by the unnaming of Algren Street). He will be a "Chicago writer" only in a historical sense. Having already split his time for many years between the Near Northwest Side and a lakefront exurb in Indiana, Algren left Chicago for good in 1975, going east to New Jersey and then to Long Island, where he died in 1981. He became one of postindustrial Chicago's ghosts—Suttles calls him one of its "casualties"[4]—rising up from the long-lost building at 1523 Wabansia to haunt Art Shay in the landscape of expressways and skyscrapers.

Algren was an early and definitive mythographer of postwar urban decline, committed to plotting one particular layer of urban development—the high-industrial order—to the exclusion of all others. *Golden Arm, City on the Make*, and Algren's other postwar Chicago writing render the decline as naturalist tragedy, taking it almost to the end of the line—the narrowing landscape, impending apocalypse, the city collapsing into Atlantean ruin. Having arrived at the end of time in *Golden Arm* and *City on the Make*, one must remind oneself that Chicago continued to produce and devour itself in the physical and discursive realms. The narrowing and collapse of Nelson Algren's Chicago exemplifies one narrative understanding of postwar Chicago, the story of the industrial city's decline told by Algren and others, but one could turn as well to complementary narratives detailing a set of expansions and rises: for instance, black Chicago, the city's suburban periphery, and the new postindustrial urban core were all booming at midcentury, competing and combining to shape the revised metropolis.

By the same token, one has to remind oneself that Algren's telling of the decline imagines itself as a culminative act of imagination: it argues that there cannot be any Chicago writers after Algren or Chicago stories after *Golden Arm–City on the Make*. Of course, postwar Chicago continued to produce writers, some of whom in turn produced a thriving city of feeling. This latter group were doing the urban intellectual's business of representing the city by repeating, reworking, and replacing the stories and figures created by Algren and his predecessors. Some of these writers who did not aspire to Algren's position at the end of a Chicago tradition, like Gwendolyn Brooks and Saul Bellow, were in the 1950s attaining precisely the kind of critical status that Algren was so rapidly losing.

In *City on the Make*, which presents his most extended account of Chicago's decline as a literary capital, Algren makes the decline's standard assertion that there are no writers left in Chicago. The city at midcentury is "a cultural Sahara" abandoned by its artists; Algren's narrating persona toils through it all alone, "with not a camel in sight."[5] Algren portrayed the artists of postheroic Chicago as shills for the progrowth coalition, bloodless academics out of touch with the world beneath the El tracks, or exiles. In an essay written in the early 1960s, Algren argued further that the postwar city's quiescent culture and the "lack of love of Chicagoans for Chicago" were made self-evident "by the fact that we make no living record of it here, and are, in fact, opposed to first-hand creativity. All we have today of the past is the poetry of Sandburg, now as remote from the Chicago of today as Wordsworth's."[6]

There is not much to be gained in holding writers responsible for keeping abreast of the work of other writers, and there is not much to be gained in pointing out in great detail how indefensible Algren's notion of a city without artists was. He was being cantankerous when he made the claim and could not have expected to sustain it against even casual counterargument. So what was he about in making the claim, and what value is there in examining it? Part of the answer is that, as I argue in chapters 1–3, he was recording the increasing strain of the relationship between an urban intellectual frozen in a prewar mold and a postwar city in dramatic transformation. Another part of the answer, which I will pursue in this chapter, has to do with the character of the urban intellectuals Algren refused to acknowledge in *City on the Make*. Algren's refusal to see others doing precisely what he thought Chicago writers should do—making literature from the materials of neighborhood life, investigating the arrangements of power and meaning that shaped neighborhood life—leads us to read those other writers for signs of literary-historical situations and generic repertoires different from Algren's. Algren's turn away from fiction and toward criticism, and the sweeping quality of his self-conception as the last of the Chicago writers, asks us to read other writers with and against him. He therefore affords us an opportunity to move beyond the decline and consider some of the literary and cultural orders that succeeded Algren's Chicago tradition in the business of representing the city.

In this chapter, then, I consider three writers—Gwendolyn Brooks, Mike Royko, and Stuart Dybek—working beyond the limits of Algren's literary sensibility. They took up the task that Algren refused to take up after midcentury: representing postindustrial Chicago. Brooks was already prominently at work in and on the city of Chicago, especially its growing black inner city, at midcentury. Algren knew her work, and that of other artists of the period, and still chose not to see it when he imagined the city without artists.[7] In the early 1960s, Algren did choose to see Royko, a newspaper reporter, as a successor to him because Royko could trace his pedigree to both of Algren's old neighborhoods: Royko grew up on the Near Northwest Side and knew how to tell the story of Chicago's decline. But Royko left Algren and the old neighborhood behind, making a career out of both retelling the decline and exploiting its inadequacy as a representational formula. Dybek also grew up in and wrote about the kind of neighborhood that Algren once regarded as his literary domain. Dybek's body of work begins at ground zero of Algren's terminal landscape, the Polish urban village in transition, but maps a distinctively postindustrial context in which that older order takes on new life through a series of fusions with newer orders.

These urban intellectuals and many more like them, both Algren's contemporaries and his successors, confronted a transformed object created by the layering-under of the industrial city by the postindustrial. Algren narrates this transformation as a decline, the collapse of the industrial city he knew; Brooks, Royko, and Dybek offer something other than the decline. For them, the revised city enabled and demanded revised formal strategies, new stories, a modified set of meanings. Read as a group, these postwar Chicago writers make the industrial city's decline the first act in the larger story of the postindustrial city's emergence.

No Living Record

Algren's claim that there was "no living record" of Chicago in the 1950s points up the limits of his understanding of Chicago and its representative forms. The claim very aptly describes the Chicago he imagines in *Golden Arm–City on the Make*—a city abandoned by its artists and populated by barflies who do not even read comic books—and it tacitly acknowledges that Algren was losing the will and capacity to make his own literary record of Chicago. Behind the claim is a kind of stunted historical reasoning: if Algren was the last of the Chicago writers on the prewar model, as he (and others) recognized himself to be, then it was because World War II and the subsequent transformation of the city had finished Chicago as a cradle of poets, realists, and reporters. In *City on the Make*, he argues that midcentury Chicago is no longer "an artist's town. It has had its big chance, and fluffed it. Thirty years ago we gave musicians to the world; now we give drill sergeants and 'professional informants.' . . . You can't make an arsenal of a nation and yet expect its cities to produce artists."[8]

In the historical case of Chicago, and especially in the case of Chicago's black inner city, Algren's opposition of arsenals to art is dead wrong. It was precisely the conversion of Chicago into an arsenal during manufacturing booms associated with the world wars that helped attract black Southerners to the city in the twentieth century. The second, much greater migration peaked in the 1940s and 1950s but continued into the 1960s, well after the wartime boom had receded to reveal a long-term process of deindustrialization and its difficult consequences for the inner city. Among these migrants were the practitioners and initial audience for Chicago blues, that series of generic innovations in the blues form that would become postwar Chicago's most enduring contribution to American, and world, culture. In adapting Southern blues forms to Chicago, and in adapting Chicago stories to the blues form, artists like Muddy Waters, Howling Wolf, Otis Rush, Magic Sam, Buddy Guy, and Junior Wells, among hundreds more (and often in collaboration and conflict, one should note, with white ethnics like the Jewish immigrants from Poland who ran Chess Records), developed the genre of electric blues that became postwar Chicago's signature cultural form. Chicago blues—really a collection of subgenres, many of them rooted in Southern and Western hinterlands—has flourished across generations in postwar Chicago, as all manner of practitioners balance tradition and innovation in the perpetual process of generic renewal. Chicago blues is nothing if not a living record (or CD, these days) of Chicago's social and cultural history.

Golden Arm has a great deal of music in it but very little blues. Most of the music in the book takes the form of standards, like "Paper Moon," which always seem to float down rooming-house hallways from somewhere else, as if leaking into the present from the past. The novel typically uses music to mark boundaries—between past and present, between the local experience of neighborhood and a wider world beyond it—and to mark the boundaries of its own representational range. *Golden Arm* makes a gesture at representing what is probably a blues house party, for instance, but the party happens just offstage. Frankie, hiding out in the Lake Street ghetto tenement, listens to the "music-making" coming from upstairs. In a standard portrait of blues as an art form shaped by a way of life (in other words, a living record of that way of life), the tenement's mundane sounds—"a snatch of rhythm by the door, shouts from porch to porch and laughter rocking down the stairs"—build through the week into "a single Saturday night shout, when the whole house shook with Negro roistering. To the din above his head, Frankie would tap away on his practice board though hardly able to hear the radio's beat for the slap and slam, the shambling and the clattering of heavy feet, right overhead all night long."[9] Frankie Machine, drumming along with music he can barely hear that filters downstairs to him from a place he cannot see, aptly stands in for Algren the neighborhood writer. Algren, so closely engaged with industrial orders rapidly acquiring the nostalgic charge of old songs, places the Chicago blues tradition and the emergent second ghetto (as something other than a black variant of the urban village) beyond the novel's imaginative and representational reach.

Algren was a writer, not a musician, and his notion of his cultural tradition was largely restricted to writers. If he was not equipped to recognize blues as a living record of postwar Chicago, and of black Chicago in particular, what *writers* did he see as doing that cultural work? Like many other urban intellectuals and readers who regarded the black inner city as exotic underworld, dark continent, or a variant of the urban village, Algren turned to Richard Wright for insights into it. From the perspective afforded by his self-positioning at the tail end of Chicago's industrial-era literary tradition, Algren recognized Wright as the link between black Chicago and his own bailiwick. Algren and Wright, who were friends, understood themselves to be engaged in sympathetic projects, both of them exploring the human consequences of the brutally circumscribed cultural, economic, and social opportunities afforded by the modern industrial city and its hinterlands. In *City on the Make*, Algren identifies Wright as the last "giant," "the only party of over-average height to stop off here awhile since the middle '20s," but takes Wright to task for joining the exodus of Chicago writers. "For the artist lucky enough to come up in Chicago there ought to be a warning engraved on the shinbone alley tenement which was once Wright's home: Tough it out, Jack, tough it out." In moving to Paris and "becoming a Café Flore intellectual," Wright had, apparently, sold his literary patrimony and failed to "tough it out."[10] Thus, Wright joins Dreiser and all the other literary giants who have moved on, given up the fight, or otherwise left to Algren the

Chicago tradition's task of representing urbanism in the neighborhoods. There was, in the aggressively blindered mode of reasoning pursued by *City on the Make*, no writer in Algren's Chicago tradition left to represent Chicago's growing black inner city.

If Wright was no longer doing the business of representing Chicago's neighborhoods, then what about Gwendolyn Brooks? Like other narrators of Chicago's literary decline, Algren never mentions Brooks in his account of the extinction of the Chicago writer, even though at midcentury she was already launched on a notable career. A shrewd handicapper might already have been betting in 1950 that she would eventually succeed Carl Sandburg as poet laureate of Illinois, which she did in 1968. By the time Algren wrote *City on the Make*, Brooks was already Chicago's most illustrious practicing poet. She won the Pulitzer for *Annie Allen* in 1950 (beating out Robert Frost and William Carlos Williams), the same year in which Algren won the National Book Award for *Golden Arm*. People like Algren who cared about such notions as "commitment" to a neighborhood could not fail to see her obvious investment in Chicago's South Side: she lived there, she wrote about it; her literary persona was, by Algren's standards, "toughing it out" with no signs of slackening attention to the lives of neighborhood people. The development of both her poetic style and her subject matter from *A Street in Bronzeville* to *Annie Allen* demonstrated that she was rising to the demands of making literature about neighborhood life in the postwar city.

Algren knew Brooks and liked her. They had been acquainted since the two of them had worked for the WPA-funded Illinois Writers' Project in the 1930s.[11] Brooks wrote in 1972 that Algren was one "notable among the whites who have befriended me and assisted me"; he had been "kindly" to her "for thirty years."[12] In particular, she credits Algren with securing her first magazine commission, to write a piece on Bronzeville for *Holiday*'s special issue on Chicago in 1950. Algren's contribution to that very issue of *Holiday*, an essay entitled "One Man's Chicago," was the first published version of the prose poem that would appear, expanded and revised, as the book *Chicago: City on the Make*. Thanks to Algren's influence with the editors, Brooks's essay was right there in *Holiday* with his own, and with Carl Sandburg's tentative version of decline ("Is Chicago less vivid?"). So why did Brooks not appear in Algren's literary landscape as he mapped it in *Holiday* and *City on the Make*? How could Algren fail to see Gwendolyn Brooks as a fellow traveler in the cultural desert?

What some people might regard as the easiest response—because Brooks was black and a woman—can only be part of the answer. Yes, Algren tended to treat the white-ethnic urban village as *the* subject of urban literature, but his failure to recognize Brooks as a Chicago writer certainly does not indicate a programmatic exclusion of blacks from Nelson Algren's Chicago. Wright was one of his heroes, the last of the "giants," and Algren would argue in 1961 that blacks in the emergent civil rights movement had picked up the standard of social justice dropped by the exiles of the failing Chicago tradition, "forcing the return of the American promise of dignity for all."[13] The argument that Algren overlooked Brooks because she was a woman has more authority but still does not satisfy. Yes, he made a practice of saying and writing stupid things about women, and he tended with other self-styled "regular guy" intellectuals of his day toward a buffoonishly masculine conception of literary work (captured in all its silliness by Algren's disappointment in Wright, whose move to France seems to render him effeminate in Algren's view), but Algren was not incapable of regarding women as social critics and artists. If he could enjoy being dismissive of "women's writing," he did count Jane Addams, Harriet Monroe, and Edna St. Vincent Millay among Chicago's giants.

So, if the narrowness of Algren's sense of a Chicago literary tradition can be explained only in part as an unwillingness to value the work of a woman writer, how else to explain *City on the Make*'s omission of Brooks from the ranks of practicing Chicago writers? We might trace differences in Brooks's and Algren's literary antecedents, but my answer has more to do with the kinds of stories Brooks told. While it is true that Brooks's sonnets and ballads advertised their connection to the English poetic canon and other traditions very different from the Chicago realists among whom Algren wished to be counted, Algren's list of his own influences (which includes Whitman, Kuprin, Dostoevsky, and Céline) was more eclectic than a simple roster of those Chicago realists. Algren could easily have chosen to find common ground with Brooks in the democratic styles and themes of Whitman or Sandburg. But he chose not to find such common ground, at least not in *City on the Make*, and we can trace an explanation for that choice in the fact that Brooks was not writing declines. Algren had in mind, as a Chicago tradition, a particular line of Chicago writers concerned with mapping a particular Chicago and exploring its meanings, and he perceived that tradition's industrial city to be in steep decline at midcentury. Algren seemed to believe that Chicago writers, as he understood that genre of urban intellectual, were at midcentury obliged to tell the story of decline, and he did not recognize as genuine any Chicago writer who did not.

One is hard pressed to find arguments at midcentury for black Chicago's decline from past glory to a reduced present, which may help to explain why Algren never mentions Brooks or anyone else writing about black Chicago after Wright's departure. In the 1940s and 1950s, Chicago's black population was growing in numbers, expanding farther into the South Side and West Side, and negotiating as a people the crucial phases of a complex transition from Southern agrarianism to Northern urbanism. "We are now constructing the baby figure of the giant mass of things to come," conclude Drake and Cayton in their massive sociological study *Black Metropolis;*[14] they sound like Dreiser describing industrial Chicago's "peculiar qualifications of growth." At midcentury, many representations of the Black Metropolis still pursued a narrative line that tended up and out, even if that tendency was frustrated by social constraint, as in Lorraine Hansberry's drama of social mobility on Chicago's South Side, *A Raisin in the Sun*. The grave disappointments associated with the failure of Northern industrial urbanism to deliver on the promise of economic and social opportunity—the failures associated with the second ghetto—had not yet become truisms, as they would during the urban crisis of the 1960s (when writers like Claude Brown would begin to assemble the elements of decline narratives about the aftermath of black migration). In detailing the inner lives of black Chicagoans, Brooks and others pointed up continuing moral and social failures readable in a racially segregated social landscape, but they were not telling the story of black Chicago's decline. Brooks therefore operated beyond Algren's literary neighborhood as it is mapped in *City on the Make*. That neighborhood, like Frankie Machine's Chicago, was shrinking around him while Brooks's dramatically expanded.

If Brooks did not write declines, she did pursue social critique, making art from the impulse to protest divisions in the social landscape and in consciousness between blacks and whites—and also between men and women, between haves and have-nots, and between fractions of each group (making color prejudice among blacks, for instance, a recurring theme of her early work). One of the principal impulses discernible in her first two books and in her *Holiday* essay is to dissipate the exotic quality of black urbanism, to expose to view the simple fact of universal humanity shared by blacks and whites. In her poetry, that simple fact struggles always to find expression against the constraints on both black and white Americans' access to and experience of blacks' humanity. The racial imagination of Brooks's early poetry manifests the balance of protest and measured optimism characteristic of the "Double V" campaign and other initiatives of the 1940s led by urban blacks, many of whom regarded the investment of American blacks in the war effort and the wartime economic boom as the basis of a postwar push for social equality. "His lesions are legion/But reaching is his rule," Brooks wrote in *Annie Allen*, an apt image of her understanding of urban blacks at midcentury.[15] This may be a humanist brand of protest—and the injuries, defeats, and bitter constraints of daily life form one of Brooks's main subjects—but it is not decline. The social landscape and imaginative world inhabited by her characters are artificially narrowed by social injustice, as residents of Chicago's burgeoning black communities in the late 1940s found themselves penned in by systematic residential segregation, but her poetry seeks and expects to explore the ways to a larger, more expansive, more fully realized future.

The sense of a narrowed landscape that pervades Brooks's early poetry should, however, remind the reader of Algren's own neighborhood vistas. The irony of Algren's inability to see Brooks as a Chicago writer is reinforced by the resonances between their writing at midcentury. The proximity of subjects is obvious: Brooks makes art out of details of daily life in the neighborhood landscape of kitchenette apartments, sidewalks, and spaces under the El, the world of men in bars and housewives. If her poetry is more inclined than Algren's to imagine moments of transcendence, and more inclined to represent the respectable poor than spectacularly ruinous losers, Brooks is still always concerned with one of Algren's central themes: the limits, imaged as a narrowing of space, imposed by urban modernity on the daily experience of people of modest means.

Reading the early Brooks with Algren in mind reveals resonances of form as well. As Algren does in his writing, Brooks uses pavement-tinged shades of gray to consider the problem of making a life in the world of rented rooms, without buffers from the street, where the city's gears grind up the powerless people of the neighborhoods most efficiently:

> We are things of dry hours and the involuntary plan,
> Grayed in and gray. "Dream" makes a giddy sound, not strong
> Like "rent," "feeding a wife," "satisfying a man."[16]

Similarly, Brooks follows the body of De Witt Williams, in its hearse on the way to Lincoln Cemetery, "Down through Forty-Seventh Street:/Underneath the El" as the poem plots the tension between the "plain black boy['s]" blind, truncated life and the expansive set of aspirations and possibilities mapped on a landscape of black migration stretching from Alabama to Bronzeville.[17] The El operates here, as it does in Algren's work, as a figure of all that delimits and constrains a young urbanite's life.

Perhaps the most resonant language suggesting the sympathies between Brooks's and Algren's work is found in the opening lines of *Annie Allen*, published in 1949, the same year as *Man with the Golden Arm* and two years before *City on the Make*. After a dedicatory poem, the story of Annie Allen begins in the poem numbered 1, "The Birth in a Narrow Room," with the lines "Weeps out of western country something new./Blurred and stupendous. Wanted and unplanned."[18] The parallel here is not to *Golden Arm* but to *City on the Make*, which begins with an image of the city that, like Annie, is a stupendous and unplanned creation shaped by desire (and its dispossessed correlative, want) and rising out of the western country:

> To the east were the moving waters as far as the eye could follow. To the west a
> sea of grass as far as wind might reach.
>
> Waters restlessly, with every motion, slipping out of used colors for new. So
> that each fresh wind off the lake washed the prairie grasses with used sea-colors:
> the prairie moved in the light like a secondhand sea.

City on the Make is Algren's definitive statement of Chicago's historical decline: this moment of natural balance will collapse when the "marked-down derelicts with dollar signs for eyes" arrive to initiate the business of urbanism, and by the poem's end the mechanized, iron-bound city they built will have used itself up.[19] *Annie Allen* starts with an eerily similar moment of birth that takes place in the expansive western country and is juxtaposed with an image (in the poem's title) of Annie's "narrow" social situation that echoes Algren's sense of social order as unnatural constraint—but *Annie Allen* travels in another direction altogether. The volume's last poem, "Men of Careful Turns, Haters of Forks in the Road," makes Brooks's most explicit statement of racial protest to that time. The poem's narrating voice asks the men of careful turns to "Grant me that I am human. . . . /Admit me to our mutual estate," a change in social and cultural relations rendered in familiar terms as an expansion of a constricted landscape: "Open my rooms, let in the light and air."[20]

It is a crowning irony of Algren's impoverished understanding of Chicago writing that "Men of Careful Turns" seems in retrospect to address him as well. Algren was no man of careful turns in the poem's sense of a white man who prefers to "sugar up our prejudice with politeness" rather than support genuine changes in the racial arrangements of American urbanism. But he was a hater of forks in the road in the sense that he responded to the transformation of Chicago under way at midcentury, a transformation that crucially involved the expansion of the black inner city and the contraction of the white-ethnic neighborhood order, as a crisis threatening his writing and his Chicago. Algren knew Brooks's work and helped her to prosper, he expressed sympathy for the struggles of Chicago's growing black population against economic and social constraint, he understood that a black writer (like Wright) or a woman (like Addams) might take up the standard in what he thought of as a literary struggle for social justice—but in *City on the Make* he did not recognize Brooks as a major artist who would carry the representational project of writing Chicago into the city's next age. Rather than narrating the decline of the city Algren knew, Brooks was developing an account of what came next, a literature that grew out of the changing terrain of the midcentury inner city. "We are lost," assert the last lines of *Annie Allen*'s last poem in a final image of this social, historical, and literary situation: "must/Wizard a track through our own screaming weed."[21]

The track was to be wizarded in all the ways that urbanism makes available and demands, including by way of a literature that found the language and narrative forms to represent the epic of black urbanization—a story inextricably intertwined with the epic of European immigration and its epilogue, the white-ethnic decline. "Men of Careful Turns" seems, ironically, to speak to Brooks's friend and admirer Algren, as well to the others who shared Algren's narrow sense of a Chicago realist tradition, enjoining these haters of forks in the literary-historical road to make room in their canons for a new order of Chicago writer who would soon enter the first rank of American poets:

> Reserve my service at the human feast.
> And let the joy continue. Do not hoard silence
> For the moment when I enter, tardily,
> To enjoy my height among you.

From midcentury until 1967, Brooks continued to make poetry that asked, insistently but politely, that blacks be admitted to the American feast. In the late 1960s, when the cumulative urban transformations of the 1950s and 1960s finally captured the national imagination (and hers) as an "urban crisis" centered on the black ghetto, her poetry took a militant turn. Poems like "Malcolm X," the sermons on "the Warpland," and a series of heroic portraits of the Blackstone Rangers street gang stopped asking so nicely, or asking at all, and began to imagine the second ghetto as a black "Nation." Brooks's poetry and politics developed in close engagement with the social and literary consequences of the inner city's transformation. That engagement with postwar Chicago was already evident in her work at midcentury, when Algren was recording the attenuation of his own engagement with the same subject.

Bungalow Man and High-Rise Man

The narrative of decline is best equipped to imagine the fall of what is, not the coming of what is next, but even the most terminal vision of decline can become the first act of subsequent accounts that represent what does come next. Algren, for all his apocalyptic self-absorption, recognized this layering of narratives and representations. By 1961, he did see one camel out there.

Algren recognized the newspaper columnist Mike Royko—a reporter singularly without literary pretensions, in keeping with Algren's portrait of the city without artists—as the most fitting successor to him among Chicago's next generation of urban intellectuals. In a rambling poetic survey of Chicago life and letters entitled "Ode to Lower Finksville" (published in 1961), Algren identifies Royko as extending the Chicago tradition's dual project of urban realism and social criticism: Royko is "not only unconcerned about the image of the city as projected by the mayor's office . . . he clouds it up." In Algren's rendering, Royko's role takes shape in opposition to the grandiose redevelopment schemes of Daley's progrowth coalition, which believes that a city is made great by "a seventy-million-dollar exhibition hall rising from the ashes of a thirty-million-dollar exhibition hall . . . an airport in the lake to accommodate out-of-towners . . . any improvement of thruways, subways, opera houses or construction in the Loop which accommodates investors."[22] Royko's work, then, will be to write against the grain of the progrowth coalition's redevelopment-obsessed imagination, to tell stories continuous with those told by Algren and the Chicago tradition— stories about the grinding of individuals in the gears of urban process, about the unaccountable persistence of humor and sentiment in the quintessential city of the machine. These stories can be found in the interstices and shadows of the monumental new landscape of redevelopment, the same landscape that Algren cannot recognize as a sustaining literary subject, and Royko's job will be to cover them.

Royko became Chicago's leading newspaper columnist in the 1960s; and from the publication in 1971 of his book *Boss* until his death in 1997 he was the dean of America's white-ethnic urban newspaper columnists (although he became increasingly erratic in the 1990s, when even many of his faithful readers believed he ought to retire). These "regular guy" columnists form an influential subset of those urban intellectuals who position themselves on the ground of "the old neighborhood," that mythic space derived from the urban village. From that vantage, deep among the postindustrial city's industrial roots, they claim authoritative insight into contemporary urbanism.

Boss, a biography of Mayor Richard J. Daley, offers an inspired account of twentieth-century Chicago. Daley's character emerges from the prewar neighborhood order but takes shape in its engagement with racial succession and redevelopment, the two principal narrative lines defining the inner city's postwar transformation. As I argued in chapter 2, *Boss* depicts Daley as a "small-town boy" from the early twentieth-century urban village. This is the world in which Royko (born in 1932) was raised, like Daley (1902) and Algren (1909) a generation before him, the world that Algren made his literary turf, and the world that Daley helped to disassemble as a leader of the progrowth coalition. *Boss* made Royko's a definitive "old neighborhood" persona coming to grips with the task of writing the new inner city that Algren assigned to him.

Over the years, Royko has been dutiful in identifying Algren as his literary godfather. Royko's 1981 obituary for Algren makes the case most succinctly:

> I remember almost to the moment the first time I saw the name Nelson Algren.
>
> It was in a tent in Korea about three decades ago. The guy in the next bunk flipped a paperback book at me and said: "Hey, here's a book about Chicago. You want it?"
>
> I glanced over the blurbs on the jacket to see what it was about. The blurb said something to the effect that the book was set in a "slum" in Chicago. And it described the slum as being the Division Street area.
>
> Slum? I was offended. That was no slum. That was my neighborhood.[23]

Having placed himself in Algren's neighborhood on the map of Chicago's social landscape, Royko presents Algren as providing entry into the literary neighborhood of Chicago writing on the genre map of American letters. "It had never occurred to me, growing up in that neighborhood, that it contained the stuff a great book can be made of." The great book under discussion here is Algren's; but in showing how Royko's own writing persona emerged from that neighborhood (and was tempered, like Algren's, by military service) the story also explains the existence of another great book, Royko's own *Boss*. Algren serves, in this light, as more than the terminus of an exhausted line of writers. Appearing in Royko's account of his own literary origins, Algren enables a succeeding order of writing that springs from its roots in both of Algren's old neighborhoods—the Polish preserve around Division Street and the tradition of Chicago realism as Algren understood and practiced it.[24]

Working from a story of literary origins founded on Algren's example, Royko fashioned for himself the role of commentator on the emergence of the contemporary metropolis and its encounter with the industrial inner city it supplanted. For more than three decades, he told pieces of a story that has as its first act the story of decline that Algren rendered as epic in *Golden Arm*. That first act was a crucial part of his stock-in-trade (and it was Royko's mastery of the decline that Algren recognized as genuine "Chicago" writing). In a newspaper column in 1967, for instance, Royko rewrote Sandburg's industrial chestnut "Chicago." Royko's parodic updating shows the personified city's decline from producer to consumer, from industrial giant to "smooth salesman," from "Hog Butcher for the World,/Tool Maker, Stacker of Wheat,/Player with Railroads and the Nation's Freight Handler" to "Hi-Rise for the World/Party-goer, stacker of stereo tapes,/Player with Home Pool Table and the Nation's Jets." Joining, rather than challenging, "those who sneer at this my city," pointing out that Sandburg is the name of an upscale housing development (Sandburg Village) rather than a poet, he endorses as well as makes sport of the decline narrative that argues Chicago has gone "to hell in a martini mixer":

> Come and show me another city with razor-cut head singing so proud to have a
>   mustang and a white turtleneck and reservations for dinner.
> Fierce as a poodle with tongue lapping for dog yummies.
> Wig-headed,
> Skiing,
> Spending,
> Twisting,
> Tipping,
> Purchasing, discarding, repurchasing.[25]

The story of decline conventionally genders and moralizes the postindustrial transformation as a loss of civic manhood. Royko's bewigged, poodlelike consumer—as opposed to Sandburg's laboring producer, who manifests all the raw vigor of "a dog with tongue lapping for action"—advances the effeminacy of the personified city already evident in Frankie Machine, who produces nothing. In "Ode to Lower Finksville," the poetic essay in which Algren anointed Royko his successor, Sandburg's "painted women under the gas lamps luring the farm boys" become undercover cops in drag entrapping harmless drifters; in Royko's version they become transvestite hustlers, "painted men tossed in jail" for luring the farm boys. Royko, then, extends Algren's personification of Chicago in decline by continuing to invert and deflate the conventions of robust manhood established in Sandburg's iconic poem.

Nothing is easier than dismantling Sandburg's poem like this, and for Royko that task is only a preliminary step in a larger, more demanding project. In succeeding Sandburg and Algren, Royko also developed a body of writing that moves beyond the decline formula to detail the thickness and irony of daily life accruing in that seemingly oxymoronic place—postindustrial Chicago. For all his poking fun at the types he associates with postindustrial Chicago, especially the service-professional type he calls High-Rise Man, Royko differs from Algren in placing himself within the landscape of this revised city and in seeing the city's contradictions and new orders at play in himself. Some of Royko's best columns are those describing the alternately belligerent and sympathetic accommodation of his old neighborhood-trained persona to a maturing postindustrial Chicago. Those columns assemble a city of feeling populated not only by old neighborhood types—white-ethnic aldermen, developers, barflies, and reporters increasingly cut off from the half-remembered urban villages that produced them—but also by Southern blacks and their descendants, by what Royko used to think of as hippies and liberated women who have found their way to City Hall, by Asian immigrants and their Ukrainian landlords negotiating the terms of a changing inner-city urbanism, by High-Rise Man in many incarnations.

Royko's portrait of his own movements in the landscape of this city points up his tendency to look for ironies in the overlaps that make up both the city of feeling and the city of fact. In a column entitled "Why I Moved to the Lakefront," he describes his own transformation into High-Rise Man for the purposes of pseudo–social scientific inquiry into a new and widely influential kind of urbanism native to the redeveloped core. "I was born Bungalow Man. Or Bungalow Baby," he begins, then traces his evolutionary movements through the low-rise landscape of the old neighborhood order: he evolves into Basement Flat Child, Flat Above A Tavern Youth, Barracks Man as a soldier, then Attic Flat Man, Two-flat Man, then Bungalow Man again as a husband and father. He is "familiar with the ways" of all these "species that form the general classification Neighborhood Man. That's because I was one, from my shot glass to my long underwear from Sears to my new linoleum."[26] But the late twentieth-century city creates new objects of inquiry—Suburb Man, for instance, and High-Rise Man—and, as an urban intellectual dedicated to representing the metropolis, Royko heeds the call to become a participant-observer in the Chicago School tradition. He goes among the lakefront's Mustang-owning, martini-drinking service professionals, preserving his old neighborhood guy's critical detachment but also becoming familiar with the ways of his new neighbors. A mock-ethnographic photograph bristling with numbers and labels accompanies the column. It shows Royko, with a supercilious look incongruously pasted on his homely Division Street mug, lounging with two young women in a well-appointed lakefront apartment packed with all the accoutrements of High-Rise Man's consumption-intensive way of life.

In placing himself in the landscape, then, Royko adds an explicitly literary chapter to his account of the emergence of postindustrial urbanism in Chicago. Royko writes precisely about the overlap of Chicagos in space and time, the tensions to be found in the overlaps, and he shows himself moving, living, and *writing* in those overlaps. Algren, the narrator of decline, uses the metaphor of his own and his characters' relation to the landscape to show himself silenced by postindustrial transformation; Royko, who builds the decline into a narrative of transformation, uses the same metaphor to show how postindustrial transformation makes him who he is and gives him something to say.

Royko, a relentless ironist, plays his own situation for laughs. The joke of "Why I Moved to the Lakefront" rests on the shabbiness of Royko's explanation for his move, on the way in which he scrambles to account for an apparent lapse from regular-guy orthodoxy as he enters the "walled city" of privilege. Royko made it his business to foreground the authoritative old neighborhood persona, the standard voice that articulates the decline, as a self-interested strategy pursued by urban intellectuals like himself. He distrusted those who deploy the persona without any sense of its inherent contradictions — literal-minded drones like the *Boston Globe*'s studiously regular Mike Barnicle or ex-would-be ethnic shaman turned free-enterprise apostle Michael Novak.[27] Royko distinguished himself from them with his rich sense of the ironic distance between the textual neighborhood inhabited by his authorial persona and the material neighborhoods he admittedly mythologized. In *Boss*, Royko sums up his evocation of the white-ethnic industrial neighborhood order with a characteristic tension between the virtues our narrators of decline increasingly choose to remember and the dynamics of class mobility and cultural ambivalence they often choose to forget: "So, for a variety of reasons, ranging from convenience to fear to economics, people stayed in their own neighborhood, loving it, enjoying the closeness, the friendliness, the familiarity, and trying to save enough money to move out."[28] God, capital, or black migration did not just break up the old neighborhood from "outside"; that transformation required the participation of the very same people, Daley and Royko among them, who claimed to represent the old ways.

Similarly, part of what makes *Boss* a great book is Royko's exploration of the ironic distance between Daley's stereotypically "old neighborhood" political persona and his leading role in disassembling the industrial neighborhood order that produced him. As Daley prepared to make way for new postindustrial infrastructure (the new Circle Campus of the University of Illinois) by tearing down the Valley, a classically Italian neighborhood of industrial vintage he had promised to preserve, he said one thing and did another. "With the elections [of 1960] behind him," Royko writes in *Boss*, "Daley returned to the task of making life better in his city, a city of neighborhoods, by plotting the elimination of one of the city's oldest and most colorful neighborhoods."[29] Reproducing Daley's mantric "city of neighborhoods" rhetoric in this ironizing context, Royko warns the reader that old neighborhood personas like Daley's and Royko's, and the narratives of decline (or decline reversed, in Daley's case) they purvey, are historically and politically situated constructions to be read with care.

Royko's old neighborhood muses, his biographical subject Richard J. Daley and his literary godfather Nelson Algren, make an instructive pair: both born in the century's first decade, both in the business of representing (Daley in the political sense, Algren in the literary) the white-ethnic neighborhood order, they told opposed stories of Chicago's transformation. Daley spoke the pro-growth coalition's language of decline reversed into progress and prosperity, albeit in the machined accents of the regular guy: he argued that the city of neighborhoods would rise to "higher and higher platitudes" under his care (to cite one of his most famous malapropisms), even as he concentrated his efforts on redeveloping the downtown core and getting reelected.[30] Algren spoke a language of exhaustion and failure that readily lent itself to telling stories of the old neighborhood's decline: he liked to say that he countered the city's official motto, "I Will," with an unofficial one, "But What If I Can't?" Daley and Algren represented and derived authority from orders that took form in the industrial city and still invoke its memory by association—the white-ethnic political machine, the Chicago realist tradition, paragons of the industrial neighborhood order like Irish Bridgeport and the Polish Triangle. Both men, however, came to prominence through their engagement with postwar Chicago in transition. They are transitional figures, major players in the redevelopment of the Chicago of fact and the Chicago of feeling that grew from it. For urban intellectuals engaged with the industrial neighborhood order and its enclaved postindustrial remnants, Algren and Daley are principal authors of the palimpsest that is postwar Chicago.

That palimpsest is a complex of persistences and successions, the tensions between which demand and enable representation. Royko puts Bungalow Man and High-Rise Man in the same landscape, in the same authorial persona, and in conversation with one another. That is, he maps a city of feeling in which the ghost of Nelson Algren, rising up disembodied from the ruins of 1523

Wabansia and industrial urbanism, can find its way downtown from the old neighborhood to serve as Royko's muse.

Hail ta Dee, Blight Spirit

If Mike Royko is one leading successor to Algren the realist and social critic, then Stuart Dybek—born a decade after Royko—is one leading successor to Algren the writer of neighborhood-inflected literature. Writers like Algren "demonstrate that it's possible to make poetry of urban dialects and city rhythms," Dybek explained in a writers' roundtable discussion. "One doesn't necessarily say, 'Well, I'm going to write like Algren,' . . . but one says this opportunity for poetry in urban language *exists*."[31] Dybek, born in 1942 (the year that Algren's novel *Never Come Morning* was published), grew up in Pilsen/Little Village, an area southwest of the Loop but similar to Algren's Near Northwest Side in its industrial infrastructure and Polish-Hispanic-black succession. Having come out of the same kind of neighborhood milieu that Algren so definitively mapped, Dybek engages with Algren's Chicago while at the same time seeking to get past Algren and his association with a terminal narrative of industrial urbanism's decline. Like Royko's newspaper columns and *Boss*, Dybek's short stories are charged with meaning by the narrative of decline but ultimately work against its grain; like Royko, Dybek both engages with the ghost of Nelson Algren's Chicago and lays it to rest.

Dybek's short stories, collected in *Childhood and Other Neighborhoods* (1986) and *The Coast of Chicago* (1990), are full of ghosts. As Algren confronts Shay on the Kennedy Expressway, the ghosts of an older city appear to Dybek's characters as "apparitions in broad daylight" of a peddler with horse and wagon or a "mute knife sharpener pushing his screeching whetstone up alleys"; El trestles, bridges, and tenements encased in decades of pigeon droppings; a Brigadoon-like restaurant that serves life-saving sauerkraut soup.[32] Landscapes and characters out of previous historical and literary moments crowd Dybek's postindustrial inner city, which is thick with accrued urban forms. The central drama of Dybek's writing, like the most sophisticated of Royko's, involves his and his characters' search through those accrued forms, sorting and absorbing disparate pieces to create a viable postindustrial urbanism that is rooted in the old city and equipped to engage with the new.

Dybek, again like Royko, turns to Richard J. Daley to explore the relation between old city and new. In Dybek's story "Blight," Mayor Daley pervades and broods over a landscape in transition, where even the boarded-up grocery stores and cleared lots bear his signature. Set in "those years between Korea and Vietnam, when rock and roll was being perfected" and when the narrator's neighborhood "was proclaimed an Official Blight Area," "Blight" is suffused with Daley's presence. Ziggy Zilinsky, an "unreliable" purveyor of postindustrial magical realism even before being beaned with a thrown bat by Stanley "Pepper" Rosado during a game of "it," has constant visions of Daley—on the street, scrounging through garbage, "riding down Twenty-third Place in a black limousine flying one of those little purple pennants from funerals, except his said WHITE SOX on it." In this latter apparition, the mayor sits "in the backseat sorrowfully shaking his head as if to say 'Jeez!' as he stared out the bulletproof window at the winos drinking on the corner by the boarded-up grocery." The narrator concedes that "Mayor Daley *was* everywhere" during the early 1960s: "The city was tearing down buildings for urban renewal and tearing up streets for a new expressway," and every sign announcing civic improvements prominently featured Daley's name.[33]

"Blight" shows how the narrator, Dave, and his friends weather the transformation of inner-city urbanism in the 1950s and early 1960s, when both rock and roll and the notion of "blight" requiring "renewal" were being perfected. In a nameless Chicago neighborhood modeled on Pilsen/Little Village, in an aging and predominantly industrial landscape of "factories, railroad tracks, truck docks, industrial dumps, scrapyards, expressways, and the drainage canal," Poles and the Mexicans and blacks who are succeeding them have "managed to wedge in their everyday lives."[34] The expressways are the dissonant element—a postwar intrusion of suburban-downtown linkage grafted onto this landscape of prewar vintage. The obsolescence of its industrial infrastructure has earned the neighborhood its blighted status: like Algren's Near Northwest Side, it falls within the region of blight designated in the 1950s by planners concerned with making the downtown core the vital center of a suburbanized metropolis. With lots cleared for urban renewal, grocery stores boarded up, and a growing division between those who look to the suburbs for entry into the American middle classes and those increasingly at loose ends in the neighborhood, the immigrant-ethnic neighborhood order has begun to break up. Dave's childhood heroes, the older boys who ruled the neighborhood in the 1940s and went to fight in Korea, now hang out under an Algrenian pall of imprecisely defined, anonymous doom—"at corner taverns, working on beer bellies," playing softball every once in a while "on teams that lacked both uniforms and names."[35]

Dave's crew of friends navigates this difficult historical moment and this layered urban space, managing to wedge into it both everyday and ecstatic experience as they draw upon the mix of materials available to them. Dybek's characters and his prose are resolutely syncretic: older orders in contraction make room for new material gathered by his characters from the social landscape in which they move. The play of persistence and succession, the range of old and new material made available by postindustrial Chicago, opens the way for ecstatic experience, the search for which forms one of Dybek's principal literary projects. That syncretic search for ecstatic experience voices a larger pattern within the postwar cultural history of the immigrant-ethnic neighborhood order. Dave and his friends, born during and after the war, form a leading edge of what James T. Fisher has called "a Catholic lost generation" that cobbled together its own cultural hybrid out of spare parts available to it.[36] White-ethnic urban Catholics like Dave are formed in the contact between the constraining but reassuring immigrant-ethnic church and a free-wheeling, if not free-falling, encounter with the cultural opportunities made available by the postwar city: new contacts with black urbanisms (of the kind that produced, for instance, bebop, free jazz, and rock and roll) and Hispanic urbanisms (especially New World religious traditions), postwar orientalism in the form of beat-flavored Asian religiosity, a rich sense of living simultaneously in both the deeply structured Old World (via the old neighborhood) and a postmodern soup of weakly rooted identity making.

The protagonists move along paths well worn by working- and lower-middle-class males of the Catholic "lost generation." Deejo Decampo gives up plans to become a great novelist and after a fling with beat poetry becomes a mediocre bluesman instead; Pepper Rosado gives up the drums and joins the Marines; Ziggy Zilinsky, tormented by quasi-religious apocalyptic visions of winking saints and Mayor Daley, and finally unhinged by Fire Commissioner Quinn's ill-advised decision to turn on the air-raid sirens when the White Sox won the pennant in 1959, gives up talking and sets out hitchhiking to Gethsemane. At the story's end, Dave takes shelter from the draft in the late 1960s at a community college, where a professor nicknamed "the Spitter" has led him to believe that there's "blight all through Dickens and Blake" and other great literature. The Spitter has a phony Oxford accent, "but the more excitedly he read and spit, the more I could detect the South Side of Chicago underneath the veneer, as if his th's had been worked over with a drill press. When he read us Shelley's 'To a Skylark,' which began 'Hail to thee, blithe spirit' [i.e., 'Hail ta dee, blight spirit'], I thought he was talking about blight again until I looked it up."[37]

The appearance of blight in canonical Western literature—in the amalgam of visionary, romantic, and urban writing provided by Blake, Shelley, and Dickens—forms the climax of the story's literary argument. "Blight" is not a narrative of decline: it is, rather, a requiem for the narrative of decline because it is about developing a cultural tradition equipped to represent the postindustrial inner city. "Blight"'s account of emergent postindustrial urbanism becomes also the drama of the emergence of new stories, including literary writing, told by urban intellectuals—like Dave the narrator and Stuart Dybek—with distinctively postwar training. Dave and his friends are all in some way artists—musicians, writers, visionaries—who encounter ecstatic moments of heightened clarity when layers of urban order and meaning reveal themselves in otherwise mundane urban space. In those moments, they confront the possibility of turning the decline into act one of a revised story. Finding the links between the old neighborhood and the community college classroom, a place where aspiring urban intellectuals with his background typically find "literature," Dave has equipped himself to do what Dybek does: to meld blithe and blight in tackling his generation's great urban subject, the fall of the old neighborhood and the rise of new urban possibilities.

"Blight," therefore, explicitly imagines the fusion of pre– and post–World War II Chicago's representative forms. One of its main postadolescent characters, Deejo Decampo, tries to write a Chicago novel entitled *Blight*. Deejo has completed only the first sentence—"The dawn rises like sick old men playing on the rooftops in their underwear"—but has stalled after this magnificent start in the Algrenian mode of expressive landscaping, and he never completes the book. *Blight* does not become the next great Chicago novel. Since *Golden Arm*'s publication, the notion of a next great Chicago novel has fallen out of circulation, as have most of the books on the canonical list of great Chicago novels. Tellingly, after an extended flirtation with beat culture, Deejo records a Delta-style blues entitled "Hard-Hearted Woman," "whining through his nose" and "strumming his three chords" as did young white men all over America during the 1960s. The narrator wishes that Deejo had instead put the first line of his novel to the tune of "Hard Hearted Woman".

> The dawn rises
> Uuuhhh,
> Like sick old men,
> Oh, Lord,
> Playing on the rooftops in their underwear,
> Yeah. . . .[38]

"Blight" therefore imagines the fusion of Chicago novel and Chicago blues into a syncretic form representing a neighborhood and a historical moment in the 1950s and 1960s when the old inner city gave way to the new, when both the ideology of blight and the genre of Chicago blues (which underlies rock and roll) were in their heydays, before the final stages of ethnic succession in which the narrator's family moved out of the neighborhood. That moment is most importantly one of fusion leading to new forms rather than decline and fall leading to ruins. Reversing *Golden Arm*'s use of music to mark the impassable borders of its narrowing world, "Blight" proposes musical metaphors of fusion across the permeable boundaries of its urban world in flux: the perfection of rock and roll, the uncanny resemblances between Polish and Mexican jukebox music, a night scene in which Dave and his friends encounter a group of black doo-wop singers at the other end of a viaduct. (The viaduct scene, as opposed to the house party scene in *Golden Arm* it closely resembles, removes most of the interference between the groups so that they can see one another and make a musical exchange: "though at first we tried outshouting them, we finally shut up and listened," Dave reports, "except for Pepper keeping the beat.")[39] Dave, reversing Deejo's artistic development as he travels from the saxophone to literature in his effort to make art from time and place, traverses an emerging syncretic urbanism.

In its most extreme form, this pervasive syncretism reveals a magical realist edge. If Algren and the neighborhood realists might be whispering in one of Dybek's ears, and the Catholic lost generation's signature ecstatic influences from John Coltrane to Jack Kerouac might be whispering in the other, Dybek's true literary godparents might be the Latin American magical realists. Gabriel Garcia Marquez, Alejio Carpentier, Miguel Angel Asturias, Isabel Allende, and others made syncretism their great subject in fashioning a literary tradition out of the encounter between New World and Old. The magical realism for which they are best known—a woman floating up into the sky while doing her laundry, a Caribbean dictator selling the sea to Americans who cart it off in labeled pieces, a grandmother who visits indiscriminately with the living and the dead[40]—acquires its charge by combining, deadpan and seamlessly, the languages of nineteenth-century European realism and a variety of indigenous folk traditions. The Latin American magical realists, writing about the leading edge of American-style industrialization as it drove south in waves, provide a model of syncretic writing about making a culture out of the overlap of orders, and in that sense they provide inspiration for postindustrial magical realists like Dybek writing from the *back* edge of deindustrialization. Apparitional encounters with mute knife sharpeners and the great city-remaker Daley, like encounters with Spanish galleons in the jungle and streams of blood that flow with supernatural purposefulness through the streets of Macondo, occur precisely in the zone of overlap between orders.

Ringing Changes

To understand, finally, how Dybek engages with Algren in turning the language of decline into the language of syncretism, let us return for a moment to the virtuoso first movement of Algren's *Man with the Golden Arm* discussed in chapters 1 and 3. Sophie Majcinek sits in her wheelchair at the window, looking out on her Polish neighborhood in decline. Drifting in and out of sleep, Sophie remembers an idealized version of the neighborhood in the 1920s and 1930s, when "everything was so well arranged" and God was immanent in the old neighborhood order, weighing "virtue and sin . . . like Majurcek the Grocer weighed sugar."[41] Between that time and the present, something has gone wrong in a large and hard-to-figure way: part of it is that the neighborhood's "gettin' smokier," as Sophie puts it, as blacks encroach on the Polish preserve; part of it is that the old ways seem to be breaking up in the postwar moment.

Waking in her chair as church bells toll midnight over the neighborhood, Sophie hears "the last echo of St. Stephen's fading across this present midnight's dreaming roofs. And her whole life, from her careless girlhood until this crippled night, seemed caught within that fading chime. . . . September had come and gone and the wind was blowing the flies away." The overlapping bells, remembered and present, bring her out of reverie and into a moment of apocalyptic insight: "'God has forgotten us all,' Sophie told herself quietly."[42]

The church bells make music charged with the diffuse sense of dread associated with an autumnal historical moment. Sophie, like the novel and its author, feels in the air the imminent reconfiguration of a familiar social and cultural landscape into something new and strange. Algren, like his literary ally Budd Schulberg, whose 1955 novel *Waterfront* covers similar territory, was not a Catholic, nor was he interested in Catholicism as a religious tradition. Rather, Algren, Schulberg, and others drew from a menu of Catholic imagery—using the church as an icon for the white-ethnic urban village—to figure the experiential and institutional complexity of an urbanism that many observers in the 1950s increasingly saw as in decline. "God has forgotten us all" means, in this context, that the network of orders enabling and defining industrial urbanism has begun to break up: there goes the neighborhood.

Now let us turn to Dave, the draft avoiding narrator of "Blight," who has been inspired by his college literature class to take another look at the old neighborhood his family has left behind. (His parents have moved to Berwyn, an inner-ring suburb favored by diasporic inner-city Poles, and Dave has moved away too, presumably to the professional-bohemian North Side.) Having gotten off the El—that ever-present reminder of Carrie's railroad city—and dropped into a tavern where the Mexican songs on the jukebox sound suspiciously like polkas, Dave has a vision that suggests the capacity of the narrative of syncretism to absorb the narrative of decline:

> Then the jukebox stopped playing, and through the open door I could hear the bells from three different churches tolling the hour. They didn't agree on the precise moment. Their rings overlapped and echoed one another. . . . [S]omething about the overlapping of those bells made me remember how many times I'd had dreams . . . in which I was back in my neighborhood, but lost, everything at once familiar and strange, and I knew if I tried to run, my feet would be like lead, and if I stepped off a curb, I'd drop through space, and then in the dream I would come to a corner that would feel so timeless and peaceful, like the Carta Blanca with the bells fading and the sunlight streaking through, that for a moment it would feel as if I'd wandered into an Official Blithe Area.[43]

I would not argue that Dybek is consciously revoicing Algren here—as opposed to Royko, who explicitly revoices Algren and Sandburg—but in this passage, as in the passage from *Golden Arm*, we encounter a flash of insight in which the landscape of the old neighborhood becomes charged with possibility. The charge is apocalyptic in Algren's rendering, initially threatening but ultimately ecstatic in Dybek's. The two sets of overlapping church bells, *Golden Arm*'s and "Blight"'s, ring one set of changes over which the two texts play very different melodic lines. Algren plays the definitive decline: the city done for with everyone in it, what he calls "a requiem for everyone trapped" in the old neighborhood.[44] The overlapping bells in "Blight," on the other hand, signal the vertigo-inducing but ecstatic opportunities made available by the overlapping of old city and new. (Compare, similarly, the jukebox refueled with heterogeneous music in "Blight" to the jukebox in *Golden Arm*, which warns the Majcineks of impending disaster, and a jukebox "running down in a deserted bar" in *City on the Make*,[45] a machine playing dirges as it winds down to silence.) The opportunities confronting Dave are explicitly literary—courtesy of Blake, Shelley, Dickens, and the Spitter—underscoring "Blight"'s drive to absorb the decline and its signifying landscape into a literature of engagement with the postindustrial city, from which Algren turned away after he had laid industrial urbanism to rest in scenes like Sophie's midnight reverie.

"Blight," then, plays inspired improvisations on the decline, turning it into something else entirely. While the menu of neighborhood imagery in classic declines like *Golden Arm* offers ways to figure what is lost in the postindustrial transformation, in "Blight" that imagery offers a model of what might be gained. Dave finds his way via the classroom and the old neighborhood—rather than via being beaned with a baseball bat, as Ziggy was—to the experience of inner-city urbanism as a series of miraculous events producing a set of meanings that flood the postindustrial landscape with cultural possibility. Winking saints, ghosts of the industrial era muttering in Polish, the mystical omnipresence of Richard J. Daley—all these are signs reminding us that literary raw materials run in rich veins through the fabric of postindustrial urbanism, which is ripe for development and redevelopment by enterprising young artists with syncretic tendencies. Like Royko, Dave finds his material and his narrating voice by confronting the transformation of the city, and its literature, into something that Algren was not prepared to recognize as his neighborhood.

Dybek, like Brooks and Royko, shapes the materials of postwar Chicago into a language that can be employed to say something other than (or, in Royko's case, something more than) "there goes the neighborhood." *Golden Arm* and *City on the Make*, however, develop the artistic possibilities of "there goes the neighborhood" on the grand scale. (This is another reason to pay closer critical attention to Algren: the language used by Americans to represent cities since World War II has developed more ways of saying "there goes the neighborhood" than of saying anything else, and Algren's version of decline explores deeply the literary properties of that language.) I do not wish to propose that Dybek's writing is somehow more open-minded or subtle than

Algren's; nothing could be less interesting or less germane to this argument. Rather, I want to suggest the confluence of imaginative repertoire and historical moment that produces the city of feeling. Complex as it can be, the city of feeling is a drastic simplification, allowing all the messy and open-ended complexity of a city of fact to reside within the constant boundaries of a text. What Algren and others pictured as a golden age followed by collapse into ruin is one long process, nowhere near complete and never to be completed, in which the Chicago that took shape between the Great Fire and World War II gradually disappears under new urban layers. The story of decline is itself a legacy of midcentury, and the work of Chicago writers like Brooks, Royko, and Dybek has similarly layered new and complementary chapters of narrative, landscapes, and character types over Algren's decline and the city it imagines. The textual Chicago Algren constructed in his writing has become in time both a persistent and a succeeded presence in the literary landscape, just as the Chicago he observed and lived in persists—interstitially, in resonantly recontextualized fragments—in the social landscape that has succeeded it.

Part 2 of this study similarly builds upon the story of decline to examine the mapping in literature of the postindustrial inner city as it emerged and matured after World War II. Part 2 also extends the map of the older white-ethnic neighborhood order into the zone of contact where white-ethnic enclave, redeveloped downtown, and black inner city meet; similarly, just as part 1 read Algren together with Brooks, part 2 explores in greater detail the postwar literature of black urbanism and its zone of contact with the literature of white-ethnic decline. Finally, part 2 begins to generalize this study's argument by extending it to a second city, leaving Milwaukee Avenue and Chicago behind and examining a set of texts that converge on Philadelphia's South Street. In reading a South Street canon against an account of the postindustrial transformation of Philadelphia, then, part 2 extends and fills in this chapter's schematic outline of the cities of feeling that imagine not just older neighborhood orders in decline but also the emergence in the decades after World War II of a new object of literary attention: a profoundly transformed inner city.

Part 2

The Neighborhood Novel and the Transformation of the Inner City

Exposition: South Street and the Neighborhood Novel

South Street runs east and west between the Delaware and Schuylkill rivers at the southern edge of Philadelphia's Center City (see figs. 5 and 6 for locations referred to in part 2). It runs as well through a textual city constructed by a body of literature that engages imaginatively with the transformation of American urbanism in the decades after World War II. The South Street milieu is a contact zone where different Philadelphias meet: the nineteenth-century industrial city and the late twentieth-century, postindustrial metropolitan region; the old neighborhoods of South Philadelphia and the business, government, and upscale residential core of Center City; white and black Philadelphia and different arrangements of white and black in different periods.[1] The writers whose work converges on South Street explore the social and literary implications of urban processes that shape city life: the constantly negotiated fit between people and place that constitutes neighborhood, the dynamic interplay between local and metropolitan orders, the redevelopment of property that puts the landscape in motion under the feet and over the heads of city people. The postindustrial inner city took shape along South Street in the 1950s and 1960s, and continues to take shape today, in a complex of persistences and successions that structure a literature as well as a social landscape. Having traditionally formed both an edge where different orders meet and a spine along which neighborhoods take shape, South Street cuts across Philadelphia in ways that lay bare the structure and shaping processes of both the city of fact and the city of feeling.

Neighborhood has been the organizing principle of South Philadelphia's social history, and the central problem of that history is the relation of neighborhoods' local orders to the metropolitan orders headquartered in Center

City's office towers and City Hall. The constitutive relationship between people and place creates a neighborhood, a complex artifact always balanced between formation and dissolution. South Philadelphia, which is separated from Center City by South Street, has traditionally been the ground of ethnic neighborhoods—principally Irish, Italian, black, and Jewish but also Eastern European, Hispanic, Laotian. Local forces like investment in homes, businesses, and institutions, individual and communal responses to interventions from outside the neighborhood, and face-to-face exchanges of ideologies and worldviews can pull a neighborhood together or apart as they affect the relationship of people to one another and to place. The same is true of metropolitan forces as varied as the regional real estate market, the city's position in national and international flows of people and resources, and the exercise of governmental power—all of which shaped the postwar history of the neighborhoods of South Philadelphia. These neighborhoods, descended directly from the industrial neighborhood order, still crowd right up to South Street from the south: the once white-ethnic enclave of Queen Village, now heavily gentrified, on the eastern end of South; black neighborhoods with nineteenth-century roots (and post–World War II trauma in the form of high-rise housing projects) in the center and west; the Irish preserves of Grays Ferry and Schuylkill (increasingly gentrified) on the far western end. At midcentury, before five decades of renewal and redevelopment, the urban villages of upper South Philly extended north of South in a ragged front into Center City, but the southward expansion of Center City has rolled back what is left of them. Today, the renovated townhouses and rowhouses of Center City's service-professional neighborhoods reach down to South Street from the core of high-rise workplaces and residences and in some places extend south of South. In the late 1950s, Philadelphia's City Planning Commission envisioned a solid mass of "healthy housing extending from river to river and meeting the core cleanly without a layer of blight between," a vision of gentrification as civic "health" that is being fulfilled as the redevelopment of Center City fills in the remaining pockets above South.[2]

The problem of neighborhood has also been the organizing principle of South Street's postwar literature. In part 2 I will examine five novels that map the South Street contact zone: Jack Dunphy's *John Fury* (1946), William Gardner Smith's *South Street* (1954), David Bradley's *South Street* (1975), Pete Dexter's *God's Pocket* (1983), and Diane McKinney-Whetstone's *Tumbling* (1996). (For the sake of brevity, I will call these novels "the South Street literature," by which I mean "literature that explores the world of and around the South Street contact zone." Two of the novels are set on South Street proper; two in neighborhoods just north of it; one in a neighborhood deep in South Philadelphia.) These novels fall into various generic categories—there are family narratives, white-ethnic declines, novels of black community (at least one of which is labeled a "protest" novel), and more than one story of the making or unmaking of urban intellectuals—but they are also parts of one composite text. The novels share so many formal and thematic characteristics that the conventional disciplinary division of South Street literature into "black" writing (novels by Smith, Bradley, and McKinney-Whetstone) and "white" writing (novels by Dunphy and Dexter) would do violence to what is clearly one profoundly unified body of work telling one larger story shared by black and white neighborhoods, writers, and characters. The various pieces of the story encompass a larger landscape and a larger set of narratives including slavery, black migration, and ghettoization on the one hand and European immigration, Americanization, and the decline of the urban village on the other, but these landscapes and narratives flow together in the South Street literature to form a story of postindustrial transformation told on the scale of family and neighborhood.

The South Street literature is a relatively local canon; it has not commanded the kind of national attention devoted to the Chicago realists or the Harlem writers to be discussed in part 3. Some of the South Street novels have circulated more widely than others, but none of them has a place in anyone's notion of a postwar urban canon. Why, then, have I chosen to devote part 2 to the composite story of postindustrial transformation via South Street and the work of Jack Dunphy, William Gardner Smith, David Bradley, Pete Dexter, and Diane McKinney-Whetstone rather than via, say, Ralph Ellison, Anne Petry, Saul Bellow, and the rest of the usual suspects (to the extent that the still-formative field of postwar urban literature has produced usual suspects)? First, the South Street contact zone offers a unique perspective on the drama of local and metropolitan orders in conflict, a drama absolutely central to the story of postwar urbanism. That tension between orders is particularly revealed on South Street because, unlike other urban places more typically traversed by literary criticism, South Street touches all three conventional elements of the postindustrial social landscape as it developed in Northern industrial cities—the redeveloped downtown, the second ghetto, and the white-ethnic enclave. South Street thereby offers a chance to study the emerging postindustrial inner city in compact microcosm. Second, the South Street literature's derivative and generic qualities allow me to generalize the argument and the narrative of this study. The South Street literature manifests a number of generic connections not only to the texts discussed in parts 1 and 3 but also to a larger, national urban literature that includes the decline and the protest novel, influential sociological studies, crime stories, seminal policy debates about planning and renewal, and the works of the "usual suspects." Those bodies of writing flow together in the South Street literature in ways that suggest a more general convergence, a way to read a broader range of urban texts together under the rubric of postindustrial transformation. Finally, the relative obscurity of the South Street novels constitutes part of their value in generalizing my argument. Readers of urban literature are forever cobbling together such local canons in their heads: for example, Cleveland stories, or subway stories, or, to go farther afield to a Western analog of the old industrial cities, the literature of California's old fruit-picking centers. Part 2 seeks, via the South Street novels, to connect that largely submerged mass of the urban-literary iceberg to the parts that typically ride above the critical waters—like the Chicago of the neighborhood novelists and the Harlem of the urban crisis.

This chapter, then, will serve to introduce the South Street literature and to sketch the history of South Street. These two frames, literary and historical, will organize the readings of the novels made in the two chapters that follow.

A South Street Literature

South Street has attracted urban intellectuals in a variety of disciplines. Social scientists, especially those affiliated with the University of Pennsylvania just across the Schuylkill, have been drawn to South Street by the area's complex social landscape, in which a variety of races, ethnic groups, social classes, and neighborhood types can be found in a close but segmented mix. If there is no "Philadelphia School" of sociology with the hegemonic status enjoyed by the Chicago School in the early twentieth century, Penn, Temple, and other Philadelphia institutions have produced a distinguished body of urban social science.[3] Part of that work has been the social scientific mapping of the neighborhoods around South, producing studies of black urbanism—beginning with W. E. B. Du Bois's distinguished early work, *The Philadelphia Negro*, and including Roger Abrahams's studies of urban folklore initiated in *Deep Down in the Jungle*—and white-ethnic neighborhood formations.[4] City planners serving progrowth forces, whose thwarted schemes to turn South Street into an expressway were crucial to the postwar history of the area, have produced innumerable representations of South Street as it was and as they wanted it to be. Residents, business owners, lawyers, professors, and others who opposed the city planners have produced their own counterliterature of studies, polemics, and alternative plans. Together, these nonliterary representations add up to an account of the social, economic, political, and cultural forces that shape the inner city and are shaped by it.

I will draw upon this account later in this chapter in assembling a historical portrait of postwar South Street, but my task in this section is to introduce the account of South Street composed by the literary intellectuals who command my primary attention. Since World War II, the South Street area has inspired novelists, especially first-time novelists. Some were homegrown: Jack Dunphy grew up between the wars in the Irish urban villages of South Philly, William Gardner Smith in black South Philadelphia during the 1930s and 1940s. Some writers were attracted from elsewhere: David Bradley came to the University of

Pennsylvania from a small Pennsylvania town in the 1960s and found his way to South Street when college life proved disappointing; Pete Dexter, raised in South Dakota, found the material for his first novel in South Philadelphia when he worked as a reporter for the *Philadelphia Daily News*. Diane McKinney-Whetstone was both homegrown and an outsider: she was still very young when her parents left South Philadelphia in the 1950s and moved to West Philadelphia, where she grew up, but she returned to South Philadelphia in her first novel. Four of the five South Street novels are first novels—and the exception, Smith's *South Street* (his third), was published when its precocious author was all of twenty-seven years old—which suggests that the South Street milieu has convinced young writers (and publishers) looking for good material that they have found the makings of stories worth telling.

Together, they have rendered those stories—that story, in aggregate—in a body of work that explores the literary implications of the inner city's postwar transformation. The South Street writers confronted South Philadelphia and Center City—and, most important, the contact zone where the two regions meet—as a place from which literature can be made. Their response to it is also a response to the problems that faced Nelson Algren at midcentury: how and who to write about the changing inner city.

How to write about South Street? The answer has come in the form of novels—more precisely, "neighborhood novels"—shaped formally and thematically by showing how the conditions of a particular historical period or moment throw urban communities into crisis. The notion of neighborhood is essential to these novels and to the ways they hang together as a group. "Neighborhood," like genre, is a fluid term: it suggests both a quality of civic life and a bounded area larger than a household but smaller than a district. The term is also at least slightly inflected with positive content: especially for city people surrounded by strangers, to think of someone as a neighbor acknowledges an obligation or regard not necessarily extended to everyone they encounter. I will, then, provisionally define a neighborhood as an urban place occupied by a community of people who regard themselves as a community, who share clear ideas of the place's boundaries, who regard the people in the surrounding areas as members of separate communities, and who might plausibly encounter one another in the course of the weekly round. The people of *a* neighborhood maintain the *quality* of neighborhood via these shared assumptions and activities. A neighborhood can be as small as a block, although it is rare that an individual block becomes distinctive or insular enough to discourage its residents from regarding people on any of the adjoining blocks as neighbors, and a neighborhood can be very large—if (as is the case with Hyde Park in Chicago or Park Slope in Brooklyn) the contrast with the surrounding areas is relatively great and the general sense within the neighborhood of living in an indivisible geographic and social unit is relatively great. Neighborhood, then, is a quality as much as it is an artifact, and it is mutable and slippery. Growing up in Chicago, I would never have thought of the people on the other side of Jeffery Boulevard as my neighbors, but I would today if I ran into one of them next week in Ulan Bator or at a scholarly conference. Let us sum up this struggle with a greased concept by concluding that neighborhood is the first geographic and conceptual level of urban community beyond the household, embracing both loved ones and strangers, and as such it is a basic unit of urban community.

Neighborhood novels concern themselves with the local conjunction of people and place that makes up a lived urban order, attached to a particular piece of urban terrain. The problem of neighborhood, of defining and sustaining a particular way of life on that terrain, becomes an organizing logic for these novels, leading them to consider how a particular equation of people and place can over time be made, broken, contested, shifted. Neighborhood crises take place in space: problems of boundary and incursion arise at the neighborhood's borders, the fit between local and metropolitan orders shapes the neighborhood in relation to the city around it. The crises take place, as well, in time: dramas of succession, rise, and decline lead to narratives about change over time; crises of reproduction, in which the neighborhood succeeds or fails in perpetuating itself into the next generation, lead to narratives about the precarious persistence of orders. The urban intellectuals who move through the South Street novels as characters also consider parallel crises in the writing of the neighborhood, dramas of reproduction and representation in the literary sense. The irruption and resolution (or lack of resolution) of these various social and literary crises help to organize these novels generically, to make them "neighborhood novels" devoting significant, patterned energies to depicting and accounting for the human orders that infuse a particular urban space with meanings, thereby turning it into a place.

Each South Street novel concerns itself with describing and accounting for the status of a neighborhood within the social landscape it constructs and imagines two sets of reasons for change: the local neighborhood order's internal logic and city-structuring metropolitan forces typically operating beyond the characters' (and sometimes the novel's) horizons of perception. Each novel's ability to imagine and figure these forces tells us something about the historical moment of its writing. Dunphy's *John Fury* and Smith's *South Street* map the late industrial neighborhood order at midcentury. *John Fury*, like Algren's *Man with the Golden Arm*, bends a 1930s-vintage account of the neighborhood order's erosive internal contradictions into a midcentury narrative of that order's decline, told in the novel as the passing of the "horse-and-wagon" Philadelphia built by Irish immigrants. Smith's South Street neighborhood must resolve divisive internal disputes in order to confront a complex of external pressures typical of the early 1950s: tension between a rapidly growing black population and white ethnics, increasing agitation by blacks for equal civil rights, the redrawing of racial and political boundaries in the changing inner city. Bradley's *South Street* and Dexter's *God's Pocket*, written in the 1970s and 1980s in the aftermath of the urban crisis that was brewing at midcentury, provide epilogues to Dunphy and Smith. Bradley's black South Streeters sustain the vestiges of community against a background of urban renewal and redevelopment, a powerful transformative impetus operating at a scale that dwarfs the neighborhood. The people of Dexter's God's Pocket, an anachronistic survival of the white-ethnic urban village tucked between South Street and Center City, respond with violence and bewilderment to incursions from "outside" that point up the neighborhood's increasingly ghostly presence in the postindustrial city. McKinney-Whetstone's *Tumbling* returns in the form of historical romance to Smith's social terrain, the black neighborhoods bracketing South Street during the 1940s and 1950s, imagining (as did Smith) a vital community that heals its internal wounds, this time by resisting the external threats of urban renewal and gentrification.

The neighborhood novel does not, of course, confine itself to the formal problem of representing neighborhood and the thematic problems of neighborhood raised by crises in the local order. As it frames and works through these problems of neighborhood, the neighborhood novel erects a flexible structure that can encompass corollary matters ranging across the variety of subjects intersecting with urbanism. (If it sometimes seems that post–urban crisis American culture tends to restrict that range of subjects to one—race—it bears noting that the mapping of racial conflict on the inner city has become a way to discuss freedom and moral order, market forces and social good, individual rights and responsibility to a community, and other large, vexed questions traditionally associated with city life.) Typically, neighborhood novels assemble a local context from a set of exemplary characters, families, pieces of urban terrain, and so on, generalizing outward from this context of neighborhood to broader notions of place, peoplehood, politics, history, and so on. Neighborhood thus provides a manageable vocabulary and scale with which to condense a city, a region, a people, a set of principles into an expressive setting and a system of individual characters.

The South Street literature, continuing the project of the Chicago neighborhood novel into the postwar era, uses the frame of neighborhood to consider the postindustrial inner city. In the 1930s and 1940s, Farrell, Wright, and Algren took up the genre of neighborhood novel developed in the nineteenth century by European and American realists and gave it powerfully influential form. In their hands, the American neighborhood novel came definitively to be about industrial urbanism as it was lived at street level in the urban village and Black Metropolis. The South Street novels share much with the Chicago neighborhood novels: an interest in those people who have the least protection from the effects of urban process; an emphasis on the disjuncture between urban process at the grand scale and the circumscribed horizons of neighborhood types; a tendency to argue (especially, in the South Street novels, via the successes and failures of writer-characters) for a literature of observation on the sociological model. *John Fury*, written before Algren's *Golden Arm* and in the long shadow of Farrell's influence on representations of the urban Irish, follows most closely on the Chicago model, proposing a modest formal extension of the genre with its exaggeratedly spare prose style. Smith's *South Street*, written at midcentury by a young writer uncomfortable with Wright's equally powerful influence over representations of urban blacks, begins to push the neighborhood novel toward representation of postwar urban transformations. (One can group Smith's book, in this regard, with Anne Petry's *The Street* [1946] and Ralph Ellison's *Invisible Man* [1952], a picaresque novel that collapses into an apocalyptic neighborhood novel.) The rest of the South Street novels develop subtexts in Dunphy and Smith as they push the neighborhood novel into its postindustrial phase, engaging with the revised inner city that succeeded the Chicago tradition's congeries of industrial villages.

The striking recurrence in the South Street literature of particular formal and thematic strategies reinforces one's sense that the novels form a collective engagement with a changing city, a single composite story spread among several texts. Although the South Street novelists do not seem to have read and influenced one another, the answer to the question of how to write the inner city is remarkably consistent as one reads through the half-century of prose spanning *John Fury* and *Tumbling*.[5]

The South Street novels are structured around family narratives and their problems of community and reproduction. These novels make families the building blocks of neighborhoods—families occupy the rowhouses, build the city, produce the next generation—and family crises become clear figures of neighborhood crises (as in *Golden Arm*, in which Vi's two families encapsulate the urban village's generational decline). In every novel, marriages are collapsing, barren, sexless, cursed with bad feeling or ill health or poor luck. Bad offspring pervade the literature, threatening to bring a family, a neighborhood, an urban people to ruin as they fritter away their inheritance. The only sons of steady-working men will not work (*John Fury, God's Pocket*), marking the terminus of working-class traditions rooted in the industrial village. Upwardly mobile daughters grow away from parents (*John Fury, Tumbling*), threatening to bring down the neighborhood with them: this is most clearly dramatized in *Tumbling*, in which one independent-minded daughter's pathological plaster-eating habit, not to mention her plan to sell her rowhouse to the city so it can build a highway, literally undermines the structure of the neighborhood. In Smith's *South Street*, three brothers aspire to sustain and lead a black community through perilous midcentury transitions, but their position of leadership is deeply undercut by their inability to form or sustain families. Bradley's *South*

Street, the only novel in which marriage dramas are not central, is also the novel with the least traditional notion of neighborhood, and part of its project is precisely to depict a vital community, surviving in the aftermath of two decades of neighborhood-breaking urban renewal, that does not conform to traditional notions of community. Yet even Bradley deploys the marriage strategy in important, conventional ways: his portrait of a childless community robbed of past and future rests significantly on two marriages in crisis (a preacher's and an ex-prostitute's); his account of an urban intellectual's engagement with the inner city takes the form of a poet's shuttling between two opposed domestic arrangements.

The South Street novels also share (again with *Golden Arm*) a habit of constructing expressive cityscapes that fit the travails of a few characters into larger accounts of urban peoples caught up in the sweep of history. The cities constructed in these novels are signifying forms, and in each of them one can read the history of a people and a place. The rowhouses of South Philadelphia, small and packed end to end in block-long fronts, consistently serve as a figure of an urbanism rooted in the industrial neighborhood order. A stock narrative line is compressed into the rowhouse form: migration (from Europe or the American South), skilled manual work, family formation, saving, commitment to traditional neighborhood institutions (church, tavern, school), an expectation of upward social mobility, and a countervailing expectation that neighborhood is a crucial value that must be preserved not only against outside influence but also against interior forces of dissolution like upward social mobility and generational drift. This is the baseline map of urbanism on which all the South Street novels build their stories of postindustrial transformation. All of them map the rowhouse world and its churches and taverns (Bradley, again, foregrounds the churches and taverns but removes the rowhouses to show the extent of the social damage caused by renewal); all of them use expressive cityscapes—scenes of demolition, collapse, construction—to show how rowhouse urbanism weathers the shocks of urban process. Some of the novels (especially *God's Pocket* and Bradley's *South Street*) also extend their signifying landscapes beyond the neighborhood to sketch greater Philadelphia's postwar history: high-rise housing projects tell the second ghetto's story of migration, conflict, and containment; the groomed precincts of Rittenhouse Square and Society Hill impress the principles of age-old social distance and postwar gentrification upon interlopers from South Philly; Center City's brooding City Hall and towering skyscrapers are the seats of metropolitan power from which anonymous managers, hidden from view, guide the city's transformation.

Always, the encounter of individual characters with the cityscape connects the novel's plot lines to the larger web of histories readable in that cityscape. This tendency is dramatized in a kind of scene repeated throughout the South Street literature: the "runaway," in which a character is borne against his or her will through a familiar landscape made strange until fetching up against some kind of limit. Whether it be a runaway horse and wagon tearing through South Philly until it reaches the railroad tracks (*John Fury*, Smith's *South Street*), a bus ride through a ruinous landscape that ends at the Schuylkill Expressway (Bradley's *South Street*), or a chase on foot after a refrigerator truck until it collides spectacularly with a city bus (*God's Pocket*), each runaway sums up the relationship between a character's individual will exercised at the local scale and infinitely more powerful, impersonal processes operating at the metropolitan scale—processes that shape the fates of characters and the neighborhoods and urbanisms they stand for. (*Tumbling*, the lone exception, helps to prove the runaway rule. The closest it comes to a runaway is a traumatic memory of a brutal abduction and gang rape in rural Florida rather than an urban scene, but the novel is unique in the South Street literature for explicitly imagining the exercise of personal will as securing the neighborhood against the effects of impersonal processes like redevelopment. The lingering trauma of the rape, like the lingering threat of the planned highway, is expunged as the neighborhood heals itself.)

The runaway gathers together the formal strategies and themes that unite the South Street literature. It typically marks a crisis in family narrative: John Fury has a vision of a runaway wagon at his first wife's deathbed; the runaway wagon in Smith's *South Street* goes out of control when Slim, a neighborhood hero, passes the reins to his young nephew. The runaway takes the reader through a landscape that links characters to larger historical narratives: Bradley's protagonist surveys the results of urban renewal from his bus window; the chase after the truck in *God's Pocket* surveys a long stretch of South Philly before ending in a crash that raises echoes of the Majcineks' wreck. In each runaway scene, a character confronts the neighborhood, the metropolis, and the relationship between them that forms the South Street literature's main theme. This clash or fusion of scales, local and metropolitan, imparts a dreamlike quality to the runaway, the sense of a familiar place rendered strange in a moment of vertiginous insight.

These moments of insight—of reading urban form and grasping the big picture—are significant departures for the characters involved, episodes in which a coal wagon driver (Fury), numbers writer (Slim), or mob-connected truck driver (Mickey Scarpato in *God's Pocket*) does the kind of work that urban intellectuals do. For other characters in the literature, though, reading and writing the city of fact is a full-time job: the South Street literature devotes significant energies to imagining what kinds of urban intellectuals are made or broken by the South Street milieu. The South Street novels' answers to this question of "who writes the inner city?" fashion a composite portrait of the urban intellectual's relationship to the inner city during the postwar era of transformation and crisis. The presence of writer-characters in three of the novels—

both *South Street*s and *God's Pocket*—is another repeated element binding together the South Street novels into a larger whole.

Writer-characters move through the literature, confronting urban change with the same sense of bewilderment and crisis evidenced by other characters trying to comprehend the disturbances in their familiar worlds. These writer-characters' dramas of reproduction and representation raise a set of literary-historical problems for them that also faced American urban intellectuals after World War II: who are the urban intellectuals equipped to take up the task of representing the transformed inner city, what should they write, and what constitutes their training and authority to do that work? Both *South Street*s plot on their neighborhood maps a story in which the postwar social landscape produces an urban intellectual suited to the task of representing it. Smith's protagonist Claude Bowers struggles to make sense of the inner city at midcentury, to decide on the right course and lead his neighborhood (and, by extension, urban blacks in general), to understand and write about black Americans in a time of migration and growing political awareness. Bradley's poet-hero Adlai Stevenson Brown, buffeted by forces of redevelopment and urban crisis that gutted South Street in the 1960s, struggles against sociological dogma and his own middle-class social trajectory to stay on South Street at all, to sustain access to the neighborhood characters, rats, roaches, and garbage that constitute the subject matter of his postapocalyptic poetry. Dexter's *God's Pocket* provides a gloss on the story of Nelson Algren's literary exhaustion by plotting the failure of an urban intellectual, a burnt-out shell of a newspaper columnist named Richard Shellburn, to understand the relationship between enclaved survivals of the industrial city and the postindustrial city that contains them.

The stakes in the struggle to represent the South Street milieu are high: writer-characters in the South Street literature tend to succeed or die. Claude Bowers and Adlai Brown fight their way to productive vantage points on the inner city, but Claude's brother Philip, an aspiring novelist, is killed by an aggrieved young man with a rock, and Shellburn is beaten to death by a mob incensed by his phrasing of a decline narrative. The violence visited upon writers in the South Street literature conveys a sense of the upheaval and drama associated with the act of observing and writing about a city in constant, feverish motion. As powerful forces mold the changing social landscape around South Street—eroding older forms of urbanism and enabling new ones, raising the stakes on neighborhoods and individuals—the characters who aspire to make sense of the complex relations among people, place, and process run the risk of writing the wrong thing or failing to write anything at all. Violent little parables of literary life, in which urban intellectuals confront their subject in the streets, identify the South Street literature as caught up in the same urban processes—the same networks of interest and contest—that shaped the South Street of fact.

Writers are not the only victims of violence in the South Street novels, which are awash in beatings, punchouts, knifings, rape, gang fights, riots, and all manner of domestic violence. This pervasive violence does more than mark the South Street literature as conventionally urban and American, it also constitutes a pervasive metaphor of the violence of urban process: family members war against one another as conflicts sweep through the household and the neighborhood it represents in microcosm; neighborhoods war against one another as the social landscape shifts beneath them; social classes and class fractions struggle over land on the edge of Center City; temperatures rise and tempers grow short as older and newer urbanisms crowd against one another. Much, but not all, of this violence is inflected by racial difference, as any reading of postwar urban history would lead one to expect.[6] From workplace fights (*John Fury, God's Pocket*) to gang wars and full-scale riots (Smith's *South Street*), a pattern of violence marks the contact between black and white Philadelphia in the novels.

That pattern of violence marks racial division in the South Street literature's city of feeling and refers to such division in the Philadelphia of fact, but it helps to unite the "black" and "white" South Street novels into a single literature. Scenes of racial violence, and the very assumption of strict separation that underlies them, are part of the stitchery that binds together the South Street literature's patchwork of white-ethnic declines and narratives of black community into the larger story of postindustrial transformation. The pattern of racial violence shared by the novels—like the shared patterns of family narratives, expressive cityscapes, runaway scenes, writer-characters, and local-metropolitan tensions—is another measure of literary likeness. This does not render the South Street literature as some kind of postracial utopia; for the most part, in fact, the white South Street authors write about white characters, black authors write about blacks, and each novel stays in its own generic neighborhood. But the South Street literature demonstrates how "black" and "white" genres of urban literature, like black and white neighborhoods in the social landscape, can be parts of a greater whole—even if the people who police their borders do not want them to be.

The violence of the South Street literature also reflects the conflict and dislocation running through South Street's postwar history. The South Street writers have been inspired by observation of a social landscape in dramatic, even violent, motion.

South Street and Greater Philadelphia

The forces shaping South Street's postwar history flow into the neighborhoods from downtown. Postwar city planning in Philadelphia, codified in the

City Planning Commission's *Comprehensive Plan* (1960) and supplementary *Plan for Center City* (1963), begins from this basic premise:

> The well being of Center City Philadelphia is basic to the well being of the entire Delaware Valley region.
>
> Center City must always remain the principal place for doing business, much of which, after all, depends on person-to-person contact; for purchase of those special things which give richness to our lives and for those great cultural activities which set the tone of our contemporary civilization.
>
> In addition, Center City serves as the springboard from which waves of revitalization spread outward as suburban families are reattracted to urban living.[7]

In 1960, Philadelphia's City Planning Commission delivered to Mayor Richardson Dilworth and the City Council its comprehensive plan, a "blueprint for the Philadelphia of tomorrow." It envisioned "a new kind of city, its beginning already in evidence, which is within the financial and physical means of Philadelphia's people to bring to full realization in the remaining decades of this century."[8] The plan undertook to structure Philadelphia's engagement with forces shaping postwar America, remaking the city in ways that would allow it to compete successfully with other cities and, more important, with its own booming suburbs. The principal struggle would be against the decentralization of capital and the increasing tendency of private investors to look elsewhere than downtown for economic opportunities. Recognizing that "the term 'Philadelphia,' as customarily used today, refers to a complex reaching far beyond the City proper," the plan outlined strategies for retaining and attracting business, jobs, and middle-class taxpayers that would otherwise be lost to the suburbs.[9] Putting the plan into action would cost the city at least $3.5 billion, but the alternative was decline and slow death.

The city the plan envisioned took shape around a vigorous downtown serving its historic function as the center of the Delaware Valley region's networks of business, government, and culture.[10] The plan framed its principal arguments as a case for "revitalizing" Center City in order that it continue to attract capital on every level: corporate investment, upscale residence, the suburban family's consumer dollars. Mustering historical support for—or anachronizing—the image of suburbanites commuting downtown to work, shop, attend a concert, or eat out, the plan invoked William Penn's colonial-era Philadelphia as "the seat of a great rural region, farmed by large landholders, each living on his own farm," who "looked to Philadelphia not only as a market for their goods and a source of supply, but also as the center of much of their social and cultural activity."[11] The plan sought to make certain that Center City Philadelphia, occupying the site of Penn's original city, sustained itself in this traditional relation to its region well into the next century.

The plan for Center City, a second volume devoted to the comprehensive plan's key Center City component, detailed the massive transportation network and physical redevelopment required to remake Center City: "A basic policy which underlies the Center City Plan is to provide the limited core area with the richest possible series of interrelated transportation facilities serving all parts of the region and encouraging the concentration of all major region-oriented activities within walking distance of these transportation centers."[12] More than half of the comprehensive plan's total expenditure would go to fund an elaborate system of expressways designed to carry traffic from the region's furthest reaches (and beyond, via the interstates) into Center City, where new parking facilities and rail stations would absorb the cars and commuters. The flows of cars from periphery to center would intersect with three progressively larger highway rings—the Center City, Five Mile, and Ten Mile loops—cut through the metropolis. This complex transportation network would channel people and money into a new urban core of tall office buildings, refurbished shopping strips, major cultural centers, pedestrian walks on the rivers, and fashionable residential areas like Rittenhouse Square and Society Hill. Bracketed east and west by the Delaware and Schuylkill rivers, buffered from lower-income residential areas to the north and south by the Vine Street and Crosstown expressways, Center City would be a showpiece central place, a self-contained walking city for the next century.

This 1950s-vintage vision of a "limited core area" was realized in important and lasting ways; however, it is crucial to the story of South Street that the plan was not, and probably never will be, executed in its entirety. In particular, many components of its expressway network were never built—among them, notably, the Crosstown Expressway, which would have erased South Street from the map (figs. 7 and 8). The rise of suburban centers rivaling, rather than subsidiary to, Center City made for less periphery-to-downtown traffic flow than the plan expected. Also, the plan's ability to pay for itself rested on overly optimistic projections of growth in inner-city population, economic vigor, and a continuing and stability-encouraging "reasonable balance of income groups, family sizes, and races."[13] The erosion of Philadelphia's tax base, combined with the formation in the 1960s of local groups opposed to urban renewal projects, weakened the public sector's ability to complete those projects. Government-assisted private development in the "limited core area," like office towers and shopping complexes, continued to flourish, but necessarily public-sector projects (like the Crosstown Expressway) ran into unforeseen difficulties.

The plan made clear that the private sector, not city government, had the leading role in their partnership. Although the plan had been assembled by a government agency, its authors noted that "much that is in it already has been planned or built by private initiative, and many of its ideas had their origin in the minds of professional or business men."[14] Two alliances, forming the two main elements of the progrowth coalition, were behind this exercise of private initiative in the public sphere. First, in 1951, the postwar Democratic alliance of latter-day Progressives, trade unions, blacks, and the party's white-ethnic "rowhouse regulars" defeated the Republican machine that had dominated Philadelphia since the city's political consolidation in 1854. The Democratic alliance's tenuous network of common interest soon began to dissolve under the multiple pressures of industrial decline, a changing calculus of racial and ethnic politics, and the discrediting of the urban renewal agenda, but while it lasted the Democratic alliance provided political support for a second, private-sector alliance of planners, bankers, lawyers, and other business and professional interests committed to fostering downtown redevelopment.[15] Elite activist business groups like the Citizens' Council on City Planning (CCCP) and its successor, the Greater Philadelphia Movement (GPM), undertook, in close cooperation with city government, to reshape the city's physical plant, transportation networks, and governmental order for a postindustrial age. The City Planning Commission's two-volume plan codified the vision of the CCCP and GPM.[16] The plan continued to serve as a blueprint for postindustrial Philadelphia into the 1980s, and further redevelopment proceeded in keeping with the plan's concentration on Center City.[17] Although planning-oriented reform mayors held office from 1951 to only 1962, the coalition of interests represented by CCCP/GPM continued to determine the shape of redevelopment. Private dollars, not governmental administrative decisions, had the ultimate say in the success or failure of necessarily cooperative redevelopment projects, and private investors heavily concentrated their commitment of capital in Center City projects.[18]

The progrowth coalition felt that Philadelphia needed to take such drastic measures to ensure its future economic and social viability. One of the nineteenth century's great manufacturing centers, Philadelphia took mature industrial form in the period 1880–1930, bequeathing to the twentieth century a cityscape of loft buildings, warehouses, narrow streets and alleys, two- and three-story rowhouses, an aging port and rail network. Like industrial Chicago, Philadelphia in this period was a city of urban villages: a patchwork of ethnic blocs grouped around factory workplaces, the whole surrounding a downtown government center and ringed in turn by streetcar suburbs. Again, as in Chicago, a common reliance on manufacturing and the brokering influence of the entrenched political machine (Republican in Philadelphia; Democratic in Chicago) stabilized this distinctively industrial urban system.

Philadelphia's manufacturing economy was especially reliant on small manufacturers of nondurable goods—as opposed to the vast plants that characterized heavy industry in Chicago or Detroit—a condition that only increased the speed and effects of postwar deindustrialization. Small manufacturers were particularly responsive to the notion that the relative cost of doing business, from taxes to union wages, in the inner city had become too high: they were less tied to place than larger manufacturers (who tended to make significant investments in fixed equipment and real estate), and smaller businesses tended to place a premium on paying lower wages. Between 1955 and 1975, Philadelphia lost three out of four of its manufacturing jobs, a particularly sharp fall within a general decline of manufacturing in America's older industrial centers after World War II.[19] In the late 1950s and early 1960s, with decentralization of capital and population clearly in evidence during the great suburban boom, the plan's authors saw themselves entering into a crucial competition with the suburbs and other cities for remaining manufacturing jobs and the industries of the growing service sector.

Philadelphia, like Chicago, had matured as an industrial city, and postindustrial transformation reshaped the city's fundamental arrangements of people, resources, power, and space. John Mollenkopf's general assessment of this transformation, applied earlier to the case of Chicago, is worth repeating here: postwar change "dismantled the mosaic of blue collar ethnic segmentation which developed within the occupational and residential order of the older industrial cities."[20] Again, as in Chicago, the progrowth coalition worked to reconcentrate capital downtown, revaluing land in and around Center City. On the southern fringe of Center City, South Street came to be poised on an edge created by these processes: between the decline and contraction of South Philadelphia's industrial-era neighborhood order and the postindustrial refashioning and expansion of Center City.

In the 1950s and 1960s, South Street became an "inner-city" thoroughfare in a distinctively postindustrial sense of the term. As was the case in postwar Chicago, a substantial black migration from the South to Philadelphia in the 1940s and 1950s combined with the outflow of money, whites, and middle-class blacks to the periphery to set the stage for the transformation of Philadelphia's inner city. The new black Philadelphians entered the city— drawn by manufacturing, especially defense, jobs available during and just after the war—at a time when, as one account puts it, "many Philadelphians were looking outside of the city for both their housing and their employment."[21] At the same time, Philadelphia's established black communities were becoming destabilized by population growth, changes in the structure of job opportunities, and redevelopment. Economic and cultural constraints on blacks helped to confine them to the inner city, which in the 1950s and 1960s began to take on distinctive postindustrial form: white-ethnic enclaves, redeveloped core, and second ghettos. South Street traversed this emergent landscape, the three principal terrains of which met along the thoroughfare.

Forming a traditional spine for Philadelphia's most established and relatively affluent communities of blacks, South Street touched upon a Black Metropolis of nineteenth-century vintage, black neighborhoods shaped to fit into the industrial city's mosaic of urban villages. Straddling the central portion of South

Street, especially, were solidly respectable neighborhoods in which black middle- and working-class families owned and patronized local businesses, attended churches and clubs, and saved to buy rowhouses. This established order underwent a series of upheavals as the Crosstown Expressway plan drove down property values and Center City moved south into the real estate "vacuum." Beginning in the 1950s and increasingly in the 1960s, with the entire area under the threat of being gutted by the planned highway, South Street's preexisting black neighborhoods eroded significantly. Those who could moved out, and a new population with nowhere else to go drifted into flophouses, furnished rooms, and condemned buildings that proliferated around central and western South Street. The breakdown of South Street's prewar black neighborhood order in the 1950s and 1960s left a mishmash of survivals—enclaved remnants of the old order, housing projects, transients—that seemed at the time to augur the formation of the second ghetto. The city did erect high-rise housing projects, the second ghetto's signature form, just below South Street in the 1960s, but the proximity of Center City and its southward movement obliged public and private authorities to prevent the second ghetto of South Philadelphia from developing on the same scale as in North Philadelphia.

Black South Philadelphia had been part of an ethnic and racial patchwork in which white ethnics predominated. Forming the northern edge of South Philadelphia, South Street touched white-ethnic neighborhoods, relics of the urban villages of crowded rowhouse blocks that had been shaped during the decades of peak European immigration before 1920. In the 1960s, these neighborhoods came to be seen as aging white enclaves squeezed between second ghetto and gentrified core. As Center City expanded south after the war and black neighborhoods along South Street were thrown into upheaval, many of South Philadelphia's white ethnics moved away from South Street: farther down into the heart of South Philly, to other, more stable neighborhoods in Northeast Philadelphia, or to the suburbs. This unraveling of the urban village in a generally prosperous, suburbanizing period was part of a larger historical process of acculturation: as the descendants of European immigrants continued to negotiate the complex generational process of shedding immigrant-ethnic status, they followed the general flow of capital and opportunity away from the old neighborhood. The comprehensive plan, drawn up before the urban crisis took the form of a racial crisis in the mid-1960s, admitted that there would be aggregate outflow from inner-city areas (and tacitly admitted that whites would be the ones moving out) but could not conceive of such movement at the scale and pace it assumed in the 1960s. Expanding black neighborhoods and the panic associated with riots and crime (and, on South Street, the dislocations attendant upon the Crosstown Expressway scheme) accelerated this movement into what has been called white flight—shorthand for the elevation of push factors (getting out of the inner city) over pull factors (entering America's suburban middle class) in the departure of white ethnics from the inner city. Some merchants on South Street, white and black, came to support the Crosstown plan, hoping to cut their losses by selling out to the city.[22]

The pressure on both white-ethnic and black communities around South Street was coming from Center City. Forming the southern edge of Center City, South Street ran along the border of one of the nation's showcases of downtown redevelopment: not just the office towers and large municipal buildings that house business, government, and cultural centers but also elite residential neighborhoods with access to restaurants, shops, and other cosmopolitan attractions. Rehabilitated eighteenth- and nineteenth-century houses and Society Hill's trio of skyscrapers, designed by the celebrated modernist architect I. M. Pei and built in the early 1960s, became architectural symbols of stylish downtown living. Philadelphia's chief planner, Edmund Bacon, likening the Pei towers to Pope Sixtus's obelisks in Rome, saw them as defining the new Center City's image and articulating the successful integration of past and future cityscapes: the towers were formally sensitive to "the delicate eighteenth- and nineteenth-century structures that form their foreground on the west and south, yet at the same time they serve as a powerful articulation point in relation to the fast movement on the Delaware Expressway dominating the sweep of the regional flow of the Delaware River."[23] The towers marked the heart of the postindustrial metropolis defined by expressways and "regional flow," but they also acknowledged the historical richness of the preindustrial and industrial layers of cityscape uniquely available to Center City's residents. Similarly, the style of life pursued by this new, preponderantly white workforce of professionals, managers, and office workers in service industries constituted a kind of postindustrial urbanism distinct from the white-ethnic, black, and bohemian urbanisms that it simultaneously displaced and drew upon for cosmopolitan texture.[24]

By the early 1970s, the industrial city was becoming a persistent but succeeded component of the postindustrial landscape around South Street. The old neighborhoods around South Street were not yet redeveloped and gentrified by Center City's service professionals, yet it was clear that they would be in time. They could no longer be identified as industrial villages, but the physical, social, and cultural orders typical of those villages were still in evidence. The old neighborhood order was in disarray, but the new order was not yet in place. South Street occupied yet another edge position, this one between phases of urban change.

The key to South Street's postwar history of change is an unbuilt expressway. South Street did not appear on the comprehensive and Center City plans' maps and views of the future. In its place, an expressway would form the southern verge of Center City, feeding cars into Center City and connecting I-95 on the east to the Cobb's Creek Expressway farther to the west across the Schuylkill (figs. 7 and 8). The planned South Street expressway—which had different names over the years but is best known as the Crosstown—would also serve to divide Center City from the variously gritty, seedy, and solid neighborhoods of South Philadelphia: the commission intended that the "Vine Street and Crosstown Expressways will reinforce the margins of Center City to the north and south."[25] The decision to build the Crosstown along South Street, made in the 1950s and reversed in the 1960s, became the great determining fact of South Street's history from that point on.

South Street has a longer history than do most American streets, extending back to the 1682 survey commissioned by William Penn for the purpose of establishing the city, of which it formed the southern edge.[26] Philadelphia's blacks, particularly the black middle class, had established themselves around South Street in the nineteenth century, and since the 1850s there had been a concentration of Jewish merchants on South, especially between Second and Fifth streets.[27] Along with Girard Avenue to the north of Center City, South was one of the main shopping streets for industrial Philadelphia's wage-earning populations. The intricately layered and intermixed Polish, Italian, Jewish, black, and Irish populations of South Philadelphia made for a heterogeneous shopping strip, with ethnic businesses and enclaves strung along South "like heads on a string," in the words of urban planner Denise Scott Brown.[28] Although some of its industrial-era merchants sold to a fashionable carriage trade drawn from aristocratic Rittenhouse Square just to the north (a trade that was diminished by an early wave of suburbanization in the 1920s), the white-ethnic and black neighborhoods of South Philadelphia provided South Street with its principal constituency.

The Great Depression, World War II, and postwar suburbanization combined to diminish South Street as a shopping street, especially as residents in surrounding neighborhoods moved out, but South was still a lively commercial strip in the early 1950s. A regional trade of ethnic shoppers returned to patronize favorite stores from the old neighborhood, and, especially west of Broad Street, South Philadelphia's growing black population used South Street as its principal commercial avenue. Denise Scott Brown argues that after World War II South Street "could, in fact, be called the main street of Philadelphia's center-city black community."[29]

If the urban planner Brown saw South Street as the commercial backbone of at least one community, the City Planning Commission's blueprints for the future conceived of it as the border of Center City—in planning parlance, an "edge" rather than a "seam." Starting in the late 1950s, as the threat of the Crosstown put a stop to local investment in the South Street area, owners of homes and businesses sold out, prospective buyers from the neighborhoods looked elsewhere, many stores closed, and only a few businesses opened to replace them. Center City's encroachment from the north accelerated the breakup of upper South Philadelphia's neighborhood orders, leaving the area's decreasing population older, poorer, and more black.[30] This typically early-1960s limbo between slum clearance and redevelopment became a lasting condition for South Street over the next two decades because the Crosstown, an idea that had transformed South Street, was never built.

A loose but increasingly effective alliance of neighborhood representatives and urban professionals opposed the expressway, one of many such local blocs formed in response to urban renewal projects throughout urban America in the 1960s. Black leaders from neighborhoods around central and western South Street made a rough common cause with representatives of two preponderantly white groups: the proprietors of new arts-and-crafts shops and cafés on eastern South Street, known to some as "the South Street Renaissance" and to others as "the hippies"; and a crew of lawyers, professors, and planners interested in fighting City Hall. A 1964 riot in North Philadelphia and recurring rumors of impending violence in South Philadelphia lent new urgency to both the city's case for a southern buffer for Center City and the continuing exodus of businesses and taxpayers from the neighborhoods around South Street. But the Crosstown's opponents raised difficult questions about the highway's displacement of 5,000–6,000 mostly poor people, the scarcity of affordable relocation housing, and the wisdom of placing another visible barrier between City Hall and black neighborhoods.[31]

By the late 1960s, the national mood had turned against urban renewal as it was conceived in the 1950s, and the increasingly sophisticated anti-Crosstown forces could draw upon a growing national and local critique of urban renewal's equity and efficacy.[32] Robert Mitchell, a University of Pennsylvania professor who had been one of the transportation plan's original architects in the 1940s and 1950s, argued against the Crosstown in 1967, describing it as a relic of the transportation-obsessed planning of the 1950s that neglected "the social aspects." In 1970, a consultant hired by the city reported that the Crosstown would be underutilized and overpriced and that its necessity had been predicated on drastic overestimates of population increase and retail employment downtown.[33] Despite these authoritative judgments, and even though other highways to which it was supposed to connect were never completed, ambitious planners and developers were still periodically reviving the Crosstown proposal into the 1970s, and neighborhood organizations were still successfully opposing them.

In 1968, members of the anti-Crosstown coalition asked the architectural firm of Venturi and Rauch to draw up a counterplan for South Street that codified their ideas. The firm, which in the late 1960s and 1970s became one of the most important influences in the field of urban planning, had a historical connection to South Street: Robert Venturi's parents had made their living selling produce from a South Street storefront, and Denise Scott Brown, the architectural firm's principal planner and Venturi's wife, has said that in the firm's fledgling period "the fruit business supported the architecture business."[34] Brown, who was in charge of drawing up the South Street counterplan, saw herself as part of a new generation of planners, influenced by populist critics of traditional city planning like Herbert Gans and Jane Jacobs and opposed to the 1950s model of the "value-free technician" working in a social vacuum. She argued that, in the absence of "governmental and societal commitment to social programs . . . Bauhaus ideals as well as our most recent large-scale architectural urbanistic dreams will be used as they were on South Street to betray rather than support the social concerns from which they sprang." Her counterplan envisioned South Street as the "strip center of a vital commercial, cultural, civic life" supported by programs to increase local employment and ownership of businesses and homes. Brown saw South Street as positioned within the metropolis to serve local clienteles (blacks, remaining white ethnics, Center City urbanites) and a regional market of ex–South Philadelphians returning to the inner city from the suburbs for weekend shopping.[35]

The contest over the Crosstown, codified in metropolitan plan and local counterplan, was a contest between two visions of South Street as a relic of industrial Philadelphia. If the anti-Crosstown forces prevailed in their argument that South Street was the spine of a community or communities, it was, from the point of view of the preexisting neighborhood formations, a qualified victory. By the 1970s, more than twenty years of disinvestment, uncertainty, and decay had emptied storefronts, destabilized the surrounding neighborhoods, and dispersed the regional shopping trade. On its eastern end, South Street, bracketed by Society Hill to the north and Queen Village to the south, was becoming a commercial and entertainment strip for the new Center City urbanites. In the center and west, Center City was extending feelers —"urban pioneers" fixing up old houses, landlords stockpiling properties for the coming revival—into what had been the hearts of black and Irish neighborhoods. "Precursors of the yuppies," Brown writes, "were approaching from both ends and the centre."[36] The city, having done everything possible to discourage landlords from investing in the blocks around South Street, stepped up enforcement of building codes to encourage those landlords to sell out to Center City urbanites and the speculators who facilitated their southward movement.

If the pro-Crosstown forces failed to build a clear southern bulwark for Center City, the threat of the Crosstown helped to lower land values and open the way for the urban pioneers and fixer-uppers who gradually moved the zone of gentrification down to and past South in the 1980s. A character in *Tumbling*, discussed in chapter 7, goes so far as to argue that the city never intended to actually build the Crosstown, that the expressway plan was never more than a way to clear the ground for the affluent householders of Center City. As Center

City in the 1990s fills in the areas around South Street and extends south toward Washington Avenue, expanding beyond the limits the planners drew for it with the Crosstown plan in the 1950s, it absorbs a revived South Street. The main shopping street of South Philadelphia's industrial villages now provides food, clothing, books, entertainment, edgy merchandise (a condom store, body piercing), a "historic" industrial infrastructure of "atmospheric" brick walk-ups widely regarded as congenial to arts-and-craft uses, and strollers' ambience to service the consumer profiles of postindustrial urbanism.

The two chapters that follow examine the South Street literature's imaginative engagement with this city in transition. Chapter 6 situates *John Fury* and Smith's *South Street* in a midcentury moment of incipient transformation; chapter 7 traces the literary reverberations of that transformation through the 1970s (Bradley's *South Street*), 1980s (*God's Pocket*), and 1990s (*Tumbling*).

In what follows, I will shuttle back and forth between more local and more global scales of analysis in at least three ways. First, the relationship of South Street to the city of Philadelphia, the problematic fit of the local to the metropolitan, commands a good deal of my and the authors' attention. In their novels, the tension between local order and city-structuring process always informs the problem of neighborhood, both literary and social. Second, I will ask individual texts to speak to the composite text I assemble from the novels and satellite documents—histories, plans, maps. Among other things, this allows characters and figures to participate in the composite postwar narrative and to move through the composite city of feeling, traveling in edifying ways beyond the horizons of their historical moment or the text in which they appear. If at times it seems that I am being "unfair" to a novel by introducing characters and ideas from other texts into it or by expanding upon the blind spots in its imaginative range, I do so in the service of tracing and reading the larger narrative to which all the texts contribute.

Third, the discussion that follows will suggest various ways in which stories of South Street and Philadelphia have meaning that can be applied to other cities and their literatures. By the early 1960s, Philadelphia enjoyed a national reputation as a model for how cities might navigate the stresses and traumas of postwar urban change. National magazine stories and professional journal articles on urban renewal featured Philadelphia's reform mayors, its "business community," and its celebrated chief planner, Edmund Bacon. Martin Meyerson observed that "no municipal reform movement more captured the imagination of observers, both nationally and locally, than did that of Philadelphia . . . during the mid-fifties and early sixties."[37] To the extent that the story of Center City is exemplary (as success or as failure, depending upon whom you might ask and when), representations of South Street might also be exemplary, suggesting resonances with representations of the multiple and particular localities that add up to urban America. The readings of the South Street literature that follow in the next two chapters argue, among other things, that narratives of white-ethnic decline and black community formation are inextricably entangled with one another—both formally and in their relation to a shared urban history. That generic entanglement, traced on the terrain mapped by the South Street literature, suggests in microcosm the stormy and fruitful encounter of white-ethnic and black urbanisms that has been at the center of postindustrial life in America's old industrial capitals.

Urban Village and Black Metropolis: *John Fury* and *South Street*

Ah, she said and she sank to the pavement. It's all
over with us, she said.
Jack Dunphy, John Fury

South Street, great blood vein of a people.
William Gardner Smith, South Street

The postwar South Street literature begins with two midcentury novels that, like Algren's *Man with the Golden Arm*, imagine the industrial neighborhood order in crisis: Jack Dunphy's *John Fury* and William Gardner Smith's *South Street*. Both Dunphy and Smith grew up in South Philadelphia, absorbing the material for their novels from the Irish urban village and Black Metropolis in which they respectively lived. They shared roots in an industrial city that at midcentury was already showing signs of transforming into something new and strange—the postindustrial inner city. Smith's neighborhood, pushed by the influx of Southerners in the 1940s and the stirrings of a postwar initiative to win social justice for urban blacks, seemed at midcentury to be on the brink of an explosion. Dunphy's, still conforming at midcentury to the template of the immigrant-ethnic village, was just beginning to feel the effects of a diffusion and contraction that would accelerate in the 1960s. The two authors, both of whom read widely from an early age, also shared an engagement with the Chicago neighborhood novelists: Dunphy's spare, prose-poetic style glossed James T. Farrell's definitive portrait of Irish industrial urbanism with enough novelty to attract Farrell's displeasure; Smith set out to write protest novels that would develop the literary possibilities of social critique beyond what he called the "wooden, Dreiser-esque" example of Richard Wright.[1]

Jack Dunphy, born in Atlantic City in 1914, grew up poor in St. Monica's parish, an area of particularly narrow streets and weathered rowhouses deep in South Philadelphia. His father was a linotype operator; his mother kept house. As Dunphy and his siblings described the Irish urban village to Gerald Clarke, a biographer of Dunphy's longtime companion Truman Capote, "the residents of those drab little row houses regarded themselves as members of a clan and held in fine disdain anyone who wanted to leave for the wider world outside." The making of an urban intellectual can be a violent process under such circumstances, especially in a neighborhood suspicious of boys who like opera and books more than sports. Dunphy's sister Olive tells of an episode in which a local boy taunted her bookish brother Jack, shouting "Come on down and play, Mary" until Jack threw down his book, "leaped over the porch railing and attacked him, smashing his head again and again against the sidewalk."[2] Dunphy left high school to work in factories but found his way out of the industrial grind through dance. After studying dance, Dunphy toured with the Balanchine company in South America, performed at the 1939 World's Fair in New York, and had a small part in the original *Oklahoma* on Broadway. He served in the army in Europe from 1944 to 1946, the year *John Fury* was published. A self-taught writer, and inspired by a reading of Gertrude Stein's *The Making of Americans*, he had begun writing the novel years before while on tour in South America. *John Fury* was the first, and by most accounts the best, of his several books, setting the pattern for subsequent novels' examination of Irish Catholic family life.[3] He also wrote plays, but his modest career as a writer after *John Fury* took place almost entirely in the shadow cast by Capote, his companion of thirty-five years. After separating from his wife, the dancer Joan McCracken, Dunphy met Capote in 1948, and they were together until Capote's death in 1988. Dunphy died in 1992. Dance, writing, and Capote took Dunphy a long way from South Philadelphia: to New York City's high life, to extensive travel in Europe, and to Sagaponack on Long Island, where the Nature Conservancy's Capote-Dunphy Preserve memorializes their resting place.

William Gardner Smith, born in 1927, grew up in family homes on Ninth Street, Wilder Street, and Twentieth Street, all within the black neighborhoods of South Philadelphia that bracketed South Street. His stepfather earned modest pay as a custodian, and the family had to make do in a climate of poverty. Smith reminisced in print about stuffing newspapers in the holes in his shoes, losing belongings when a firetrap house burned down, and going to war as a member of the local street gang against the Irish gangs of Grays Ferry, the Italians across Reed Street, and other black gangs.[4] Educated in the Philadelphia public schools, he was an early reader and took early to writing as well: he was producing copy for the *Pittsburgh Courier*, one of the nation's leading black newspapers, while still in high school; and he wrote his first novel, *Last of the Conquerors*, at the age of twenty upon his return from an eight-month tour of duty with the army in occupied Europe. *South Street* was his third novel (following *Anger at Innocence*) and his greatest critical and popular success. By the time of its publication in 1954, he had been living in Paris for three years, settled into the community of expatriate American black artists that included prominent urban intellectuals Richard Wright, James Baldwin, and Chester Himes. He lived in Paris, working for Agence France-Presse and writing one more published novel (*The Stone Face*), until his death in 1974. He left Europe for only one extended period—to serve as an administrator of state television and the Institute of Journalism in Ghana, another meeting place for expatriate black intellectuals, from 1964 until Nkrumah was overthrown by a military coup in 1966. He also made two short visits to the United States, for a month at the height of the urban crisis in 1967 and again in 1968, gathering the materials for his last book, a journalistic account entitled *Return to Black America* (1970).[5]

Dunphy and Smith, two homegrown South Philadelphia talents who went far afield into the literary life, initiated the exploration of larger subjects in their South Street novels. Dunphy's exploration of the urban village's inner life in *John Fury* provided the template for one of the central themes of his artistic and personal life: the shock of Irish Catholic urban villagers' encounter with a wider world of high culture, wealth, and models of family and morality far removed from neighborhood norms. That theme finds fittingly confusing expression in the interpolation of an invented priest in crisis, a fictional character who seems to be a double of Dunphy, into *Dear Genius*, Dunphy's otherwise nonfictional account of his relationship with Capote. Smith's local exploration of the Black Metropolis in the postwar moment of protest and growth established the starting point for a literary and journalistic career dominated by the theme of urban black Americans' engagement with a larger world: the possibilities suggested by European race relations and culture; the postcolonial possibilities, suggested by Ghana, for reconstituting black locality under the auspices of black internationalism; the responsibility of black intellectuals to apply the lessons of Africa and Europe to the American inner city. Those themes were given final expression in *Return to Black America*, in which a much-changed Smith returns after sixteen years abroad to find his old neighborhood transformed by the urban crisis into a nascent postcolonial nation besieged by imperial America.

Dunphy's and Smith's literary journeys begin in the industrial neighborhood order of South Philadelphia at midcentury, the world given imaginative life in *John Fury* and *South Street*. This world, on the verge of postindustrial transformation, attracted and focused the attention of these two homegrown urban intellectuals: in that sense, it produced them, bringing them to literary maturity just in time to imagine its passing.

John Fury (1946)

The composite story of the postwar South Street literature begins deep in South Philadelphia with a white-ethnic decline. As the way of life native to the industrial villages of South Philadelphia began to contract, unravel, and disperse, versions of white-ethnic decline predictably appeared. *John Fury*, set in St. Monica's parish, imagines the decline of an urban people's way of life—that of prewar Philadelphia's Irish Catholic industrial workers—through the failure of John Fury, a close-mouthed and serious-minded "steady working man," to sustain his family and his way of life into the next generation. Spanning a period of perhaps thirty years that begins roughly at the turn of the century, from Fury's young manhood to his death at fifty-four, the novel proceeds as a series of family dramas: Fury's marriage to his first wife, Mame; the launching of their household and family; her death of consumption; the souring of Fury's second marriage; the familial shocks and separations as his daughters marry and his son goes bad; Fury's expulsion from the home, leading to his death. Fury dies after falling from his front steps while attempting to batter down his front door with an iron pipe, his second wife, Bridget, having locked the house against him in a dramatization of familial collapse.

In the novel's final lines, Fury's literal fall, culminating that of his family, further generalizes itself as the figurative fall of a people. His death sends a kind of impulse through the neighborhood—up two blocks on Twenty-third Street from Seigal Street to the corner of Moore Street[6]—where it seems to transfix Mrs. Harrigan, a neighbor also driven into the streets and bewildered by the collapse of her household:

> Ah, she said and though it pained her what she felt and though she held herself with the pain, her fist clenched hard and her fist's knuckles blue, jammed between her sagging breasts, she smiled.
> Ah, she said and she sank to the pavement. It's all over with us, she said.[7]

In those final lines, the novel completes its argument for Fury as an exemplar of a particular people caught in a particular place and time.[8]

John Fury frames the microhistory of Fury's decline within an imagined historical moment—or, more precisely, within a heavily freighted myth-historical moment: the passing of a horse-and-wagon Philadelphia in which people like John Fury, exemplar of the Irish who came to America to build its industrial cities, could work and raise families that sustained their way of life. A paragraph-long preamble to the novel, offering in miniature the kind of historical concordance that *City on the Make* supplies for *Golden Arm*, suggests in portentous mock-epic tones that *John Fury* is about this slipping into the past of Fury's Philadelphia. Introducing a novel of what happened when the city had been built and begun to change, the preamble concludes by describing the fate of the Irish in urban America: "they landed and a shovel was placed in their hands or a hammer or spade and they built Boston and New York and Chicago and Philadelphia. And in the evenings they walked home in the leaning shadows of the gray stone to their one room or two rooms and fell into bewildered sleep."[9] The preamble thus promises a novel about the home life of these immigrant laborers, which *John Fury* surely is, but it also puts in motion a historical narrative. When the kind of work required by that earlier moment of city building is done, the way of life defined by that kind of work begins to fall to pieces along long-standing internal fault lines, much as does Fury's second marriage.

As a decline narrative, *John Fury* has a rich sense of the past and in fact projects a postwar moment of decline into the prewar past, but it has very little corresponding sense of the future as anything more than the extended decay of past and present. Familial barrenness serves as the central metaphor of this sense of winding down to a terminus. Even though Fury's daughters, Lizzie and Katie (both borne by his first wife, Mame), produce children into the next generation, Fury's family proves barren in the sense that it cannot reproduce its patriarch's way of life. Lizzie marries well and leaves the neighborhood, climbing toward a middle-class life in North Philadelphia; Katie marries badly, to a lace-curtain snob who reviles her family and eventually breaks with them in their last stages of violent decline. Fury's second marriage produces a son, John Jr., a drunkard and idler who sponges off his indulgent mother, will not work, and does not marry. Fury's only son, his father's physical duplicate but otherwise his antithesis, appears to be the end of the Fury name and the history of migration, neighborhood-based urbanism, and city-building hard work associated with it.

This familial barrenness comes to light in a series of emotionally and physically violent conflicts staged for the most part in Philadelphia's signature domestic landscape — the plain, orderly interiors of two-story rowhouses. Familial collapse as the collapse of an entire people's way of life takes final form in the paired figures of Fury and Mrs. Harrigan, each of whom is driven from a troubled rowhouse home to fall in the street. The argument that the Fury family stands for a people, that their inability to reproduce their way of life stands for a people's inability, is made clearest in those moments in which the novel takes to the streets of South Philadelphia.

John Fury plots its narrative on a high-industrial cityscape in the streets south of South: modest rowhouse blocks, railroad tracks running down Washington Avenue at grade, horse-and-wagon traffic intermixed with cars and trucks. Fury's revealing walks through this world allow the reader to discern the meanings legible in its form. Denied work at his trade — driving a coal wagon — by the foreman at his old job, Fury walks south on Nineteenth Street from Washington Avenue to his daughter Katie's house on Roseberry, a narrow side street. Fury's passage through it allows Roseberry Street to speak its message, to the reader if not to him:

> It's [sic] houses smothered close together, jammed two stories high, and with small wooden porches hung on their fronts, looked like stony red-faced criminals serving a life sentence. Stuck together and dependent one upon the other, they seemed to live in constant fear that someday and somehow one would be pardoned and leave and so jeopardize the rest of them. They stood then, those square red bricked houses, and there were many of them in Philadelphia, tortured row upon row of them, doing penitence and allowing life with its worn semblance of freedom to crowd within them.
>
> Only in summer with the sun beating upon their roofs and with the screaming of all the children and the women's nagging tongues did they seem to sag one row toward the other. Then, and who can blame them, did they appear to say, Let us fall all together. We have stood long enough. (219)

In moments like this, the cityscape argues for generalizing Fury's failure. Driven from his home and unable to work, Fury walks in the street with the two foundations of his way of life collapsing beneath him. Roseberry Street's fanciful collapse takes the form of rowhouses falling, because one "leave[s]" or because they "fall all together." The collapsing houses enact the implications of Fury's crumbling household, and the communal character of the collapse images the classic case for the way an ethnic neighborhood "goes," despite and because of its sense of solidarity: first one household, then all at once. The figure expands to include many similar blocks of Philadelphia and the neighborhood order for which they stand, the way of life they "crowd within them." In this way, the houses on Roseberry Street speak for the passing of an urbanism exemplified by Fury's household. It is therefore fitting that the bitter argument that marks this family's final, irrevocable collapse occurs at Katie's house on Roseberry, at a christening party.

That collapse begins early in the novel, just as, the preamble implies, the eventual collapse of the city-building immigrants' way of life is fated from the moment of their arrival. Fury's life goes wrong when his first wife, Mame, dies young. Standing outside the door of her bedroom at the moment of her death, he has a vision: "Suddenly with train whistles screeching, he felt himself racing his horses alongside the Washington Avenue tracks and beating the horses to go faster and faster and holding in one sweating hand the leathery reins which kept stretching away from him." The reins continue to elongate and the train rushes past, "far up the tracks and his horses and wagon after it, leaving Fury stumbling behind dragging in the last of the long leathery reins" (51). When he returns to himself, she has died.

In that runaway scene, as in the moment of Fury's death, the novel elegizes the immigrant-ethnic urbanism made by Irish industrial workers. Fury's race with the train is not about the industrial train replacing the preindustrial horse, a progression familiar from Westerns. After all, the pervasiveness of trains in the Chicago literature reminds us that the railroad is an integral element of the industrial city inhabited by characters as different as John Fury and Sister Carrie. Rather, the race with the train provides an image of arrival at an urban limit, a moment we encounter throughout the literature of South Street in which some underlying and life-shaping urban logic impresses itself in palpable form on a character moving in the cityscape. The race with the train, like the replacement of the coal wagon by the "motorized truck" that helps put him out of work, allows Fury an insight into the impotence of his individual will: the order of work and family crowded within the rowhouse world depends not on his ability as working man, husband, and father to sustain it but on vast urban-industrial processes of technological change and business as usual that rush on and leave him behind. There may be individuals exercising their considerably more powerful wills to guide such processes, but they are hidden from the view of people like John Fury, whose experience of change is of seeing through the "worn semblance of freedom" to the metropolitan processes that shape life in the neighborhoods. The period in which his services were required having ended, the industrial city rushes on to the next thing, leaving him holding reins that do not control anything. Like Algren's Chicagoans—although none of those two-bit hustlers qualifies as a steady worker—Fury comes up against an iron logic expressed in the built form of the city's rail lines, which defeat him and delimit his world. In the parallel failures of family and work, figured in the scene of Mame's death via the hallucinated juxtaposition of domestic interior and industrial cityscape, the novel encapsulates the human dimensions of an urban order and its passing.

John Fury, then, is a standard white-ethnic decline, a generic sibling of *Golden Arm* and a forerunner of many, many declines to follow (including *God's Pocket*, discussed in chapter 7). Like *Golden Arm*, *John Fury* draws upon the language and themes used by the Chicago neighborhood novelists to represent industrial urbanism: a narrow landscape that expresses both social constraint and the characters' restricted understanding of their place in the urban system; violent familial collapse that dramatizes the injuries of class; individual will crushed or twisted to self-destructive ends by the encounter with powerful economic and cultural forces. Like *Golden Arm*, *John Fury* refits that prewar repertoire to the purposes of a postwar formula, the white-ethnic decline that turns from social critique to something more like elegy. One can perceive signs of that refitting in Dunphy's prose style.

John Fury's formal innovations mark its relation to a literature of industrial urbanism defined for many readers by a fellow chronicler of the Irish in America, the Chicago neighborhood novelist James T. Farrell. The volumes in Farrell's massive Studs Lonigan trilogy were canonical Chicago neighborhood novels, occupying the center of an established tradition of representing the world of the Irish and European "new immigrants" and their descendants in the urban village. Dunphy, writing in the 1940s, played off the expectations raised by working Farrell's literary turf.[10] Showing the influence of Gertrude Stein, Dunphy turns Farrell's flat, descriptive "sociological" style into a kind of prose poetry by ostentatiously stripping it down to the bone: leaving out many commas, quotation marks, apostrophes, paragraph indentations, most of the main plot points, and about 250 pages of the naturalistic period detail one would expect in Chicago neighborhood novels, *John Fury* seems to expect that readers can fill in the details from their generic knowledge of Irish-American and proletarian narratives.[11] That process helps to give the novel its elegiac charge: the worn familiarity of the industrial city of feeling, like that of industrial urbanism in general, marks its arrival at the end of the line. Farrell did not appreciate the intimation of decline or the backhanded acknowledgment of influence, finding *John Fury*'s "relative brevity" and "impressionistic, sketchy manner" unfit for its subject. Predictably, he understood that subject to be not an elegy for industrial urbanism but rather another attempt to critique it in the manner he helped codify in the 1930s. "If [Fury] is to be presented as a passive victim of exploitation," he argued, "then the story would demand a fuller and broader use of detail, a use of detail which would bring more of his working life into the narrative."[12] Farrell wanted those 250 pages back in the novel. So did Jack Conroy, another writer of Farrell's and Algren's circle, who seconded this opinion in a review that identified Dunphy's "typographical effects" (which smacked of "surrealistic or ultramodernistic writing") as "an annoying impediment" to telling the powerful, familiar story of the "poverty-harried Celt."[13] These reviewers registered discomfort with the signs of a generic progression: Dunphy was machining the older orders of the proletarian novel into the decline, and some Chicago neighborhood novelists did not like the signs of change in their literary neighborhood.

Those signs of change in the city of feeling paralleled changes in the city of fact. The industrial neighborhood order of South Philadelphia was still in full flower in the late 1940s, but postwar transformations were already on the horizon. One salient aspect of those multiple, interconnected changes was the growth of the black inner city. Conflict at the boundaries of black and white-ethnic neighborhoods was as old as racial prejudice but also as new as the postwar migrations of people and capital that put the social landscape of the inner city in motion. Violent struggles between white ethnics and blacks in postwar South Philadelphia were some of the most obvious signs of a deeper, thoroughgoing change in urbanism that embraced both whites and blacks, both urban village and Black Metropolis.[14] By the same token, the pattern of racial violence traceable in all of the South Street literature indicates an appreciation of the violence of urban process shared by novels of white-ethnic neighborhood life and novels of black neighborhood life.

Following the tracery of violence, one can see how the story of decline enters into conversation with complementary stories figuring the black inner city's postwar expansion and transformation, a process that became evident to observers in the 1940s and 1950s and eventually became the central matter of the urban crisis in the 1960s. One episode in *John Fury* opens a narrative link between the white-ethnic decline and the stories linked to the second ghetto's growth and maturation told by Smith, Bradley, and McKinney-Whetstone (and the authors discussed in part 3): early in the novel, on the day Mame gives birth to their first child, Fury knocks down a black driver who cuts in ahead of Fury's wagon at the company stable. The black driver responds by slashing Fury with a razor, after which another white driver takes away the razor and gives the black man a beating. In that violent moment—and in the judgment of Bridget's brother Thomas that Fury is an obstacle to her social advancement because he "never has a word t'say but goes around thrashin niggers" (79)—*John Fury* suggests how we can begin to move through the narrative of white-ethnic decline into the complementary acts and extended landscape of postwar South Street's composite drama. *John Fury*, like John Fury, has no interest in black urbanism—the black character is there only to be beaten—but the contours of John Fury's story fit with those of black characters in the South Street literature to follow.

South Street (1954)

If *John Fury* is about the gradual end of a people's way of life, William Gardner Smith's *South Street*, published eight years later in 1954, wants to be about the persistence and internal cohesion of community. If *John Fury* sees a neighborhood in decline—and even, in the novel's darker moments of insight, collapsing all at once—then *South Street* wants to see a neighborhood regenerating itself and reaffirming the continuing connection of people to place as it grows. Mapping a self-sustaining black community that resolves crises of internal division in order to meet the external threat of attack from John Fury's people, *South Street* takes up the problems of neighborhood raised by the mid-century battles fought at the boundaries of America's inner-city neighborhoods and workplaces. The growth of the city's black population and expansion of black neighborhoods, the initial stages of contraction and unraveling in the system of white-ethnic urban villages, and the conflicts that arose out of these linked processes were all part of the larger transformation of urbanism after the war. The progrowth coalition of business and government responded to that larger transformation with the blueprint for postindustrial Philadelphia embodied in the comprehensive plan, which included the Crosstown scheme. Published just as the progrowth coalition was making plans that would drastically reshape Center City's (and thus South Street's) future, *South Street* occupies a historical moment that inflects the novel with a special irony. Projecting the future of the black inner city from a late-1940s template, the novel imagines its local heroes assuring black South Street's place in the industrial neighborhood order. But that arrangement of orders, John Mollenkopf's "blue-collar mosaic" undone by postindustrial transformation, was already breaking up under pressure from forces operating at the metropolitan, even the international, scale.

South Street takes place in an early stage of the overlap between the smaller and relatively stable prewar black neighborhood order and the second ghetto that would take mature form by the early 1960s. In the northern industrial cities, Philadelphia and Chicago prominent among them, the second ghetto was shaped by a volatile mix of factors: massive in-migration of Southern blacks during the war years and after; continuing residential racial segregation, leading to enormous population pressure in black neighborhoods; the economic and physical redevelopment of inner cities in response to deindustrialization and suburbanization; and politically charged efforts to respond to this urban racial crisis with government-funded slum clearance, relocation, and housing projects. *South Street* maps a neighborhood in which some of these transformative circumstances have begun to converge but have not yet coalesced into a new order.

The novel *shows* us a South Street that seems to fit the prewar model of Philadelphia's most established black neighborhoods. The middle classes are invested in the area for the foreseeable future (a condition encouraged by the strictness of forced residential segregation); there is a thriving commercial strip of black-owned stores, clubs, bars, and other businesses; the modest industrial-era housing stock is privately owned, low-rise, and for the most part well maintained. Despite the presence of classic 1950s juvenile delinquents, men and women stroll through the neighborhood at night with no particular fear of violence, and the only instance of drug use takes place among middle-aged jazz musicians. This older Black Metropolis, similar to Bronzeville on Chicago's South Side, was one among the ethnic villages ("like beads on a string" along South Street, in Denise Scott Brown's phrase) that made up industrial Philadelphia's neighborhood order. Deindustrialization and suburbanization, which had such a powerful influence on the postwar erosion of white-ethnic neighborhoods, exerted an equally powerful but drastically different effect on black neighborhoods: as jobs and capital were redistributed toward the metropolitan periphery and its downtown center, inner-city blacks found it difficult to redistribute themselves as freely. They found themselves penned behind the second ·ghetto's "invisible walls."

The novel *tells* us, often in awkwardly informative asides, that historical pressures leading to the formation of the second ghetto have begun to transform the neighborhood and its relation to the city:

> Since the great influx of workers from the South to defense plants during the war, the usual Negro sections of the city had become intolerably congested: even the wholesale transformation of houses into rooming houses, and the letting of rooms in private homes, and the building of housing projects (Government financed) on vacant ground, had done almost nothing to ease the situation. So, slowly, the Negro areas had been pushing *outward*, encroaching on territory formerly exclusively for white people; and those of the white population in this threatened area who could, hastily packed their bags and moved much further back, away from the "front lines." Some could not move. Between these, and the pressing Negroes, grew up conflict.[15]

The parenthesis, "(Government financed)," is an awkward digression within a paragraph that awkwardly digresses from the novel's plot. The novel stops what it is doing, which is showing us a melodramatic feud between two major characters, to tell us about sociohistorical developments in midcentury Philadelphia. Written in the early 1950s and from an expatriate's perspective,˙ *South Street* comes equipped to imagine the old neighborhood under strain, not the place it will become. The writers its characters invoke by name—poets of the Harlem Renaissance, Willard Motley, the early Chester Himes, and especially Richard Wright—are writers of the Black Metropolis. (Writing about the second ghetto, Himes later became a very different writer indeed.) The in-betweenness of the novel's historical moment finds expression in the gap between what the novel can show—how it can imagine its city and what it has precedent for showing—and what it can only tell us about the still-emerging postwar inner city. The language to represent that emergent inner city, especially its black neighborhoods in the throes of transformation, was still developing at midcentury. The novel's awkwardnesses are not just part of its tone and its charm—they are marks of its literary-historical moment.

Although *South Street* takes note of developments that will lead to the second ghetto's formation, it is still a novel of the Black Metropolis, and its spatial and political imaginations express that orientation. Embodying the external threat to South Street in young white-ethnic toughs very much like John Fury Jr., *South Street* turns its back on Center City to attend to the dynamics of neighborhood in South Philadelphia. It concerns itself with relations between the industrial city's neighborhoods, a subject condensed in black South Street's violent encounter with the Irish of Grays Ferry. Center City does receive mention as a seat of power, but only in the abstract as the locus of machine government, the function of which is to help contain black South Street's expansion and autonomy. *South Street*, mapping a community in order to plot its campaign for self-preservation against other elements of the industrial neighborhood order, is therefore not positioned in time or space to conceive of the terrific blow about to take black South Philadelphia in the back in the form of the Crosstown Expressway plan. Not, of course, that the novel, or any work of fiction, is obliged to anticipate or prepare for such a blow from the city of fact. However, the novel's place in the South Street literature's composite narrative of postindustrial transformation creates opportunities to read it against a larger backdrop, including a future obviously unavailable to its author. Also, we are encouraged to read *South Street* in relation to its historical moment for two reasons that form main lines of analysis in my reading of the novel.

First, *South Street*'s story of three brothers finding the means to ensure their neighborhood's integrity into the next generation—a passionately local, parochial subject—is undermined not only by what we know of the novel's historical moment but also (as I argue later in this chapter) by a line of counterargument within the text itself. Winding through the story of the three Bowers brothers' struggle to resolve linked family and neighborhood crises is a critique of the resolutions they accomplish. *South Street* suspects that forces beyond the imagination or control of its heroic urban-intellectual protagonists will render their triumph contrived and temporary. The subsequent history of South Street develops that theme in ways the novel could not imagine.

Second, the question of the relation of literary writing and literary intellectuals to their historical moment was at the center of Smith's work. *South Street* thinks at length about the black intellectual's relation to the inner city he represents, a subject Smith expanded upon in a critical essay—published in *Phylon*—on Wright, Himes, and the black intellectual's "duty" to avoid "social detachment."[16] The story of Smith's heroes the Bowers brothers is about the formation of engaged black intellectuals suited to the task of representing the postwar inner city, and one of its governing themes is the problem of constructing a city of feeling from materials provided by the city of fact. We are therefore encouraged to perform a similar reading of the novel against the city of fact upon which it drew. Written during the great postwar wave of ghettoization and suburbanization, but more than a decade before that wave would crest in American cultural and social life during the ghetto-centered urban crisis of the 1960s, the novel's account of a crisis (ironically) resolved in the black inner city asks to be read against its historical moment.

The Neighborhood Reproduction Drama

South Street proceeds by shifting among the subjectivities of a large network of characters as they move through a landscape of streets, homes, and bars centered on South Street. It is a novel of long walks and long talks, with some of the principal walkers and talkers being Lil, the neighborhood's most coveted woman; Lil's boyfriend Slim, a successful hustler employed by the Italian numbers syndicate; the Old Man, an unspecified political machine's local black functionary; and a broadly archetypal blueswoman called simply the Blues Singer. At the novel's center are the Bowers brothers: Claude, a nationally prominent writer and civil rights activist; Michael, a Negro nationalist firebrand; and Philip, a would-be poet. They form a miniature character system around which the others revolve. The novel's various family and neighborhood crises—couplings and uncouplings, struggles against the Irish of Grays Ferry, problems of sustaining the neighborhood into the next generation—are resolved by the temporarily exiled Claude's return to South Street. Walking on South Street at the novel's dramatic climax, he returns to the neighborhood-based identity that enables his intellectual work, throwing off the moral and intellectual paralysis that has threatened him during his self-imposed exile from the neighborhood: "endless, baffling Time and endless, terrifying Space? One could, should, be aware of them, in wonder and in awe. But one could not live in their contemplation; one could not live according to their all-paralyzing commentary. One lived—whether one wanted to or not—in the bounded time and the bounded space of one's own life and one's own world" (310–11). Having ventured into the larger time and space of the metropolis, Claude returns to the "bounded" time and space of the neighborhood to avert a riot at the novel's end. This exercise of leadership marks him as a fully engaged urban intellectual with the power and responsibility to protect his "own world."

Like John Fury's, the Bowers brothers' family history (further condensed, as with Fury and his no-good son, in the paternal line) encapsulates that of a people, extending from the moment of their father's lynching in the South to their various struggles to make a viable future for themselves in the urban North. Claude's romance with Kristin, a white classical musician, and his climactic decision to choose South Street over her; Michael's romance with black nationalism, unsatisfyingly consummated with acts of violence; Philip's romance with bohemia and highbrow detachment, which ends abruptly with his violent death—these narratives of family crisis and the making of inner-city intellectuals structure the novel as each brother tries to make sense of the neighborhood and his place in it. Each brother seeks a synthetic understanding of the kaleidoscopic bits and pieces of urban experience presented by the novel's episodic form and shifting subjectivities. Philip dies trying; Michael fails but helps Claude to succeed.

South Street's action extends through the streets above and below South Street, into Center City, to distant Philadelphia locations, and briefly as far as New York and Montreal, but South Street forms its spatial backbone and center. Specifically, the novel's South Street extends roughly ten blocks east to west, from about Twelfth Street (east of which were predominantly white-ethnic neighborhoods) to the three-way intersection of Grays Ferry Avenue, Twenty-third Street, and South. That intersection forms the community's best-defined border, marked by a post against which Claude Bowers leans, drinking a beer, "staring off, alone, thinking, dreaming, toward Grays Ferry" (171), the novel's white-ethnic terra incognita. Although there were white-owned businesses and white shoppers on this stretch of South Street in the 1950s, and although a rich variety of ethnic groups lived cheek by jowl in the areas around it, *South Street* renders South Street as an all-black space ending abruptly at a clearly marked border with an unmapped and homogeneously Irish Grays Ferry.[17] This simplicity of spatial form and racial scheme allows the novel to pursue complexity where it wishes to—in the inner life of the black community it selectively assembles.

That community takes shape on the pavements of South Street. The novel opens with the first of many street scenes: "It was a hot Saturday in July, and South Street was crowded: people promenading, vendors with their wares, streetcars clanging, automobiles crawling slowly and honking their horns. The brown pedestrians wore, for the most part, no coats or ties; their shirts were open at the neck and their sleeves rolled up above their elbows. Slim burned in the heat, walking slowly" (3). The pedestrians we can see are brown (and, apparently, male); if there are whites, they do not rate a mention. Here, the crowd indicates the neighborhood's vigorous good health—the commercial liveliness of a good business day, the robust health of working people. Similarly, the figure of the crowded street in other scenes indicates cultural vigor, a viability of tradition and community. South Street's spring festival, especially, serves as a ritual of renewal in which the crowd ratifies the neighborhood's status as a community. Although "no one in the neighborhood knew exactly when, or under what conditions, the custom of having a festival had originated," the montage of marching bands, dance bands, beer drinking, politicians courting votes, speakers invoking "'the days of our forefathers'" (139), and contestants for the Elocution Prize reading poets of the Harlem Renaissance arrives at a moment of communal plenitude and integrity:

They listened, then, the audience—listened, even the youngsters, as they shuffle-danced to the music which was the soul-beat of a people:
  I hate to see that evenin' sun go down
    dancing, and the old people and the young, with cold beer running down their throats, and the knowledge of the neighborhood which was the world and the peo-

ple who were the universe, and fish burning tongue, and ice cream cold, and
Holiday. (142–43)

The novel argues that South Street forms the spatial ground of this people's
being, just as the blues forms its spiritual ground. In roping off the street and
dancing in it, the crowd enacts the connection between the quality of neighborhood—proceeding from a shared way of life—and the neighborhood as a
place in which that shared life takes form.

The "knowledge of the neighborhood which was the world" requires urban
intellectuals who can grasp and articulate that knowledge. Their job, performed
by the Blues Singer in the festival scene, is to reinforce and reproduce the
neighborhood order by reminding the crowd that it is a self-contained, unified
entity—"the people who were the universe." The festival passage achieves final
refinement in a chaos of sharply defined impressions—"and fish burning
tongue, and ice cream cold, and Holiday"—that somehow contain within them
the meaning of neighborhood. Those who would take up the responsibility of
representing the neighborhood, in both the literary and the political senses,
must give form to those bits and pieces of neighborhood content. In doing so,
these representers impart coherence to the neighborhood. There is, of course, a
global component to this local responsibility: the bonds of race and social class,
culture, and history that make the people of South Street a people are the same
bonds that make black Americans a people. The intellectuals who wish to represent the neighborhood aspire to represent a race. Three candidates, the three
Bowers brothers, aspire to that responsibility as writers.

If the crowd stands for a people, the Bowers family narrative both encapsulates that people's story and produces candidates for the task of writing it.
Claude makes the case explicit in his own writing: "'A nation throws up its
heroes, in whom are concentrated all of the group ideals, the group feelings, the
group courage. The hero is himself nothing; he is a focal point, a galvanizer of
the energies already latent in his people; his voice is not his voice at all, but
their voices concentrated. And anything the hero does or says—it is they, his
people, who do or say it'" (91). The Bowers family narrative considers the relation of three brothers—writers, intellectuals, potential leaders—to the notions
of place and peoplehood conjoined in the term "South Street." Through a series
of movements back and forth between South Street and other terrains, and by
articulating the brothers' various relationships to the crowd on South Street,
their stories are made to exemplify three versions of crisis in the formation of
urban intellectuals accredited to represent the black inner city. In working out
the writer's place in the world of South Street, the Bowers brothers provide a
triple structural spine running through the novel along which its fragmentary
forms and meanings—its writing—arrange themselves.

The aspiring poet and bohemian Philip, the youngest, proves himself inadequate as an urban intellectual by insisting on separating literature from South Street. The novel makes this clear by cross-cutting between South Street and the indeterminately located apartment in which Philip ("one of the two Negroes present") meets his circle of "actual or aspiring writers, painters, teachers or the like." The men of this group, "with coats off and sleeves rolled up," make a pale bohemian imitation of the shirt-sleeved South Street crowd presented in the novel's opening scene. They reach a rough consensus on the separation of the intellectual from the social order and historical circumstances embodied by the crowd, especially when "social stress and strain" compel him to "escape the convulsions and violence" of his historical moment. They agree that the intellectual "has *always* been detached from the mainstream of society" (87–88). Their endorsement of "detachment" marks their conclusion as precisely the opposite of the position that Smith took in his *Phylon* essay on the responsibilities of Negro writers, and *South Street* deploys its energies to demolish the misguided ideas of Philip's associates.

Their conversation, joined in midstream and departed in midsentence, forms a separate chapter significantly bracketed by two neighborhood vignettes that identify Philip as the wrong kind of urban intellectual. The preceding chapter describes how Lil's father had over the years made a habit of entering her room at night, culminating in an attempted rape, which Lil resisted by braining him with an ash stand—echoing Lutie Johnson's culminative act of violence in Ann Petry's *The Street*. The chapter following the intellectuals' discussion consists of three short paragraphs, reminiscent of *Native Son*'s opening scene and markedly closer than the rest of the novel to Wright's starker setting and tone, in which a nameless tubercular woman, living in a South Street tenement and abandoned by her drunken husband, discovers a rat in her child's crib: "she felt the hideous biting and squirming in her hand, then she dashed the rat, with all her strength, against the wall" (90). Philip's notions of detachment, presented as an inability to accept the social and historical hard facts of South Street as the ground of his intellectual being, cut him off from Lil and the nameless woman. Were he the right kind of urban intellectual, Philip would know that his calling should be to speak their stories, in the manner theorized by Claude's notion of the hero, practiced by the Blues Singer in her music, and practiced as well by Petry and Wright in the novels to which *South Street* apparently refers via ash stand and rat. Philip's failure to recognize that calling, to understand the neighborhood's "bounded space and bounded time" as limits to be crossed at his peril, render him and South Street of no sustaining use to one another. That he dies just before his wedding day helps mark him as a barren element of the Bowers line, in that sense the John Fury Jr. of this family drama.

Philip's relation to the crowd must therefore ring false. Moving through it during the festival, he enjoys a mistaken feeling of connectedness: "He had never felt such strength before: moral and physical. He *felt* himself expand. . . .

Now, new-born, a new Philip moved in the world! He was *with* people now!" (149–50). The tinny, facile quality of this realization undercuts the moment, however, and Philip draws precisely the wrong conclusion. He feels that to be "*with* people" he must throw over his literary self: "Had that been life, the immersion into books, into endless discussions, into Freud, into Kafka, into Dostoievsky?" (147). Because he understands writing as removing himself from the neighborhood, his subsequent and inevitable return to literature, in the form of a retreat to his circle of literary friends and a library job, entails a complementary distancing from South Street. Philip's straying from home takes the spatial form of an ill-advised walk to the borders of Grays Ferry, where he fatally encounters a hard fact in the shape of a rock thrown by an Irish youth from the other side of the frontier. He is the first but not the last urban intellectual in the South Street literature to get hit in the head for misunderstanding his relation to the social landscape and the stories it houses.

Michael, the middle brother, "breathe[s] Negro nationalism" (193) and doles out, rather than receives, physical punishment. The family's advocate of direct political action, he writes speeches, not poetry. Unlike his brothers, Michael leaves South Street rarely and briefly and usually with violent results: he punches out a white man on Market Street in Center City; he leads punitive expeditions against the Irish youth gangs of Grays Ferry. Michael's violent tendencies point up his great weakness as an urban intellectual—an inability to grasp that South Street means a way of life to be nurtured and sustained by articulating its internal logic, not just territory to be defended. The faction-ridden Negro Action Society he founds never becomes a significant force because he cannot recognize, make coherent, and invoke the bonds of community that must underlie the kinds of political action he aspires to direct.

Michael, however, shows a nascent promise as an urban intellectual, a promising fit to the social landscape in which he moves, that Philip never does. Michael's capacity for direct action, combined with his eleventh-hour reconciliation with Claude (the brothers having broken over Claude's marriage to Kristin), suggests that Michael, while yet misguided, might grow under Claude's influence into a viable leader. This future takes embryonic shape in the initial raid on Grays Ferry, when Michael joins forces with teenage gang members to retaliate for an Irish gang's attack on a black man. The political leader working hand in hand with gang members was to be one of Smith's enduring dreams. Sixteen years after the publication of *South Street*, having come from his home in France to survey black America in crisis, Smith articulated that dream at greater length in his nonfiction work *Return to Black America*. He saw a possible politicization of youth gangs as "one of the most significant phenomena I noted during my tour of the United States," suggesting to him a new convergence of interest among political leaders and violent young men around defense of the community. One gang member he interviewed imagined a fantasy scenario that reads like a racially politicized variant of that in Sol Yurick's teen-gang epic *The Warriors*: the gang member envisioned a "'federation of gangs. All the black gangs in Philadelphia. Then, there ain't gonna be no more gang fights. Just one black army.'"[18]

To Smith in the late 1960s, Michael would appear in retrospect as an early visionary, anticipating by more than a decade this transformation of youthful delinquents into actors in the arena of racial politics. In a sense, Michael is prepared and "saved" for such a future by a protest novel of the 1950s written at a time when that future, the urban crisis of the 1960s, could be conceived in only germinal form. However, the time for Michael's brand of leadership has not yet arrived in the world of *South Street*. His potential productivity, his capacity to lead the neighborhood in defending and reproducing itself by harnessing the energies of its youth, takes misguided form in the raid on Grays Ferry, which in turn leads directly to Philip's death: an Irish boy nursing a beating from a gang raid decides to get even by throwing the fatal rock. In that sense, Michael kills Philip.

The novel's climax is the return of Claude, the oldest Bowers brother, to South Street. Having left the neighborhood's circle of community to be with Kristin, he has been living with her in her studio near the city's edge. Although Claude has resisted the pull of South Street, Philip's death makes clear to him the necessity of his return. Claude's decision to commit himself anew to South Street asserts itself as the event that organizes and makes sense of the many bits and pieces—narrative threads, shifting subjectivities, fragments of anecdote and imagery—that make up the novel's portrait of South Street. Walking on South Street after Philip's death and his own break with Kristin, Claude understands that meaning must be pursued "in the bounded time and the bounded space of one's own life and one's own world, within the bounded nature of one's spiritual core." That is, he feels himself to be *placed:* "This was his blooded world, his cross, his love, his challenge—South Street" (311).

In Claude, South Street ultimately possesses an intellectual embodying Claude's own model of the race hero, singularly equipped to synthesize and express the experiences and needs of the people he encounters on his climactic walk—"an old man with white hair; couples chuckling; . . . a youth, with pork-pie hat and wide-legged trousers" (310). This reverse generational progression of age, coupling, and youth suggests in shorthand the range of South Street's character system: the Blues Singer and Michael, the juvenile delinquents and the Negro Action Society, Lil and the nameless tubercular woman, an old manual laborer who tells Claude about Marcus Garvey and a young law student who tells Claude that he wants to try cases before the Supreme Court —a line extending all the way back to the South and the Bowers brothers' martyred father. The novel's succession drama ends with the emergence of a figure who can effectively represent the neighborhood. Claude combines the formal sophistication of Philip's aesthetic impulse and the social engagement of Michael's political imperative. Each element cancels the other's negative charge—Philip's social detachment, Michael's blindness to culture as the key to community—so that only Claude can encompass and speak for the way of life rendered schematically as the novel's character system and the street on which it is deployed. Claude, the only Bowers brother whose writing has reached a wider audience, is therefore the only character who can stop the self-destructive riot brewing after Philip's death: "'I tried to stop it,'" Michael says, "'but no one listened to me. They listened to Claude. They always listen to Claude'" (305–6).

South Street's last line offers an image of the neighborhood's continuing vitality: "The Blues Singer threw back her head and opened her mouth and began to sing" (312). That portrait of the most "organic" of urban intellectuals doing her cultural work—reinforcing the cultural ties that bind—clinches the novel's argument for South Street as a sustaining conjunction of place and peoplehood. The critical internal division represented by Michael's feud with Claude has resolved itself, and the Bowers family romance has resolved the neighborhood's crisis of reproduction by putting Claude in a position to represent South Street and lead it into the next generation.

The Counterargument

Looked at from another angle, however, the resolution of this crisis smacks of irony and incompleteness. After all, if family narrative provides the central metaphor of the community's reproduction, the Bowers brothers prove to be if anything more barren than the Furys: Philip dies before he can marry his fiancée; Michael's grim courtship of Philip's erstwhile fiancée, Margaret, who worships Claude, promises to remain loveless; and Claude, the only married brother, makes leaving his wife, Kristin, the condition for his return to South Street. The male Bowers line (about whose mother we know nothing) has purified itself through crisis and sacrifice but has not formed a subsequent generation of family groups. If the neighborhood's crisis of reproduction seems to end in resolution, with Claude on South Street and the Blues Singer singing, the male Bowers family's crisis of reproduction—which has been offered to us as the microcosm of a people's—ends in a kind of Pyrrhic spinsterhood, with no prospect of producing even the next batch of Bowers men.

Kristin provides a key to the novel's counterargument, which unravels the Bowers family narrative's argument for reproduction and continuity. Claude's solution to the novel's central problem, leaving Kristin, does not succeed in the fantasy project of erecting a hermetic barrier around the closed communal circle of South Street. Lines of what Michael and even Claude would understand as "outside" influence persist in shaping life on South Street, a state of affairs that the novel acknowledges in several ways.

Kristin is one of several whites who move through the festival crowd, each representing a significant external influence that modifies or threatens the ideal of a self-sustaining, all-black South Street. The Italian gangster Pete, who dances with Lil at the street festival before taking up with her, represents the shadow government of organized crime. He underpays and abuses Slim and the other black numbers writers and finally has Slim, who is Lil's boyfriend and one of South Street's leading figures, beaten for insubordination. Similarly, the city's mayor (who opens the festival) and various policemen represent legitimate government. Paralleling Slim's fealty to Pete, the Old Man's authority on South Street proceeds in large part from his fealty to white politicians downtown. Like Pete's humiliation of Slim, episodes of police harassment and brutality—one of the issues around which Michael's Negro Action Society tries to organize neighborhood opinion—make it violently clear that metropolitan authority shapes the inner life of South Street in important ways.

It is, however, the gentle violinist Kristin, not the powers represented by gangsters or police, who poses the greatest threat to the Bowers brothers' reconstituted South Street. That the novel's climactic moment boils down to Claude's choosing South Street and the crowd over Kristin marks her as the novel's central problem. This is a curious framing of the problem for at least two reasons. First, the novel presents her as its only racial innocent, unable to see color as anything more than an aesthetic category: "Her problem was simple—she could not *understand* the great uproar that arose out of the color of a skin. . . . Why, brown was a beautiful color, for all that, and, looking over groups of Negroes, noticing the infinite variety of shades—of textures, even—she had often felt a positive envy that her skin was a colorless white!" (204). Second, she endorses the Bowers brothers' vision of black South Street as a vital, closed circle. While she moves among the "groups of Negroes" in the festival crowds on South Street, her subjective experience catches the bits and pieces of imagery that make up the building blocks of a community: "Her eyes caught everything: 'beautiful' faces, odd-angled dancers, a man in ecstasy playing the saxophone." Her response to these raw materials of neighborhood endorses the novel's argument for South Street as the incarnation of a thriving way of life: "*Life!* There was *life* in the air of South Street." Watching the crowd dance in the street, she feels a "sharp wave of pain that she was outside of this nation of people, a stranger looking on" (146), ratifying by her discomfort the self-containment and boundedness of peoplehood—she sees a "nation"—that this dancing has been posited to mean.

Without color prejudice, attracted by the neighborhood's folkways, Kristin aspires to acceptance by the crowd. When the Blues Singer invites her to join the dancing crowd on South Street, Kristin feels that "for this moment—she *belonged*" (146). Just at the moment when Kristin feels that she has stepped within the closed circle of black community, the novel marks her as its central problem. The mark takes the form of a wink. The Blues Singer winks at Claude from behind Kristin, an unreadable gesture (mockery? conspiratorial good will? irony?) until it is rhymed later in the novel with another wink at Claude, this one from a white newsvendor who has previously made clear his disapproval of Claude's marriage to Kristin. Near the end of the novel, having decided to leave Kristin, Claude stops at a red light not far from her studio: "the newsvendor at his stand suddenly caught Claude's eye and winked and waved. Claude looked at the newsvendor. With a slight smile, he waved back. He remembered, now, from where it was that he knew the newsvendor" (308). How does the memory of the Blues Singer's wink allow Claude to "know" the newsvendor, a minor character who exists in the novel only to react unpleasantly to the idea of interracial marriage? In order to understand how Claude's marriage to Kristin unites the newsvendor and the Blues Singer, who is the living embodiment of black community, we need to understand how Kristin threatens South Street. The novel's characters discuss at least two ways to formulate an answer, and the history of South Street suggests a third.

Michael Bowers argues, in the protest novel's clankingly analytical register, that Kristin is a white American above and beyond anything else she might be: "Is Kristin a woman of steel? Is her spirit wrapped in some new alloy which is absolutely impervious to all the superstitions about us that are held by her society, her parents, her friends?" (227). Following this reasoning, her manifest racial innocence and saintliness are therefore all the more pernicious in that they might encourage Claude to forget the unalterable social fact of her whiteness. She threatens South Street, in Michael's view, as an agent of white America, and Claude's marriage to her would therefore denature him as an urban intellectual by driving a wedge of difference between him and his people. The newsvendor's and the Blues Singer's winks endorse this logic of strict separation: the two find common ground in seeing Claude's place as South Street and Kristin's as anywhere else.

In the end, Claude does not accept Michael's argument in full, remaining convinced that Kristin lives, as her brother puts it, "in a vacuum," a world of music and form in which color has only an aesthetic meaning, but he accepts Michael's essential point. Claude concludes that his liaison with Kristin inevitably creates distance between him and the neighborhood. The novel suggests a historical reason for Claude and Kristin's inability to find an apartment near South Street or in any black neighborhood: newly arrived Southern migrants have crammed these neighborhoods so that "some families of four or five were living in a single room at rents as high as those charged for houses" (87). The Blues Singer's wink suggests a more important thematic reason that

Kristin cannot live on South Street: the circle of community Kristin encounters at the festival remains closed to her. Unable to rent an apartment together in a white neighborhood, either, Claude and Kristin therefore have to take up residence in her studio, which lies at the edge of the city in a largely undeveloped area—a spatial expression of the artist's detachment from social order in which Philip misguidedly believes. Claude finds himself living in a place that is not a neighborhood, a spatial vacuum to match the racial vacuum in which Kristin lives, far from the South Street milieu that he will finally come to see as "the bounded time and bounded space" of his "own life" and his "own world." Choosing Kristin would eventually drive Claude, South Street's leading intellectual and an influential voice in national and international discussions of race, from America altogether. He and Kristin are in fact planning to flee to Canada when Philip's violent death forces Claude's return to South Street.

These two explanations of what Kristin represents—Michael's strict construction of her as white America and Claude's looser construction of her as unfortunately not black and thus not of South Street—lead to the same point: Claude's marriage to Kristin constitutes a major crisis in the Bowers family narrative and thus (by the novel's logic) in that of the South Street neighborhood and the black America it stands for. Kristin's entry into the Bowers line would necessarily explode the fantasy of a hermetic, self reproducing black world, a fantasy promulgated by people like Michael, enacted by the crowd in the street, and argued for in the novel's final image of the Blues Singer making the special music of a self-contained people. Claude seems to resolve the crisis by his return to South Street, where Kristin cannot follow, making it possible to again imagine an all-black Bowers family, an all-black South Street, a closed circle of community and culture.

The continuing presence on South Street of white men like Pete and the police, however, seriously compromises this community's hermetic integrity. The sight of Pete dancing in the street with Lil at the festival, precisely on the sacred ground and at the key ritual time of the novel's construction of a self-contained black world, suggests that the novel knows itself to be imagining an ideal of racial separation it cannot sustain even as fantasy. In that sense, even though Claude leaves her, the crisis caused by Kristin (also seen dancing in the street) continues to point up the inadequacy of the Bowers family narrative's proposed resolution by showing that the reconstituted fantasy of a self-contained black South Street is dangerously parochial. The fantasy blinds itself to lines of force and influence that extend across the borders of that local world from the metropolitan orders operating at a greater scale beyond it.

The gendering of the Bowers family narrative speaks to this point. Given that the South Street community's drama of leadership and succession takes the form of a family narrative, a childless all-male resolution asserts its own incompleteness. The character of Margaret helps to underscore the point, as the three Bowers brothers orbit tellingly around her: she rejects Philip, worships Claude from afar without success, and, although she finally takes up with Michael, she appears dissatisfied with his strictly political passions. The novel's female characters, more generally, suggest the limitations of the male characters' authority to sustain and reproduce the neighborhood order. Lil, having attacked Pete with a razor to avenge the beating he gave Slim, immediately leaves town for good (heading out on a Chicago-bound train, again a parallel to Petry's Lutie Johnson) because she knows South Street will not shelter her from Pete's cronies. The Blues Singer, high on heroin, curses the Old Man as a transparent fraud: "Your whole goddamn life's a lie! Open your goddamn eyes! Face it!" (289). Just as his hollow sexual advances fail to conceal his age and timidity, the Old Man's air of political insiderhood fails to mask the impotence of a local functionary controlled and disdained by City Hall. Lil and the Blues Singer, then, suggest that Claude, having finally arrived at a moment of heroic plenitude by eliminating Kristin, remains blind to the ways in which white people still shape black South Street.

If the gendering of South Street's succession drama undercuts the Bowers brothers' victory, then Kristin's extratextual "return" to South Street further reveals the futility of regarding her elimination from South Street as an exorcism of outside influences. As a type, she figures in a succession drama, extending far beyond the novel's horizons to the present day, in which the southward march of Center City's new postwar population made it impossible to sustain even the myth of South Street as a locally self-determining conjunction of place and peoplehood.

We might see Kristin as a far advanced outrider for an approaching army who, rushing into the "void" left by the Crosstown plan, would remake South Street in the 1970s and 1980s as downtown Philadelphia's "alternative" main street. Their way of living, an urbanism built by pointedly non- or postethnic service professionals and artists (Pete is an Italian gangster; Kristin, a violinist, is just white), was still in its nascent stages in the 1950s. In 1954, the year South Street was published, the City Planning Commission and its powerful mentors in the private sector began work on what was to become the comprehensive plan.[19] The plan envisioned a Center City designed to attract the more cosmopolitan element of the growing service sector's largely white professional workforce, people who would live conveniently near to the office towers in which they worked, the universities in which they taught, and the upscale businesses they would own and support. Center City's "secondary uses, such as small restaurants, specialty stores, and galleries," would thrive in concert with a new generation of housing—new apartment houses, rehabilitated rowhouses, and town houses forming the plan's desired "band of healthy housing extending from river to river and meeting the core cleanly without a layer of blight between."[20]

To establish the advance outposts for this order, there had to be pioneers much like Kristin, an adventurous, open-minded, mildly bohemian artist with a rich, perhaps patronizingly aesthetic appreciation of lively streets and black culture. Were they to remain together, she and Claude— a musician and a writer, probably with young children—would have been ideal buyers for a rowhouse that needed work on a transitional block somewhere near South Street.[21] If they weathered the racial tensions and disinvestment of the 1960s, they would have been natural leaders for the neighborhood-based anti-Crosstown coalition that eventually scuttled the expressway project. But by depressing property values and increasing the rate of decay, abandonment, and turnover of building stock, the Crosstown plan helped to make possible the gradual southward movement of the new inner-city urbanites to South Street. The unbuilt Crosstown made it possible for them to colonize much of South Street in the 1970s and 1980s as their local commercial strip—upscale on the east, atmospherically "gritty" further west.

Old neighborhood hands like Kristin and Claude would no doubt decry the coming of "yuppies" and wax nostalgic for a lost golden age of community, but today's South Street is the product of a process begun in part by people sharing Kristin's sensibilities and background. Mounting a defense of the Black Metropolis in transition, *South Street* posits Kristin as an interloper to be banished, but the novel's counterargument opens the way for her return and the larger drama of succession that return suggests.

South Street and Greater Philadelphia

Seen in its historical moment, in the shadow of Center City and the second ghetto, Claude's epiphany on South Street—"great blood vein of a people" (310)—seems dwarfed by the scale of forces at play in the metropolis. His return to South Street pales in light of our knowledge that in the following decades significant breaks will occur in the connection of people to place that the novel so passionately and selectively constructs—a connection the novel asks Claude, the model urban intellectual, to sustain into the future. The Bowers brothers, principals of the novel's argument, share an inward communal turn and a limited sense of political geography—figuring "white" territory as Grays Ferry rather than Center City or the suburbs—that, while surely appropriate to the neighborhood boundary disputes of midcentury, seem naively parochial in light of the forces already in motion on South Street. The novel's counterargument presents those forces—embodied in Kristin, Pete, and the Mayor—as in fact *not* external even to the mythic neighborhood formation constructed by the novel's argument. The Citizens' Council on City Planning and the Greater Philadelphia Movement came into being to influence the outcomes of vast metropolitan processes like suburbanization and redevelopment, a drastic reshap-

ing of the city as part of a significant spatial redistribution of capital and population. These are not "outside" forces; rather, they operate at a grander scale
than that of the neighborhood, and *South Street* shows that the Bowers brothers
remain unequipped by their unrelievedly local sense of neighborhood to grasp
this fact in the way that Lil and the Blues Singer do.

Read against the scale of time and space on which the comprehensive plan
pursues its vision of the metropolitan future, Claude's epic struggle to return to
the local becomes a retreat. Let us return once more to his climactic walk on
South Street, when he concludes that this return provides a way to throw off
moral and intellectual paralysis by stepping within a charmed communal circle:
"endless, baffling Time and endless, terrifying Space? One could, should, be
aware of them, in wonder and in awe. But one could not live in their contemplation; one could not live according to their all-paralyzing commentary. One
lived—whether one wanted to or not—in the bounded time and the bounded
space of one's own life and one's own world" (311). The grotesquely inflated
language makes us wonder, here and elsewhere, whether *South Street* is *being*
pretentious or poking fun *at* its characters' pretensions, but it is clear that Lil
and the Blues Singer have suggested a deflating irony that extends to Claude as
well. Without a grasp of the scale at which South Street's future was at that
moment being determined—and, in fact, retreating from any understanding of
that "baffling," "terrifying" scale—Claude is an urban intellectual destined to
receive a nasty surprise from his historical moment.

Looking back to *John Fury* and forward to the coming upheavals of the
1960s, we might begin moving toward subsequent acts of South Street's composite drama by imagining *South Street*'s historical moment more broadly. We
can read the novel as carrying us from horse-and-wagon Philadelphia, the
industrial city in which Smith's and the Bowers brothers' South Street thrived,
to the eve of a round of race riots ignited by stresses of the postwar period in
which that industrial neighborhood formation would suffer from disinvestment
and disruption. That historical sweep is figured in a runaway wagon episode
similar to Fury's vision at Mame's deathbed.

In the novel's first chapter, Slim's nephew Joe (later to receive a terrible
beating from the Grays Ferry Irish) loses control of a horse pulling a wagon
loaded with his friends. The runaway wagon makes a tour of the neighborhood,
west on Carpenter and north on Nineteenth, at the last with its wheels caught in
the streetcar tracks, before Slim regains control. Read with Fury's vision,
which depicts a personal defeat that *John Fury* expands into a communal and
generational one, the scene takes on new meaning. The defeat is again communal—with passengers aboard—and familial and generational, as the transfer of reins from Slim to his nephew Joe produces chaos. The wagon caught in
the streetcar tracks, like Fury's wagon racing along the railroad tracks and like

Algren's bewildered survivors contained by the El structure, images a people arriving at an urban limit. Like Fury's vision, this episode suggests that the passage of time, the unfolding of a future in the urban space delineated by the horse's route, will go hard on the community invested in that piece of terrain. Slim gets the reins back from Joe, but a deeper lack of control is foreshadowed: "outsiders" beat Joe, but Slim will be reminded of the arrangements of power within the neighborhood by a beating from his boss Pete, and in the aftermath Slim's girlfriend Lil will be forced to leave the city entirely.

The novel's final chapters introduce a still-germinating urban crisis, as Claude and Michael head off a riot brewing in the aftermath of Philip's death. The reader has been told that the riot has its origins in tensions particular to the moment: population pressure at the borders of an increasingly overcrowded ghetto, organized and violent teenage gangs, new currents of black nationalism. Claude and Michael must stop this riot before it destroys the neighborhood. (By the late 1960s, however, Smith's *Return to Black America* follows the logic of urban crisis in depicting the intellectual's duty as transforming the self-destructive riot into a well-planned insurrection, in large part by harnessing the violence of youth gangs.) *South Street*, then, wants to balance runaway urban process with local control as its community of characters effects a passage from horse-and-wagon Philadelphia to the postindustrial inner city on the sacred ground of their neighborhood.[22]

If John Fury "never has a word t'say but goes around thrashin niggers," we might say something similar of Michael Bowers, amending the phrase to reflect his incessant speech making and altering the racial epithet to describe whites. Rather than the raids on Grays Ferry, it is Michael's attack on a white man in the heart of Center City that points the way to the next phases of the South Street literature's composite drama.

Out walking on Market Street, Michael and Philip happen upon an argument between a white man and a black man, and, without ascertaining the issue at hand or what either party has to say, Michael pushes through the bystanders and levels the white man with a sucker punch. That moment of casual violence visited upon a white man on Market Street by a black man from South Philadelphia represents the Center City planners' worst nightmare, an obverse face of the cosmopolitan Center City urbanism so invitingly sketched out by the comprehensive plan. Unlike the sharply delineated frontier at Grays Ferry Avenue, *South Street* renders the border between Center City and South Philadelphia as vague and permeable. Philip and Michael wander up to Market Street for a movie and a bit of unscheduled racial violence; Philip and Margaret also stroll up to Market Street for a movie and walk back through Rittenhouse Square, "past the pleasant streets, then across Lombard and South again, and on into the gloomier neighborhoods" (21).

Philadelphia's planners intended the Crosstown Expressway not only to carry traffic but to form Center City's clearly defined southern boundary, to "reinforce the margins," helping to produce "a clear and forceful image of a desirable physical environment, related to some definite physical symbol."[23] A product of the 1950s, the plan thought primarily in terms of traffic flows and of elegant design on the grand scale. Reinforcing the margins of Center City should not be read as a transparently coded rationale for building the expressway to keep black people (and other South Philadelphians) out. But as the 1960s wore on, and especially after Philadelphia's riot of 1964 helped to usher in the urban crisis, planners and business activists on one side and anti-Crosstown forces on the other did come to see the Crosstown as just such a social barrier. The plan was not ready to consider (and never mentioned) the fear of criminal violence, whether in the form of riot or mugging, that would during the urban crisis of the 1960s become a principal figure of inner-city social pathology and a principal rebuttal to the plan's vision of the urban future.

Racial violence, and violence in general, has been a favored means of representing postindustrial urbanism, the abrupt emergence of which was attended not only by violence in the streets but also by parallel wrenches and dislocations in the city of feeling. Michael's punch, and its repercussions in the novel and in the composite narrative recounted by the South Street literature, is charged with the deep-sunk force of postindustrial transformation. The further consequences of that transformation, coming into view as the postindustrial inner city matured in the 1970s, 1980s, and 1990s, are sketched by the three novels that make up the South Street literature's postindustrial phase.

The Literature of Post-industrial South Street

The street lay like a snake sleeping; dull-dusty, gray-black.

David Bradley, *South Street*

Reading the South Street literature from midcentury into the 1970s, 1980s, and 1990s, during and after the playing out of the transformations still on the horizon at midcentury, one sees a mixture of persistence and succession in both literary form and urban order. Even though the language changes, sex and violence become abundantly more explicit and carry more and more of the burden of meaning, and, most important, fifty years of urban history leave marks on plot and landscape, many of the literary forms familiar from *John Fury* and Smith's *South Street* persist. Neighborhood novels continue to explore the tension between the metropolitan and the local via family narratives, expressive landscapes, runaway scenes, and the presence of writer-characters struggling to make sense of the neighborhood in crisis and its relation to the metropolis. In spite of the enormous changes wrought by postindustrial transformation, elements of familiar neighborhood orders persist as well. The semidesolate black community of David Bradley's South Street, blasted by urban renewal in the 1950s and 1960s, still sustains in its bars and churches the vitality identified by William Gardner Smith. The rowhoused white-ethnic enclave of God's Pocket, fiercely struggling against the grain of urban change, descends directly from John Fury's immigrant-ethnic industrial village. *Tumbling* returns to Smith's Black Metropolis to trace a black family's and a black neighborhood's struggles against history in the form of the Crosstown Expressway plan. Bradley's *South*

Street, Pete Dexter's *God's Pocket*, and Diane McKinney-Whetstone's *Tumbling* spin out the human meanings of the urban transformation still impending in the midcentury novels: their unifying context is the tension between persistence and succession of urban orders during the maturing of the postindustrial inner city.

Unlike Jack Dunphy and William Gardner Smith, both of whom grew up in South Philadelphia's industrial neighborhood order and left it to pursue the literary life in faraway places, their three successors converged on postindustrial South Street from all over the map. Neither Dunphy nor Smith had a college degree (Smith dropped out of Temple University to write full-time), and both served in the armed forces, a standard route to middle-class status for children of the working class in the 1940s. Their three successors all have college degrees and did no military service. Dunphy and Smith wrote their way out of the neighborhood into a wider world; their three successors began their literary careers by writing their way *into* the neighborhoods of South Philadelphia and the bony substructure of urbanism to be found in them.

David Bradley, born in 1950 and raised in a minister's family in the small town of Bedford on the edge of Pennsylvania's soft-coal country, crossed the Schuylkill River to South Street in the late 1960s. Uncomfortable with life as a black undergraduate at the University of Pennsylvania, where he found no satisfaction in the company of politically engaged black students or in studying the stock portraits of "pathological" ghetto life offered by the booming field of urban studies, he found his way to the downscale community of South Street's bars. In the wake of almost two decades of disinvestment and neighborhood erosion, the seedy, transient quality of western South Street's flophouses and bars was a long way from the Ivy League campus, and Bradley could get there in fifteen minutes' walking. He began writing *South Street*, his first published novel, while still an undergraduate. His second novel, *The Chaneysville Incident*, a meditation on history and race—via an account of the Underground Railroad—that has been widely acclaimed and regarded as a more "mature" work, returned to the setting of small-town Pennsylvania.[1]

Pete Dexter, who is white, came from even further afield to find the material for his first novel in South Philadelphia. Born in Michigan in 1943, raised in Georgia and South Dakota, fitfully educated at the University of South Dakota, having driven a truck, worked construction, sorted mail, and tried to be a salesman, he found his way into reporting in Florida and ended up at the *Philadelphia Daily News* in the 1970s. The often-repeated story of how he took up novel writing as a serious vocation turns on a beating administered to him—and a friend, the catcher's mitt–faced heavyweight boxer Randall "Tex" Cobb—by a group of bat- and tire-iron-wielding readers. They were displeased with a column Dexter had written about a drug-related murder in their neighborhood, a small enclave known as Devil's Pocket located below South Street on the extreme western edge of South Philadelphia. As Dexter tells it, the blows that broke his back and hip were less life-changing than those to his head, which altered his sense of taste permanently. Now that alcohol "tasted like battery acid" to him and he no longer had any desire to spend his spare time in bars, he had the equivalent of several workdays' extra time per week on his hands and devoted it to finishing his first novel and writing several more.[2] *God's Pocket*, that first novel, is set in South Philadelphia and culminates in the fatal beating of a reporter. That beating resembles the one Dexter suffered, but Richard Shellburn, the character in the novel, does not resemble Dexter; Shellburn has run dry, and the men who kill him are in a sense helping him to give up the struggle of writing; Dexter, on the other hand, became a prolific novelist in the 1980s and 1990s, shifting among regions (South Philly in *God's Pocket* and *Brotherly Love*, the Wild West in *Deadwood*, the small-town South in *Paris Trout*, Florida's swamp country in *The Paperboy*) and subjects (although returning often to racial conflict and the inner lives of working people), garnering awards (including the National Book Award for *Paris Trout*), a wide readership, and the inevitable invitations to write screenplays for Hollywood movies. In Dexter's autobiographical account of the making of a reporter into a writer, the blows visited upon him in the street literalize the shaping influence of the city of fact on the city of feeling: one can almost picture him taking notes as his antagonists hammer away.

Diane McKinney-Whetstone, born in the early 1950s, moved away from South Philadelphia when she was a small child. Her parents, responding to rumors of the Crosstown plan, sold the family's rowhouse at Sixteenth and Fitzwater in the 1950s and bought a larger house on Chestnut Street in West Philadelphia, part of the postwar exodus of the black middle class from South Philadelphia to what they hoped were more stable neighborhoods. Her mother was a native South Philadelphian, raised in Queen Village; her father came north from Atlanta in the 1940s. The family prospered in Philadelphia: their catering business on Catharine Street did well, and the father got into Democratic politics, eventually serving two terms in the state Senate. Diane McKinney-Whetstone got her college degree from the University of Pennsylvania, started a career as a public affairs officer for the federal government, and came to fiction writing through a class at Penn, a writers' workshop, and enthusiastic reading in the black urban canon (Wright, Ellison, Baldwin, Morrison, Naylor). *Tumbling*, her first novel and indeed her first attempt at a sustained writing project, began as a contemporary story, but she found herself pulled back to the 1940s and 1950s by period detail and her parents' memories of the old neighborhood.[3]

Unlike the first, this second generation of South Street writers was not homegrown. Their convergence on the neighborhoods of upper South Philadelphia from various directions reinforces two important points about the relation of writers to the neighborhoods they map. First, the relation is not a matter of breeding. Writers do not magically grow from the places and the people they represent in their neighborhood novels. Writers make their way to their subject by various routes through the social landscape and their reading and training, and the encounters of all three writers discussed in this chapter with the postindustrial inner city have been conditioned by some of the same forces that shape the neighborhoods in their novels. Second, the neighborhood is as much a starting point as a destination, even for writers who come to it from somewhere else. All three of the books discussed in this chapter are first novels, and Bradley and Dexter have gone on to write considerably more celebrated books about places and people far removed from the South Philadelphia neighborhoods mapped in their first novels. (McKinney-Whetstone has just embarked on a promising career; at this writing, she is at work on a second novel, set in West Philadelphia in the 1960s.) The South Street literature has been a kind of staging ground in which urban intellectuals take credentialing first steps into literary life. The novels imagine those steps as fraught with the possibilities and danger native to the postindustrial inner city—Bradley's poet-protagonist gets knifed, Dexter's reporter gets killed—so that the work of urban intellectuals forms part of the novels' dramatic action. All of the novels consider explicitly or implicitly the relationship of the urban intellectual to the social landscape, itself in motion, in which he or she moves.

South Street (1975)

David Bradley's *South Street*, like Smith's novel of the same name of twenty-one years before, opens with a pass down South Street ending, in the second paragraph, at a bar.[4]

> The street lay like a snake sleeping; dull-dusty, gray-black in the dingy darkness. At the three-way intersection of Twenty-second Street, Grays Ferry Avenue, and South Street a fountain, erected once-upon-a-year by a ladies' guild in fond remembrance of some dear departed altruist, stood cracked and dry, full of dead leaves and cigarette butts and bent beer cans, forgotten by the city and the ladies' guild, functionless, except as a minor memorial to how They Won't Take Care Of Nice Things. . . .
> There was no one on the corner where Grays Ferry met Twenty-second and Twenty-second met South: the police, spying any of the local citizens, assumed they were there to rob the liquor store or the food market, and ran the duly convicted offender away. But a little way downtown, near the junction of a nameless alley and South Street was a dim entranceway, a hole in the wall with a thick wooden door hanging open, and out of it came belches of heavy-beating jukebox music and stale tobacco smoke.[5]

Smith's street has changed in the intervening years. The crowds of shirt-sleeved "brown pedestrians" are gone; the war with the Irish of Grays Ferry seems to be over; Smith's bright, populous day has given way to gray-black, depopulated evening. The three-way intersection at Grays Ferry Avenue and South Street (Bradley makes Twenty-second, rather than Twenty-third, the cross street) serves not as a frontier in space but in time—marked not by the post that separated black South Street from Irish Grays Ferry (a boundary consecrated with Philip Bowers's blood) but by the fountain that separates an age of Nice Things and ladies' guilds from one of garbage and liquor store holdups.[6] Claude Bowers, drinking his beer and looking dreamily down the avenue into Grays Ferry, would never even think of tossing his empty in the fountain; his counterpart in Bradley's novel, the poet Adlai Stevenson Brown, idly tosses empty bottles wherever he pleases or "airmails" garbage bags from his window into the alley, where they burst and add their contents to the detritus collected there. The "great blood vein of a people" has become "a snake sleeping": the street, and the representative urban intellectual to be found on it, has molted in significant ways in the two decades since Claude Bowers's neighborhood-affirming walk down South Street.

Bradley's *South Street*, being a subtly efficient novel beneath its tendency to sprawl, suggests in its third paragraph a reason for the change: "The traffic light at the intersection changed. A flood of cars accelerated away from the corner, their lowered headlights reflecting in pools of the soft tar of the street" (6). One of these cars runs over a stray cat, leading to an extended scene of miscommunication, built around the phrase "some cat," in which the patrons of the "hole in the wall" bar (Lightnin' Ed's) understand the car's driver, a well-intentioned white man, to mean that he has just run over a black man in the street and wants a shovel with which to hide the body in a garbage can. On Smith's midcentury street, "brown pedestrians" dominated the traffic; cars, with racially unspecified drivers, crawled along honking their horns. On Bradley's postcrisis street, a "flood of cars" rushes through the void, carrying white people to distant metropolitan destinations. Although the Crosstown Expressway was never built, South Street has been reshaped by metropolitan imperatives, embodied in the suburbanite's murderous car, that the Crosstown was intended to serve. The novel's opening episode closes with the driver leaving the scene: "As the car accelerated, turned the corner, vanished into the night, the bloody remains of the cat dropped off the fender and onto the street" (9).

One can imagine a neighborhood novel written after the 1960s that shows the success of local resistance to urban renewal and redevelopment, a novel about a changing neighborhood's ability to reproduce itself and determine to some degree its own future. *Tumbling*, discussed below, is that kind of novel. Bradley's *South Street*, set primarily on South Street's most run-down and least conventionally neighborly western end, is emphatically not such a novel, undertaking instead to figure the "bloody remains" of South Street—what is left after

Smith's neighborhood has been run over and left, back-broken, for dead by the comprehensive plan. These remains, surprisingly, are yet twitching with the vitality of neighborhood, although the Bowers brothers' fantasy of hermetic and self-sustaining localism has been exploded by two decades of engagement with large-scale processes of urban change.

Bradley's South Street twitches as well with literary vitality. Like Smith's novel, Bradley's takes form around the problem of placing the right kind of urban intellectual on South Street so that he can do the work of representing it. When we read the two novels together, the poet Brown becomes an extension and in some ways a critique of the Bowers brothers. Bradley wrote his South Street novel in the late 1960s and early 1970s, after the Crosstown plan, the urban crisis, the redevelopment of Center City, and other elements of Philadelphia's postindustrial transformation had made it clear that forces operating on the metropolitan scale could overwhelm Claude Bowers's intensely local notions of neighborhood. Adlai Brown's central task and achievement, as the protagonist of Bradley's *South Street*, is to negotiate the play of historical forces and urban processes on both the metropolitan and the local scales in such a way as to place himself, an urban intellectual with pen in hand, within the transformed but still-vital neighborhood order of South Street. So positioned, Brown is ready to enter into conversation with a variety of American culture makers, from television news producers to the urban sociologists that Bradley read and despised at the University of Pennsylvania, who have since the urban crisis of the 1960s portrayed the black inner city as a "pathological" ghetto defined by the absence of those community-building orders that give the quality of neighborhood to an urban place.

Opening in a wasteland but finding its way soon enough to the music and smoke of Lightnin' Ed's, the novel immediately asserts one of its fundamental premises, which we might summarize as an updating of Smith's phrase to read: "*Life!* There is *still* life in the air of South Street!" We might read its complicated character system and several threads of narrative, some more or less integrated into larger stories and some resolved in relative isolation from the others, as designed to accrue the quality of neighborhood, the texture and depth of a way of life. The coming to South Street of Adlai Brown, a bad poet but an accomplished drunk; Brown's feud with the pimp and hustler Leroy Briggs; the troubles between Rayburn, a janitor, and his wife, Leslie, who leaves him for Leroy; the intertwined sorrows and little victories of the ex-prostitute Vanessa and the veteran prostitute Big Betsy, the wino Jake, and Leo, owner of Lightnin' Ed's; the fall of the shifty Reverend Sloan and the moral salvation of Sloan's successor Brother Fletcher by Leo the barman—if all these pieces are not made to add up to a single culminative moment like Claude Bowers's return to South Street, they do weave loosely together to suggest the messy vitality of a community subsisting where at first glance there seem to be only ruins and casualties.

This neighborhood takes spatial form around what one reader has aptly described as the novel's "three social and cultural centers": Lightnin' Ed's bar, the Elysium Hotel (Leroy's headquarters), and Reverend Sloan's (and ultimately Brother Fletcher's) Word of Life church.[7] The majority of the novel's characters move from grubby walk-up apartments in the area's decaying industrial-era building stock through desolate streetscapes to Lightnin' Ed's or the Elysium, where they drink and mix with the others, returning home to fight, fornicate, and perform other closely detailed bodily functions. If Smith's largely faceless crowd has dispersed—one gets the sense that the named characters of Bradley's novel form a significant proportion of South Street's remaining residents—the interweaving paths of the remaining few in their ceaseless travel up and down South Street create a spare but complex network of community.

William Gardner Smith's South Street community took shape over and against an outside order expressed spatially by the clearly delineated border with Grays Ferry. If Kristin proved over time to be the greater "threat" to black South Street, it was still Grays Ferry that embodied a neighboring "outside" terrain against which Smith's South Street cohered. Bradley's South Street borders the high-rise Philadelphia of Center City. The boundary between South Street and Center City, left vague and permeable in the geographical imagination of Smith's novel, becomes crisply delineated in Bradley's. Crossing it is almost a bodily experience. Walking south from the redeveloped upscale preserve of Rittenhouse Square, Brown enters the buffer zone between Center City and South Philadelphia, "the half block of dilapidation that preceded South Street." The change happens without modulation, "like the snapping of a switch, the crossing of a threshold." It feels "as if, crossing the visible border, Brown left something like a piece of luggage in a coin locker, and on the other side he picked up the piece of luggage he had deposited there at his last crossing" (143–44). Compare this to the mild frisson felt by Philip Bowers as he makes the exact same crossing in an earlier period: "A gentle depression flitted briefly across Philip's heart; it was banished as soon as he pressed Margaret's hand."[8] Brown and Vanessa do more than hold hands, and, rather than mitigating the force of this threshold sensation, Vanessa's body *reminds* Brown of the poverty and decay that define South Street as a distinct place. "'You wanted to know what I thought about when I looked at you,'" Brown says after she reads some of his poetry. "'There it is.'" Vanessa answers: "'Yeah. Garbage. Rats. Roaches. Drunks. Jesus, Brown'" (192).

Movement across the sharply defined threshold dividing South Street from Center City allows the novel's terrain to make available explanations for the forms it takes, especially through its imagining of metropolitan forces shaping South Street. Bradley's novel laughs off the local "threat" from white ethnics with the device of Leroy's unfounded worry that an "Italian army" of Brown's supposed allies will invade South Street at any moment, but the novel takes very seriously the power of city-shaping forces concentrated in Center City banks to arrange the novel's world. In other words, it reverses the priorities of Smith's novel by turning its back on Grays Ferry and the other white-ethnic remnants of the industrial neighborhood order to attend to South Street's encounter with Center City.

The key figure in this regard is Rayburn, a hard-drinking and relentlessly cuckolded janitor who cleans the executive suites of a bank in a high-rise office building on Market Street. First, Rayburn's walks to and from work reveal the novel's split streetscape: a declining foreground of dilapidated or demolished industrial-era buildings against a prospective background of high rises under construction. On Fifth Street, for instance, "an uneven lane of cobblestones and trolley tracks that dated from sometime before the Civil War," a demolition project clears the "blight" of the post–Civil War industrial city from the flanks of redeveloped Society Hill. A giant wrecking crane dominates the scene, and "there was no traffic now except for the dump trucks trundling away loads of rubble from the buildings being razed in an urban-redevelopment project. . . . Beyond the hulks of the houses was a pit where a high-rise apartment building would one day stand" (18–19). Second, the Center City bank at which Rayburn works suggests the logic ordering this landscape, the concatenation of interests and motives driving the remaking of Center City Philadelphia. The novel's split cityscape expresses a simplified vision of the postindustrial city: high rises and rehabilitated housing on one side of the split, the surviving unrehabilitated building stock of previous eras on the other. For Rayburn, the service economy means crossing the divide to clean toilets in the workplaces where professionals handle information for a living. Images of Rayburn at the bank after hours —on his knees in the bathrooms of the executive suite, lounging at the president's desk while fantasizing emptily about having power—make clear South Street's relation to the logic structuring this new city. The pattern of decisions pursued by the big downtown banks in the 1960s, which invested in Center City projects and disinvested from marginal areas like South Street, plays a crucial role in remaking the city and thus in shaping life on South Street.

The neighborhood's political, social, and economic relation to the metropolis is not in question: Center City and the suburbanites who drive to it have run over South Street and left it for dead, and the people of South Street are almost completely without power. As Bradley described them in an interview, "Their lives were terrible—they just lived with the situation and made the best of it."[9] If Bradley's novel wants to show how they improvise a community in these circumstances, it does not have any illusions about that community's power to determine its own destiny. The active, unresolved problem that makes the novel go is the literary, not the social, problem of neighborhood: the poet Brown has to find a way to the South Street neighborhood—so that he can write about it—

through a postindustrial metropolis seemingly bent on frustrating his literary project.

Placing Brown

The central problem of Bradley's novel, to the extent that it has one, strikingly resembles the literary problem of neighborhood in Smith's novel: an urban intellectual, the poet Brown, must be *placed* on South Street. This involves getting him out of a high-rise apartment and embedding him within the low-rise neighborhood textures of South Street in such a way that he can begin to write about it. It also involves Brown's abandoning Alicia, who, although she is black, is the novel's Kristin: Brown must stay away from South Street in order to be with Alicia, a well-to-do educated woman associated with the University of Pennsylvania, who plans to help him meet editors and get published. He therefore trades her for the unlettered Vanessa, who could not care less about his poetry but lives amid the rats and roaches of South Street he wants to write about. The resolution of the problem built around Brown intertwines with the novel's principal narrative lines and their resolutions: Rayburn finally breaks with his wife Leslie, who is then run out of town by the pimp Leroy as part of a new austerity program in the wake of his troubles with Brown; the wino Jake, who has been looking into Brown's background for the barman Leo, serendipitously turns up evidence of the Reverend Sloan's criminal past, causing Sloan's replacement by the humble Brother Fletcher; Brown's commitment to South Street, and thus to Vanessa (whose body we have seen rhymed with the street's physical form), coincides with Vanessa's ultimate success in achieving a long-sought-after orgasm; and so on.

However, unlike the placing of Claude Bowers, the placing of Brown on South Street does not present itself as an order-producing or -reproducing moment—organizing around it both the text's various pieces and its neighborhood—to which the novel has been building. Bradley's *South Street* arranges itself only loosely around the narrative spine formed by the placing of Brown, who is, after all, just a struggling poet who drinks too much. Brown's ambition to represent South Street stops at the limits of the representational. He does not aspire to the cultural and political representativeness that equips Claude Bowers and in some ways even Michael Bowers to speak *for*, rather than about, a people. Seen against the character system of the Bowers brothers, Brown appears as rather an inversion of Philip, a writer with purely literary ambitions pursuing precisely the enabling connection of literature to South Street that Philip failed to cultivate. If Brown in a sense replaces the wino Jake on South Street—since Jake's death frames Brown's final move to South Street—that replacement yields explicitly literary results: we see Brown at work rewriting a foul-mouthed doggerel "pome" that Jake recited to him. *South Street* makes no argument about succession or representativeness in the progression from Jake to Brown (unless one argues that Brown, if he succeeds as a writer, will, like Kristin and Claude Bowers, be a good candidate to buy and renovate a brownstone in advance of the coming gentrification). Brown's presence on South Street does not bind the neighborhood's generations into a continuing line as Claude's purports to do.

There are, in fact, no generations to speak of. Unlike *John Fury*, William Gardner Smith's *South Street*, and the other South Street novels, Bradley's *South Street* does not employ the family narrative form to consider its neighborhood. The coupling of Brown and Vanessa does serve as the principal figure for Brown's placement on South Street, but the novel does not take up questions of succession, generation, and rise and decline typical of family narrative. The convention of good sex, rather than good children, indicates the fruitfulness of Brown's consummated arrival on South Street. This anomaly in the South Street literature makes a certain historical sense: Bradley's novel, written out of close (if selective) observation of South Street's older neighborhood formations in their moment of greatest disorder, imagines a South Street suspended in the present. The neighborhood's past has been erased by urban renewal projects and related dislocations; its future is still to be determined by flows of capital directed from Center City. Unlike Smith's, Bradley's novel does not conceive of its central problem's resolution as an event ordering or indicative of South Street's future. There are couples and households in crisis in Bradley's novel, and those crises are resolved in ways that indicate the neighborhood's continuing vitality—Brother Fletcher regains his wife's respect by taking over the church, Brown regains his self-respect by choosing Vanessa over Alicia—but these families and couples do not offer a model of generational succession. If Smith's novel is equally childless (pointing to the Kristin-centered counterargument's undermining of the Claude-centered argument for self-sustaining community), it at least explicitly imagines a generational progression and puts forward leaders to guide the community into the future.

By crossing the river to South Street, then, Brown enters into a spatially bounded network of stories and characters—a neighborhood formation—that he has no ability to order, not (yet) even in his writing. That crossing, however, begins to make Brown into an efficacious urban intellectual. The kitchen drawer full of poems and notes in his South Street apartment suggests that he will in time evolve the representational skills required by his subject matter, the fragment of black inner city at the heart of postindustrial Philadelphia's social landscape.

Brown crosses and recrosses the Schuylkill, passing back and forth between urban worlds, until he crosses it for good in the novel's last scene. The three-towered form of Alicia's high-rise apartment complex encapsulates the world he leaves. This "trio of high-rise apartment buildings that erupted from the asphalt like acne blemishes" (45) calls to mind I. M. Pei's triple high-rise centerpiece for the Society Hill development, one of the earliest and most widely applauded efforts to remake the residential landscape of Center City for a population of new urbanites. The novel places that distinctive three-tower complex—a form that signified redevelopment for many Philadelphians in the 1960s—on Spruce Street west of the Schuylkill, near the University of Pennsylvania campus, where no such private development with that distinctive monumental form existed. By "moving" the three-towered form from the eastern edge of Center City to the western edge, by melding Center City and Penn, the novel neatly schematizes its split Philadelphia along the single axis formed by South and Spruce streets. Brown, as a black urban intellectual, is thus "always" on South Street, even when separated from South Street proper by the river, the change of street name to Spruce, the high-rise remove of Alicia's apartment, and association with the university that forms one of the centers of the city's postindustrial economy.

In shuttling between three-towered Philadelphia, where he lives, and South Street, where he drinks, Brown has literally to turn his back on South Street to reach Alicia's building: "He walked to the corner of Thirty-third, contemplating an accident of the city's geography: on his left was South Street; on his right, the same street was Spruce. Brown looked to his left. Then he turned the other way and began to move west on Spruce, breaking into a jog as if he were in a rush to get away from the intersection" (45). The city's geography forces him to decide between antithetical options, propelling him "in a rush" away from the uncomfortable point where both confront him. The retreat to Alicia's apartment, however, produces a crisis for Brown as a writer. Although he is figuratively still on South Street, he finds himself engaging with the city at a grand metropolitan scale, the scale available to the information-handling classes who get their training at universities and inhabit luxury high rises, that denies him access to the raw materials of his subject matter. The crisis can only be resolved by the opposite movement, back across the dividing line to South Street and the local scale, where those materials can be recognized and confronted.

Brown's move to South Street happens as a series of steps away from the understanding of the city to be gained from Alicia's apartment. High up on her balcony, Brown on two occasions looks out upon the city's geography. His first survey takes in refineries to the south, Fairmount Park to the north, and Center City to the east (both Fairmount Park and Center City being showpieces of Philadelphia's postwar refashioning) but averts itself from South Street: "Brown's eyes wandered slightly south, along Spruce Street until it reached the Schuylkill. He snorted and turned away" (47). His second survey from the balcony, two days later, essays the opposite course, forgoing the panoramic view and narrowing itself to the Spruce-South axis. Brown's gaze follows a bus headed east on Spruce "as it creeped across the bridge and dipped down onto South Street. Brown stared after it as it gradually lost itself in traffic." The effort to follow the bus from his elevation as it disappears into the street-level fabric of South Street makes the whiskey he has been drinking turn to acid in his stomach, inducing a powerful wave of nausea. He lets "the bottle fall away, twenty-four stories, to shatter beyond recognition in the street below" (96). The next and last time Brown surveys this view, he does so from the modest elevation of the South Street bridge—an intimate vantage point almost within the streetscape itself—and when he leaves the bridge it is to walk east, descending into South Street itself for good.

Brown's movement between landscapes constitutes not only a shift from redeveloped core to ghetto but also a shift in scales, from the generality of metropolitan Philadelphia to the locality of the street. The expansive geography available to him from Alicia's balcony obscures from view his (and the novel's) literary subject, expressed as South Street's detritus-strewn streetscape. He wants to "write poems about rats and roaches and garbage" (327) and in so doing to write about what Alicia's doorman calls the "sorry-ass niggers that couldn't afford nothin' else" (46), but he cannot see the street from Alicia's balcony: the bottle he throws from Alicia's balcony passes from view as it moves to the scale of the street, ending up "beyond recognition in the street below." Brown's shuttling between landscapes produces an incapacitating dissonance between the metropolitan and local scales and between the violently antithetical worlds of the three-towered apartment complex and the garbage-strewn neighborhood street. His nausea, triggered by an attempt to see South Street as part of the landscape made available from Alicia's balcony, expresses a kind of authorial vertigo produced by this dissonance. Brown's only literary ambition or capacity is to write about South Street. Presented as a strict neighborhood realist who must literally keep his subject matter in view in order to write about it (much like Nelson Algren, who always maintained that "the only way I can work is up close"), he must cross the river once and for all to gain access to the material that constitutes his subject matter.[10]

In the novel's last scene, Brown's final crossing of the South Street bridge takes the form, familiar in the South Street literature, of a runaway and arrival at an urban limit. Having promised a doubtful Vanessa that he will return to her and South Street, Brown walks a block up to Lombard Street to catch a westbound bus to a cocktail party at Alicia's apartment across the river. To get back to Alicia's he must cross the significant South–Spruce divide, returning to three-towered Philadelphia. From the bus, Brown catches stroboscopic views of South Street through gaps in the gentrifying landscape of Lombard Street, indicating that Brown finds himself poised one last time between the two urban worlds. The appearance on the bus of the janitor Rayburn, soiled and stinking from a night's drinking, ushers in the novel's final crisis. Rayburn, whose fan-

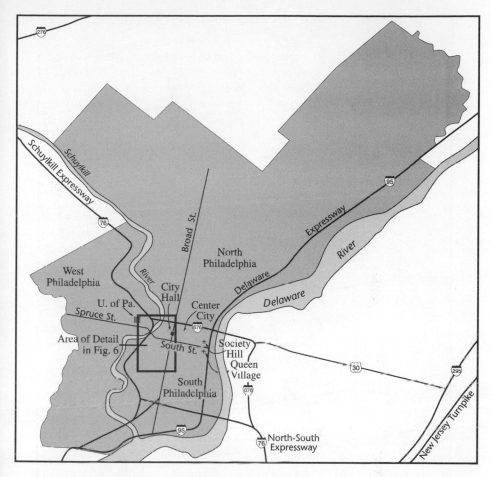

Figure 5. Philadelphia. University of Wisconsin Cartographic Laboratory.

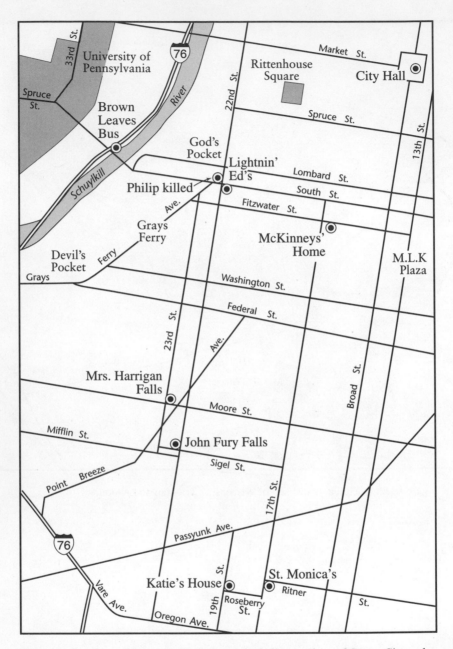

Figure 6. Detail map of western South Street, including portions of Center City and South Philadelphia. University of Wisconsin Cartographic Laboratory.

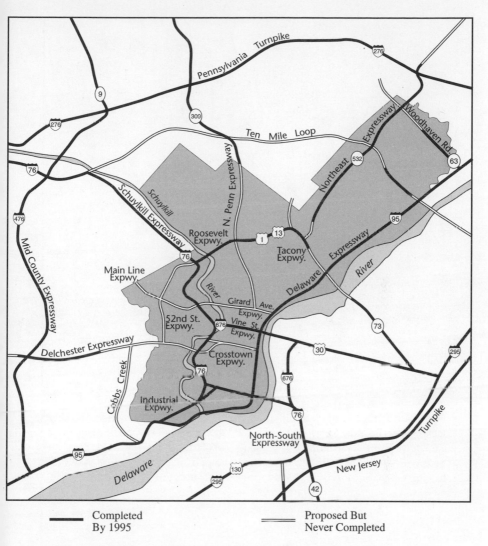

Figure 7. Philadelphia expressways as proposed in 1960. The planned Crosstown Expressway is at lower center. University of Wisconsin Cartographic Laboratory.

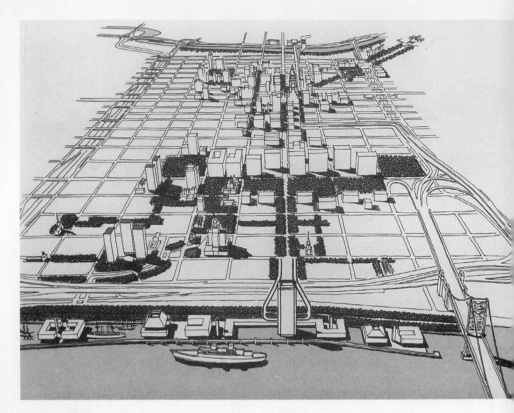

Figure 8. "The Image of Philadelphia," from the *Center City Plan*. An idealized view looking west from the Delaware River toward the Schuylkill River. The planned Crosstown Expressway forms the left (southern) border of the view; I. M. Pei's trio of Society Hill towers is in the left foreground. (From Edmund Bacon, *Design of Cities*, p. 249.) GBQC Architects. Reprinted with permission of GBQC Architects.

tasy life revolves around leaving his unfaithful wife and going far away from South Street, tells Brown that this time he means to leave for good: "'I gots to be flyin'. I got ma transfer.' He held it up. 'You see, I'm on my way'" (339). Brown responds, "'I see,'" and, suddenly seeing clearly the danger of transferring or separating from South Street, decides to get off the bus, which has by now crossed the river by the South Street bridge and arrived at the traffic light controlling entrance to the Schuylkill Expressway.

In that moment, Brown's bus ride has reached an urban limit, with the postindustrial expressway updating a function served by the industrial railroad tracks in the runaway wagon scenes in *John Fury* and Smith's *South Street*. A carefully choreographed sequence has carried Brown through the novel's signifying split landscape to the place where the Crosstown would have begun; just beyond is the place where South becomes Spruce. The Schuylkill Expressway marks the point where Brown's will, operating at a local street-level scale, intersects with the metropolitan-scale forces—figured by the expressway in this scene, the high-rise office towers in others—that shape the city in which he moves. Brown makes the driver let him out, although there is no official stop there, and walks back across the river to South Street. Brown's success in placing himself on South Street takes the form of a final decision *not* to cross the dividing line. Unlike Fury and Slim on their runaway wagons, Brown exercises his will to stop the runaway and get what he wants. The difference is that what he wants is to write, not to safeguard and sustain the neighborhood's way of life: in fact, the more spectacular the decay of the old neighborhood's way of life, the better for a poet who seeks out the romantic ruins of dying urban orders. Like Kristin, another artistic proto-yuppie and a fellow connoisseur of urban grit, Brown has to work hard to get *inside* the ambit of his urban limit, to enter the neighborhood landscape. Thus his failure to recross that limit can be presented as an important exercise of will. Brown has learned the lessons taught by Kristin and the South Street literature's previous runaways, though: unlike Claude Bowers, Brown returns to the South Street neighborhood equipped with a rich sense of its limits as constituted by, rather than shutting out, the metropolis.

The Accreditation Drama

Brown's climactic return to South Street clinches *South Street*'s argument about the writer's relation to the postindustrial city it has imagined, presenting South Street as the place that enables and produces the literature of neighborhood. The three-way intersection at Grays Ferry Avenue and South Street serves as yet another kind of boundary, in this case between not writing and writing. It marks the place where literature—this novel itself, as well as Brown's access to his subject matter—begins as we repeat the movement of the novel's opening scene in a descent eastward into South Street from the South Street bridge. Having gotten off the bus and begun one last descent from the bridge as the novel ends, Brown will pass through this airlock and enact once more his move into the local scale, the streetscape richly strewn with fetid details (versus the unwritable, because invisible, streetscape below Alicia's balcony), and the neighborhood order marked by the outpost of Lightnin' Ed's just off to his right. He will pass, therefore, into the novel's literature-producing landscape, the place that determines his ability to write even about the rest of the city, which only has meaning in relation to South Street—reversing in literary terms the lesson of conflicting urban scales, which is that South Street's meaning and social fate depend on its relation to the metropolis. *South Street* thus puts forward an argument for South Street as enabling and accrediting a specific kind of inner-city intellectual—a realist writer—that Brown will struggle to become (and that Bradley, by virtue of writing the novel, can lay claim to being). The novel thereby extends the South Street literature's project of imagining the formation of urban intellectuals suited to the task of writing the inner city. The novel's climax occurs when the poet Brown, turning back at the expressway, saves himself—not the neighborhood.

The problem of the novel is not the survival of a neighborhood but the question of whether and how Brown will write. Voices in the novel link the "wrong" kind of writing to urban sociology, canonical in the 1960s (and since then), that labeled black inner-city neighborhoods as ghettos defined by pathologies and lack of sustaining order. The critic Albert Murray has derided this stock portrait of the second ghetto—an antineighborhood, antithetical to the immigrant-ethnic "ghetto of opportunity"—as "social science fiction," written by and for people steeped in conventional wisdom, that serves to reinforce the most addled and sensational myths about cities and race.[11] Both Alicia and Vanessa accuse Brown, a poet, of being a sociologist or anthropologist of the participant-observer type associated with the Chicago School's inquiry into city life. The imputation here is that he is writing social science fiction, and the charge leveled against him is one of inauthenticity: if Brown continues to see South Street from the perspective of a slumming researcher, the kind of distanced view available from Alicia's balcony, then he will not write South Street as anything other than a set of sociological truisms and stock images of pathology and disorder.

The question of authenticity provides the dramatic tension in Brown's climactic bus ride, during which he significantly encounters an acquaintance: Earl, "a thin, well-dressed black man" reading the *New York Times Book Review*, a kind of updated version of Philip Bowers's literary cronies. Earl's greeting, "'Hey, brother, I hear you been way down in the jungle, as the sayin' goes'" (336), echoes the title of Roger Abrahams's *Deep Down in the Jungle* (1964), a scholarly study of black urban folklore collected in the marginal neighborhoods around South Street. This book first directed Bradley's interest to South Street, and its emphasis on African survivals in a thriving neighborhood culture would seem to promise just the kind of portrait of black community that Bradley sought in response to the period's standard sociological portraits of the black inner city.[12] Indeed, Bradley has suggested that one motivation for writing about South Street was to find a position opposed to the emphasis of sociologists like Daniel Patrick Moynihan on ghetto pathology. "The book was sort of a reaction to my sociology professors" and "sociology à la Moynihan," Bradley said in 1990.[13] But Bradley did not see urban folklorists like Abrahams as allies in this project: their efforts to identify a peculiarly African or African American brand of community in the black inner city nettle Bradley, who has often spoken against the folklorists' naive antiurbanism and their tendency to see African survivals preserved in amber where he sees a living urban heterogeny.[14] (Criticizing Abrahams's naiveté in particular, Bradley claims that several people on South Street assured him they told Abrahams whatever he wanted to hear about the African roots of verse forms and Southern folk life in order to keep flowing the wine he provided.)[15] Earl's greeting, then, throws him together with both the folklorists and the social pathologists against whom Bradley, the disgruntled University of Pennsylvania undergraduate, saw himself as writing *South Street*. Earl's "jungle" image condenses *both* standard, often opposed, understandings of the ghetto: the social pathologists' (ghetto as opposed to civilization) and the folklorists' (ghetto as primal Africa). Brown, therefore, must get away from Earl, which he does when he gets off the bus.

Brown represents that elusive third position Bradley sought: more sophisticated than the folklorists about the shaping forces and deceptions of the metropolis, more attuned to the quality of neighborhood than the social pathologists. The novel indicates Brown's attainment of that position in a series of figures of violence and sexual prowess. The point of these depictions of Brown's bodily engagement with the landscape is to establish him within the network of exchanges that constitutes the South Street community, not on Alicia's balcony with Earl and other readers of Moynihan or Abrahams.

South Street, extending Algren's fetish for writing "up close," wants to say that Brown is part of the world he observes, a relation to his "material" that makes for authenticity in what he writes. Earl, by way of contrast, takes pains to separate himself from the physical manifestations of South Street: he is prissily appalled by the stinking-drunk Rayburn, and he is unable to understand why Brown has left Alicia's body and Alicia's Philadelphia for Vanessa's. "'I heard a sacrificin' yourself to your art,'" Earl says on the bus, "'but that, brother, is takin' that shit too far'" (337). Brown pursues precisely the physical engagement with South Street that Earl avoids. Brown's habit of airmailing garbage bags from his window into the alley marks him as a resident, rather than an observer, of South Street. Contributing his share of garbage to the garbage-strewn streets marks Brown not just as a man who writes about garbage but also as a "producer" of garbage, a man helping to generate the raw materials and landscape—the city of fact—that constitute his literary subject. Since Brown (whose sexual politics, like the novel's, makes Nelson Algren seem like Simone de Beauvoir in comparison) sees Vanessa as South Street personified, sex with her becomes a figure of intimate bodily engagement with South Street—her long-awaited orgasm serving in this case as a predictable assurance of authenticity. Brown makes a detailed exchange of materials with South Street: drinking its liquor and delivering in exchange his own juices (urinating and vomiting in the street, having sex with Vanessa); writing its garbage and contributing his own in return.

Brown seems to be marking South Street, as would a dog, as his literary territory, and in turn South Street marks his body and thus his prose with the signs of an intimate engagement. Walking to the bus stop before his last ride, Brown sees South Street as "a knife cut slicing across the city, a surgeon's incision, oozing pus, stitched with numbered streets" (336). The knife cut on Brown's chest, legacy of an earlier disagreement with the razor-toting Rayburn, incarnates the street on Brown's body with the authenticating sign of violence (which, as I argue in part 3, took on new importance in representing the inner city and the place of urban intellectuals in it during the urban crisis of the 1960s; and which, as Pete Dexter's iconic story of beating and literary rebirth demonstrates, has become a staple of urban intellectuals' credentialing stories). Rayburn's razor, inscribing the "knife cut" on Brown himself, ratifies Brown's assertion that his move to South Street is more than a research project. Defending himself against Alicia's characterization of his move to South Street as "'a quest for reality in the capital-H heart of the capital-G ghetto with the capital-P people,'" Brown says, "'It's not a research project. And the middle of the ghetto isn't real. You don't cut with the side of a knife. Only the edge is real. And this is the edge'" (123). Insider access to that knife cut writ large as South Street accredits Brown and enables him to write past received clichés—"the middle of the ghetto"—into unmapped literary territory. The writer needs to get at this "surgeon's incision" in the urban fabric, where the metropolitan meets the local, because it reveals the structure of urban process and social fact underneath. The gaps and scars that make the landscape ugly, like the knife cut that makes Brown's body ugly, are openings from which flow history and literary possibilities. With Brown's entrance into this landscape, the futility of writing about or even looking at South Street from the metropolitan perspective of Alicia's balcony gives way to productivity, yielding the kitchen drawer crammed full of poetry about garbage, collected in bars and alleys, and written on garbage (paper bags and paper napkins). It follows that when Rayburn, the author of the knife cut on Brown's chest, appears on the bus, Brown is reminded of the proper relation between poet and street and returns once and for all to South Street.

Bradley's *South Street* places Brown on South Street so that he can write about a place, as Bradley did. Like William Gardner Smith, Bradley deploys his character system on a piece of terrain to make the conjunction of place and peoplehood, but Bradley's sense of place is conditioned by two decades of urban change. While Claude Bowers places himself, however problematically, in a community with borders to defend and a generational structure by which to further itself, Brown places himself in an urban limbo ("the middle of the ghetto isn't real") variously figured as void, edge, and incision. Claude Bowers mounts a defense of the Black Metropolis just as urban renewal, the civil rights movement, and the kinds of violence associated with riots and drugs were taking shape on its horizon. The poet Brown moves to South Street in the aftermath of Claude's future, after the failures of urban renewal, the breaking of neighborhoods by redevelopment, and the flight and desolation accelerated by the urban rioting Claude tries to prevent. But if the prewar orders of the Black Metropolis have entered into steep decline in Bradley's novel, the second ghetto has not taken standard "social science fiction" form. Bradley gives us the churches and bars and troubled homes that traditionally constitute a community in the neighborhood novel, and in his South Street milieu there are no projects, no drugs, and only one gun (Leroy's, and he does not use it). The neighborhood is in that sense a late survival of an older inner city of feeling that Bradley stubbornly opposes to the stock second ghetto pathologies formulated in the 1960s by writers of the urban crisis as different as Moynihan and Claude Brown (discussed in part 3).

If Bradley's South Street is in a curiously suspended and contradictory state, emblematized by the juxtaposition of churches and bars with the gaping holes dug for the foundations of high-rise apartment buildings to come, it is a productive one. The credentialing of Brown as a poet—by his movement onto South Street, by his flight from the campus across the river, by his rejection of social science even as he employs methods identified by other characters as social scientific—makes literature out of the process by which Bradley became a novelist. *South Street* imagines and argues for a process by which the inner city produces urban intellectuals. The inner city's signifying landscape and aging, uneducated population equip both Brown and Bradley—young, educated outsiders from across the river—to write its stories.

God's Pocket (1983)

Pete Dexter, like Bradley, spent a good deal of time in the bars of South Philadelphia, and his tongue-in-cheek accounts of the beating he received in Devil's Pocket—he calls it "the greatest bar fight in the history of South

Philadelphia," which took place in "the worst white neighborhood in America"—both poke fun at and conform to the codes that signal the credentialing of the poet Brown. If a knife cut across the chest is supposed to indicate close engagement with the city of fact, then how much more deeply do a broken back, a broken hip, ninety stitches in the scalp, and a changed sense of taste propose to inscribe Dexter's relation to South Philly on *his* body? *God's Pocket* (1983) moves the South Street literature's composite story back to the white-ethnic enclave and the decline, but the master story of postindustrial transformation—and the meditation on the urban intellectual's place in the landscape—retains its formal and thematic shape with remarkable consistency.

God's Pocket, an imaginary little neighborhood that Dexter places on Twenty-fifth, Twenty-sixth, and Twenty-seventh streets around Lombard, just north of the extreme western end of South Street, is a composite of Philadelphia's white-ethnic enclaves. Its residents, insular people of Irish and Italian descent, work in construction, at the local refineries, for the city or the mob. They drink in old-style bars like the Uptown and the Hollywood, where people "sit around and argue about the Eagles or the Flyers or the niggers . . . the things everybody agreed on." They live in dark, narrow rowhouses with "two bedrooms, one bath, four Touch Tone Princess telephones."[16] God's Pocket, then, stands for Devil's Pocket, Tasker, Whitman, Two Street, Fishtown, and other tight little enclaves descended from the world built by people like John Fury: the industrial neighborhood order's immigrant-ethnic villages. Like Bradley's "moving" the Pei towers to Spruce Street to conflate Center City and Penn, Dexter's "moving" Devil's Pocket from south of South to north of South places it right on the line where South Philly meets Center City, an encounter between declining enclave and a new urban world that will give rise to the novel's culminative act of violence.

The industrial moment has passed, and the Pocket is an anachronism in the postindustrial landscape. The financial hub and gentrified neighborhoods of Center City are just to the east, the campus of the University of Pennsylvania just to the west; the suburbs beckon to those who want to move and can afford it, and the expansion of the black inner city since World War II has created a permanent sense of crisis in the Pocket. To show how the industrial neighborhood order has been succeeded, the novel surveys the landscape of North Philadelphia, which was once a vast congeries of white-ethnic neighborhoods much like South Philly and is now dominated by the city's most notoriously immiserated second ghetto. Riding to work on a bus headed south down Broad Street through North Philadelphia, a black construction worker named Lucien Edwards notes that "someone had done a lot of good work in North Philadelphia once." As a bricklayer, he has a professional appreciation for the "good work" apparent in the surviving nineteenth- and early twentieth-century rowhouse architecture of North Philadelphia, which once housed immigrant-ethnic neighborhoods much like God's Pocket. As a skilled tradesman who makes things, he stands for an older notion of "good work" that has been in short supply for the black residents of North Philadelphia since they supplanted the white ethnics who left, along with most of the factory jobs, in the decades after the war. The white ethnics who remain in the inner city, in places like Fishtown in the north and God's Pocket in the south, see themselves as embattled and surrounded. Lucien can see the newer definition of "good work" from the windows on the other side of the bus: he likes to watch women on their way to the campus of Temple University, an enclave of professionals and aspiring professionals distinct from the neighborhoods around it and the menial service work their residents can secure. Like Penn, Temple is part of the higher education complex so crucial to a postindustrial economy based on intellectual labor and high technology. Twenty minutes later, the bus having passed through Center City and entered South Philadelphia, Lucien can compare the "good work"—meaning both the jobs and the architecture—suggested by North Philadelphia's rowhouse architecture to the Southwark Homes housing projects, part of the second ghetto built after World War II to lock the expanding black inner city in place.[17] He decides that his wife, who prays every morning for the destruction of a white race bent on corraling and exterminating the black race, must be right about the projects: Southwark Homes, a cluster of forbidding towers crowded with people cut off from economic opportunity, "couldn't be no accident" (20).

God's Pocket, then, persists in an urban landscape that has been drastically and purposefully changed, and the Pocket's residents are embalmed in the insularity and xenophobia encouraged by this dissonance. The novel's plot is set in motion when Lucien brains Leon Hubbard, a twenty-four-year-old good-for-nothing from the Pocket, with a lead pipe after Leon flies into a rage about "working for niggers" and goes after Lucien with a razor. Leon, an unemployable psychopath fueled by pharmaceuticals and paranoia, had the job only because his stepfather, Mickey Scarpato, is "connected"—he hauls meat for the local mob. Leon's death attracts the attention of Richard Shellburn, the city's best-loved newspaper columnist, who falls instantly for Leon's mother, Jeanie. At the end of a long, fantastically plotted chain of events, the two main protagonists have been banished from the inner city: Mickey is holed up in Palatka, Florida, waiting for the mob's enforcers to come for him, and Shellburn is dead—killed by patrons of the Hollywood Bar who took exception to the wording of his column about Leon Hubbard. Lucien and his foreman, a white Southerner named Peets, get back to work laying bricks but conclude that they have grown old.

God's Pocket, then, is a decline narrative, baroque to the point of self-parody. As in Man with the Golden Arm, a sense of doom pervades the novel, its sources just beyond the characters' range of perception. "'Some strange shit's goin' around,'" says Arthur "Bird" Capezio, Mickey's supplier of stolen meat, whose electricity keeps going out and whose traditional mob protectors are getting killed and slapped around by young turks on the make. "'Everywhere. I ask but, you know, it ain't on my level or something'" (59). The "strange shit" in question is, in this case, the generational collapse of the Philadelphia mob. Organized crime, like the ethnically based machine politics to which it is tied, flourished in the urban villages of the industrial city, but the sons and nephews of the old mobsters are running the business into the ground. Holed up in Florida with Bird at the end of the novel, Mickey is not even sure the mob will have the wherewithal to find him. "In the old days, you wouldn't of had to wonder" (278). The decline of the mob is part of a larger collapse of the industrial city's orders, a gradual slide readable throughout the novel's social landscape and character system. Lucien and Peets—hard-handed, steady-working, reticent men on the model of John Fury—seem to be the last two skilled manual laborers in a city full of cheap crooks, soft-handed layabouts, and other non-producers. Like everyone else in the novel, they are childless. Like *Golden Arm, John Fury*, and even Smith's *South Street* (in its self-critical moments), *God's Pocket* imagines the decline of an urban order as a family narrative that ends in barrenness. The many families of the book produce no children (except Leon, who dies), and the only inheritors of the old neighborhood are destructive bad sons on the order of John Fury Jr.: the sons and nephews who kill the old-time gangsters; and Leon Hubbard, who combines the shiftless violence of John Fury Jr. with the simpleminded uselessness of *Golden Arm*'s Poor Peter Schwabatski.

According to the patrons of the Hollywood Bar, "Leon was what the neighborhood stood for. . . . 'He was just like everybody else in here'" (79). Sharing none of the conventional virtues of his antecedents and all of their vices, Leon is an embodiment of the Pocket in steep decline, and the black-comic returns of his corpse to the street from the grave figure the Pocket's historical situation: it is dead, but it mimics the activity of life. Leon dies early in the novel, but his body keeps getting up and hitting the streets. First, the undertaker dumps him in the alley when Mickey loses the money for the funeral at the racetrack; then, after Mickey has temporarily stored the body among stolen sides of meat in the back of his refrigerator truck, a traffic accident deposits Leon on the streets once more. The resourceful residents of South Philadelphia steal all the free meat lying around in the intersection, so that by the time the police arrive "the only meat left on the street was Leon"(213). Leon is meat, and Mickey, who drives a refrigerator truck in a land where the electricity is going out, knows that "anywhere meat went bad, it never smelled the same"(139). When Leon is finally given a funeral, Mickey extends the spoiled-meat metaphor of generational decay to the whole Pocket: he discovers that the funeral home "had that same stale smell as the Hollywood. It never occurred to him before that the smell belonged to the people as much as the bar"(243). Leon, the bad son who stands for the Pocket, has spoiled; the mob's stolen meat spoiling in Bird's freezer indicates the unraveling of the old criminal order; the industrial-vintage urbanism for which God's Pocket stands is getting old and going bad.

God's Pocket narrates the decline with materials familiar to a reader of the South Street literature. It is a neighborhood novel that uses figures of family and landscape to show older orders in collapse, and it features a runaway scene that combines those representational strategies. Mickey, needing money to bury Leon, decides to sell the truck to Little Eddie, a used-car pirate whose Automotive Emporium sits among lines of rowhouses near Third Street and Emily deep in the fabric of South Philadelphia. One of Eddie's employees takes the truck for a test drive without Mickey's permission, and Mickey chases after him on foot, seemingly impelled by a need to watch over Leon's body. It is a dreamlike and unclearly motivated chase, in which Mickey follows the truck in traffic through South Philadelphia—up Third, all the way to Fitzwater, almost to South—at times almost close enough to touch it. At Fitzwater, the truck collides with a city bus just after Mickey stumbles and falls. The chase eerily repeats the horse-and-wagon runaway in *John Fury:* Mickey, disoriented and defeated in the landscape, futilely tries to keep up with an inscrutable process larger than himself. He is not sure why he is chasing the truck, only that he has to. That futile, bewildered passage through the landscape is again paired with familial collapse: Fury is at his dying wife's bedside, about to lose the family structure that stands for a neighborhood order; Mickey is chasing his dead step son Leon, the incarnation of the Pocket, who ends up in the street anyway.

Like everyone else in the novel, Mickey tries to make sense of what is happening to him and establish control over it. Chasing the truck, he blunders through an eviction scene, crashing through the furniture on the sidewalk while a woman holding a child "began to cry 'Stop' over and over. He didn't know who she meant, but he knew how she felt" (210). Like John Fury, Mickey cannot get urban processes to stop long enough for him to impose order on his experience of them. In his dash up Third Street through the rowhouse landscape of South Philly, he passes through the stage set of decline—people bewildered in the street, crying "Stop" as the world changes around them—and arrives at an urban limit: Leon and the old mafia's "meat business," two figures of God's Pocket and the declining urbanism it evokes, are the detritus left over after a crash (like the one that broke Sophie Majcinek's body, family, and neighborhood in *Golden Arm*). The local family drama is part of the larger drama of urban process. At the center of both is Leon, who goes bad despite Mickey's efforts to stop the process.

Richard Shellburn, the newspaper columnist, also finds himself chasing after a sense of control and losing ground. *God's Pocket* shares with *John Fury* a notion of *how* to write about the white-ethnic neighborhood—the decline— and engages the question of "*who* writes the inner city?" also raised by Smith and Bradley. Shellburn is one of several writer-characters (and the only white one) moving through the South Street literature. He is an urban intellectual charged with the task of representing Philadelphia by gathering material from the city of fact around him and constructing a city of feeling infused with meanings that sell newspapers. Shellburn, then, is like Mike Royko—although he is closer to Jimmy Breslin in his empurpled style and closer to Herb Caen in the nearly universal adulation he commands until his disastrous run-in with the people of God's Pocket. Like the Bowers brothers and Adlai Brown, Shellburn faces the problem of finding a productive relationship to the postwar city; like Philip Bowers, his failure kills him.

Shellburn is a writer in crisis who has had nothing new or interesting to say for twenty years. Getting by on recycled conventional material while he drinks himself to death, he has been writing what his readers want to read. He cranks out appeals to civic pride from an insider's perspective: "I love this city . . . not the sights, the city. I loved her last night, and I love her this morning, before she brushes her teeth, knowing she snores" (69). He tells stories of neighborhood decline populated by frenzied criminals and extravagantly innocent victims: "The old man had eyes as sad as the dog's. He looked into the empty rooms where he and his wife had lived their lives, quiet lives, and wondered what had happened to his neighborhood, that children would come into the house and beat up an old man for his money. 'At least they didn't hurt Hoppy,' he said" (12). His occasional paint-by-numbers representations of blacks and Puerto Ricans—the latter are "a spirited and proud people" summed up by neighborhood portraits of "burned-out houses, wine bottles, rats, naked children"—are careful never to alienate white-ethnic readers. If he writes a column criticizing the police for their treatment of Puerto Ricans, for instance, he will be sure to write one later in the week ("The Loneliest Job," or "Down Any Alley") that lionizes the police and other white-ethnic icons "for walking around a wino instead of kicking him" (70). He also writes columns decrying the coming of "the New Journalists," a vague category of younger reporters from "places like Florida" who threaten to ruin the local newspaper business in unspecified ways. These "New Journalists" are not the literary-journalistic movement of that name, identified by Tom Wolfe in the 1960s, that did change the practices of American newspaper reporting; rather, they seem to be "new" and threatening simply because they are urban intellectuals who have no trouble writing the postindustrial city and do not know or care much about places like God's Pocket.

Shellburn is losing touch, as Nelson Algren did, with the postindustrial city. Like Algren, Shellburn imagines himself to be the last good writer in town, an endangered species in a changing literary-historical ecology. Like Algren, Shellburn looks to the industrial neighborhood order—or, in the early 1980s, to survivals of it—for inspiration and his ideal readership. Looking out the window of his Center City office, Shellburn sees South Philadelphia, "where the city started. When he looked at a map, he could see how something must have tipped over there and spilled out in two giant stains, the northeast and northwest parts of the city. The source was South Philly. When it came up, he would say he could look out his window and see the people he wrote for" (72). South Philly is the starting point for Shellburn's city of feeling, as it is for Adlai Stevenson Brown's: it is the place that produces writing and readers. In that sense, South Philly produces Philadelphia for Shellburn, hence the image of the rest of Philadelphia as stains poured from South Philly. That image of spilling also captures a demographic movement underlying Shellburn's writing: the movement of white ethnics to the northeast and far northwest portions of Philadelphia since World War II is part of the story of neighborhood decline in South and North Philly that forms an essential component of his stock in trade. Shellburn thus echoes Algren in subject and even in style: Shellburn's ode to Philadelphia as a woman who shares his bed echoes Algren's comparison of loving Chicago to loving a woman with a broken nose;[18] phrases like "Down Any Alley" share Algren's tendency toward the sentimental universal. Shellburn raises the specter of Algren because he is similarly burned out, an urban intellectual running out of things to say about a city that seems strange to him.

God's Pocket, in keeping with Smith's and Bradley's dramas of placing the writer in the neighborhood, defines this urban intellectual's relationship to the changing inner city by putting Shellburn in a signifying landscape. For all his talk of communing with the people, Shellburn is comfortable only in postwar America's two favorite refuges from the inner city: his Lincoln Continental, "the safest place he had in the city" (70), and his suburban property on Chesapeake Bay, where he half-heartedly plans to build a house and settle down. He does not seem to belong in the inner city anymore. At one end of the social scale, he does not belong in the exclusive, heavily redeveloped Center City neighborhood of Society Hill. During his brief and ill-fated marriage to a socialite—who had planned to gain hegemonic leverage in Philadelphia's social scene via this "cultural juxtaposition" with a regular guy—he lived in a Society Hill townhouse, but the marriage collapsed and he moved out. At the other end of the social scale are the black and Hispanic neighborhoods of North Philadelphia, and Shellburn sends his legman Billy to do his reporting there. Unlike Adlai Brown, who has to see his material up close to write poetry, Shellburn does not really need to do any reporting to trot out the rats, roaches, and naked children of generic ghetto reportage. Billy's diligence allows Shellburn to insulate himself from the inner city, to avoid his readership. When Shellburn finally confronts those readers in God's Pocket, somewhere between Society Hill and North Philadelphia on the social scale, they are toting baseball bats and looking for blood.

In a darkly comic rendering of the urban intellectual's relationship to his subject and readership, Shellburn is beaten to death in the street by expert readers to whom he wishes to pander. Shellburn's column on Leon Hubbard's death uses the decline to conflate the reporter's grievances with those of the Pocket's residents: "Until the coming of the New Journalism . . . you only got to die once in this city, even if you came from God's Pocket. . . . There was a time . . . when a 24-year-old working man could die once, have the event noticed in his local newspaper, and then move on to his reward, without the complications of an additional death" (255–56). Shellburn's account repeats *City on the Make*'s strategy of positioning writers like himself alongside the decent working people of the old neighborhoods. Both groups have had indignities visited upon them by "the New Journalists": his own paper reported Leon's death at the construction site and the body's reappearance in the truck accident as two different deaths, a professional embarrassment to Shellburn and a social embarrassment to Leon's mother. Shellburn stands up for "the working man" here, his standard pose. What is it about the column, then, that sparks a wave of angry phone calls to the paper, leading to Shellburn's ill-fated peace-making trip to the Hollywood Bar?

Shellburn is guilty of two major offenses. The first is generic. In his column, he portrays Leon as the type of all the "workingmen of God's Pocket"— "small, dirty-faced, neat as a pin inside," just like the rowhouses in which the simple people of God's Pocket live. Leon and the rowhouses look the same because they are both exemplars of a way of life imbued with the dignity of hard work and simple, blue-collar pleasures, like a "drink at the Hollywood Bar or the Uptown, small, dirty-faced little places deep in the city" where the good people of the Pocket argue "about things they don't understand. Politics, race, religion" (257). As the callers and Billy explain, Shellburn is telling the wrong kind of decline here. Dirty *hands* is the appropriately clichéd image of hard work; "'Dirty-faced is you don't take a bath'" (264). Shellburn has equated God's Pocket with the generic North Philadelphia of his columns, where the people are soiled by poverty and pathological culture rather than honest hard work. The people of God's Pocket also do not want to hear that they do not understand politics, race, and religion. In their preferred story of decline, they are not ignorant anachronisms adrift in a world that has passed them by; rather, they are traditionalists clinging to a proven set of political, racial, and religious beliefs in an increasingly incoherent and valueless world populated by maniacs like the children who attack defenseless old people in Shellburn's columns.

Second, by constantly making Leon's death fresh and more absurd, Shellburn, like Mickey Scarpato, is guilty of telling the Pocket that it is not so much in embattled decline as dead—and grotesquely, comically dead at that. Since Leon is held up by the Hollywood's patrons as everything the Pocket stands for, and the novel offers the recurring presence of Leon's body in the street as a comic figure of the white-ethnic enclave's zombielike state of life after death, the newspaper and Mickey are telling the neighborhood a joke it does not want to hear. Early in the novel, after the foreman Peets lies to the police and claims Leon was killed in a workplace accident, a "fat kid" named Dick objects to the details of the newspaper's account of Leon's first death. "'They put it like that in the *Daily Times*,'" complains Dick, "'everybody in the whole fuckin' city sees it, thinks we're a bunch of jerk-offs down here. Walkin' around fallin' off shit all the time'" (100). Dick's animus against the newspaper seems to proceed from a sense that the paper, operating on a metropolitan scale far beyond that of the neighborhood, broadcasts the Pocket's demise as an undignified comic whimper—a matter of "fallin' off shit"—rather than a bang in which the old order makes a last stand against chaos. It is Dick, bat in hand 170 pages later, who announces to the crowd at the Hollywood that Shellburn has "'come down here to get fucked up'" (270). Mickey tries to stop the beating, fails, and is forced to leave the Pocket. The neighborhood has thus punished and eliminated Shellburn and Mickey, both of whom are responsible for holding up a mirror to a living corpse.

"'What the fuck?'" asks Mickey as the crowd closes in on Shellburn, "'Over something he *wrote?*'" (271). *God's Pocket* makes the writing of the inner city part of the violent action of the novel. Shellburn, like Mickey in pursuit of his truck, is another of the many characters adrift and disoriented in the signifying landscape of the postindustrial inner city. Like fellow writer-character Philip Bowers, killed by the fathers of the mob at the Hollywood Bar, Shellburn dies violently because he is improperly suited to the task of reading the social landscape through which he moves and representing it on paper. "The truest thing in the world," for Shellburn and other urban intellectuals committed to writing from close observation of the world around them, "was that you showed who you were" in writing a column. "It was almost incidental, what you had for issues. But how you saw things, how physical things went into your eyes and what your brain took and what it threw back, that told who you were" (255). Shellburn's literary relationship to the city through which he moves is nearly exhausted. His electricity, like Bird's, is going out; he is spoiled meat, pale and gray and soaked with bad chemicals. *God's Pocket* finally puts him, as dead as Leon, on the street in the Pocket, as if to suggest that his sense of how to be an urban intellectual is as parochial and limited as the neighborhood's sense of itself. In the end, the embalmed neighborhood and the doomed urban intellectual deserve one another.

Tumbling (1996)

There is no runaway scene in Diane McKinney-Whetstone's *Tumbling*. The only scene that comes close to the runaway's out-of-control movement through the landscape of the novel occurs when Noon, the main female character, remembers being dragged into the woods and raped by devil worshipers when she was growing up in Florida. That buried trauma generates much of the novel's family narrative: she has never consummated her marriage to her husband, Herbie, a circumstance that drives him to cheat on her with Ethel, a jazz and blues singer; Noon and Herbie, who want a family, adopt two girls left on their doorstep several years apart, and various dramas unfold around the maturing of these two girls, Fannie and Liz. At the same time, a second plot line expands the family narrative into one of neighborhood crisis: as the girls mature in the 1950s, city planners and other bureaucrats begin maneuvering to clear the ground for a planned highway (the Crosstown), threatening to uproot and disperse Herbie, Noon, and their neighbors. The equation of urban renewal with rape—parallel violations of the neighborhood's and the individual's body and spirit—is consistently made in critiques of redevelopment. The South Street literature is rich with images of redevelopment and urban change in general as assaults on the body, from the imagined collapse of anthropomorphic rowhouses in *John Fury* to the equation of vacant lots and streets to missing teeth and knife cuts in Bradley's *South Street*. *Tumbling*, then, is a neighborhood novel built around family narrative, an expressive landscape violated by processes of change, and the problem of the local versus the metropolitan, all squarely in keeping with the South Street literature's formal and thematic tendencies. But there is no true runaway scene in *Tumbling*, a novel about the successful exercise of personal and communal will to resist and even reverse urban processes that threaten the integrity of individuals, the family, and the neighborhood. In the end, the therapeutic structures of family and neighborhood allow Noon to make peace with her memories and thus with Herbie (good children *and* good sex indicating the family's and neighborhood's vitality), and Noon helps lead the neighborhood's fight against the expressway. The novel ends with echoes of proletarian strike melodramas: "They would not be moved. No way, no way."[19]

Tumbling returns to the Black Metropolis mapped by William Gardner Smith. McKinney-Whetstone did not read Smith's novel before writing her own, but there are striking similarities of setting, plot (substitute the war against the Crosstown for the war with Grays Ferry), and character (down to the resemblance of the jazz singer Ethel to Smith's Blues Singer). As in Smith's novel, the first lines of *Tumbling* introduce a vital segment of the industrial neighborhood order occupied by black working people who own and care for their urban world:

> The black predawn air was filled with movement. Its thin coolness rushed through the streets of South Philly, encircling the tight, sturdy row houses. In 1940 the blocks were clean and close. The people who lived here scrubbed their

steps every morning until the sand in the concrete sparkled like diamond pins. Then they went to work mopping floors and cooking meals for rich folks, or cleaning fish at the dock, or stitching fine leather shoes or pinch-pleated draperies at the factories on the north side. Some answered phones or crumpled paper for the government. Some tended house and nursed babies. A few were really nurses. One or two taught school. (3)

Herbie and Noon are exemplars of this time and place. He is a redcap at Thirtieth Street Station, doing the low-end, manual service work often done by blacks for the railroad, that backbone of the industrial city's infrastructure. She keeps house with a rigor that the novel's opening identifies as unique to time and place, participates with special vigor in the spiritual and social life of the church, and otherwise does her part to sustain the neighborhood. Like other working- and middle-class people in the neighborhood, Herbie and Noon own the modest rowhouse in which they live. (McKinney-Whetstone leaves the exact location of their home vague, but it is on Lombard, probably around Ninth Street.) The cobbled-together quality of the family—Liz is Ethel's orphaned niece and, unknown to all but Ethel, Fannie is Herbie and Ethel's daughter— helps to identify it as a microcosmic element of the neighborhood: the ties that bind Herbie and Noon and their daughters go further than blood into the sphere of community obligation. Ethel's anonymous contribution of money for the girls' upbringing makes even the family's economic life into a neighborhood project. The family and the rowhouse neighborhood for which it stands will be thrown into disarray by the forces that turned the world mapped by William Gardner Smith's *South Street* into the postcrisis world mapped by David Bradley's *South Street*.

The expressway plan threatens to break down the neighborhood's structuring orders. Neighbors begin selling their homes, businesses close, the transitional landscape of vacant or rundown rowhouses begins to mix in with the neat-as-a-pin remnants of the neighborhood's older order. The pressure driving the change is both external and internal. Not only does the downtown- and suburb-centered logic behind the plan bring the metropolitan into conflict with the local, but the federal and private money behind the plan flows into social cleavages already present in the neighborhood and exaggerates them. Noon's minister, who has been trying to help her mend her marriage with Herbie, takes payoffs from the city that distance him from his congregation. Fine Willie Mann, a local heartthrob who works at the neighborhood's most important nightclub, becomes an operative of the progrowth coalition in order to pay off outstanding debts. Willie Mann's romances with both of Herbie and Noon's adopted daughters cause trouble in the family, creating a rhyme between seductions of the body and of capital. The razing of a church marks the gravity of the threat: the overwhelming political and economic power behind the expressway plan, the compromising of community leaders like the minister, the removal of institutional structures that reinforce the neighborhood's cohesion. Addressing the bewildered congregation in the ruins of the church, Willie Mann explains that all the progrowth coalition wanted "was your space" (314). The destruction of the way of life rooted in that space will be both a strategy to clear the space and a result of clearing it.

The neighborhood, then, is faced with a crisis of reproduction familiar in the South Street literature, and that crisis is given fullest expression through the familiar strategy of mapping a family's relationship to the landscape in which it lives. When Fannie and Liz begin college, embarking on the trajectory into middle-class life mapped for them by their hard-working parents, they move into a rowhouse around the corner from Herbie and Noon, who buy it from a neighbor driven out by rumors of the Crosstown plan. The parents' investments in the neighborhood and in their adopted daughters converge in this rowhouse, so that the family and neighborhood narratives come to a head together when Liz (who has been sleeping with Willie Mann) considers selling it and clearing out of the neighborhood. Liz is the novel's candidate to join the ranks of bad offspring in the South Street literature. Not only does she want to sell the house, but she is literally tearing it down from within: her evocative plaster-eating compulsion becomes a full-blown madness as the novel proceeds, so that when her family finally breaks into her room near the end they find an entire wall gone. As in *John Fury*, the rowhouses that stand for a neighborhood order are about to fall, first one at a time and then all at once.

Tumbling, however, is unique in the South Street literature in imagining a resolution of neighborhood and family crisis in which both sustain themselves into the next generation. The therapeutic resolutions multiply interconnectedly. Noon works through her sexual block (with the anonymous help of Ethel) and saves her marriage with Herbie. Noon and Herbie begin having sex all over the house, a kind of ritual that anoints the rowhouse with the signs of the family's (and thus the neighborhood's) order-reproducing good health. Liz tries to kill Fannie with a hammer, reaches the breaking point, repents and admits she is on the path to self-destruction, and returns to the fold of the family for help. The catastrophically bad daughter becomes a good one. The enraged congregation stones Willie Mann with the rubble of their church, driving him back to his lair beneath the Club Royale, another ritual that demonstrates Noon and her neighbors have committed in earnest to the fight to save the half-bulldozed neighborhood.

These resolutions are gathered under the rubric of individual and communal will triumphing over the seemingly ineluctable processes that have always buffeted characters in the South Street literature and in urban literature more generally: the rhyming flows of capital and hormones. The key moment in that triumph comes when Fannie, who has a kind of second sight, discovers that not all of her visions of the future must come true. She has a lustful vision of giving in, as her sister Liz has, to the seductions of Willie Mann, but when the moment of truth arrives she finds the power to reject him. The lesson she learns is that, while human will cannot change the course of "birth and death and storms and luck of fortune," it can shape the course of desire and power. Jeanie, an older neighbor who speaks the language of civil rights and community action, advises Fannie, "You always had control of your own will. . . . Strong will. Will stronger than Willie Mann. . . . You got the power to make your vision not true" (254). At the novel's end, Jeanie and Noon are prepared to lead the neighborhood in the political contest of wills with Willie Mann's puppeteer, Philadelphia's progrowth coalition. *Tumbling*, then, is a story of runaways narrowly averted: Noon mends the damage done by the rape; Fannie asserts control over her body and life; the family and neighborhood resolve that they will not be moved.

What resolution—necessarily temporary, since there will no doubt be more South Street novels to come—does *Tumbling* provide for the composite story of postindustrial transformation told by the South Street literature? The answer is twofold and draws together two principal lines of development that organize the literature. First, *Tumbling* is an epic in the sense that it imagines the beginning of a new formation: the postindustrial black middle class. Herbie and Noon are paragons of the industrial neighborhood order, but their daughters are not. College educated, holding property given to them by their parents, one likely to be a designer (Liz) and the other some kind of creative intellectual (Fannie, who has the makings of a writer), the two daughters are on track to become higher-end service professionals from a neighborhood that traditionally provided service workers only at the lower end of the employment ladder— toters of bags, cleaners of rich folks' houses and offices. At the novel's end, the daughters' upward social trajectory is firmly rooted in their parents' neighborhood and in the migration-to-elevation narrative traditionally compressed in the figure of the rowhouse. Identifying the Black Metropolis as the source and model of black social mobility, turning the Black Metropolis into a "ghetto of opportunity," *Tumbling* counters the stock image of the dead-end second ghetto as a place from which the black middle class has fled.

Second, *Tumbling* also contains the elements of a decline narrative: internal and external threats to the neighborhood, metropolitan change threatening local arrangements, the sense of one period giving way to the next. Historical markers like Murray's hair pomade and Jackie Robinson's arrival in town suggest larger historical groundswells that form a context for local dramas. Discussions in the novel of "the up-and-coming Cassius Clay [and] the demise of Lady Day" intermix with and double discussions of "South Street, the way it used to bounce in the old days before all the talk of the highway had people closing up shop" (220). If Cassius Clay has come to the attention of black South Street, then Muhammad Ali and the urban crisis—and the eclipse of both the Republican integrationist Jackie Robinson in the era of black power and of Murray's hair pomade in the days of the afro—cannot be far behind. If Billie Holiday is gone, then the soul divas are in the wings, ready to provide the soundtrack of social upheaval in the 1960s. South Street as Herbie and Noon knew it has lost its bounce because the Black Metropolis, rooted in the nineteenth-century city, is reaching the end of its period. That decline parallels the decline of the white-ethnic urban village, as both elements of the social landscape are swept up in postindustrial transformation. Like the white-ethnic decline, the narrative of the Black Metropolis in decline is driven by prosperity (Liz wants to move somewhere "better") as well as by Algren's great subject: the relative powerlessness of the neighborhood in the face of capital and people in motion. The silent bells of the razed church in *Tumbling*, a silence that warns Noon of the gravity of her situation, are close cousins to the church bells playing the requiem in *Golden Arm*.

The two elements, the emergence of the postindustrial black middle class and the decline of the old neighborhood, are in a kind of creative tension in the novel. As in Stuart Dybek's Chicago writing, in which the declining order is always part of and paired with an emergent order, the novel's magical realist elements tend to occur where that tension is strongest. Fannie has a prophetic vision in which she sees "no road" in the future—that is, no Crosstown Expressway—only "brick houses, bright, new, red brick" (173–74). On the one hand, this is a vision of the neighborhood sustained into the future. Fannie evokes an old-neighborhood mysticism of seeing eyes and working roots extending back into the Southern cultural heritage, traditionally identified as the source of shared, community-shaping traditions like the black church and the blues that have been so important in the urban North. On the other hand, Fannie's vision points up the historical irony lurking in the novel's periodization. *Tumbling* ends in the early 1960s at a moment, perhaps the last moment, when the novel can still imagine the old neighborhood proceeding relatively intact into the next generation. If we turn to the history of South Street, we can see that, even though the struggle against the Crosstown was eventually won, Willie Mann is the true visionary in explaining that ground will be cleared for a new urban order. Today there are new and newly refurbished brick rowhouses in the blocks around South Street between Queen Village and Broad Street, just as Fannie envisioned them, but the old neighborhood—as a full-blown complex of people and place adding up to a way of life—is long gone. There are still some well-scrubbed rowhouse blocks and parts of blocks occupied by working- and middle-class black families, and the big AME church remains, but the landscape tells the story of urban crisis and postindustrial transformation. Above South, preponderantly white service professionals are paying top dollar for rowhouses in Society Hill and west of it; below South, "urban pioneers" looking for a better deal or grittier texture than Society Hill or (increasingly) Queen Village can offer are extending the line of renovation and gentrification west from Queen Village and south from Center City. South of South, just east of Broad Street, the Martin Luther King Plaza projects, erected on the bulldozed site of Philadelphia's oldest black neighborhood, form a moraine left when the second ghetto flowed over the Black Metropolis. *Tumbling* ends just at a moment when the people of the novel's neighborhood can imagine the world as they know it weathering the world-changing processes—not just redevelopment but also social mobility—now inscribed in the transformed landscape.

One can see throughout *Tumbling* the marks of this journey backward from the 1990s through the veil of the urban crisis to the period before it. Characters in the novel speak anachronistically of "lifestyle" and "gentrification," words popularized during and after the urban crisis as part of the lexicon of postindustrial urbanism. The generic "tangle of pathology," popularized by Moynihan and other students of the ghetto in the 1960s, is present in the fragmentation of families, but the novel reinterprets this fragmentation as a sign of communal strength: that Herbie and Noon raise Fannie, the child Herbie had with Ethel, is a sign of a strong neighborhood sharing fundamental values. More important to the novel's organizing ideas, one can see in it a powerful impulse to rewrite William Gardner Smith's period in light of David Bradley's. In the 1950s, Smith trained the political impulse of the protest novel on the problems raised for urban blacks by the postwar migration and the emergent second ghetto; in the late 1960s and early 1970s, Bradley was attracted to South Street after the crisis precisely because the people there, having been run over and left for dead in the 1960s, "had absolutely no power" but struggled nevertheless to sustain their sense of community. McKinney-Whetstone imagines Smith's neighborhood girding itself to fight the "right" war—against the coming of the second ghetto and the service professionals, not Grays Ferry—that is already lost in Bradley's novel. The external threat against which the black neighborhood must fight, a project that requires the neighborhood to resolve its internal tensions, comes not from the white-ethnic urban village but from the progrowth coalition. The two-dimensional white antagonists who briefly pass through the novel are not white-ethnic toughs or old-time political bosses—they are bureaucrats who answer to the city and the faceless private interests who need to clear away the industrial city's orders. *Tumbling* passes back through the veil of history to the moment when people like Herbie and Noon and Diane McKinney-Whetstone's parents decided to move out of the old neighborhoods of South Philadelphia, hastening the separation of the black middle class from the second ghetto as it

formed. In a novel of traumas unearthed and healed, this return to the historical fork in the road serves as a kind of therapeutic fiction: a return to a place
where the decline of the industrial city meets the epic of the postindustrial city's
emergence, a place where one can recover a healthy model of efficacious community before the fall.

There is a gap between the generations of South Street literature. The reader
jumps from the two midcentury novels to novels of the 1970s, 1980s, and
1990s. The gap comes in the 1960s, the moment in which the complex of
changes in postwar cities of fact and feeling gathered momentum and coalesced
as "the urban crisis." To borrow David Bradley's reptilian metaphor, urbanism
sloughed off its old form and revealed its new one in the decades after World
War II, and the urban crisis of the 1960s was the moment in which American
culture spotted the snake and started screaming. The South Street literature
weaves together two principal narrative lines that shaped the urban crisis—the
decline of the industrial city and the emergence of the postindustrial metropolis—and considers as well the pressing problem of how to tell, and who can
tell, the stories of urban orders in decline and on the make. The South Street literature also suggests how this larger context of urban transformation contains
and qualifies the distinctions of race and gender (white and black literature,
male and female authors) that provide the literary-historical pigeonholes in
which postwar literature has been conventionally sorted.

But the South Street novels, as a group, pass over the urban crisis itself, presenting a set of before and after accounts that bracket the 1960s, so we are
obliged to move on to another city and another neighborhood to fill in the gap.
We got to Philadelphia and the South Street literature from Chicago, the quintessential industrial city and the cradle of an industrial literary urbanism that
influenced Dunphy, Smith, and, more generally, the writing of the twentieth-
century city. The continuities of literary form and theme between the Chicago
writing in part 1 and the Philadelphia writing in part 2 suggest the more general application of my account of material and textual cities transformed. Part
1 primarily explores the literature of decline and the white-ethnic urban village;
part 2 pairs the decline with complementary stories of persistent and emergent
urban orders and puts the old neighborhoods (white and black) in conversation
with the redeveloped downtown. Part 3 continues on to New York, to Harlem,
to examine the principal ground of the urban crisis. Turning to accounts of the
emergent second ghetto and the postindustrial urbanism it has so powerfully
dominated, part 3 completes this study's spatial survey of the postindustrial
inner city of feeling. Part 3 completes, as well, this study's historical account of

the postwar period: from the incipient decline of the industrial city that inspired Nelson Algren's best work, through the traumas of juxtaposed persistence and succession that drive the South Street literature, to widespread recognition and representation of the postindustrial inner city's emergence as not the end of the world but rather the stormy arrival of the urban future.

Part 3

The City of Feeling
in Crisis

8

Exposition:
That Separate World

"That separate world in which the American Negro has his being is now, after 100 years, coming under scrutiny—and by all disciplines, all sorts of people, and for an enormous variety of purposes."[1] Warren Miller, reviewing Claude Brown's *Manchild in the Promised Land* in 1965, began by framing Brown's Harlem memoir within a growing literature of Northern, urban "black America" to which Miller himself had contributed two novels. In arguing that this "separate world" was "*now* . . . coming under scrutiny," Miller was not affecting to dismiss a tradition of writing by and about black Americans that stretched back "100 years" to the end of the Civil War (and, of course, further back than that). Rather, he was dramatizing the suddenness and urgency with which the postindustrial inner city, and especially its emergent second ghetto, was moving to cultural center stage in concert with the notion of a national urban crisis. In the late summer of 1965, in the aftermath of the Watts riot, that notion was rapidly developing into mature form.

Long-developing changes like postindustrial transformation become crises when a significant number of people take notice of them, and that usually happens when the consequences of gradual change are displayed all at once in what feels like a sudden, violent disruption. The urban crisis of the 1960s was, among other things, a national recognition of the facts and consequences of postindustrial transformation, and the element of the postindustrial social landscape that drew most of the attention was the second ghetto. Sometimes dramatic and sometimes almost imperceptible, the postindustrial migrations of capital and population—and policy responses to them—had by 1965 produced full-blown second ghettos in American cities. These segregated black districts, expanded by two decades of massive black migration from the South to the urban North, were increasingly cut off from the rest of the metropolis, and from economic well-being as well, by capital flight to the suburbs and redeveloped downtowns, deindustrialization, selective governmental abandonment, poor schooling and health care, racial segregation and discrimination in the work-place and in housing, high incidence of violent crime, departure of the black middle class . . . the list extended into infinity. The distinctive high-rise form of notoriously dangerous and unclean postwar housing projects marked the efforts of policy makers to fix the second ghetto in place as it grew, and the projects served as beacons warning the rest of the metropolis—residents and busi-nesses—to stay well away from the black inner city.

At the same time, however, those beacons attracted urban intellectuals and their audiences. By 1965, the second ghetto was acquiring new status in the minds of Americans as the principal terrain of "black America," just as "the Negro problem" came to a boil after two decades of increasingly more vigor-ous simmering. The continuing upheavals surrounding the civil rights move-ment combined with two forms of anxiety-producing urban violence—a much-publicized rise in reported street crime during the late 1950s and early 1960s and a series of ghetto riots beginning in 1964—to encourage urban intellectu-als from across the political and generic spectrum to accept almost without exception the convergence of "the Negro problem" with an urban crisis cen-tered in the black ghetto. Harlem (see fig. 9 for locations referred to in this sec-tion), which had for several decades been widely known as a "capital of black America," became a leading example of the postwar ghetto in crisis, and there accrued around Harlem in the late 1950s and 1960s a rapidly growing body of new representations ranging across (as Miller put it) many disciplines and viewpoints.[2]

The social drama of cities in transition attracted urban intellectuals like Warren Miller. Miller was the kind of engaged writer who undertook to make literature—quickly and well—out of the age's principal social and moral crises. Born in 1921 and raised in the Pennsylvania Dutch country around Pottstown, educated at the University of Iowa in the late 1940s, Miller became a New York writer, moving in the overlapping circles of left-liberal urban intel-lectuals in a continuum formed by *Dissent*, the *Nation* (for which he was a lit-erary editor), the *New Yorker*, and the *Saturday Review*. At home in both liter-ary and political life, publishing in both widely read and intellectually prestigious venues, well connected in the Village, Jewish (although he did not make much of it), Miller had much in common with that loose grouping of "New York intellectuals," most of them better known than him, who styled themselves the house intelligentsia of the postwar American metropolis. When Miller died relatively young in 1966, a perceptive *Newsweek* obituarist summed up his brief, prolific literary career by identifying him as a writer "fully

engaged in the moral drama of his time." If he had not written a big novel or
notable criticism, he was "one of that band of novelists who provide a literary
period, not necessarily with its principal sources of light and power, but with its
texture and density."[3] In a decade of publishing, Miller's writing had surveyed
pressing issues of his time: he had to his credit not only the two Harlem novels
(*The Cool World* and *The Siege of Harlem*) that occupy my attention in this section but also novels of McCarthyism (*The Sleep of Reason*), the psychological
fallout of Cold War (*Looking for the General*), U.S.-Cuban relations (*Flush
Times*, as well as the nonfiction account *Ninety Miles from Home*), and the area
of overlap in which youth culture encountered the bohemian scene (*The Bright
Young Things, Love Me Little, The Way We Live Now*). Even his children's
books, on which he collaborated with the artist Edward Sorel, offered social
critique: *The Goings-On at Little Wishful* gently skewered the rhetoric of
progrowth coalitions; *Pablo Paints a Picture* meditated on the artist's relationship to the city and to his public's short attention span. In the late 1950s and
1960s, Miller made a modest reputation for himself as a purveyor of literate and
literary social critique.

He also made a name for himself as a mimic. Miller specialized in a tour de
force style of dialect tale that employed patterns of speech unique to subcultures, especially those of young people. Each of his novels, he told an interviewer in 1959, "was, in a sense, an exercise in reproducing the language of the
society I wrote about."[4] His novels of young bohemian life in Greenwich
Village, two published under the pseudonym Amanda Vail, were told from the
standpoint of young women on the make; his narrating character in *Looking for
the General* is an articulately unreliable spokesman for Cold War cultural
malaise. His Harlem novels delved into semiliterate delinquent cant, the smooth
talk of politically sophisticated hipsters, and something perilously (for a sensitive white writer) close to blackface minstrelsy.

So it was not only the social drama but also the exotic language of the second ghetto that engaged Miller's roving attention. In addition to reviewing others' books on the subject (a matter to which I will return in chapter 12), Miller
contributed two novels to the literature of the second ghetto. *Cool World* (1959),
about juvenile delinquents in Harlem, established Miller as a literary specialist
in urban matters. *Siege of Harlem* (1964), a broad social satire that imagined
Harlem's secession from the United States, recorded Miller's engagement with
the increasingly apocalyptic logic and language of urban crisis. Both novels
received special notice for the urgency of their subject matter and for the highly
stylized language in which they were narrated.

Cool World, Miller's biggest success, is a kind of orthographic dialect novel,
a long and expressively miswritten letter from its fourteen-year-old black protagonist, gang leader Duke Custis, to a reform school psychologist. The letter
explains the geography of the delinquent's inner life to "Doc Levine" in a styl-

ized version of Duke's speech: "They aint law on the streets. No an none in the houses. You ask me why an I tellin you why we do whut we have to do. Because when they aint law you gotta make law. Other wise evry thing wild Man an you dont belong an you alone. . . . So we go in the gang."[5] Detailing Duke's delinquency, his rise to gang leadership, a big rumble, a killing, then reform school, *Cool World* stays close to standard formulas of a highly developed and immensely popular literature of juvenile delinquency. In the 1950s, especially, Americans were fascinated, frightened, and exhilarated by juvenile delinquency, which commanded a great deal of cultural attention and impressed observers as a key to divining the future of postwar America. Representations of delinquency, pursuing insight into the troubled generation born in the late 1930s and 1940s, illuminated as well the troubled social landscape, and especially the transformed inner city, in which the delinquents moved. Readers and critics therefore received *Cool World* as both a signal literary achievement and a powerful, important document of life in the inner city in transition—especially its older slums, decaying as the industrial neighborhood order unraveled, and the second ghettos that abutted and supplanted them.

In the early 1960s, Miller followed the conventional line of his period's thinking, the developing notion of ghetto-centered urban crisis, in moving from a primary emphasis on youth and delinquency to an elevation of race as the defining urban subject matter. *Siege of Harlem*, published just as the urban crisis began to take canonical shape as a racial crisis, recounts the postcolonial struggle that ensues after Harlem's secession from the United States of America. Despite its military premise, the novel is at heart a comedy, meditating with gentle irony on a growing tendency—manifested across the political spectrum—to understand "that separate world" inhabited by black Americans as a distinct ghetto nation at war with the rest of America. Engaging with the separatisms of black nationalists on the one hand and white-flight-encouraging conservatives on the other, *Siege of Harlem* both replicates and critiques the assumption of a radical division between races so central to the notion of urban crisis as it developed in the mid-1960s.

The novel also explores the implications of urban crisis for urban intellectuals, who experienced their own peculiar disarray and ferment during the upheavals of the 1960s. Not only did the urban crisis and the larger postindustrial transformation behind it signal the advent of a new urbanism, requiring revised stories, new language, and new forms of expertise, but the violence of the crisis reminded everyone that the city of feeling might also be divided along the same stark lines traceable in the city of fact. The logic of separation underlying the urban crisis suggested that if the black inner city and the white housed two radically different and mutually incomprehensible urbanisms, two different languages, then it followed that there should be two different ways—one black and one white—to engage with the corollary problem of how and who to write about cities. *Siege of Harlem* records the growing sense of racialized urban crisis not only in its map of a violently divided metropolis, with a double line of fortifications running along East Ninety-seventh Street, but also in its winkingly self-critical dialect strategy: echoes of Joel Chandler Harris's Uncle Remus stories foreground the elaborate disguises and credentials presented by a white author entering a black narrator's speaking voice, showing how the logic of separation, even as espoused by radical critics of American social order, hardens rather than erodes long-standing racial boundaries. *Siege of Harlem* thus argues for the increasing difficulty of passage across new barriers of racialized rhetoric that the urban crisis erected at the boundaries of "black America" as they were mapped by American letters. By the mid-1960s, Miller considered the universal assumption of racial separation to have cut him off from writing about the second ghetto, which was by then accepted as ground zero of the period's most compelling domestic problem.

Endorsing these rhetorical walls around "that separate world" of the ghetto and the putatively distinct urbanism it housed, the logic of urban crisis therefore called for a new set of black urban intellectuals to take up the task of mapping it in prose. If whites could not gain access to "black America," blacks could write about it from within, and the authority of these informants would proceed from their demonstrated intimacy with the second ghetto. The great migrations from South to North, and the urban crisis that capped them, produced and inspired black writers in great numbers, and many of them got published: black authors writing about the urban crisis and related issues carved out new avenues of access to major publishing houses and periodicals. Although these authors wrote about all manner of subjects in all manner of ways, national attention to the urban crisis tended to channel their reception into the well-traveled grooves of "problem" literature about the second ghetto. For all the reasons that a genre achieves cohesion—internal reasons (writers reading one another, shared influences, shared social and intellectual milieu) and external reasons (publishers seeking more of what already succeeded in a competitive market, readers and critics rewarding favored models)—the ghetto narratives of the urban crisis developed consistent generic properties. Among those properties were a foregrounding of "raw" first-person voices (even in very sophisticated analytical writing); a narrow angle of difference between narrator and author; analytical and experiential emphasis on those "pathologies" (irregular family life, criminal behavior, moral degradation) generically associated with the second ghetto; a willingness to explain root causes and propose comprehensive solutions.

Claude Brown's Harlem autobiography *Manchild in the Promised Land*, which not only fits but helped to establish these parameters, was published in 1965, appearing in bookstores at just about the same time as the Watts riots and news of a serious increase in violent crime moved the urban crisis to the top of the domestic agenda. Also published in the same year were *The Autobiography of Malcolm X*, which *Manchild* at first eclipsed in popular and critical circles, and Kenneth Clark's *Dark Ghetto*, a path-marking social-psychological study of Harlem. All three books circulated widely among popular audiences and urban intellectuals, becoming standard texts in the literature of urban crisis. *Dark Ghetto*, especially, became a kind of concordance for *Manchild*, providing a social scientific template against which to read Brown's richly digressive ghetto memoir-bildungsroman.[6] *Manchild* thus not only participated in the growing literature of "the American Negro" identified by Miller, it also formed part of a new genre of writing that mapped the content of urban crisis on a ghetto of feeling to which people like Miller believed white outsiders had little or no access except as readers. Brown was part of a new generation of urban intellectuals whose writing and public personas, staking out the ghetto as their bailiwick, cooperated with many whites (including their most conservative antagonists) to develop the notion of a distinct ghetto identity. This group included Clark, Malcolm X, Stokely Carmichael, H. Rap Brown, Eldridge Cleaver, George Jackson, Angela Davis, Ron Karenga, Sonny Carson, James and Grace Boggs, LeRoi Jones (Amiri Baraka), Julius Lester, Sonia Sanchez, and many, many more. *Manchild* made important opening moves in the literary formulation of a composite, indeed a generic, second ghetto—its social landscape, the principal narratives to be found in it, the character and import of the problem it posed for America in the 1960s.

Claude Brown, who in 1965 was a twenty-eight-year-old novice author with a recent B.A. from Howard University, told in *Manchild* the story of an urban intellectual shaped by the postwar ghetto and uniquely accredited to represent it. Unlike Warren Miller, Brown was not by training a professional writer. The child of poor Southern migrants, he had grown up in Harlem and various upstate correctional facilities. His "Career" entry in *Contemporary Authors* reads, in part: "Member of Harlem Buccaneers Gang's 'Forty Thieves' division and served three terms at Warwick School . . . during 1940s; worked confidence games and dealt in drugs, New York City, 1953–54; worked as a busboy, watch crystal fitter, shipping clerk and jazz pianist in Greenwich Village, 1954–57; writer and lecturer."[7] Aspiring to encompass and survey "the experiences of a misplaced generation, of a misplaced people," *Manchild* builds the story of Brown's delinquency and reform (much like that of Duke Custis in *Cool World*) into a much larger story that surveys a number of standard or soon-to-be-standard second ghetto narratives and types: the career and reform of a delinquent, drug dealer, or hustler; the making of a musician, boxer, artist, bohemian, or entrepreneur; the reengagement with the ghetto of an intellectual, social reformer, political or religious activist.[8] Plotting Brown's movements in and out of Harlem, reform school, and Greenwich Village, *Manchild* maps in great detail not only the second ghetto but its vexed relationship to the city around it. Violent and profane, written in the mixed register of a street voice

incompletely tempered by higher education, *Manchild* was predictably har-
rowing and challenging to digest for a large reading public drawn with increasing anxiety to Harlem and the urban crisis. For the vast majority of readers who
never went near Harlem or any place like it, *Manchild*'s portraits of delinquency, crime, drug use, precocious sex, reform school, and Southern country
people adrift in the big city were at once profoundly alien (did people really
live, and talk, like that in America?) and familiar from the newspaper, the talk
of concerned neighbors, and other problem literature (especially the literature
of delinquency).

Manchild enjoyed enormous popular success and critical response. Its initial
readers saw matters of the utmost social and literary importance in *Manchild*'s
account of the emergence of a new kind of urban intellectual to represent the
ghetto in crisis. The editors of *Newsweek*, for instance, identified *Manchild* as
one of the most important books of 1965:

> There is no elegant Baldwinian rhetoric and none of Langston Hughes's charm-
> ing folksiness or LeRoi Jones's college-bred temper tantrums. In their place is
> unmistakable authenticity—the news brought out of the ghetto by a battered but
> miraculously intact survivor of our unending civil war, a message to Whitey about
> what hell feels like from the inside of the furnace. Though the scene takes place
> 3,000 miles away, Brown's best pages could have told Governor Brown more
> about Watts than all the reports compiled by all the McCone commissions, past,
> present and—inevitably—yet to come.[9]

The Watts riot and the McCone Commission's effort to explain it lent special
force to Brown's representation of Harlem in ways that elevated it above those
written by literary sophisticates like Baldwin, Hughes, and Jones (not to mention Warren Miller), all of whom suddenly appeared to be out of touch with
what was happening on the streets of contemporary cities. Brown was one of
four authors whose photos appeared in *Newsweek*'s year-end literary roundup
for 1965 (in which the above-quoted passage appeared). The other three made
heady company for an ex-delinquent novice writer whose editors asked him to
stop using so many four-letter words: Günter Grass, the martyred president
John F. Kennedy, and Norman Mailer, who supplied a blurb on the front cover
of the paperback edition of *Manchild* describing it as the "first thing I ever read
which gave me an idea of what it would be like *day to day* if I'd grown up in
Harlem."

Manchild offered not only an impeccably credentialed insider's account of
ghetto street life (and, at over 400 authenticatingly unedited-feeling pages, that
account did have a "*day to day*" density of bruisingly repetitive detail) but also
the story of how one apparently foredoomed young delinquent had changed his
fate and "got out" of the ghetto. *Manchild*, then, promised not only to develop
postwar ghetto narratives, languages, and maps of the inner city that broke new

ground in the much-traversed literary territory of Harlem but also to shed light on sociological and political questions that the urban crisis had raised to the top of the domestic agenda: what caused the complex, intractable problems posed by the second ghetto and what the solutions might be.

Claude Brown and Warren Miller were part of a community of intellectuals thrown into crisis and into the limelight in the late 1950s and 1960s. The urban crisis, and the postindustrial transformation of cities that led up to it, put enormous pressures on urban intellectuals even as it offered new opportunities—aesthetic, generic, professional—for them to exploit. The development of the crisis caused upheavals and realignments in the ranks of urban intellectuals, who struggled (as we have seen in parts 1 and 2) to represent the changing inner city and manage the traffic in representations. Both Miller's and Brown's books devote important parts of their energies to thinking explicitly about the problem of who writes the ghetto—and how—as it becomes the postindustrial inner city's defining terrain. *Cool World* and *Siege of Harlem* both feature subtexts figuring a white author's entry into Harlem and the complementary emergence of black voices from Harlem. *Manchild*'s sprawling story is organized by the theme of a black author's emergence from the ghetto. All three books are in important ways *about* the need for representations of the ghetto and about the art and politics of meeting that need in a cultural climate supercharged by urban crisis. Each text's physical plot of Harlem and narrative plot of its protagonist's activities enter into a mutually shaping relationship with the author's persona and the possibilities for writing the second ghetto.

This is not to reduce complex, multifaceted texts of considerable artistry to a set of professional maneuvers in the scramble for notoriety and influence occasioned by the urban crisis. Rather, in thinking out the changing calculus of authorship and the terms by which the inner city might be represented—what language to use, what maps to draw, what stories to tell, what manner of narrating personas to position in the ghetto spaces thus delineated—these texts address the relation between textual and material cities in a historical moment when both were seen to be entering into a state of crisis.

Miller, Brown, and the supporting cast of authors assembled around them in this section wrote about Harlem during the period when American culture, spurred by "the Negro problem," developed a comprehensive conceptual response to the urban transformations of the postwar period. That response, the concept of urban crisis, set the pattern for the way Americans have thought, written, and read about cities since then. Miller's and Brown's literary personas, shuttling back and forth in prose across the boundaries of the generic ghetto of feeling as it was mapped by American culture, therefore reveal in their movements the contours of an important historical moment: the subsuming of other sources of urban anxiety, like juvenile delinquency, by the racially ordered rubric of urban crisis; the conventional logic of urban crisis guiding the two writers' and their readers' changing assumptions about the relation between urban literature and urban life; the combined literary and nonliterary standard, entailed by the pressure of urban crisis as both conceptual process and social fact, to which their writing (and critics' reading of their writing) responds; the rules of movement and credentialing evolved by the community of urban intellectuals in response to the inner city's transformation.

Parts 1 and 2 explored the literature of the urban village and the Black Metropolis in transition and their relationship to the redeveloped downtown; this section treats the literary encounter between Miller and Brown as an episode through which we can begin to understand a third aspect of the transformation of literary urbanism tied to the transformation of American cities. Like most Americans at the time (and today), Miller and Brown regarded Harlem as an ideal type of the second ghetto. The two authors participated in the mapping of the second ghetto in relation to the rest of the metropolis— which is why in its spatial emphasis part 3 will devote more attention to the edges of the second ghetto, and their relative permeability, than it does to Harlem's interior landscape   as "the ghetto" came to dominate thinking about the character and meanings of urbanism in the postindustrial metropolis.

Chapter 9 describes what should by now be a familiar set of economic, demographic, and physical changes that framed the emergence of the second ghetto in New York City. It describes as well some of the most important habits of language and thought that characterized the writing of that ghetto, especially the tendency to see the transformation of cities as a sudden, violent process, the meanings of which might be found in analyzing the antisocial behavior of young black men like Duke Custis and Claude Brown. In tracing the parallel contours of change in New York and the writing of New York, chapter 9 therefore provides the background for readings (in chapters 10–12) of Miller's two Harlem novels and Brown's novelistic autobiography—and, crucially, of readers' responses to Miller and Brown.

Violence, the Second Ghetto, and the Logic of Urban Crisis

Of the many problems disrupting the present and
threatening the future of this city, none is more
critical than this growing concern and fear over the
increase of fear and violence in the streets, the
subways, the elevators and the parks of New York.
                        "New York City in Crisis,"
            New York Herald-Tribune, 5 February 1965

This study describes a complex set of postindustrial transformations occurring
in the city of fact and in the city of feeling from the late 1940s through the mid-
1960s—an extended "crisis" defined as much by the problem of how to think
and write about cities as by physical and social change in cities. But the term
"*the* urban crisis," as used in popular and scholarly conversation, has a more
limited meaning. The term usually describes a period of particularly violent
social upheaval in inner cities, accompanied by appropriately extreme rhetorical habits, lasting from the mid-1960s to about 1970. Conventional accounts
trace the sources of this urban crisis to a convergence of many factors. Some of
them were aspects of the continuing postindustrial transformation of inner
cities: black migration to the Northern inner city, largely white and middle-
class exodus to the suburbs, the flight of capital and especially manufacturing
jobs from urban neighborhoods. These structural changes formed the context
for upheavals surrounding the civil rights movement, rising expectations of

urban blacks in tension with social and physical conditions in the second ghetto, and the inadequate or misdirected responses of the state to the continuing problems of racial conflict, poverty, inequities in housing and education, and increases in criminal violence. Urban riots, fear of muggers, and proliferation of the drug trade gave special significance to "crime," by which most people usually meant face-to-face violence and theft, in the litany of second ghetto ills. While it lasted, the urban crisis shared space at the top of the American agenda with the Vietnam War and the more vaguely defined problem of youth culture.

Although the list of contributing factors tends to be long and various, the widely recognized urban crisis of the 1960s—when the term itself came into general use—was and is constructed as fundamentally a matter of violent racial conflict. Its most compelling element was typically described as a "rising tide of violence" in the nation's black ghettos, which did not seem to be party to the general prosperity and economic growth the nation as a whole enjoyed in the 1950s and 1960s. As Robert Beauregard puts it in *Voices of Decline*,

> What made the years between roughly 1960 and the recession of 1973–5 unique in the discourse on urban decline was the emergence of a single theme that unified its various fragments and turned urban decline into a society-wide problem. The theme was race, the problem was the concentration, misery, and rebellion of Negroes in central cities, and the reaction was one of fear and eventually panic.[1]

The language of crisis achieved even greater compression in its foregrounding of criminal violence. In addition to commanding attention in its own right, explicitly racial violence (like the "race riot") and racially coded violence (in common usage after about 1960, the figure of "the mugger" is implicitly assumed to be black or Hispanic) became rubrics under which to reduce the complexity of urban transformation to sharply representable and narratable form. The widespread tendency to understand the relationship between whites and blacks in the postindustrial inner city as primarily a problem of too little law and order in the ghetto (or too much, as critics on the left argued) led to what Sharon Zukin has called "the institutionalization of urban fear" as a defining principle of urbanism during and after the urban crisis.[2]

Urban America was in some ways a more violent place in the 1960s than it had been in the 1950s, and representations of the inner city reflected that change, but the period's cultural fixation on urban violence also marks a collective rude awakening to a gradual change of urban orders. The endless repetition and interpretation of images of "urban disorder"—riots, muggings, police and National Guard responses—chart the sudden shock of Americans' encounter with the slower, duller, more obscure disorder of shifting economic and social arrangements. The racial logic and violence that dominated the canonical urban crisis gave Americans a way to think about, or not think about, historical processes like the emergence of postindustrial urbanism. One way to understand the urban crisis of the 1960s is to regard it as the period in which Americans—especially Americans who steered clear of the black inner city— were forced to confront that emergent urbanism. The "crisis" ended when they had developed routines for understanding and responding to it. They were used to it, settling into generic understandings of this once-new and strange prospect, by the time the riots petered out at the end of the 1960s.

The urban crisis, then, brought together two traditional sources of American social concern: disorienting urban change and the American dilemma of race flowed together, and the second ghetto—understood to be the point of conflu-ence—moved to cultural center stage. As Beauregard puts it, "Urban decline eventually became fused to the Negro ghetto."[3] The ghetto came to dominate consideration of American urbanism and of the still-emerging postindustrial city, and the Northern ghetto gradually eclipsed the rural and urban South as the principal representative terrain of what Warren Miller called "that separate world in which the American Negro has his being." The report of the National Advisory Commission on Civil Disorders (the Kerner Commission), one of the canonical texts of the urban crisis, articulated and helped to reinforce the con-fluence of urban and racial discourses. "Our nation is moving toward two soci-eties," the report's most famous sentence argues, "one black, one white—sep-arate and unequal."[4] Defining the urban crisis as it sought to explain the causes and implications of rioting in the inner city, the Kerner Commission report mapped those two separate societies as, in essence, the ghetto and the rest of the country.

Condensing the city into the ghetto and the ghetto into the problem of crim-inal violence, the Kerner Commission report demonstrates how the logic of urban crisis made analysis of violence in the streets a key to unearthing the racial sources of urban problems. In accounting for rioting in the ghetto, the report notes economic transformations leading to the decline of blue-collar employment opportunities for unskilled workers, and it recognizes that subur-banization may be more complex than simple white flight, but it nevertheless concludes that "white racism is essentially responsible for the explosive mix-ture which has been accumulating in our cities since the end of World War II."[5] If other observers pursued other readings of the causes and meanings of urban riots, they tended to share with the Kerner Commission an acceptance of riots as somehow communicating the racial essence of what was wrong with American cities. For instance, Stokely Carmichael and Charles V. Hamilton's *Black Power*, another widely read formulation of urban crisis (and an influence on the Kerner Commission), pursues a class-based analysis that nevertheless arrives at an almost identical assessment of the root problem: "The dynamite" in the ghettos "was placed there by white racism and it was ignited by white racist indifference and unwillingness to act justly."[6] The discourse of urban crisis rendered the complex and many-faceted postwar transformation of American cities as a simplified, divided landscape in which distinct "white" and "black" urbanisms produced violent sparks wherever they met.

Writing about one of the nation's most written-about ghettos in transition, Warren Miller and Claude Brown were advantageously positioned in the late 1950s and early 1960s to participate in the formulation of urban crisis. The pages that follow describe the world in which Miller's and Brown's characters move: the historical and rhetorical dimensions of diffuse urban change as it became sharply defined as urban crisis, the character of the crisis in New York, and, more specifically, the place in that crisis of Harlem, the exemplary ghetto. "After the uprising of 1964," writes James de Jongh in his history of Harlem's place in the American literary imagination, "the symbol of Harlem crystallized questions of racial being in America once again, and the Harlem motif was associated with the riot itself. In the decade after 1964, the fact of rioting in Harlem was a pervasive historical influence and a dominant metaphoric presence associated with the motif of black Harlem."[7] The pages that follow also explore the crucial representational role played by figures of criminal violence in imagining Harlem in particular and the breakdown and emergence of urban orders in general. Violent delinquents like Miller's Duke Custis and Brown's autobiographical persona became lenses—often fantastically distortive lenses— through which to observe the changing inner city.

Postwar New York City in Transition

Americans, especially New Yorkers, tend to regard New York City as sui generis, citing its singular scale, complexity, and "world capital" status in support of the notion that New York is exceptional in all ways. In its general outlines, however, New York's postindustrial transformation recapitulates those of Chicago and Philadelphia. Although many observers did not register the decline of New York's manufacturing complex (the nation's largest, despite being anachronistically dominated by small businesses rather than steel mills or auto plants) and the parallel growth of its service industries until the city's fiscal crisis of the mid-1970s, the transformation was well under way by the mid-1960s. As John Mollenkopf argues, the recessions and fiscal crisis of the 1970s "accelerated and crystallized . . . secular trends" discernible throughout the postwar history of New York:

New York City's economy and society have undergone a profound and often painful transformation since the mid-1950s. At the end of World War II, New York was clearly a white, ethnic, blue collar, industrial city, despite the importance of its office sector. Today [in the late 1980s], high level business service activities drive the city's economy and its industrial base suffers from seemingly endless decline.[8]

The other principal elements of this story, familiar from the accounts of postwar Chicago and Philadelphia in parts 1 and 2, are a parallel set of physical reconfigurations and ethnic successions. Proliferating steel-and-glass towers in Manhattan, regional highways, housing projects, and the decay of the waterfront and other industrial-era building stock combined with the absolute and relative growth of black, Hispanic, and (later) Asian populations to remake the city's social landscape.

If in its physical, demographic, and economic arrangements "New York in 1940 appeared much as it had for more than a half-century," New York in the late 1960s was a very different place: a service city as much as a manufacturing center, with the balance shifting toward service industries; an increasingly black and Hispanic city; an increasingly postindustrial landscape in which postwar development and redevelopment (concentrating especially in the core) recast the prewar template.[9] In the decade spanning the mid-1950s to the mid-1960s, this recasting began to make itself evident in partial and disorienting ways.

The city builder and neighborhood breaker Robert Moses has often served in popular and scholarly narrative as the personification of transformative forces acting upon "old" New York.[10] Stories of the industrial city's decline single Moses out as the man who tore down a prewar New York distinguished (in the more rhapsodic versions) by the productive vitality of its white-ethnic urban villages, the cultural achievements of its black districts (especially jazz-age Harlem), the scrupulous respect accorded to female pedestrians at all hours and in all parts of the city, and the heroic excellence of its public schools and baseball teams. But Moses, for all his considerable power and vision, is a character symbolic of forces that extend far beyond the capacities of any individual. One can, on the one hand, find causes of postwar New York's transformation operating on the world-historical scale. Jason Epstein's essay "The Last Days of New York," an evocatively titled decline narrative and a classic account of the roots of New York's 1975 fiscal crisis, lists "a general crisis in capitalism; . . . the gradual westward shift of the American population; . . . new technologies and cheaper labor markets."[11] One can, on the other hand, trace the sources of transformation in the machinations of blocs of political and economic players, especially New York's versions of an alliance we have encountered in both Chicago and Philadelphia: the redevelopment-oriented progrowth coalition of local, state, and federal political operatives in league with developers and planners, construction companies and trade unions, bankers and money managers—a large, interconnected interest group with which Moses did business. However one casts the relation between global and local engines driving the change, Epstein argues that by the middle sixties you could see the city and its people changing all around you. New construction was going up everywhere, herding the old residents and their businesses into ever narrower enclaves, or driving them out of the city altogether. Meanwhile the expanding ghettos were overflowing with refugees driven here by the mechanization of Southern agriculture and by Southern welfare practices that made Northern cities seem deceptively generous by contrast. . . . Between 1960 and 1970 the proportion of blacks in the city had risen from 14 percent to 21 percent, most of them blacks trapped here by a city that didn't need their labor and that had, in fact, begun to export its menial and routine work to less costly labor markets, often to the same areas which these new arrivals had recently abandoned.[12]

For Epstein, as for many others, the story of postwar New York lies in the reduction of the industrial city's residential, economic, physical, and cultural orders to a set of narrow enclaves squeezed among expanding suburbs, spreading ghettos, and a densely redeveloped core. As in the cases of Chicago and Philadelphia, postindustrial transformation and ethnic and racial succession play the leading roles in shaping the postwar city's history and social landscape. The New York City Planning Commission's *Plan for New York City* of 1969, researched and written during the urban crisis and bearing the marks of its historical moment, concurs with Epstein in its mapping of cleavages in the present and future social landscape: "Greatest of all is the problem of the slums. . . . The blacks and Puerto Ricans crowded in them have been finding the way blocked in a way groups before them did not."[13] As Epstein points out, the ethnic succession of the 1960s coincided with the erosion of the traditional structure of economic opportunities offered by the industrial city, making for the specter of permanent central ghettos that even the plan of 1969—anything but a narrative of decline—identifies as the single most important urban problem.

The plan of 1969 respectfully acknowledges the "fear and hostility"of "blue-collar whites" and "middle class neighborhoods" threatened by the departure of industrial jobs and the expansion of black and Hispanic ghettos.[14] These nervous taxpayers are service professionals and especially white ethnics: some entrenched in their inner-city enclaves "on the edge of" black and Hispanic ghettos (as the plan sees them), more in diasporic movement along the track of upward social mobility from the old European-immigrant slums to the periphery. They are headed for the outer neighborhoods of Brooklyn, Queens, the Bronx, and Staten Island and beyond into a vast arc of suburbs encompassing Long Island, southern Connecticut, upstate New York, and New Jersey.[15] In the plan's view, these whites are responding with natural fear and doubt to a massive process of ethnic succession. New York City's non-Hispanic white population declined by about 2 million during the 1950s and 1960s, during which time whites in the city proper also tended to move toward its edges or concentrate in Manhattan below Ninety-sixth Street. At the same time, migration from the

South and from Puerto Rico helped to increase New York's black and Hispanic populations by about a million each, many of them concentrated around the core in areas that had once housed white-ethnic urban villages.[16]

If the specter of permanent ghettoes was what was most importantly wrong with New York in the 1960s, however, the plan of 1969 hastened to point out "a great deal that is very right with New York City." First, the densely redeveloped core of New York remained an international capital in which were concentrated corporate headquarters, financial markets, communications, advertising, publishing, the arts, theater, and the fashion industry. Second, New York offered on an unrivaled scale the semi-intangible urban quality of "life—more different kinds of people, more specialized services, more stores, more galleries, more restaurants, more possibilities of the unexpected." This weighing of the problem of the ghetto against a set of strengths located in the core and enclaves has a particularly postindustrial ring to it. The plan's introductory list of the city's strengths makes no mention of manufacturing but locates "the engine" of future growth and prosperity in service industries, cultural life, and the "phenomenal" rate at which new office space was being constructed in midtown and downtown Manhattan.[17] Glossing over a contracting but still vital industrial order, the plan stakes its rosy outlook on the service city's growth.

The central problem facing the plan's postindustrial city, the central problem of urbanism in transition as imagined by many of the urban intellectuals who together formulated the notion of urban crisis in the 1960s, was to manage the tension between the ghetto and the rest of the metropolis. As Fainstein, Fainstein, and Schwartz point out, the plan operated on the fundamental assumption that

> New York could be redeveloped in an orderly fashion for the rising service industries of the 1970s, as long as its restive minority population did not destabilize the city. . . . The central concern of government [as opposed to private investors in partnership with it] was not so much creating economic development as eliminating slums, providing public infrastructure, and assisting the disadvantaged to receive their share of its benefits.[18]

New York's planners drew a familiar map of complex urban transformations detailed in the first two parts of this study: the breakup, dispersal, and reduction to enclaves of the industrial neighborhood order; the emergence of a new social landscape centered on a densely redeveloped business core and complementary residential areas occupied by service-professional office workers; and the emergence of the second ghetto as the principal terrain of urban crisis, which threatened to destabilize the whole arrangement.

Harlem was, for most observers, the quintessential second ghetto. Although Brooklyn's Bedford-Stuyvesant and Brownsville districts, both of which had once been slums of opportunity for Jewish and other white-ethnic immigrants, served as important examples of the ghetto in the 1960s, Harlem played the more important role in representations not only of New York's ghettos but of "black America" in crisis.

The Capital of Black America

The *Plan for New York City* of 1969 framed its consideration of Harlem with two assertions that help to explain Harlem's role as an exemplary ghetto: "Central Harlem is the capital of black America" and Harlem's "physical and social problems" are so " massive and deep-rooted" that "only a total commitment by government and the community can solve them." The plan provided a thumbnail history of Harlem's turnover from German, Irish, Jewish, and Italian to black during the first quarter of the twentieth century, gesturing in capsule form to the turnover from white ethnic to black that formed one cornerstone of inner-city narrative after midcentury. The artistic, intellectual, and political renaissance of the 1920s following the moment of black succession— "Harlem's brightest period"—elevated Harlem to both representative and exceptional status among black urban communities. The plan understood Harlem to be in decline since the 1930s, attributing the decline to the exaggerated effect of the Great Depression on the employment and living conditions of blacks, overcrowding exacerbated by residential segregation, substantial migration from the South, and the community's increasing "frustration and disenchantment" (stock terms indicating rioting and other unrest) in the postwar years. [19]

Harlem in the 1960s had become, in the plan's formulation, a textbook second ghetto characterized by a definitive concentration of what were called "pathologies": high rates of poverty, unemployment, drug addiction, homicide, juvenile delinquency, maternal and infant mortality, venereal disease, and "family instability"; poor health conditions, deteriorating and blighted housing, and poor performance in schools; a weak business community dominated by "small stores in poor condition serving a local clientele," interspersed with abandoned and gutted retail space; and, of course, the isolation of blacks (and, in East Harlem, of Puerto Ricans) from the rest of the metropolis. The plan subscribed to the notion, popularized by Daniel Patrick Moynihan a few years before, of a "tangle of pathology" so knotty that only drastic intervention could break its grip on Harlemites. Accordingly, city, state, and federal governments had concentrated in Harlem a variety of ameliorative efforts—poverty programs, job training, expenditures on school buildings, and especially housing projects. Since World War II, large sections of Harlem's prewar landscape of brownstones and tenement residences interspersed with small businesses had been torn down and rebuilt in classic second ghetto form: high-rise apartment slabs, built in superblocks, set obliquely to the street. Harlem had the greatest concentration of public housing in the city, yet it was obvious that renovation of the physical landscape (especially renovation that involved tearing down existing neighborhoods and local businesses) was not going to be sufficient to ensure social peace. The plan of 1969, a document designed to put the city's best foot forward during a period of extraordinary pessimism about the urban future, could only promise that "the City is firmly committed to physical and social renewal" in Harlem. But if Harlem was indeed the capital of black America, then even this most congenitally optimistic of urban analyses could not, in 1969, bring itself to foresee anything but the persistence of the ghetto's "massive and deep-rooted" problems as the central social fact of the urban future.[20]

Although there were dissenting voices (like that of the novelist and critic Albert Murray, who will reappear in subsequent chapters) arguing that Harlem was neither typical nor a ghetto, the plan's formulation of Harlem as the core terrain of urban crisis went with the grain of Americans' representational habits in the 1960s.[21] There were at least three reasons for Harlem's status as, in the words of one standard urban history, "the ghetto that in this period consistently seemed to stand for all others."[22]

First, even though Harlem had not become a Black Metropolis until the 1920s, it had rapidly become in both popular culture and American letters an instantaneously "traditional" locus of black American urbanism. Because of Harlem, New York shared with Chicago and perhaps Detroit the status of housing a representative community of black Southerners come North to pursue the promise of steady work and social mobility extended by the industrial city to European peasants and other immigrants. Each of these cities was associated in the postwar period with a distinctive musical form identified as quintessentially black culture—New York with bebop, Chicago with blues, Detroit with Motown—but Harlem had since the Harlem Renaissance enjoyed a special status in American letters. A concentration of black writers, artists, and critics had aided Harlem's ascent to representative status by generating a body of work that encouraged black and white Americans to look to Harlem for authoritative black urban culture. After the war, Harlem continued to attract newcomers looking for work and intellectuals—black and white—looking for a vantage point from which to view the changes sweeping American inner cities.

Second, postwar Harlem remained a good position from which to enter into the national urban conversation, in which (for better or worse) New York City played a uniquely important role. In the 120 or so blocks south of Harlem's well-defined lower borders were concentrated disproportionate numbers of nationally accredited urban intellectuals, the nation's main publishing center for periodicals and books, one of two central headquarters for the entertainment and information industries, and a newspaper accepted by many readers across the nation and the world as the "paper of record." These various producers of urban literatures looked to Harlem, and only secondarily to Brooklyn, as the handiest avatar of black America, close by (perhaps too close for some) and yet a world apart. Thus, a socially engaged writer with Miller's modest but established record had only to move uptown to the edge of Harlem to collect material for a nationally acclaimed novel of the inner city. An ex-delinquent with Claude Brown's impressive experiential credentials had a better chance to publish his writing because Ernst Papanek, director of an upstate reform school in which Brown had served time as a boy, moved in the same circles as the prominent New York intellectuals who edited the journal *Dissent*, where Brown published his first autobiographical piece on Harlem in 1961.[23] Harlem in the 1960s (like South Central Los Angeles in 1992) had unique access to the national limelight by virtue of its position near the core of a city with outsize influence in discussions of American urbanism and by virtue of its proximity to sites where national culture was produced and disseminated.

Third, Harlem provided an object lesson in urban change. The bankruptcy of the promised land's promise could be read in the collapse of the Black Metropolis of the 1920s into the postwar second ghetto. Ralph Ellison tells a version of that story of generational disappointment in his essay "Harlem Is Nowhere," in which he visits Harlem's Lafargue Clinic, where Fredric Wertham specialized in psychiatric treatment of violent delinquents. The landscape around the clinic "is a ruin" of "crumbling buildings with littered areaways, ill-smelling halls and vermin-invaded rooms," and in these details one can read "the cultural history of Negroes in the North." Their story "reads like the legend of some tragic people out of mythology, a people which aspired to escape from its own unhappy homeland to the apparent peace of a distant mountain; but which, in migrating, made some fatal error of judgment and fell into a great chasm of mazelike passages that promise ever to lead to the mountain but end over against a wall."[24] Representations of Harlem could map the form and meanings of the bewildering, "mazelike" inner city by following the sensationalized bad behavior of the inheritors of this "fatal error," violent delinquent children of the postwar inner city like Duke Custis, Claude Brown, and Wertham's patients. Precisely because Harlem had enjoyed the status of America's most modern and sophisticated Black Metropolis, defined by its aspiration to cultural leadership, the casting of Harlem as one among many ghettos defined by its pathologies carried particular ironic or tragic force. Harlem thus suggested itself as a place to engage with the emergence of the postwar inner city by asking what had happened to "black America."

The cover of *Manchild* (fig. 10) posed that question as well. The hardback edition features a handsome cover photo of three young men at the intersection of Seventh Avenue with 125th Street, Harlem's main thoroughfare (and therefore a main thoroughfare of "black America"). Sporting variously skewed hats, hands stuffed into jacket pockets, striding in a loose, challenging row, they command the attention of an older man approaching them from the opposite direction. With his back to the camera, and therefore sharing the reader's perspective, he appears to turn his head a bit to eye them—with interest and per-haps apprehension—as they pass. These young men, successors to the postwar generation of what Ralph Ellison called "transitional boys," move through the heart of Harlem in transition. The young men's situation is marked in time by an advertisement for a televised boxing match between Cassius Clay and Sonny Liston. (Liston's top billing and the use of the name Clay, rather than Ali, iden-tify it as probably the first of their two fights, held in February 1964.) Like the delinquent Malcolm Little's transformation into the political and religious leader Malcolm X, Cassius Clay's public transformation into Muhammad Ali registered his engagement with the political and cultural currents of the period that shaped Claude Brown and his cohorts (including Brown's friend Doug Jones, called "Turk" in *Manchild*, a heavyweight who lost a close decision to Clay in 1963). The young men's situation is marked in space by the split back-drop against which they move: to the right, a bustling crowd, an industrial-era building with the traditional (for New York City) fire escape running down its street facade, a movie theater, a liquor store, a bowling alley, bar, and restau-rant; to the left, austere slab-style housing projects (the General Grant Houses, built in 1955) set at an angle to the street. If the right side of the frame evokes the traditional vigor and bustle of the past of the Black Metropolis, the left side seems to indicate an ominous, inscrutable future. The boys move through the world that hangs in the balance.

Claude Brown's cultural work, and Warren Miller's before him, was to fig-ure and explain that world by using the eyes and voices of these young men to traverse the changing landscape of Harlem. Both addressed an initial reading audience steeped in the notion of urban violence as a sign of larger urban changes, an audience that avidly eyed the "transitional boys" with a mix of unease and fascination.

From the Delinquency Panic to the Urban Crisis

Claude Brown (born in 1937) and *Cool World*'s narrating protagonist Duke Custis (born sometime around the end of World War II) offered themselves as representative members of the first generation to come of age in the postwar inner city, a generation in whose behavior observers sought to read the conse-quences of urban America's postwar transformation. Brown and Duke, born in Harlem and raised there by parents who migrated from the South, are part of what Brown called "the first Northern urban generation of Negroes," by which he meant the first generation of black Americans raised in the Northern inner city as the spatial and demographic center of "black America" shifted from the South to the urban North. Brown and Duke are also violent young male delin-quents, a crucial aspect of their credentialing as actors on the urban stage who do the cultural work of representing their generation's leading role in the remaking of urbanism.[25] Changing images of violence offer us a way to read the continuities between the delinquency panic of the 1950s and the urban crisis of the 1960s, creating a single stream of violence that ran through representations of postindustrial urbanism as it emerged.

Duke is a juvenile delinquent first and a young black man second. Keeping to the conventions of teen gang formula, *Cool World* sits squarely in the generic mainstream of a vast literature of the 1950s that represented, exploited, and sought the meanings of juvenile delinquency. Written in the late 1950s, the novel considers race as an important factor underlying the geography of Duke's world and consciousness, but Miller's ultimate responsibility in *Cool World* is to rendering an account of Duke's membership in a gang as an existential condition. For Miller in the late 1950s, the problem of delinquency organized the dependent variable of race. Along with many other urban intellectuals, however, Miller in the 1960s reversed the relation between delinquency and race, making race the defining urban problem that drove consideration of previously independent problems like delinquency. By 1965, when *Manchild in the Promised Land* appeared, a large readership was prepared to receive Claude Brown, who claimed to speak for his generation of young inner-city blacks, as a writer who addressed the heart of urban concern and spoke for all black Americans. Brown undertook to map the second ghetto from the inside, to explain what it was like to be a black American by exploring the urban terrain on which that experience was understood to take shape. Brown, then, was black first and delinquent second, his delinquency (like Malcolm X's) serving as the most compelling of the ghetto pathologies that were seen to characterize life in "that separate world" of "black America."

Miller and Brown help to demonstrate how the problem of juvenile delinquency, which played such an important role in discussions of the inner city during the 1950s and early 1960s, was subsumed by the problem of race that defined the urban crisis during the 1960s. In the time between the publication of *Cool World* in 1959 and *Manchild in the Promised Land* in 1965, conventional representations of the problem of urban street crime and violence moved the focus from the figure of the street gang (composed of lower-class boys, and girls, of all races and ethnicities) to the figure of the young black man as mugger and rioter. The classic delinquent gang's odd combination of anarchic violence and pseudo-military posturings—at once "disorganized," in the Chicago School's sense of insufficient socialization, and too organized, in a manner that spoke darkly to some postwar observers of incipient fascism—gradually ceased to be an issue of national concern in the early 1960s.[26] A more general concern with "youth culture," embracing both ghetto and campus, succeeded it.[27] But the same paradoxical blend of under- and over-organization characterized the figure of the riot that captured the public imagination from 1964 through the end of the decade. The riot, like the gang, combined the threat of random savagery embodied in the figures of the mugger and the rapist—young men unable or unwilling to control basic drives—with the threat of organized insurgency theatrically fostered by the paramilitary rhetoric and trappings of black "revolutionaries" and campus radicals. The conventions of the delinquency problem had flowed into both the problem of race and the national fascination with youth culture by the mid-1960s, tending to obscure the prior importance of juvenile delinquency, which had been in its own right an overarching national concern that intersected with discussion of the changing city and helped to guide it.

Before race became *the* urban subject in the mid-1960s, juvenile delinquency provided the images of violence in the streets used to represent the inner city in transition. A national concern with delinquency, originally linked to the familial dislocations occasioned by the war effort, gathered momentum during World War II and gradually built up to panic proportions in the mid- and late 1950s, becoming one of the period's defining subjects. The threat of a delinquent generation—a "shook-up generation," as the journalist Harrison Salisbury called it[28]—condensed a whole range of anxieties about postwar America, from the power of mass culture to the erosion of traditional sources of authority to the psychic disruptions of the Cold War, but those anxieties also intersected in significant ways with the reordering of American urbanism. The booming suburban periphery, where traditional authorities succumbed to prosperity and mass culture, and the decaying inner city, where poor, undereducated black and Hispanic in-migrants came into violent contact with the contracting white-ethnic neighborhood order, served as the two principal terrains in which the drama of delinquency was enacted.

If delinquency was seen to be dispersed across the American landscape, it was also seen in important ways to proceed from the inner city. Middle-class teenagers in suburbs and small towns seemed to be adopting habits of mind and behavior associated with the urban lower classes. In addition, the inner city was home to the powerfully compelling figure of the violent teen gang. Portrayed in uniform—club jackets, zoot suits, or the more understated "conservative" styles—and given to acts of almost inexplicable cruelty and destructiveness, displaying no allegiance to family or country, opposed to school and other forms of socialization, the gang served as the principal icon of a separate juvenile order with intractably alien systems of value and belief. By examining the gang's behavior and motivations—quintessentially by investigating the violence of the gang's inner life as expressed in heinous criminal offenses perpetrated in public spaces—one could begin to understand the transformed urban world in which delinquency "grew" (as communism was supposed to "grow") like a weed, cancer, or contagion. The redevelopment-minded business leaders and planners of the Greater Philadelphia Movement, for instance, followed this logic in concluding that part of their duty in planning the future of downtown

Philadelphia involved providing funds for journalist Roul Tunley to visit several American cities, as well as Moscow, Bangkok, Tokyo, Tel Aviv, and Cairo, to prepare a report on delinquency and methods of controlling it (published later, in 1962, as *Kids, Crime and Chaos*).

On the one hand, the delinquency panic can be seen as a response to a complex of metaphorical associations carried by the delinquent, including associations with urban change, rather than as a response to a genuine crime wave. In *A Cycle of Outrage*, James Gilbert calls the apparent rise in juvenile crime "an arithmetic observation" that "inspired geometric fears."[29] There had been gangs, juvenile delinquents, and criminal violence in American inner cities before the 1950s, and it is not clear that the cultural prominence during the 1950s of the problem of delinquency was caused by an actual increase in serious crime. Gilbert points out that what looked like a juvenile crime wave might in fact have been a product of changes in the enforcement and definition of crime, combined with the mass entry of Americans below the age of consent into a set of market relations and cultural styles that make up "youth culture." The statistical increase in crime during the 1950s can be traced in part to a surge in status crimes, which involve young people behaving in ways traditionally reserved for adults (drinking, having sex, staying out late), rather than to a surge in violent crimes.[30]

On the other hand, it may be that the proliferation of zip gun shootings, knifings, rumbles, and gang rapes that formed the backbone of delinquency as represented in movies, comic books, and newspaper accounts *did* actually refer to an increase in certain forms of urban violence. What matters here is that compressed into the subtext of these representations of violence were responses to social and cultural change on the grand scale—not only the flowering of mass culture and the rise of youth culture but also the processes of suburbanization, ghettoization, and ethnic succession that marked the decline of the industrial neighborhood order and the formation of new inner-city orders. Gangs of teenagers committing acts of violence in the streets presented a social problem, but the stock figures of such violence offered as well a repertoire of forms with which to consider and represent—among other complex, often indistinct processes—the transformation of the urban social landscape and the urbanisms it housed.

The language of the delinquency panic therefore had important resonances for urbanists. For instance, in *The Death and Life of Great American Cities* (1961), a profoundly influential attack on the conventional wisdoms of city planners and redevelopers, Jane Jacobs uses "the barbaric concept of Turf" to describe a destructive ethos of territorial aggressiveness associated with "hoodlum gangs" but shared by "developers of the rebuilt city"—progrowth coalitions. That is, she infuses "turf," one of the slang keywords of the delinquency literature, not only with the violent territoriality of the gang but also with the territoriality of redevelopment. She concludes that "wherever the rebuilt city rises the barbaric concept of Turf must follow, because the rebuilt city has junked a basic function of the city street and with it, necessarily, the freedom of the city."[31] For Jacobs, who was one of Robert Moses's most prominent antagonists, the city's vital functions (circulation of people, goods, capital) and defining qualities (density, flow between private and public spaces) depend on citizens' confidence in the safety of their streets. Violent juvenile delinquents destroy citizens' sense of freedom of movement in the street, but the delinquents' brand of street violence only expresses in visceral form a more powerful territorial logic. City planners, developers, and government officials destroy the intricately developed, life-giving tissue of urbanism by limiting "the freedom of the city" on the grand scale with housing projects, highways, and the bulldozing of neighborhoods.

Jacobs's use of violence in the street as a metaphor of the principles underlying urban transformation also offers a way to bridge the delinquency panic and the urban crisis. In the course of making her attack on the kind of city planning that was reshaping Chicago's Milwaukee Avenue corridor, Philadelphia's South Street and Center City, and old New York, Jacobs identifies what she calls "the drama of civilization versus barbarism in cities" as the most important story in which to read the content of urban crisis. Jacobs did not yet, in 1961, feel obliged to organize that content under the rubric of race. Writing in the late 1950s and 1960, Jacobs casts the physical threat on the street as a matter of "delinquency and crime," downplaying the role of racial and class differences in the way citizens formulate their city-killing sense of fear. Jacobs's notion of "barbarism" straddles the delinquency panic of the 1950s and the urban crisis of the 1960s, during which the racial ghetto became the conventional site of barbarous violence. Jacobs may, in fact, have believed that differences in race and class did not matter in the calculus of urban fear—she did not find it "illuminating to tag minority groups, or the poor, or the outcast with responsibility for city danger"—but others did find such explanatory categories illuminating. Jacobs herself points out that when we speak of one's sense of relative safety, believing makes it so: "Today barbarism has taken over many city streets, or people fear it has, which comes to much the same thing in the end."[32] She was soon in the distinct minority in separating the "drama of civilization versus barbarism in the cities" from the ghetto-centered drama of racial succession and conflict.

"It all began in about 1963," writes James Q. Wilson in *Thinking About Crime:* "That was the year, to overdramatize a bit, that a decade began to fall apart." Wilson is describing an increase in crime rates, one "sign of social malaise," that helped to "shatter" the "mood of contentment and confidence in which the decade began."[33] In more measured tones, Stuart Scheingold's *The Politics of Law and Order* offers a similar periodization: "Beginning in the mid-

1960s, crime, especially street crime, became a political issue of considerable importance at both the local and the national levels."[34] Street crime became, as well, perhaps the most important source of compelling images in which to read and consider the meanings of the divided metropolis. Glossing the Kerner Commission, Wilson explains, "we were becoming two societies—one affluent and worried, the other pathological and predatory." For Wilson, whose addition of "predatory" plays up the fear of the ghetto that the Kerner Commission played down by emphasizing white racism, the latter of these two societies was, in essence, identical with the black inner city.[35]

"Pathological and predatory" might also describe Americans' growing sense of themselves as a people in the 1960s. In the second half of the decade, especially, American culture became particularly obsessed with the idea of Americans' own exceptional, definitive, and racially inflected violence—not just as expressed in street crime, police brutality, and race rioting but also as expressed in the high-tech savagery of the Vietnam War, the assassination of political figures (John and Robert Kennedy, Malcolm X, Martin Luther King), and a great deal of violent talk (and, occasionally, even violent behavior) on college campuses. President Johnson felt obliged to appoint a National Commission on the Causes and Prevention of Violence to expand the Kerner Commission's investigation of urban riots into an effort to explain the larger problem of American violence, and the many studies overseen by the "Violence Commission" constituted one of the most comprehensive of the period's many efforts to read the meanings and provenance of Americans' exceptional barbarism.[36] Johnson's appointment of the Violence Commission is one sign of a general recognition evident during the 1960s, registered across the political spectrum and in the highest reaches of government, of a need to grapple interpretively with violence (or to be seen doing so as a sign of responsiveness to national trauma). The problem of violence in the streets, giving dramatic expression to the many factors underlying the urban crisis, played a central part in the period's obsessive attention to American social violence.

Violence in the streets also played a crucial role in the formulation of urban crisis. In addition to expressing a general sense of violently sudden change in the inner cities, violence in the streets provided occasions to consider in particular the complex of racial successions and physical reconfigurations that shaped the postwar inner city's social landscape. Rioting and street crime, apparently boiling out from a permanent and increasingly immiserated second ghetto, served as the most visible sign of conflict and social cleavage attendant upon urban transformation. The round of ghetto riots that catalyzed the notion of urban crisis began in 1963; there was rioting in Harlem, among other places, in 1964; larger riots followed in Los Angeles, Detroit, Newark, Chicago, echoed by a variety of disorders in smaller and usually more placid cities, until the end of the decade. In the mid-1960s, also, a significant annual increase in the urban crime rate, measured in the FBI's Uniform Crime Reports (UCR), began to figure prominently in the urban conversation as a "crime wave" centering on the ghetto. *Newsweek* explained in August 1965 that, according to the UCR, "every category of crime was on the increase" and that since 1958 "serious crime has spiraled upward at a rate of five times that of the population."[37] The inner city appeared to be a more violent place than it had been in the past.

As in the case of the delinquency crisis of the 1950s, violent crime surged so dramatically into a leading place in public discourse in the 1960s that some observers questioned the basis of anxiety in hard facts. Even *Newsweek*'s dramatic cover story in August 1965, which replicated and exploited the talk of a "rising tide" of "crime in the streets," paused to question the relation between violence in the city of fact and in the city of feeling ("How true is the impression?"), quoting dissenting experts who wanted to know how the statistical increases had been affected by changes in the reporting rather than the incidence of crime.[38] But the UCR indexes of assault, robbery, rape, murder, and other face-to-face crime did rise alarmingly, especially in cities. Various experts and lay commentators traced the increase to a statistical bulge in the crime-prone population of young men in general and especially to the shaping influence on young black men of problems that were supposedly native to the second ghetto: the spread of heroin addiction, the increasing dissonance between general prosperity and the permanence of the ghetto, "the culture of poverty," bad schools, and a collapse of parental authority often discussed as the problem of "the Negro family." The same explanations were available to account for urban rioters, whose behavior became a national trauma endlessly rehearsed on television. Street crime and rioting, and the "wave" of both that suffused the news media during the urban crisis, did accelerate the dispersal of the middle class and capital to the suburbs, but one ought to bear in mind that such violence did not for the most part spill out of ghettos into the rest of the metropolis. Most of the damage and suffering took place in the ghettos themselves, largely involving black citizens and the police officers paid by society to contain the shocks of ghetto life. In certain ways, the inner city was more unsafe in the 1960s than it had been before (especially if one lived *in* the ghetto), but an increasingly suburbanized nation reacted as if the entire inner city had become a free-fire zone. Increases in certain highly charged and representable kinds of violence in the ghetto were received as a general increase in violence that was a fundamental component of American urbanism.[39]

Whatever the relation between actual and perceived increases in urban violence, it is clear that in the early 1960s violent crime and the fear of it rose to the status of a defining urban problem, flowing as such into the racial logic of urban crisis. The second ghetto was widely regarded as the source of violent disorders—or, one might say, as a place in which to measure the traumatic emergence of new urban orders—that spread fear throughout the metropolis.

The conceptual condensations that made up the Negro-ghetto-violence equation, implicit in the subtexts of the word "ghetto" as it came to be used during the urban crisis, were in 1965 just ascending to received status, to be underscored in the next three years by the reports of the President's Commission on Law Enforcement and Administration of Justice, the Kerner Commission, and the Violence Commission. Like so many other previously independent sources of urban concern, crime and juvenile delinquency and other ways to consider the problem of violence in the streets found places within the organizing racial logic of the urban crisis.

Postwar Harlem was, of course, a logical place to look for meaningful violence during both the delinquency panic and the urban crisis. Fredric Wertham, perhaps the most important analyst of juvenile delinquency in the 1950s, did his research on the effects of mass culture on socialization at the Lafargue Clinic. He found that black and Hispanic children, who were more likely than whites to be poor and poorly educated, were particularly susceptible to the dehumanizing effects of comic-book reading. The peculiar cruelty of delinquents' violent behavior, and their insufficient remorse, was the centerpiece of Wertham's critique of mass culture as a root cause of delinquency. Like Wertham, Kenneth Clark conducted his profoundly influential research on "youth in the ghetto" in Harlem. The genesis of Clark's *Dark Ghetto* shows how during the urban crisis the problem of race subsumed delinquency. As Clark describes it, *Dark Ghetto* grew "directly from the two years which the author spent as chief project consultant and chairman of the board of directors of the planning stage of the Harlem Youth Opportunities Unlimited" (HARYOU), a group funded by the City of New York and, more important, by the President's Committee on Juvenile Delinquency. Clark's original report, *Youth in the Ghetto*, described "the conditions of youth in Harlem as background for a comprehensive program for these young people," but he drastically condensed and revised *Youth in the Ghetto* in preparing *Dark Ghetto* as "a book for the general public . . . broader and deeper in scope and purpose." Thus, while the original HARYOU report "emphasized the plight of youth in Harlem, the present book concentrates on the problems of ghetto communities everywhere and with all the inhabitants of the ghettos, not with youth alone."[40] Youth flowed into race, delinquency flowed into the ghetto-centered urban crisis, urban intellectuals continued to model the relation between criminal violence and urban change—and all these movements were plotted on the ground of postwar Harlem.

New York City in Crisis

Having established a series of historical frames—the emergence of postindustrial New York, the centrality of Harlem in discussions of urbanism in transition, the continuing importance of criminal violence in representing these changes—I want to suggest how such matters found their way into cultural circulation. Complex urban change is in some ways hard to see (e.g., globalization of markets) and in other ways impossible to miss (e.g., police shooting at fleeing looters on television), and signs of it circulate in the coded form of compressed, formulaic, even ritual representations. To recover some of the texture of those signs and formulas, I will consider how a reader of the *New York Herald-Tribune* would have experienced them in 1965. Before turning in following chapters to the writing of Warren Miller and Claude Brown, which develops at book length the literary possibilities afforded by postwar urbanism in transition, let us establish one more frame for that inquiry by reading the daily newspaper.

On 25 January 1965, the *Herald-Tribune* began publishing a series of investigative stories collectively entitled "New York City in Crisis." The series, developed over several weeks and in dozens of stories flagged with a somber image of the New York skyline and harbor in shadow, painted a portrait of a city too weakly governed to survive the massive postwar transformations visible in every aspect of its life. Proceeding from a pair of assumptions typical of New Yorkers' examinations of their city—"New York is the greatest city in the world . . . and everything is wrong with it"—the *Herald-Tribune* series emphasized the damage done to New York by suburbanization, the decline of manufacturing, rising crime, intractable poverty, and the failures of urban renewal. Jane Jacobs and Kenneth Clark, urban intellectuals who rose to prominence through their treatment of these matters, offered pithy quotations that frame an introductory outline of the premises and agenda of the "New York City in Crisis" series in the 25 January issue. Jacobs, the critic of urban renewal and city planning, warns of popular discontent: "The people are being utterly disregarded." Clark, the expert on ghetto pathologies and youth, warns of impending catastrophe: "Time is running out for this city."[41]

The investigation was, among other things, a political hatchet job. Relentlessly attacking Mayor Wagner, a Democrat, the liberal Republican *Herald-Tribune* respectfully turned whenever possible to the opinions of Manhattan's liberal Republican congressman John Lindsay, who was later to become the paper's chosen candidate and, eventually, Wagner's successor in Gracie Mansion. Above Jacobs's and Clark's properly apocalyptic sentiments in the 25 January issue were juxtaposed two more framing quotations: a defensive-sounding plea from Wagner ("I'm willing to listen to anybody") and a more dynamic line from Lindsay ("New York has lost its will power"). Barry Gottehrer, who headed the "New York City in Crisis" investigative team, later joined Lindsay's campaign staff and then became one of Mayor Lindsay's most important advisers, especially during periods of tension and upheaval in New York's ghettos.[42] Gottehrer's *Herald-Tribune* series lost few chances to play up Lindsay as a reformist alternative to business as usual and to present Wagner's administration as an obsolescent, corrupt pack of clubhouse regulars un-equipped to face a developing urban crisis.

"New York City in Crisis," then, offers a narrative arguing for the decline of the prewar inner city and its orders—a manufacturing-based economy, a social landscape dominated by white-ethnic urban villages, and the regular Demo-cratic coalition rooted in the fraying structure of the industrial neighborhood order. That narrative, intertwining with the rise to cultural prominence of the increasingly city-centered "Negro problem," helped the reporters and editors of the *Herald-Tribune*, as well as its readers (some of whom recorded their responses in letters to the editor), to define a historical moment.

Reading the *Herald-Tribune* as the investigation develops through January and February of 1965, one has the sense of passing in a rush through the post-war period. The inaugural article of the series squeezed continuing coverage of Winston Churchill's recent death to the margins of page 1. His prominence as a hero of the Cold War notwithstanding, Churchill's name and the eulogies accorded him invoke associations with World War II and with FDR (and thus the Great Depression and New Deal) that seem to recede swiftly into the his-torical background as the War on Poverty and the Vietnam War rise up in the foreground. Throughout early 1965, "New York City in Crisis" shared the front page with news of America's deepening involvement in Vietnam—stories char-acterized by a Cold War blend of measured containment, high-tech annihila-tion, and ambiguous commitment that seems worlds apart from the language of the Good War.[43] Next to the daily bulletins from the battle fronts of Vietnam and the inner cities, Churchill's war and FDR's America—the war in which even Frankie Machine fought, the prewar urban America in which Nelson Algren, Gwendolyn Brooks, Jack Dunphy, and William Gardner Smith grew up—become ancient history. By late February, the "New York City in Crisis" articles were also sharing the front page with another death: that of Malcolm X, who was as much a "political figure" as Churchill but in a particularly 1960s sense of the term. Malcolm X, an ex-delinquent turned urban intellectual whose public persona was grounded in the terrain of the second ghetto, had risen to prominence as the notion of urban crisis became a point of confluence for discussions of postwar urban change and racial conflict.

The *Herald-Tribune* suggests that confluence by juxtaposing Malcolm X's sensational death in Harlem with information on structural changes in urban-ism. On 24 February 1965, page 1 of the *Herald-Tribune* featured a follow-up story on the assassination of Malcolm X, exploring the meaning of his politi-cal and cultural influence. A discussion of various theories about the motives of Malcolm X's killers leads to a consideration of black separatism or nationalism as responses to the ghettoization of blacks—that is, to their confinement in the most deteriorated, blighted parts of the city, where economic opportunity is least accessible and most rapidly diminished by deindustrialization. Economic opportunity in decline was the subject of another story on page 1 that day, this one under the "New York City in Crisis" graphic. Under the headline "For N.Y., Another Grim Report," Barry Gottehrer detailed the findings of a "long-awaited" consultant's "study of the city's extreme industrial and manufacturing problems." The consultant's report outlines a set of economic conditions structuring the inner city and the urban crisis, as declines in manufacturing lead to erosion of the city's tax base and "increasing deterioration and blight."[44] The logic of urban crisis incorporated both economic change and racial conflict and offered ways to read them together.

The stories resonate with one another, but a number-laden consultant's report did not carry the popular representational charge found in the bloody martyrdom of a controversial public figure. The consultant's report was dutifully noted and logged, but one can see the passion over Malcolm X in the tension between eulogies in the *Herald-Tribune* of 24 February: on the one hand, American and African political leaders call him a statesman, "the American Lumumba"; on the other hand, he is identified as a member of "the Negro fringe" whose death could lead to what columnist Jimmy Breslin calls "a tong war" among Black Muslims or to more generalized rioting in "potential trouble spots across the nation."[45] Discrete, violent events like murder and riots lend themselves readily to American representational habits, traditions shared by those texts labeled "news" and those labeled "literature." When gunfire in Harlem took center stage, the complex of urban transformations described in the consultant's report on manufacturing became deep background to the story of Malcolm X's life and death. Complex change that over time had produced the second ghetto became terrifically compressed in the figure of Malcolm X, a character infused with the content of crisis. Warren Miller had argued, in his review of the delinquent memoir *Out of the Burning* a few years before, that "there is a need for stories like this . . . that present us with a life rather than with statistics (which are hard to read and easy to ignore)," but it is hard to recover the consultant's analysis in any depth in the analysis of a murder.[46]

Malcolm X's violent death was one more episode confirming the widely received understanding of Harlem as a dangerous place full to bursting with well-armed and violently disaffected young black men. That death, and the perception that Malcolm X was responsible for fomenting racial violence, further elaborated the constantly repeated motif of street violence recurring in "New York City in Crisis." There had been a riot in Harlem in 1964, which Gottehrer's team interpreted as a response to worsening social conditions: "an already troubled Negro population learned last summer that City Hall could be made to listen."[47] Street crime was also on the rise in Harlem as unemployed young men, casting around for ways to make money, hit upon the drug trade and muggings. (One of them, profiled by Gottehrer, had not worked since 1961, except "as an extra in the movie 'The Cool World' and as a porter at CCNY" for two months.)[48] Reporters, police experts, and other commentators worried that a tide of drug- and poverty-driven muggings was spilling out from the ghetto to change the character of urbanism throughout the metropolis. Several "New York City in Crisis" stories, and the letters to the editor they elicited, described a fear of leaving one's home after dark, especially in once-safe neighborhoods, as a novel and salient feature of urbanism in the 1960s.[49] The *Herald-Tribune* offered a narrative of declining civility in which the quantity of violence increased and the spaces and times of citizens' vulnerability to violence expanded: "Today it is no longer only the slum streets and the darkened parks that create this fear. Increasingly, as major crimes of violence continue to rise, New Yorkers have become afraid everywhere in the city—in their streets, in their parks, in their subways, in their own homes, at night and during the day."[50]

The *Herald-Tribune* printed a number of letters from readers who also understood this increase in fear of violent crime as significant and central to contemporary urbanism. The letters offered visions of "a city besieged" and wished for a return to civility in which women could "walk after dark without fear or molestation." One respondent, having moved to Valley Stream, Long Island, explained that his family had for many years "lived reasonably content in a mixed neighborhood on the edge of the Negro ghetto," accepting as normal an escalating fear of assault, robbery, and burglary. Finally, the "city fathers" had gone too far in declaring that "our children must attend school with slum dwellers" even though "middle-class Negroes" had "long since fled our neighborhood" to protect their own children from "such a fate"—and the writer had joined the flow of middle-class whites moving from inner city to suburbs. "We have left New York City," the writer concluded. Sketching a generic narrative of what many called "white flight," he explained that the city had lost "one industrious, law-abiding, taxpaying family" as a result of its failure to control pathological ghetto types—"the drug addict, the thief, the prostitute, the sponger, the degenerate"—and the criminal threat they posed to the well-being and property of other urbanites.[51]

Reported violent crime had, in fact, increased substantially during the late 1950s and early 1960s, as a "New York City in Crisis" article reported under the headline "New Figures on Crime: Up, Up, Up," but fear of violence also carried a powerful symbolic charge that extended far beyond a simple response to increases in some criminal activities.[52] Powerfully evocative figures of violence offered ways to consider and respond to the emergence of a new set of urban orders. Riots, muggings, assassinations, and experts' talk of crisis trailed deep roots in processes like long-term economic and demographic change, corporate and governmental decision making, subtle but comprehensive reconfigurations of the city's social landscape. The *Herald-Tribune*'s coverage of Malcolm X's violent death and the recurring language of urban violence and fear that runs through the "New York City in Crisis" series show how the motif of violent crime served as a way to imagine the traumatic emergence of the second ghetto and other shocks presented by the advent of postindustrial urbanism.

"New York City in Crisis" is a period piece. Not only a portrait of one American metropolis in 1965, caught in motion, it is also an example of the logic and language of urban crisis, which was just then acquiring a canonical status it still enjoys. "New York City in Crisis" thus helps to create a frame of reference for the literature of urban crisis. A regular reader of the *Herald-Tribune*, having followed the series into the spring of 1965, would have a background in mind against which to read the excerpts of *Manchild in the Promised Land* the paper ran in July of that year. This hypothetical regular reader would, in particular, be encouraged by "New York City in Crisis" to desire entry into the subjective experience of a leading character in the urban drama, the violent black man represented not only by Brown but also by the delinquents and some Harlem secessionists in Warren Miller's novels. The *Herald-Tribune*'s investigation spun out a bewildering complex of analytical lines in describing the extent of urban crisis, but the increase in criminal violence—which, like the growth of the inner city's black population, was just one aspect of urban change—enabled a powerful simplifying strategy by which the complexity could be condensed and made accessible. Thus, Gottehrer's investigative team could assert that "of the many problems disrupting the present and threatening the future of this city, none is more critical than this growing concern and fear over the increase of fear and violence in the streets, the subways, the elevators and the parks of New York."[53]

Ralph Ellison's *Invisible Man* (1952), a novel built around a series of violent acts and culminating in a Harlem riot, considers the representational potentialities and limits of street violence in its opening episode. The Invisible Man, on a nighttime excursion from his cellar retreat just outside the border of Harlem ("on the edge of the Negro ghetto," as the letter by the *Herald-Tribune*'s reader from Long Island would put it), runs afoul of a white man and ends up administering a savage beating to him. "The next day," the Invisible Man tells us, "I saw his picture in the *Daily News*, beneath a caption stating that he had been 'mugged.'"[54]

In one sense, that brief news item makes the Invisible Man visible, or at least legible, by inserting him into a generic event. Although it is his victim who appears in the photograph, the Invisible Man assumes representable form as a stock figure, the mugger emerging from the ghetto to make the city's streets unsafe for pedestrians. In another sense, though, the newspaper story about a mugging renders the Invisible Man invisible once more by condensing to the point of illegibility a much larger story, his tour of midcentury America. His participation in the black migration from the agrarian South to the Northern inner cities; his disastrous entry into the racially divided workplace; his survey of political responses to the American racial order, ranging from the assimilationism of his Southern college to the radical separatism of Ras the Exhorter; his cultural cartography, surveying the efforts of black Americans to "enter history" in their dress, music, and speech—all these encounters with larger movements and processes that shape the Invisible Man's experience, his inner life, and the postwar inner city move beneath the surface of the *Daily News* story. So far beneath the surface do these contents move, however, that the generic story of a mugging cannot hope to bring them to light. They become almost invisible to a reader of the *Daily News* at the same time as the Invisible Man becomes almost visible as a mugger.

Assaulting the white man in the novel's first episode, three paragraphs into the prologue, the Invisible Man inaugurates his encyclopedic narrative with an act of violence. He also makes possible yet another story in the paper about a mugging near the second ghetto, a fragmentary example of the language of fear and violence used to articulate the arrival of postwar urbanism. A growing anxiety about violence in the street joins the Invisible Man's urban world in transition of the 1940s and 1950s to the urban world in crisis of the 1960s. The dutiful reader of the *Daily News* would, in the early 1950s when the novel was published, have generically assumed that the mugger was one of Ellison's uprooted, zoot-suited, delinquent "transitional boys" who inherited the postwar inner city to which their parents migrated. That same reader in the mid-1960s would assume the mugger was driven by a different set of stock motivations identified by the *Herald-Tribune*'s letter writer from Long Island—drug addiction, moral disorientation produced by ghetto pathologies and permissive governmental response to them, racial antipathy edged with political radicalism. This hypothetical reader would be responding to a portrait of postindustrial urbanism as it was gleaned from the daily papers—in bits and pieces, inflected by received wisdoms and ideological nuances, its meanings simultaneously articulated and garbled by generic formula.

Still, the Invisible Man's prodigious story and the brief, almost opaque item in the paper contain one another—just as the Invisible Man and the mugger contain one another. Although the Invisible Man protests that he is "a man of substance" and not "one of your Hollywood-movie ectoplasms," in his role as mugger he flows easily into a representational niche made available by institutions of culture—in this case the newspapers—and thus marks with violence his passage through the inner city and into history.[55] The postwar generation of "transitional boys" like Duke Custis and Claude Brown likewise occupied a representational niche in violent, formulaic stories infused with the content of urban crisis.

Checkpoint Frederick Douglass: Warren Miller and the Boundaries of the Ghetto

You look aroun you see I not the only one who found
the way to break thru. They a lot of us an we no
worse then some of those down town who just
dreamin about it an dont have the nerve for it.
                    Warren Miller, *The Cool World*

As the obituarist put it in summing up Warren Miller's literary career in 1966, Miller was "one of that band of novelists who provide a literary period, not necessarily with its principal sources of light and power, but with its texture and density."[1] In Miller's two Harlem novels, *The Cool World* (1959) and *The Siege of Harlem* (1964), one can read some of the texture of the urban crisis as it developed in the late 1950s and early 1960s. One can see how the complex and extended transformation of inner cities shaped changes in the literary representation of cities and how urban intellectuals like himself engaged with the material made available to them by the historical moment. Precisely because Miller was an observant, intelligent, but not particularly original writer who worked by exploiting the possibilities presented by genre and the daily newspapers, he makes a portrait of the period's urban orthodoxies as he maneuvers along their forward edge.

Miller reveals, in particular, the mechanics of the fit between authorship and the changing social landscape. One can trace secondary dramas in Miller's Harlem novels, readable in their manipulations of dialect and in their images of various traffic across the boundaries of the ghetto, in which Warren Miller the author enters the ghetto and the subjectivity of his black narrators. The narrating voices move in a generic landscape of familiar Harlem landmarks and speak formulaic ghetto languages with which the second ghetto can be described from the inside by characters that readers would recognize as exemplary types. The deployment of this authenticating language effects and certifies Miller's, the novel's, and the reader's entry into the ghetto. Like everything else in the urban literature, this motif of authorial entry into Harlem became freighted with the content of crisis in the 1960s: as the reader passes from the signifying landscape of *Cool World* to that of *Siege of Harlem*, the erection of fortified barriers around the ghetto argues for its increasingly violent and absolute separation from the rest of the metropolis. Miller, who was nothing if not up to date in his thinking about cities and the emergent politics of identity, understood this development to constrain his, or any other white author's, ability to cross in prose into the ghetto of feeling. As juvenile delinquency flowed into the problem of race and was subsumed by it during the early 1960s, Warren Miller, who had made a name for himself as an urban intellectual in the late 1950s by contributing to the literature of delinquency, found himself repositioned in relation to Harlem and the makings of literature to be found there.

Miller's passionate engagement with the leading social problems of the day gives a special ironic edge to the notion that the urban crisis made it increasingly inappropriate for a white man to write serious literature about Harlem in a "black" voice. Both the delinquency panic and the logic of urban crisis identified Harlem as a place in which the city's deepest structuring forces might be unearthed and seen at work; thus, the literature of Harlem, mapping the Harlem of feeling, commanded a privileged view of urbanism in crisis. Because Miller was so caught up in the cultural "texture and density" of the moment, he found himself in the position of arguing for and subscribing to a racial logic of urban crisis that tended over time to erect barriers to his own entry into literary Harlem, thus pushing him to the margins of the urban conversation. Voices in *Cool World*, an otherwise relatively standard contribution to the literature of juvenile delinquency that flourished before the urban crisis became a racial crisis, argue that the problem of race structures other urban problems, including those typically compressed in the figure of the delinquent. *Siege of Harlem*, published just as the canonical urban crisis began to achieve widespread recognition, manifests a tension between critiquing and affirming Americans' growing tendency to assume an absolute divide between white and black as the basis of late twentieth-century urbanism. Like many well-intentioned people during the urban crisis, Miller found himself curiously torn by the violent social and intellectual conflicts staged in the ghettos of fact and feeling. The signs in his writing of those larger struggles are what make Miller's two Harlem novels so powerfully evocative of period and place.

Even, or especially, the violence evokes period. *Cool World* builds through knife fights and beatings to a climactic rumble; *Siege of Harlem* tells a story of insurrection, war, and cold war between Harlem and America: both novels offer and analyze the images of escalating violence so central to postwar urbanism. Miller tends toward the left-liberal reading of this violence: the rumble is rooted in the limitation of young ghetto dwellers' economic and cultural horizons rather than in weak government, moral decline, or individual failures of character or intellect; *Siege of Harlem*'s ghetto insurrection anticipates a reading of the 1960s riots as postcolonial uprising rather than as mass chaos suggesting a culture of poverty, the apotheosis of "crime in the streets," or reasons for moving to the suburbs. Miller, who above all wanted to write topical, timely books that moved readers to engagement with the issues of the day, turned to violence in the streets as the way to represent and account for the emerging postindustrial inner city and the stories it had to offer.

The Literature of Delinquency and the Inner City

In 1959, the publication and critical acceptance of *Cool World* made a name for Miller as both a literary stylist and an observer of the city. Through his treatment of delinquency, he became a recognized urban intellectual, engaged with social and cultural transformations that would in the mid-1960s become central elements of the urban crisis. *Cool World* was important to its initial readers because it contributed to the vast network of discourses that converged in the 1950s and early 1960s on the problem of juvenile delinquency in the inner city, a problem personified above all in teenage gang members like its protagonist Duke Custis. *Cool World* entered a stream of representations of delinquency in a variety of forums—newspapers, magazines, scholarly studies, popular and self-consciously "serious" novels, the movies, comic books—comprising a literature that played an important role in representing the inner city. As I argued in the previous chapter, the youth gangs that occupied the center of the delinquency panic inhabited and seemed to be produced by an urban world in crisis: in the 1950s, to understand one was to understand the other.

Of the various explanation systems proposed to account for delinquency, several called attention to what were seen as quintessentially urban problems: uprooted blacks and Hispanics newly arrived and ghettoized in the cities, the enfeebling of "traditional" structures of authority (family, church, school) as part of the breakup of the industrial neighborhood order, organized crime, ignorance and cultural deprivation proceeding from inadequate education and socialization. If Estes Kefauver's Senate Subcommittee to Study Juvenile

Delinquency in the United States entertained the experts' general critique of mass culture and its effect on all American youth, Kefauver was drawn in particular to the notion that organized gangs of teenage criminals posed a dangerous alternative to the social order of America's cities.[2] If in the 1950s variously accredited intellectuals like Erik Erikson and Paul Goodman were reconsidering the meaning and character of youth and the proper formation of young citizens, the delinquency panic sustained itself in the public forum with more visceral fare: a steady diet of stories detailing heinous crimes, usually committed in urban areas, that located in the violent delinquent gang a complex knot of social and cultural malaise.

The violent gang moved through an urban world in transition. In *The Shook-Up Generation* (1958), a book-length study of delinquent gangs adapted from a seven-part series of investigative reports in the *New York Times*, respected journalist Harrison Salisbury wrote that suburban New Yorkers traversing the inner city on commuter trains and new highways saw the physical signs of a new social landscape: "phalanxes of new structures . . . new brick towers. . . . You can hardly recognize Harlem. The East Side has been transformed. Driving out the Gowanus Super-Highway they admire the rectangular patterns of Fort Greene Houses, Gowanus Houses, Red Hook Houses, Queensbridge Houses."[3] Like the housing projects that have replaced the prewar tenements, the elevated structure of the Gowanus Super-Highway, casting its shadow over Brooklyn's Red Hook (a terrain much traversed in gang literature), becomes a sign of the times. The elevated highway, completed in 1941 and articulating with other highways built during the massive postwar effort to link redeveloped central business districts to the suburban periphery, is a dramatic physical sign of the urban change that forms the context for the gang's delinquency. In Salisbury's account, the historical moment that has produced the projects of the new Harlem and the Gowanus Super-Highway has dislocated a generation of young people, leading to the present crisis. Although Salisbury points to other conventional explanations of delinquency, like the power of mass culture and the weakening of family structure, and although he takes a characteristically global view in accounting for juvenile delinquency (suggesting that the specter of the bomb breeds psychic dislocations; drawing analogies between American and Soviet delinquents, housing projects, and violence), the core of his analysis takes shape around the emergence of the postindustrial metropolis. Salisbury, best known as a foreign correspondent and political reporter, treated delinquency and the urban transformations that framed it as a domestic crisis on par with and linked to the continuing international crisis of the Cold War.[4]

The postwar inner city presented experts with a "new delinquency," for which they had to evolve new models and explanations. The Chicago School's classic immigrant-ethnic jackroller or thief of the 1920s and 1930s, gone astray in the interstices of the industrial city's social organization, no longer provided an adequate type for delinquents in the emerging postindustrial inner city. Albert Cohen led a movement to rethink delinquency as a subculture at odds with the values and institutions of the expanding postwar middle class. This logic undergirded subsequent analyses that treated delinquency as produced by deprivation of opportunity, traceable to deep race and class divisions in the urban social landscape, and that called into question the Chicago School's prewar assumption of social mobility out of the slums. Subculture theorists like Cohen sought to explain a new order of delinquent: a violent gang member in the inner city; a ghetto-dwelling black or Puerto Rican or a white ethnic "left behind" for some reason in the geography and mentality of the slums; a youth therefore unlikely to exit the delinquent subculture without comprehensive institutional assistance from professionals like youth workers, psychologists, social workers, and teachers in public and reform schools.

Rather than continuing to believe in the Chicago School's classic "delinquency area"—the temporary slum of opportunity constantly remade as immigrant groups moved up and out and new ones replaced them—the subculture theorists addressed the prospect of a permanent ghetto underclass drastically and lastingly cut off from opportunity and the rest of the metropolis by lines of racial difference and class conflict. The ghetto was not "disorganized," Cohen argued (as David Bradley would argue in *South Street*); rather, the deceptively comprehensive organization of its "vast ramifying network of informal associations among like-minded people" contributed to its status as an established, continuing subculture.[5] In *Delinquency and Opportunity* (1960), Richard Cloward and Lloyd Ohlin extended Cohen's reading of the delinquent as an indicator of deep class and racial divisions, developing the notion of the delinquent as a kind of organic social critic responding rationally to the denial of genuine economic opportunity to poor, and especially black, young men.[6]

Beginning in the early 1960s, the problem of delinquency as a youth crisis gave way to a more diffuse emphasis on youth culture, and the problem of racial segregation and conflict became the inner city's defining crisis, subsuming all others. Moving in the directions suggested by Cohen, Cloward, and Ohlin, various observers came to link the delinquent gang to the rebellious student subculture and to the emergence of racially defined identity politics in the inner city. The sedimentation of delinquency at the foundations of thinking about the ghetto helps to explain how, during the urban crisis, some delinquent gangs (like Chicago's Blackstone Rangers) succeeded in recasting themselves as political organizations. Federally funded poverty programs accepted them as community organizations through which money and effort might be directed into the ghetto.[7] But in the 1950s and early 1960s, race and urban change were still contributing factors to the independently significant problem of juvenile delinquency, in which could be read various urban and cultural subtexts.

In the 1950s and early 1960s, therefore, delinquency experts like Albert Cohen and Fredric Wertham occupied positions of cultural authority in representing the inner city. Cohen, a social scientist, and Wertham, a psychologist, came at the problem of delinquency from opposite directions—Cohen by way of an analysis of subculture and social inequality, Wertham by way of a critique of mass culture—but they converged on the inner city as the center of the problem. Cohen put the permanent ghettos of the postwar inner city in the foreground of the study of urban subcultures. His influential work, which subordinated psychoanalytical explanations of delinquency to an emphasis on social structure and cultural order, helped launch the crisis-infused urban sociology of the 1960s. Wertham's condemnation of comic books, the movies, and other mass cultural forms made him the star witness at Kefauver's Senate hearings on delinquency. (Wertham even saw himself as a potential martyr, pointing out that certain comic books had taken to advocating violence against thinly fictionalized anti-comics crusaders modeled on himself.)[8] If Cohen was ultimately interested in the nature of deviance and Wertham in the nature of violence, and if both achieved recognition as experts on delinquent youth, they were also regarded in important ways as urban intellectuals. In explaining delinquency, they helped to map and explain the inner city and its social cleavages.

Cohen's and Wertham's books, like Miller's *Cool World*, moved within a vast literature of delinquency. Like the Chicago neighborhood novels in relation to the work of the Chicago School, a body of variously fantastic and authenticated novels, movies, and first-person accounts paralleled the social scientific and journalistic treatments of delinquency. The nonfiction literature, exemplified by Salisbury's *Shook-Up Generation*, shared formulas of narrative, landscape, and theme with the genre of delinquent films that enjoyed a golden age in the 1950s, a series extending from early noir treatments like *City across the River* (1949, the film version of Irving Shulman's seminal novel *The Amboy Dukes*) through classic statements like *Rebel without a Cause* and *The Blackboard Jungle* (both 1955), the baroque excess of exploitation movies like *High School Confidential* (1958), and the exhaustion or elevation of genre (depending upon whom you ask) evident in later movies like *West Side Story* (1961). The movies resonated with luridly packaged paperback novels that formed the backbone of delinquent literature: Irving Shulman's *Amboy Dukes, Cry Tough*, and *Children of the Dark;* Harlan Ellison's novel *Rumble*, drawn from his experience as a participant-observer that also produced his fanciful "report" on gang life, *Memos from Purgatory;* the sensationalist hackwork (or genius, again depending upon whom one asks) of genre stalwarts like Wenzell Brown (*The Hoods Ride In, Gang Girl, The Big Rumble, Jail Bait Jungle*), Hal Ellson (*Duke, The Golden Spike, I Take What I Want*), Edward De Roo (*Rumble at the Housing Project, The Young Wolves, Go, Man, Go*), Frank Paley (*Rumble on the Docks*), Willard

Wiener (*The Young Killers/Four Boys and a Gun*), and Sal Lombino as "Evan Hunter" (*The Blackboard Jungle*).[9]

A brief glance at writers discussed in parts 1 and 2 will remind us that writers with reputably "serious" credentials also explored the literary possibilities of delinquency. Because the delinquency literature owed so much to Chicago realism—the naturalist constriction of slum life and the violent young male protagonists found in Algren, Wright, and Farrell; the Chicago School of sociology's portrait of prewar delinquency as a product of the industrial neighborhood order—it makes sense that Avon Publications sought to market Nelson Algren in the 1950s as a founding father of delinquent literature. Algren revised his 1942 novel *Never Come Morning* for subsequent printings in 1948 and throughout the 1950s as a novel of juvenile delinquency. Reframed on front and back covers as "TEEN-AGE TRAGEDY!" Algren's Chicago neighborhood novel gained new life as part of the literature that engaged with "the problem that has stunned all thinking Americans: Juvenile Delinquency." Similarly, Algren revised his first novel, *Somebody in Boots*, for Avon, which retitled it *The Jungle* and sold it as "a great novel of lawless youth" who "ride the rods to degradation [and] delinquency." Algren's fellow Chicago writer Gwendolyn Brooks was not recycling old material in the 1950s, but she was inspired by delinquency. One can read an intellectual history of the urban crisis in the progression from her much-read portrait of doomed pool-shooting layabouts of the late 1950s in "We Real Cool" to her ringing paeans to the Blackstone Rangers of the late 1960s: the delinquents are now "The Leaders," who help "construct, strangely, a monstrous pearl or grace" that is black urbanism.[10] One can read that same story as well in William Gardner Smith's progression in his treatment of street gangs from the destructive turf-protectors of *South Street* to the shock troops preparing for the coming race war in *Return to Black America*.

If Warren Miller preferred to keep company with the "serious" purveyors of social critique and literary stylists (and did so via good reviews in the right places), *Cool World* found an eminently marketable niche in the middle ground between their work and the gloriously overheated genre fiction of Sal Lombino and company. *Cool World* shared with this paperback formula literature a defining impulse to make imaginative forays into the mental world of the gang, delving into its subjectivity in order to address the basic question driving the delinquency panic: what possessed young people to do the terrible, apparently senseless, often titillating things they did? The formula novels told stories of gang fights, murders, rapes, and other crimes committed by and against delinquent boys and girls; they imaginatively mapped the decaying older slum order and the ghettos that succeeded it; and they pointed up the inability of parents and social institutions to control the children formed in this inner-city environment. Covering ground familiar from journalistic, social scientific, and filmic accounts, the formula novels made the most sustained attempts to see the inner city with the delinquent's eyes and speak with the delinquent's voice. In this they surpassed the movies, which tended to shy away from sustained renderings of the inarticulate delinquents' inner lives. The novels surpassed as well the nonfiction accounts, which gestured at delinquents' mentalities with obligatory glossaries of teen slang but usually tended toward the dry, distanced language of explanation favored by delinquency professionals.

An *Uncle Tom's Cabin* for the City of the Future

Warren Miller made his entry into the delinquent literature with *Cool World* in 1959, when the generic template codified a decade before by Shulman's *Amboy Dukes* (1947) was showing its age but still the dominant model. Shulman himself had parlayed a career out of his story of Jewish delinquents caught up in the decline of Brooklyn's decaying urban villages. He had ridden the developing delinquency panic out of the old neighborhood to Hollywood, and in his writing he was now traversing the small cities and suburbs of America, to which many thought delinquency had spread from the inner cities. For Hollywood, Shulman adapted Robert Lindner's *Rebel without a Cause*, a psychological case study of a violent Polish delinquent living in an Eastern industrial suburb. The movie script moved the scene to a largely de-ethnicized and middle-class suburban setting. His novelization of the same story, *Children of the Dark*, takes place in a small, dowdy Ohio city—in "the heartland," far from the ethnically and racially heterogeneous Brooklyn mapped in *Amboy Dukes*. Warren Miller followed the logic of the delinquency panic in the reverse direction, along a complementary, well-worn route *into* the much-traversed literary terrain of Harlem, and he identified the processes shaping the second ghetto as the main sources of those postwar urban ills typically identified as the conditions breeding delinquency.

Inspired by news reports of sensational teen violence, especially Edward R. Murrow's radio interviews of members of a gang accused of a murder in upper Manhattan's Washington Heights area, Miller set out to write a novel that would demonstrate the literary potential of delinquent literature and redirect its social priorities toward black (and Puerto Rican) ghettos and the problem of race. "The voices of those boys made [writing the novel] seem an urgent matter," Miller told an interviewer for the *Saturday Review*. "I kept telling myself that writing the book would be an exercise in language and no more. But what I really wanted to do was write a novel that would have all the social and political force of *Uncle Tom's Cabin*, a book that would finally break through the timidity and concealed arrogance and the aridity of the sociologists' treatises."[11] For Miller, then, *Cool World* would be timely, meshing with the latest journalistic attention to delinquency. Establishing in young people's own words why "we go in the gang,"[12] it would speak to the most basic objectives of social scientific research, providing a human face, a compelling narrative frame, and affecting explanations for the endlessly detailed statistical facts of delinquency. The delinquent's voice, the strategy of first-person dialect narration, would carry the reader inside the delinquent's mind with a depth and totality at which glossaries of slang only gestured. As a literary achievement in a culture obsessed with its disaffected adolescent boys, *Cool World* aspired in its "exercise in language" to negotiate a difficult passage into Duke Custis's subjective world, an accomplishment to rival and surpass J. D. Salinger's passage into the considerably less threatening Holden Caulfield in *Catcher in the Rye*—to which *Cool World* was often and favorably compared. Finally, Miller envisioned *Cool World* as social document, appearing at a moment when perceptive observers could discern that the second ghetto could soon come to dominate American urban and racial landscapes, that would serve as an *Uncle Tom's Cabin* for its time. The novel would do its part to shape and mobilize the attention of Americans to the inner city, where the problem of delinquency converged with the resurgent problem of race, as *Uncle Tom's Cabin* had so successfully shaped and mobilized their attention to the South and the institution of slavery a century before. Rather than following delinquency out of the inner city into the suburbs and small towns, as Shulman had done, Miller sought to make an entry into the ghetto, not yet but soon to be the city's most compelling and troubling terrain.

"Doc Levine ast me once. 'Richard.' He say. 'I want you to describe for me the street where you lived'" (69). Describing the street on which he lives becomes Richard "Duke" Custis's cultural work, the job for which he offers impeccable credentials in a chapter entitled "Who Am I?": "Duke Custis. War Lord of the Royal Crocadiles. I been knifed 7 times and I got 9 stitches in my head from where a sonofabitch Wolve bastard hit me with a radio aireal off a car. From behind" (11). Duke's reform school psychologist Doc Levine, a fictional avatar of delinquency intellectuals like Albert Cohen, is the intended recipient of the letter the novel purports to be. Both a delinquency intellectual and an ideal reader of the genre, Doc Levine wants Duke to map the inner-city delinquent's mental world and his social landscape—in so doing, Duke obligingly traces the relation of the delinquency panic to the postwar inner city.

The novel plots Duke's inner life on the turf of his gang, the Royal Crocadiles, so that the twin explorations of mentality and space become figures of one another. The notion of turf fascinated postwar students of the gang, who could not seem to get over the deep emotional and psychological investment made by delinquents in patches of inner-city terrain from which the state and private capital were disinvesting. Delinquent literature had to explain what it meant that gang members invoked turf as a primary rationale for their shocking behavior. As Jane Jacobs suggested in identifying the "barbaric concept of

Turf" as a key to the postwar inner city, an investigation of turf seemed to promise some secret knowledge of the relationship between the inner city and its inhabitants, the way in which threatening urban spaces became places infused with human meanings.

Cool World communicates the narrowness of Duke's world and a sense of his investment in it, so that Duke's delinquency and the social processes readable in the signifying terrain of postwar Harlem help to account for one another. To that end, Duke describes the gang's domain and its way of life, both of which take shape around the street and the project: "The street is three blocks long. That the territory an the Royal Crocadiles control it. . . . Mostly the street jus a dirty place. The bildings is dirty like they bin washt in dirt. It run down they faces. You sit on a stoop an look acrost the street at a house for a while an after awhile it look like that house is cryen. . . . An at the end of the street loomin up is the projeck" (67–69). The projects line the rim of this landscape, giving form to its spatial limits and to the logic of its formation: "Man when they tore down the bildings to make room for the projeck you could see all the crap them old bildings was made of. . . . Some time they goin to tare down the projeck because evry thing get taren down an it will be the same all over again" (69–70). Duke's sense of history and future history both arrive at a dead end in the second ghetto's signature form, the high-rise project. "They tore down" the prewar Black Metropolis to make the second ghetto, and the processes that shaped the second ghetto will eventually produce a subsequent form—"the same all over again"—that will likewise contain and constrain people like Duke. The projects form the limit of Duke's mentality and of his life chances: until his lightning reform in the novel's final pages, set in a rural landscape far from the city, he exemplifies and believes in the paradoxical mix of destruction (of individual lives) and endlessly renewed stasis (for the black lower class) embodied by the projects.

Within the signifying shadow of these projects, Duke lives in the street, a condition that leads inevitably to joining a gang. The delinquency narrative shares with Chicago realism an understanding of the street as the space in which the forces of urban culture and social reality reveal themselves most nakedly as they act on the urban self. Duke tells us that the homes and other private spaces of this landscape do not keep out the street: people in Harlem get dogs and put iron flanges over the hinges on their front doors, Duke notes, "but that dont stop the robbin." Self-preservation in this circumstance requires like-minded allies: only as a gang member walking in the street does he feel the possibility of exercising his will, because the Royal Crocadiles are a homemade order he can sustain by good citizenship in the gang. "They aint law on the streets," he explains. "No an none in the houses. You ask me why an I tellin you why we do whut we have to do. . . . So we go in the gang" (149–50).

The "You ask me why" in this passage refers to Doc Levine and thus to the reader of delinquent literature who seeks the "why" of delinquency. *Cool World* offers the literature's stock explanations, each plotted on the constricted ground of the street. The collapse of the old neighborhoods into the new inner city, symbolized above all by the projects "loomin up" over the remnants of old Harlem, turns weeping, dirty buildings into anthropomorphic refugees from cataclysm. The notion of "cultural deprivation," which came into general use in the 1950s to express the limited opportunities and prospects of inner-city children, finds expression in the claustrophobic geography of Duke's life—and in the character of Lu Ann, a young prostitute hired off the street by the Royal Crocadiles, who is shocked to learn that New York is on the ocean and that one can take the subway to the water. The street's relentless entry into the home signals the failure of families like those of the Royal Crocadiles' president, Blood Thurston (Northern and urban in outlook, two-parent, upwardly aspirant), and Duke (Southern and rural in outlook, without consistent male authority, without prospects for entry into the middle class) to raise their children as they wish to or should.

The high-rise housing project, an architectural form that speaks of postwar social engineering and the urban geopolitics of race, is a continuation of the street rather than protection from it. Duke's visit to the projects makes clear that they exacerbate the kind of social failure incarnated in the delinquent, that they are continuous with the social landscape compressed in the three blocks of the Royal Crocadiles' turf. Blood Thurston's family lives in a new high-rise project, in an apartment filled with books and middle-class sensibilities, where "evrything clean and so neat you afraid to sit down." Blood's father works for the post office, his sister is a nurse, and his older brother, Harrison, attends Fisk University. When Duke arrives the family is waiting for Blood to return from the supermarket, although Duke knows better: "Put some money in Bloods hands and he aint goin to no supermarket he goin to the junkman for a fix" (21). For all their striving and politesse, Blood's family cannot defeat the "Uptown Stink" that pervades the projects or keep Blood from the street, gang life, and heroin. When Duke leaves they are still waiting hopelessly for Blood's return from the streets.

Duke's, and the text's, sense of the world beyond those three blocks of street that make up the Royal Crocadiles' domain takes form in a few brief excursions, usually by subway, into a broader geography that accentuates the narrowness of Duke's domain. Chief among these is a school field trip to Wall Street, during which he sees a diorama of the City of the Future: "These rocket ships kept flyin back an forth over it. There were on wires you could see the wires. An the City of the Future it was just a big housing projeck" (16). Duke's fantasies of escape revolve around the recurring figure of soaring beyond the limits of his narrow turf, removing himself from the crushing influence of the street. (Such images recur as well in the Chicago neighborhood novels.)[13]

Riding the subway, he vividly recalls a childhood fantasy in which the subway became a rocket to the moon rather than a cousin of Algren's El that can only return him to his three blocks of Harlem. The City of the Future diorama reveals such flights of the imagination as wishful thinking: the rocket ships, like Duke's fantasy vehicle that always takes him back to Harlem, are constrained by visible wires from escaping the giant housing project that the City of the Future will become.

The model of a vast, spreading housing project is the novel's model of the urban future and of the imperatives shaping it. Displayed in the heart of Wall Street, the City of the Future appears bracketed in the narrative by two American flags—the first painted on the box of a street preacher outside the stock exchange, the second, "the biggest American Flag I ever see any where" (16), hanging on the wall above the trading floor. *Cool World* thus suggests an argument that would recur in the critiques of urban renewal and redevelopment that appeared across the political left in the 1960s: the City of the Future takes the form of projects for the poor and "luxury" high rises (which would appear to the "culturally deprived" Duke as more projects) for the rest because it is ordered by the imperatives of capital. Economic growth and development drive the urban future, and the state, acquiescing to this priority by building the projects, directs its energies to sustaining inequities of race and class rather than redistributing wealth or power. *Cool World* deploys Duke's sharp eye and authenticated speech to contradict the rhetoric of social responsibility— "decent housing for all" and a "war" on poverty—that presented urban renewal as a program of reinvestment in the inner city. Duke's narrow delinquent sensibility offers a kind of unconscious, or pastoral, social critique that glosses Jane Jacobs's equation of the gang's and the progrowth coalition's rhyming "barbarisms." Duke sees and remarks upon the signs that express the novel's understanding of postindustrial urban development—he sees the wires that give the lie to the City of the Future's promise—even though he is not equipped to self-consciously articulate that understanding for Doc Levine.

Duke likewise encounters and absorbs ways of thinking that identify race as *the* city-structuring problem, the root cause of delinquency and other subsidiary problems. Voices in *Cool World*, rendered in Duke's voice, offer race as an explanation for delinquency in ways that suggest the change in the delinquent's cultural role that would occur in the 1960s. In *Cool World*, there are no white delinquents, only blacks and Puerto Ricans. Furthermore, race runs through and helps to drive each of the other explanations of delinquency. For instance, Blood's brother Harrison, the college man, collects the failure of families and the influence of environment under the us/them rubric of race. Looking out at Harlem from the window of the project apartment, Harrison says (in Duke's rendering), "'They make us live like animals. Is it any wunder then that some of us act like animals an some of us become animals. The fantastic thing is how few of us succum to their idea of us'" (21). Harrison's analysis of the second ghetto's effect on its children is seconded by the "race man" Hermit, proprietor of a hamburger stand on the Royal Crocadiles' turf. Hermit decorates his establishment with pictures of postcolonial heroes Nasser and Nkrumah (for whom William Gardner Smith worked in Ghana), opposes Duke's trade in marijuana as "'Ruinin the Race with the products of white civilization'" (91), and urges Duke to imagine himself removed from the narrow terrain of the ghetto into the expansive promised land of Africa ("'our real home'" [91]) and Brazil (where "'they aint no color line'" [145]).

Duke's grandmother, speaking in a Christian register drawn from the Book of Revelation, connects Harrison's and Hermit's racial analysis to the urban critique offered in the City of the Future scene. Having caught Duke thieving money from her purse (in order to buy a handgun), she preaches Duke a mighty sermon on the effect of the city on their people: "'It this city this hore of Babylon. This hore city is whut happenin to you making you go bad was so sweet and good. . . . You a child of Babylon.'" Having paralleled Harrison's naturalist assumption that the urban environment is the force shaping Duke, she gestures at Harrison's and Hermit's racial language by identifying Harrison as "a credit to the Race" (Duke capitalizes the R here as he does when representing Hermit's speech). She then extends and revoices in biblical language the City of the Future scene's portrait of a city structured by capital ("merchants") rather than righteousness:

> "Come out of Babylon my people so that you don't receive of her playgs. Therefore shall her playgs come in one day. . . . You shall see the smoke of her burnin boy. . . . Alas alas that mighty city Babylon. For in 1 hour is thy judgment come. An the merchants of the earth is gonna weep because they cant buyeth they merchandise no more. Cinammon and frankincense an horses & slaves & pearls. Ointments & oil & wheat & fine linen. . . . The angel gonna throw the millstone and he sayith thus with vilence shall that great city Babylon be thrown down. For thy merchants were the great men of earth and by thy sorceries were all nations deceeved." (23–24)

Gramma Custis, with her talk of violent retribution for the failure of postwar urbanism she reads in the making of a delinquent black boy, anticipates the language of urban crisis. Were she to preach the sermon in 1965—on 125th Street or in the pages of *New Leader*—she would find no shortage of sympathetic listeners for an argument that touches upon Harrison's combined environmental and racial analysis (as in Clark's *Dark Ghetto*), Hermit's separatist racial politics (a forerunner of the Third World internationalism favored by many black nationalists), and the critique of urban social cleavage occasioned by the spectacle of violence in the streets. Gramma's sermon manages to come at this last subject, the "vilence" with which "that great city Babylon" shall "be thrown down," from both left and right: on the one hand, riots grow from intertwined class and racial conflicts produced by the uneven flow of capital, or "frankincense an horses & slaves & pearls," as argued in *Black Power;* on the other hand, escalating crime indicates moral and political failure expressed as violent chaos in the streets, as argued by law and order apostles like Chicago's Mayor Daley and Philadelphia's police chief Frank Rizzo.

The City of the Future, prophesied by both Duke and his grandmother, anticipates the generic landscape of the urban crisis. The model of the City of the Future expresses the novel's deepest concern: an urban future dominated by an expansive, delinquency-producing ghetto of blacks and Puerto Ricans, divided from the whites in the rest of the metropolis by permanent and impenetrable boundaries. *Cool World* thus plots race together with delinquency, and at times at the root of delinquency, on its map of the inner city, defining the narrowness of Duke's personal prospects and his turf—the building blocks of his delinquency—as a racial condition. As a black resident of Harlem, as well as a violent gang member, Duke can only conceive of *his* urban future in the form of the housing projects "loomin up" at the limits of his three-block world. The racial logic of social cleavage becomes the novel's most viable answer to the "why?" of delinquency. In anticipating the drift from delinquency to racial crisis while telling a familiar story of rumbles and reefers, Miller was both comfortably within the limits of the delinquent genre and just ahead of conventional wisdom.

Duke Custis and Warren Miller

If *Cool World* devotes itself to mapping a postwar inner city rapidly devolving into the City of the Future, its brief final chapter offers a glimpse of a larger landscape and a competing narrative. *Cool World* returns Duke to the Royal Crocadiles' turf from each expedition downtown and every flight of fantasy, until the climactic rumble (and a murder, committed by another Crocadile) lands him upstate in reform school, the only locale unconnected to the encompassing ghetto. Forcibly removed from the city into this retreat, he tends to thuddingly regenerative flower beds, makes friends with a Puerto Rican (who teaches him how to say in Spanish that the city is dirty), and narrates the novel in the form of the letters he writes to Doc Levine. As the novel ends, Duke is preparing to attend school in a nearby town, anxiously awaits the spring to see "how good I done" with his flower beds, and shows signs of distancing himself from the mental-geographical complex of inner-city life: "At first I miss it. But now I dont so much any more. I mean Man who need it? Man that one sue cio [his spelling of the Spanish for "dirty"] city an I dont care if I never see it again" (160).

This is how the reform variant of the delinquent story traditionally ends, with the reforming delinquent reaching escape velocity, suggesting the arc of a movement into a promised but unmapped land beyond the limits of his gang's turf. The caution mitigating Duke's potential movement into this larger landscape lies in the danger that he may prove a signal exception, one of the lucky or extraordinary few who got out. Thus Miller's invocation of *Uncle Tom's Cabin* when explaining his purpose in writing the novel: this narrative must acquire political weight in order to help change the world it maps. In the end, *Cool World* cannot *show* Duke's destination. The novel presents itself as, at best, able to suggest the possibility of an alternative to the City of the Future and to suggest that the state can intervene on Duke's behalf by providing the limited services of teachers, police, jailers, social workers, and psychologists.

The reform endings of delinquent stories, piously tacked onto enthusiastic accounts of delinquents' bad behavior, may seem contrived or weak, and *Cool World*'s resolution struck some reviewers as such. Dan Wakefield, for instance, writing in the *Nation*, interrupted his praise for the novel (rendered in an authenticatingly inner-city style of literary criticism appropriate to the late 1950s) to take issue with the ending: "Yes man, yes. All through the book I felt the impulse to keep saying 'Yes—this is what it's all about'—until I came to the final chapter, which tacks on a 'hopeful' ending."[14] However, the ending takes on further and vital meaning if we read it as the culmination of a second narrative line detailing the movement in language of Warren Miller's authorial persona through the inner city of feeling.

In the last chapter, Duke Custis, a character who moves through the world of the novel, figuratively meets and fuses with Warren Miller, the author, whose complementary moves in the city of feeling are coded in the text but executed in a world of letters extending far beyond the novel's diegesis. Duke enters into his sudden reform in the novel's final pages by becoming a writer who rethinks the narrative and spatial plot of his life. In *Cool World*'s final and climactic moment, Duke understands Doc Levine's assertion that through reading and writing Duke might challenge the prophecy of the City of the Future, that he will move from the ghetto into a larger world: "'When you can read an write why you can do any thing. Do any thing. Be any thing'" (160). Duke discovers that he can write his way across the boundaries of the ghetto. Plotting the course of his life in his letters to Doc Levine, he begins to conceive of a world beyond the limit of the projects, even as he returns in memory to the three-block world of the Royal Crocadiles. That is, he crosses into the ghetto from without to tell the story of crossing out of the ghetto from within. This double principle of boundary crossing also informs Warren Miller's moves in the urban spaces of the city of feeling, his entry into the generic terrain of Harlem. Miller had lived for a time in the 1950s in an apartment on what he describes as the "realtors' frontier" of East Ninety-sixth Street. From that vantage point in the social landscape just outside Harlem's southern border, and from the van-

tage point on textual Harlem enjoyed by a man who read copiously and followed the news, Miller gathered his material and wrote his way into the literary
ghetto. We can read in Duke's story a deflected account of Miller's imaginative
journey into Harlem, culminating at the same point: "When you can read an
write why you can do any thing, Do any thing. Be any thing." The textual device
of Duke's authorship also functions as Miller's authorial claim: Miller the
writer can speak from the ghetto as Duke, can "do" and therefore "be" Duke.

If Miller's imaginative rendering of Duke's voice felt to readers like the
voice of a fourteen-year-old black delinquent from Harlem—never mind
whether such a kid would actually *write* like that—then Miller had taken the
readers where he wanted to take them. He had presented the right credentials to
traverse in prose the boundaries of the second ghetto. In the narrative of
Miller's entry into Harlem, Duke's "Do any thing. Be any thing" climaxes a
drama in which Miller's authorial persona has gone to a place where can be
found a language of particular effectiveness in imagining and understanding the
inner city. Miller's passage into Harlem is marked, in retrospect, by the trail of
authenticating language extending behind him through the novel as he arrives,
with Duke, at the novel's culminative lines on its last page.

Duke was black and Miller was white, but in 1959 people who mattered (to
Miller and his literary circle, anyway) were comfortable with the notion that
Duke and Miller could share a voice and the complementary narrative trajec-
tories it articulated. James Baldwin, an established Harlem writer positioned to
mind its literary gates, accepted *Cool World*'s authenticating style as sufficient
credentials for entry into Harlem. "I consider it a tribute to Warren Miller," he
wrote in the *New York Times Book Review*, "that I could not be certain, when I
had read his book, whether he was white or black. I was certain, however, that
I had just read one of the finest novels about Harlem that had ever come my
way."[15] A reviewer in *Commonweal* began his evaluation by putting *Cool World*
at the head of the delinquent genre on the strength of Miller's innovative use of
Duke's voice:

> If anyone had ever suggested to me that I would be able to scurry through yet
> another novel about New York juvenile delinquents and end up liking it
> immensely, and if this hypothetical worthy had informed me that though the story
> was told entirely in dialect I should conclude this was a brilliantly sustained nar-
> rative method, I would have had doubts about his sanity. Yet it seems to me that
> Warren Miller's new novel . . . is something of a small miracle.[16]

Reviewers found a reassuring familiarity in *Cool World*'s standard gang narrative. This generic authenticity mutually reinforced the novelty of rendering the
entire text in the delinquent's own voice, a device that took the authenticating
impulse behind the genre's standard glossaries of delinquent language to its
logical extreme. The dialect strategy and Duke's narrative movement toward the

status of writer together sought to overleap in virtuoso fashion the split between professional writer (like Ira Henry Freeman, the *New York Times* reporter who wrote *Out of the Burning*) and knife-scar-authenticated teenage protagonist (like Frenchy, the reformed Brooklyn delinquent who told his story to Freeman), forming one figure more generically potent than either of them. *Cool World* made an explicit poetry out of the stiltedness that marked the genre's distinctively awkward fit between delinquent and writer, removing the quotation marks and glossary matter that separated the delinquent's language from the writer's craft. The novel asserted in its form that Duke's authorial persona flowed into Warren Miller's and vice versa.

Reviewers understood the formal success of that flow, *Cool World*'s principal generic innovation, as conferring on it special importance as both social document and literary achievement. Writing in the *Saturday Review*, one reviewer, stating his hope that "the Mayor and the Governor read this book," put Miller in the tradition of "'naturalistic' or 'socially conscious'" writers stretching back to canonical naturalist writers of the city like Crane, Norris, and Dreiser. He placed Miller as a novelist above writers of the 1930s like Caldwell, Steinbeck, and James T. Farrell, all of whom tended to obscure "the art in the vehemence of the social protest" and were guilty of prolixity, wooden characterizations, and styleless prose. Apparently on the strength of *Cool World*'s effective rendering in dialect of the transformed contemporary inner city, rather than any harsher social reality inherent in the life model, the novel's Harlem therefore made prewar literary terrains of social trauma like "Studs Lonigan's Chicago and Tom Joad's Oklahoma" look like obsolescent "playgrounds for clergymen's children."[17] Miller's rendering of Duke also enjoyed favorable comparisons to the period's literary icon of alienated youth, Salinger's Holden Caulfield, some suggesting that Miller's novel was the more powerful for bringing its narrator's youthful subjectivity to bear on the forbidding social environment of Harlem.[18]

Even when reviewers were not unanimous in ratifying *Cool World*'s literary success, they were more nearly unanimous in noting the importance of Miller's subject matter. Some readers found *Cool World* to be overly sociological at the expense of its literary qualities, a flawed "topical" novel. *Time*'s reviewer, although completely convinced by Miller's rendering of Duke ("Miller's gift for mimicking the speech of a bitter, neurotic boy is as true as Salinger's"), thought *Cool World* "too much the composite case history to be a really good novel." The reviewer argued, however, that this sociological stiltedness did not prevent the novel from succeeding as a social document: "but it is powerful reporting and impressive pamphleteering against the savagery of slum life in a great city."[19] Even negative reviews conceded that Miller had made sociological clichés and dry statistics come alive.[20] The most potentially damaging critique came from those few reviewers who found Miller's mimicry of Duke mannered and unconvincing. This small minority, with no James Baldwin in their ranks, tended to dismiss *Cool World* on literary grounds as a gimmicky experiment, thereby condemning the novel to obscurity as just another book about delinquents in New York. If Miller did not speak convincingly as Duke, then Duke's crossing out of Harlem would be uncoupled from Miller's crossing into Harlem: the novel would collapse into a blackface rehash of what was by 1959 well-rehearsed and near-exhausted delinquent material.[21]

Happily, for Miller, those few reviewers who questioned Miller's mimicry of Duke were for the most part shouted down by his many enthusiastic supporters. Miller found himself in a commanding position: at the top of the literature of delinquency and with access not only to the language of that genre but to one of the inner city's most representative and represented spaces, where one might encounter besetting urban matters like delinquency and racial conflict in uniquely revealing form. Modest stage and movie adaptations of the novel helped to sustain Miller's cultural currency, especially in the local New York circles that dominated the literature of delinquency. The film version in particular, produced by documentary filmmaker Frederick Wiseman and directed in faux-documentary style by Shirley Clarke (who also directed the well-received drug movie *The Connection*), helped to keep Miller's authorial persona circulating in connection with delinquency and Harlem In 1961, the American Academy and Institute of Arts and Letters cited Miller for "his lively imagination and deft expression, and for his willingness to try the tones of many voices while finding his own voice."[22]

Uncle Remus and Checkpoint Frederick Douglass

Miller had written his way into the delinquent canon and thus into literary Harlem, but the urban conversation was changing. Harlem was also at the core of a developing literature of urban crisis, which, even more than the literature of delinquency, would by the mid-1960s come to identify the second ghetto as the place to seek and stage the most important urban dramas. When *Cool World* appeared in 1959, a perceptive urbanist like Miller could already detect the momentum of processes by which the postwar transformation of cities and representations of them brought into being the race-driven notion of urban crisis. As race came to organize discussion of the inner city in the 1960s, the once-imperative need to account for the delinquent lost its urgency—except in that delinquent black youths were understood to be at the center of a "crime wave." Miller, above all else a writer attuned to changes in the culture around him, was not going to be left behind. Reading *The Siege of Harlem* (1964, hereafter referred to as *Siege*), and rereading *Cool World* through the lens provided by the later novel, we see the parallel development of urban crisis and Miller's changing sense of the problem of writing the inner city.

Siege retells the postwar history of black migration, the struggle for civil rights, and the formation of the second ghetto through Harlem's secession from the United States of America. A great leader named Lance Huggins, "inspired to take the national cancer and localize it for all to see," calls together blacks from all over America to the defense of Harlem in its fledgling moments as an independent nation-state.[23] American blacks stage another great migration to what becomes the literal capital of black America, a "free" Harlem surrounded on all sides by hostile forces. The action of the novel has mostly to do with the heroic efforts of Harlem to resist economic and cultural pressures exerted by the United States to force Harlem to rejoin the nation. Constrained from outright military attack by the close attention of the United Nations, especially its Third World members, the United States employs stratagems recognizable as exaggerated caricatures of Americans' attitudes toward the second ghetto. The mix of neglect and destructive exploitation of Harlem practiced by the state and private industry produces the novel's paired urban and diplomatic crises.

Thus the novel's depiction of America's attempts to stop capital from flowing into Harlem, and of state-sponsored radio broadcasts tempting Harlemites to abandon their free ghetto state with offers of consumer products, caricatures selective disinvestment from the black inner city. The siege of Harlem and a barrage of advertising intended to undermine the solidarity of its people—"tempting offers" of "a free trip to Miami; a color teevee set; a complete set of forty copper-bottomed pots; an electric swizzle stick; a lifetime subscription to *House and Garden* magazine" (16)—provide the foils for Lance Huggins's Harlem Land Reform and mass rent strike against absentee landlords, his nationalization of the hospitals, and his decision to throw open the pawn shops. The novel presents Huggins's measures as designed to counteract the effects of market forces and governmental policy on the postwar inner city.

Similarly, *Siege* lampoons the tendency to obscure the root causes of urban crisis with hysterical talk of crime in the streets. Desperate to undermine Huggins's government, the "Majority People" of the United States of America introduce black agents provocateurs into free Harlem to orchestrate a crime wave and thus generate an excuse for an armed attack on Harlem by the United States in order to protect blacks from themselves and preserve law and order in the metropolis. The United States' black agents carry the principal icons of postwar crime in the streets, guns and hypodermic needles, and the propaganda machine of the Majority People produces sensational headlines to describe the crime wave in Harlem: "HARLEM A JUNGLE, MUGGINGS AND MURDERS" (88). *Siege* offers in the episode of the agents provocateurs an argument that white Americans have constructed a pathological black male criminal to carry the blame for causing the urban crisis. The novel argues for shifting the blame for crime in the streets, that rubric under which the complexity of the urban crisis was so often simplified, from inside the ghetto to outside it. "'Products is what they were,'" says Lance Huggins in describing the cultural construction of a violent black scapegoat, "'and they had been made sick to their souls by their mechanical condition'" (130).

If the novel proposes a scenario that enacts and in some cases anticipates the rhetorical aims of militant separatist manifestos of the 1960s—like Grace Boggs and James Boggs's "The City Is the Black Man's Land" (1966) or Eldridge Cleaver's "The Land Question" (1968)—Miller's objective is broadly satirical social commentary on the status quo in American race relations rather than a self-consciously radical politics.[24] *Siege* distances its analysis from that of Harlem's most extreme separatists by amalgamating them with juvenile delinquents as "the Tribal People," gangs of knife-toting hoodlums who practice "Karate on the rooftops" and spout a Black Muslim–derived rhetoric of "blue-eyed devils" and "white dogs" (89). The Tribal People pose an interior threat to the stability of the Harlem state, established and led by ironically battle-scarred veterans of the nonviolent civil rights movement, but Huggins neutralizes the threat with a pragmatically liberal blend of tolerance and political maneuver.

The novel also critiques standard notions of racial separation by making a string of postcolonial references equating Harlem's situation with that of Algeria, Ghana, and especially Cuba. As in its treatment of the separatist argument, *Siege*'s portrayal of the ghetto as colony does not advocate the ghetto's independence so much as critique the tendency of both right and left to understand the ghetto as a colony. The Bay of Pigs–era talk of "air support" for an army of blacks recruited to invade Harlem; Huggins's boxes of Cuban cigars and his decision to set up his headquarters in Harlem's Hotel Theresa, where Castro famously stayed in 1960; the United States' sponsorship of radio propaganda portraying America as a consumer paradise and offering defecting Harlemites free trips to Miami—all these parallels to Cuba's situation invoke the colonial metaphor but also offer a critique of the overblown rhetoric of separation. In the same way, the Berlin-style Checkpoint Frederick Douglass at Ninety-seventh and Third satirizes a growing tendency of thought that divided the ghetto from the metropolis in the same kind of Manichaean division as that between East and West proposed by Cold War ideology. *Siege* wants to show with the device of Harlem's secession how the fortunes and identities of whites rest upon those of blacks and how the labor and the cultural vitality of blacks make American urbanism run. But the novel's guiding impulse is not to advocate postcolonial separation; rather, the novel critiques the growing tendency across the spectrum of urban intellectuals and representations to regard the ghetto, inextricably intertwined with the rest of the metropolis, as a separate world: colony, enemy, alien land.

Harlem has, then, been forced out of the union as much as it has seceded. "'Let me lay on the scene for you,'" Lance Huggins says to Mister Eddie, the envoy to Harlem from the United States, "'we had this secret space in us and now we have located it geographically and made it public for all the world to see'" (81). *Siege* imagines being a black American as a separate state, in both the experiential and political sense of the word, mapped in mentality as a "secret space in us" and in social space as a ghetto violently separated from the rest of the metropolis (especially the redeveloped residential and business districts south of Ninety-sixth Street). *Siege* thus extends fantastically *Cool World*'s habit of finding parallels between what Albert Cohen would call the subculture of the ghetto and the world beyond its boundaries. Duke's drug supplier, for instance, a West Indian entrepreneur named Royal Baron, speaks a hip variant of corporate jargon and compares himself to Henry Ford, pointing up the warping of free enterprise in the ghetto. In *Siege*, these parallels flower into a full-blown parallel structure, so that "black America" produces not just a drug-dealing subcultural Henry Ford but its own president, economic and foreign policy, armed forces, and history.

The secession of "black America" from America makes for a national crisis and a predictable response: committees of businessmen, professors, and ex-coaches study the problem, then the state takes steps to reincorporate Harlem into the nation. The crisis of Harlem's secession inspires the same response as did the urban crisis: the problem of the ghetto comes to be seen as one of separation that asks for reincorporation. That was the message of the Kerner Commission, a committee much like those in the novel. The Kerner Commission and many others saw the crisis as one of social dissolution proceeding from the center outward. If the ghetto was the key to the future viability of cities in an urbanized nation, to "lose" the ghetto would be to lose control of social order in one of the nation's core spaces (just as the "loss" of China in 1949, and the threat of "losing" Vietnam, threatened a parallel loss of control on the global scale). *Siege*, however, imagines a situation in which Lance Huggins and his government have established a separate and self-sufficient order in Harlem, so that the ghetto, stable behind its new walls, does not threaten violent destabilization of the metropolis. The desperation with which *Siege* imagines America responding to Harlem's secession therefore requires a different explanation. Even in the early 1960s, as the rise in urban crime was just beginning to gain widespread notoriety, there were plenty of Americans who might have thought ringing the ghetto with barbed wire and armed men was not a bad idea. *Siege*, however, imagines a situation in which America is desperate to reincorporate Harlem and many of those shut out of the ghetto long to get in. There are at least three ways to read that desperation.

First, the federal government's need to reincorporate Harlem has to do with the message the secession sends to the rest of the world. By "localizing" the "national cancer" of racial inequality and literalizing the color line, Harlem's secession threatens to undermine America's Cold War self-conception as the free world's leading power and a noncolonialist nation. "'I'm on record as being in favor of freedom and the whole world knows it,'" says Mister Eddie, but Harlem's secession refutes that argument, just as the dire conditions in pre- and postseparation Harlem refute the notion that Cold War America provides the world with an example of universal prosperity. Lance therefore responds to Mister Eddie's statement by suggesting that the secession, like urban social unrest in the 1960s, undermines America's Cold War ideology: "'When we pulled out we took the mortar with us and now your house is going to come falling down around your ears'" (81).

Second, the need of individual white New Yorkers to reestablish communication with Harlem reminds us of the interconnectedness of what Americans accepted as radically separate, mutually opposed black and white urbanisms. White New Yorkers, who miss jazz, night life, and Harlem's more illicit pleasures, suddenly realize that urbanism as a way of life depended on the fusion of "black" and "white" spheres. They also miss their housekeepers and nannies, upon whom they suddenly understand the economies and smooth operation of their households have depended: "now your house is going to come falling down around your ears." The fantasy of strict separation caricatures the distance between prevailing assumptions of separate racial spheres and the deep intertwining of black and white in urban social reality.

Third, and this is perhaps where Miller's deepest engagement with his subject can be found, the need of whites to get into Harlem expresses a need to know the black inner city. The political struggle to reincorporate Harlem models the literary struggle to map and interpret the second ghetto, and Siege meditates at length on the art and politics of crossing the boundaries of the ghetto in the city of feeling. As in Cool World, the story of the author's participation in this struggle is modeled in the novel's ostentatious dialect narration.

Miller delivers his satire in Siege by way of a rhetorical strategy tellingly different from that employed in Cool World. In the earlier novel, the author's entry into Duke Custis's subjectivity, and into Harlem, aspires to seamless totality. The author's entry into his narrating character in Siege self-consciously appropriates the form of the white Southerner Joel Chandler Harris's Uncle Remus tales (from which Miller draws the novel's epigraph). In Siege, an old black man narrates stories of his role as a young man in Harlem's break with America and its first year as an independent state, events now seventy-five years in the past. Uncle Remus addresses white children, but the narrator of Siege speaks to an audience of black children, a cosmopolitan postseparation generation of boys with Africanized names, a command of French, and a gently patronizing air toward their cranky, atavistic grandfather: "'Il est très désagréable aujourd'hui,'" Sekou whispers to Ahmed (32). Cool World sought to be an Uncle Tom's Cabin, urgently presuming to enter into the consciousness of both black literary subjects and a white readership in order to mobilize the latter on behalf of the former (an imperative that helps to explain the need for what some saw as a "sentimental" ending, to propose an objective or alternative akin to Stowe's Quaker abolitionist household). Miller's shift to the model of Uncle Remus proposes a cooler engagement of author and subject, much more cautiously mediated through conventional devices for indicating a literary crossing of racial boundaries, that calls attention to the distance rather than the intimacy between them.

The elaboration in *Siege* of Miller's characteristic strategy, the dialect tale, acknowledges that distance by foregrounding the old man's role as a mediating convention á la Uncle Remus. The old man employs a mishmash of verbal styles, intermingling hip usages of the 1950s and early 1960s ("'Lance baby, that is the language of diplomacy and protocol. It really wails'" [70]), a kind of courtly epic register ("'oh my dear friend, live and recomfort me somewhat for this grievous life I am having'" [144]), down-home-sounding aphorisms ("'Get your hand out of my pocket and your feet off my back!'" [7] is Harlem's separatist creed and the novel's opening line), and oddly spelled locutions that seem to take Uncle Remus directly as a model ("'I'll get to that bimeby, honey'" [7], "'tooby sure, honey'" [10]). This pointedly artificial mélange calls attention to the presence of dialect as a device and the increasingly complicated politics of mimicry. Where Duke's voice aspired to verisimilitude, the old man's voice aspires to a sly use of convention to comment on the necessity of such conventions.

Siege does not expect that a black urban intellectual will authenticate the novel, as Baldwin did *Cool World*, by saying that Miller has written like a black man. Instead, Miller uses the model of Uncle Remus to demonstrate in the form of the dialect tale the increasing difficulty of bridging the distance between the races, the accumulation of screens and mediating barriers at the literary boundaries of the ghetto of feeling to match the social and economic barriers that encircle the ghetto in the social landscape. The novel's landscape figures this erecting of new and more impassable barriers around the ghetto as a double line of barricades, across which armed men confront one another and distraught lovers stage tragic dialogues.

"'There were two complete and distinct sets of barriers, let me set you straight on that'" (33). The ruling image of *Siege* is the double set of barriers, manned by troops on both sides, running around the perimeter of Harlem. Populist collage barricades of "abandoned automobiles, mattresses, orange crates, and such like" (11) guard the Harlem side; government-issue barbed wire guards the Majority People's side. At Checkpoint Frederick Douglass on East Ninety-seventh Street, where Third Avenue becomes Luthuli Drive, soldiers stare at one another across the barricades and heartsick whites come on Sunday mornings to entreat resolute black ex-lovers and ex-domestics to cross the wire. The double line of fortifications around Harlem makes concrete the ghetto's figurative "invisible walls"—self-imposed as well as imposed from outside—and identifies the racial roots of urban social cleavage. The Harlem forces paint "famous sayings by our famous sons, such as, 'The problem of the twentieth century is the problem of the color line' " (33) on the barriers, identifying those barriers as a literalized color line. These images only slightly exaggerated what other observers of the time concluded about the line where the Upper East Side meets East Harlem: V. S. Pritchett, also writing in 1964, duplicated Miller's Cold War and postcolonial metaphors when he observed that East Ninety-sixth Street was "nothing less . . . than Manhattan's Berlin Wall. You stare across it as you stare over the wire at checkpoint Charlie into East Berlin, into another dispensation. You are staring into the Caribbean and Africa."[25]

In both *Cool World* and *Siege*, the traffic between dispensations at the checkpoints along the realtors' frontier is both sexual and literary: sexual commerce across the boundaries of the ghetto provides a model of the traffic in representations. The whites who come to Checkpoint Frederick Douglass manifest a set of needs first introduced in *Cool World* when Duke and other gang members sell their sexual services to white men who gather after dark in Central Park. Duke's friend Chester leaves Harlem and the Royal Crocadiles altogether to live with an older white man in a luxury high-rise well to the south of the realtors' frontier. Anticipating *Siege*, the homosexual exchange across the boundaries of the ghetto serves as a figure of exploitative commerce, to be developed into a major theme in the later novel's critique of America's economic exploitation of the ghetto. In keeping with the habits of the delinquent literature, *Cool World* covers well-traveled generic ground in detailing the precocious (and, following the period's dominant reading of homosexuality, degraded) sexuality of delinquents, part of the delinquent literature's signature combination of titillation and social critique. Seamy teen sex was exciting generic material, but it also served to express cultural deprivation, emotional impoverishment, and the lack of normative parental models and authority, all contributing to a failure to date, love, marry, and reproduce social order in the approved ways.

The delinquent's sex life becomes a figure of authorship in *Cool World* when we turn to Royal Baron's secretary and lover, a white woman Duke calls Miss Dewpont, who explains the attraction of white and black to Duke while they are lying in bed looking at their naked bodies in a ceiling mirror. Having just brought herself to orgasm using the passive Duke's hand, and having told him earlier that (in his rendering) " 'They nothin more excitin in the whole world than black skin against white skin' " (115), she explains that " 'breakin thru thats what count' ":

"I have try to be happy with my own kind an break thru with my own kind but Duke I just cant make it. When you cant make it with you own kind then you have to break thru with the kind what you can break thru with be they whatever color they may be. . . . You look aroun you see I not the only one who found the way to break thru. They a lot of us an we no worse then some of those down town who just dreamin about it an dont have the nerve for it." (117)

Miss Dewpont explains her movement into Harlem as the search for an orgasmic breakthrough and suggests that there are many more people outside the ghetto ("down town") who feel the way she does. This begins to suggest an affinity between Miss Dewpont's lust and the stated desire of Miller, a downtown intellectual, to write "a book that would break through the timidity and concealed arrogance and the aridity of the sociologists' treatises."

If *Cool World* offers a sexual metaphor of authorial entry into the ghetto from without, then Miller shows a rich appreciation for the complexity of his project. On the one hand, he is, like Miss Dewpont, shaking off the constraints of fear and convention to break through into the most exciting and satisfying of inner-city terrains. And, like Miss Dewpont, whose speech is articulated by Duke's narrating persona and authenticated by his orthography, Miller's successful breakthrough is marked by the acquisition of Duke's language. Miss Dewpont brings herself to "break thru" by taking control of Duke's hand and manipulating it, an apt analogy to Miller's strategy of writing as Duke. On the other hand (if you will pardon the ramifying pun), Miller is, like both Miss Dewpont and the men in the park who pay for Duke's services, using Duke as an instrument to satisfy himself. In Miller's case, that satisfaction lies in his credentialing himself as an urban intellectual. Miller has employed Duke, and the life models for Duke outside Miller's window when he lived near Harlem, in writing his way across the boundaries of Harlem and into the delinquent canon, the *New York Times Book Review*, and a movie deal. If Duke's realization that as a reader and writer he can "Do any thing. Be any thing" is also Miller's, then *Cool World* offers in its system of double-edged sexual metaphor an appreciation of that climactic moment's nuances of exploitation.

The forlorn whites who gather at Checkpoint Frederick Douglass in *Siege*, "old friends and lovers" bemoaning their separation from their black counterparts across the wire, take on new meaning when read against *Cool World*'s equation of sexual traffic across the boundaries of the ghetto with the traffic in representations across the boundaries of the literary ghetto. The old man tells his audience that in observing the tragedies played out at the checkpoint he learned "what separation meant" (36). Like *Siege*'s dialect strategy, the little tragedies at the checkpoint play up the consequences for urban intellectuals of the notion that the ghetto and the rest of the metropolis are two mutually incomprehensible urban realities. Miller understands both sets of barriers around the ghetto to be increasingly forbidding. Both sides in the novel are forever doubling and redoubling their border guards, just as the developing urban crisis made both whites and blacks increasingly reluctant to believe that any white novelist—especially as opposed to social scientists, educators, journalists, and others speaking the ostensibly deracinated technical language of professionals—could imaginatively enter the literary ground of "black America."

Just as *Siege* projects a fantasy of Harlem's separation from the nation, it projects as well a cultural situation in which a socially engaged, white, left-liberal writer like Miller, eagerly pursuing the logic of the cultural moment, will be obliged to consider Harlem as someone else's literary turf. The novel's last lines make the point one last time. The old man, who has throughout his narrative always told the children precisely where he was and when, concludes by saying, "but here I am in Harlem and I'm doing very well; and as dear old Lance said that time to Mister Eddie: It is magnificent to be here!" (166). Read as *Miller's* concluding statement, these lines stake the author's claim to having passed through Checkpoint Frederick Douglass, presenting winkingly trumped-up linguistic and political credentials, and into the heartland of urban crisis. The forlorn lovers beyond the wire, extending the sexual metaphor of authorship proposed in *Cool World*, give an edge to this claim by reminding us that the literary repercussions of urban crisis have made such boundary crossing especially illicit, precarious, and difficult to accomplish.

Siege begins with an epigraph from Uncle Remus's "Story of the Deluge," in which the crawfishes, wronged by the other creatures, bore into the ground so that "'de waters squirt out, en riz higher en higher twel de hills wuz kivvered, en de creeturs wuz all drownded.'" Read against that epigraph, *Siege*'s last lines acquire two darkly prescient subtexts. First, the figure of an imminent catastrophe of biblical proportions, emanating from the ground of the wronged beings (the crawfishes initiate the deluge) and constituting a judgment on those who fancy themselves superior (the creeturs who "'let on 'mong deyselves dat dey wuz bigger dan de Crawfishes'"), suggests an expectation of violent social conflict that will recast the novel's last lines as nostalgia for a better time. Second, the author's need to invoke Uncle Remus at all in order to make his entry into Harlem is an acquiescence, however ironic, to the logic of racial separation and mutual incomprehension that rapidly gained conventional status during the mid- and late 1960s.

"A Saggy Bottomed, Tangle Footed Buck and Wing"

Located in *Siege* where the Upper East Side ends and the projects begin, Checkpoint Frederick Douglass stands a block north of the realtors' frontier. Cold War resonances make the checkpoint a figure of implacable social conflict and ideological struggle. Named for a writer, the checkpoint is also an apt figure of the critical impulse to control and manage the traffic in representations across the hardening boundaries of the city of feeling.

The reception of *Siege* made clear the new difficulties of authorial movement in the city of feeling that Miller acknowledged in the novel itself. Without
the corollary issue of juvenile delinquency to legitimate its imaginative entry
into the ghetto, *Siege* fell into a kind of generic limbo. The novel went against
the grain of a time when American culture, "awakening" to the developing
urban crisis, was turning to new standards of accreditation for written voices
from the ghetto: documentary, violent, and studiously raw rather than highly
novelistic, gentle, and sly; urgent, brutal social realism rather than archly ironic
folk tales; the ostentatiously unvarnished first-person narratives of black ghetto
dwellers and the third-person analyses of accredited professional experts rather
than the polished prose of accomplished literary technicians. Critics were on
the lookout for ghetto *writing* but did not seem to be awaiting great new *novels*
of the ghetto. *Siege* became just another book about race relations by a well-
meaning white author, albeit a particularly clever (or, for others, precious) book
distinguished by an attempt at humor in what was rapidly becoming a humor-
less literature.

The reception of *Siege* was instructively mixed. *Siege* did receive respectful,
even glowing, reviews in some of the same venues that had established *Cool
World*'s place in the literature of delinquency. A *Time* review called Miller "one
of the best satirists working in the United States." *Saturday Review* held that
Miller had "done something wonderful" in giving "the most explosive issue of
our day focus in a novel—that is, brought under one roof all of the attitudes and
conceptions that still keep the races poles apart." *New Republic* saw Miller as
executing trenchant, stinging grotesques in addressing "Topic Number One" of
the day.[26]

But there were important questions about Miller's use of language, and to
question the success of *Siege*'s dialect strategy was to question Miller's credentials for entry into literary Harlem. *Cool World*'s reviewers, when it was
published in 1959, had not mentioned Miller's race except to praise his sensi-
tivity to young black people's voices and habits of mind, and the emphasis in
almost every case was on his achievement in bridging the gulf between ages
rather than races. *Siege*, by contrast, appeared in a very different moment in the
ever-mutating urban conversation, and the delicate questions of race and
authorship acknowledged in *Siege*'s self-consciously contrived narration were
very prominently at issue. Miller found his credentials evaluated by the new
standards of separation he lampooned in *Siege*, and with new unpleasant
results. Miller had said of *Cool World* in 1959, "My greatest concern now is:
What will the Negro reader think of it?"[27] Black urban intellectuals, self-
consciously writing in the mid-1960s as "the Negro reader" of *Siege*, argued
that Miller had no business in Harlem on the eve of urban crisis.

Several reviewers, among them prominent black intellectuals, took issue
with Miller's appropriation of the Uncle Remus form, some finding it unfunny

and less satirical of convention than demeaning to blacks, some merely object-
ing that it interfered with the narrative. *Cool World* had also weathered similar
criticisms (mostly from the margins), but the critique of *Siege's* language fed
into a much more powerful attack on Miller's accreditation as a writer of the
inner city. John O. Killens, a black novelist and founding member of the
Harlem Writers Workshop, actually found *Siege's* intentionally artificial dialect
to be "a fairly good imitation of Afro-Americanese" but concluded that "it
never achieves its idiomatic and historical truth."[28] When Killens reviewed
Siege in August 1964, he was still in the limelight after publishing an essay entitled "Explanation of the 'Black Psyche'" in the *New York Times Magazine* of 7
June. That essay is a classically stark formulation of identity politics typical of
the first blush of urban crisis: "Just as surely as East is East and West is West,
there is a 'black' psyche and there is a 'white' one, and the sooner we face up
to this social and cultural reality, the sooner the twain shall meet. . . . Your joy
is very often our anger and your despair our fervent hope."[29] Extending this line
of argument, Killens assumed in his review of *Siege* that Miller could write
something that looked and sounded exactly like voices from the inner city and
still fail to write from within the inner city. He located the problem, predictably,
in Miller's whiteness.

Killens made the definitive case against Miller's entry into the ghetto, erecting the barrier to keep whites out even as he praised Miller as "one of the few
American novelists of European descent who really seems to give a damn about
his country and his people." (James Jones and Norman Mailer were the others;
J. D. Salinger and John Updike exemplified those who "write page after page
of pretty precious prose about nothing of substance.") Killens's review does not
take issue with Miller's Uncle Remus strategy: on the contrary, the review
endorses the logic of separate racial spheres that informed Miller's use of
dialect, and Killens ignores or misses the possibility that *Siege* might in some
way be using dialect and other strategies to criticize that logic of separation. In
the vocabulary of urban hipster criticism that Miller's work seemed to attract
(recall Wakefield's "Yes man, yes"), Killens argues that *Siege* collapses into
insignificance because Miller cannot write his way convincingly into the language, and thus into the space, of Harlem: "he 'dug' the surface but never dug
beneath the surface, and therefore never really 'dug' the essence."[30] Killens
goes on to apply the same criticism to *Cool World*, Miller's principal credential
as an urban intellectual, which now becomes in retrospect a similarly superficial effort.

Miller becomes, in Killens's review, one of his own white characters looking
forlornly over the barrier at Checkpoint Frederick Douglass to the separate
black state beyond. Although Killens lets the "serious" and well-intentioned
Miller off the hook as an individual by regarding a white man's failure to "dig"
his way into Harlem as socially (if not genetically) foreordained, he still

concludes that Miller has failed to move into the space and language of "black America." The black man "remains a foreigner" to Miller, "an exotic 'noble savage' unreachable in depth or time or space." As long as Miller devotes himself to Topic Number One and the mimicry of black subjects, Killens condemns him to, at best, an inefficacious kind of literary tourism that cannot penetrate Harlem's invisible walls—and, at worst, to the kind of exploitative tourism Miller acknowledged in his own images of sexual traffic across the borders of Harlem. Killens directs Miller instead to his own neighborhood: "One can only wish Warren Miller cared enough to write about that great white jungle of a society which has kept the Harlems of our country in a perpetual state of siege."[31] In effect, Killens understands Miller to be attempting to hurdle the barricades and completely forecloses any prospect of irony or self-awareness in Miller's rendering of those barricades and the author's need to hurdle them. He tells Miller to stay on his own side of the line.

Killens, arguing via the logic of urban crisis that divided America into two countries, closed one gate to Harlem; Albert Murray, who dissented against the idea of racial separation, closed another gate by identifying Miller as contributing to the mutual misunderstanding that divided the races. Murray, a black novelist and critic with strong ties to Harlem, explicitly wrote against the notion of separate black and white worlds upon which Killens's reasoning and the logic of urban crisis rested. He attempted in his criticism of the 1960s, later collected in *The Omni-Americans*, to

restate the problem formulated by the *Report of the National Advisory Commission on Civil Disorders* by suggesting that the present domestic conflict and upheaval grows out of the fact that in spite of their common destiny and deeper interests, the people of the United States are being mislead [sic] by misinformation to insist on *exaggerating* their ethnic differences.[32]

This project had much in common with *Siege*'s ironizing of the rhetoric of separation, but Murray understood Miller to be *part of* the problem they both addressed. Thus, for Murray, Miller sinned by assuming that a white man had ostentatiously to put on the blackface of exaggerated dialect strategy in order to write black characters. Miller was not guilty of trying to get through the barricades at Checkpoint Frederick Douglass; he was guilty of helping to erect them in the form of the conventional mediating devices he employed in writing as and about black characters.

Murray had some odd notions about what constituted good models for whites writing about Harlem—his enthusiasm for Hemingway's treatment of Spanish characters comes immediately to mind—but, whatever the value of those models, Miller did not come up to their standard. Murray's review denies Miller at every step of the accrediting chain. Murray concludes that Miller's defender James Baldwin, who had vouched for *Cool World*'s authenticity, knows "much more about the goings on in Greenwich Village, Saint-Germain-des-Prés, and even Saint Tropez than he is ever likely to know about Harlem" and probably has more in common with Oscar Wilde than he does with Harlemites. As a literary stylist, Miller does not possess the means to write his way into Harlem. His "coyness" of language screens his bankruptcy as "an imaginative novelist. [The reader] will find a series of patently contrived situations hastily derived from the currently fashionable generalizations of the so-called social sciences."[33] Murray reduces *Cool World* to the received wisdom of social workers, reporters, purveyors of psychiatric and Marxist clichés—anything but the work of a novelist.

With *Siege*, Miller forfeits even his claim to spurious social scientific authority. Stripping away the layers of literary, journalistic, and social scientific authority that made up Miller's case for himself as a writer of Harlem, Murray reduces this second Harlem novel to that which it sought to lampoon, "a minstrel show in which the writer comes pumping on stage doing a saggy bottomed, tangle footed buck and wing in the guise of Joel Chandler Harris, which he ain't."[34] Directly asking Miller's imagined "Negro reader" to bar Miller's movement into literary Harlem, Murray concludes by suggesting that "Negroes would do well to keep an eye cocked on Warren Miller, slapdash, slapstick, and all. With your white Negro anything is possible." Miller struck Murray as the kind of intellectual who might still maneuver along various routes of expertise—in politics, jazz, narcotics, interracial romance, the civil rights movement—to gain a position in which he "could very easily be mistaken as a very genuine and understanding friend of Negroes." Extending Miller's own image of sexual traffic as literary traffic, Murray tells black readers to beware of a seducer who wants to become an expert on, among other things, "Negro sex life as it really is."[35] Given Miller's stated desire to produce social documents that made literature from the richest dramas of his historical moment, the categorical rejections by Murray and Killens read like a letter from Frederick Douglass to Harriet Beecher Stowe telling her to stay off his turf.

Having returned from a visit to Blood's family in the projects, new buildings that are nevertheless pervaded by the "Uptown Stink" of garbage and poverty, Duke Custis returns home and steals money from his grandmother's purse. Just before he decides to rob her, he searches the apartment for money but finds only an old shoe shine box deep in a closet. "I give it a kick. Dont know why I aint ever throw it out. The stink of shoe polish is the worse stink of all" (22). The Uptown Stink and the stink of shoe polish rhyme here, together outlining a systematic foreclosure of economic opportunity and imagination that structures the geography of the novel and of Duke's inner life. He steals, the novel wants to say, because the only other option connects to the historical train of degradations with which the shoe shine box has been invested. *Cool World* shows the narrowness and violence of Duke's world from an interior perspective marked by access to the space (Harlem) and language (Duke's interior monologue) of the juvenile delinquent, in whom one might read the failures and imminent crisis of the postwar city. Duke's tortured orthography gives this account of inner-city life the Uptown Stink of authenticity.

Killens's and Murray's reviews of *Siege* suggest how five years, in which the urban crisis began its move to the center of both urban and racial thinking, might change the valences of "the stink of shoe polish." As Miller's invocation of Uncle Remus itself suggested, the stink of shoe polish surrounding *Siege* proceeded from the assumption—shared by author and critics—that a white author crossing into the ghetto of feeling and speaking in a "black" voice was obliged to apply to himself the linguistic equivalent of shoe polish. The need to go through the grotesque rituals of "blacking up" had to do with the need to present credentials at the checkpoints policing those boundaries. In the late 1950s, writing within the canons of delinquent literature, Miller presented himself as trying to "pass" through the exercise of prose technique—to write as his predominantly white readers expected a young, inadequately educated black man might think, speak, or write. In the mid-1960s, writing within the emerging canons of urban crisis but in some ways against the grain of their structuring assumptions, Miller's dialect strategy itself asked why it seemed necessary for him to adopt fantastically contrived and baroque dialect masks. *Siege* asks, and tries to show in parable form, why Miller must go through the ritual steps of "a saggy bottomed, tangle footed buck and wing" in order to effect an entry into the space and language of "black America."

Of course, Miller himself had aspired to help lead the way toward the elevation of race as the urban problem structuring all others. *Cool World* argues for subsuming delinquency to race in ways that help to raise *Siege*'s slogan-decorated barriers marking the color line around Harlem as the signal feature of the urban landscape. Miller's death of cancer in 1966, freezing his encounter with the inner city before he had a chance to formulate further responses to it, preserves the sharp edges of the irony defining his relation to the advent of the urban crisis. The changing conditions of Miller's imaginative entry into Harlem in *Cool World* and *Siege*, conditions about which the novels think in complex and self-critical ways, consider the rising stakes and changing politics of writing about the inner city. The two novels together frame a moment in which urban intellectuals managed and engaged with the emergence of the second ghetto as the ground on which the urban crisis must be staged.

The Box of Groceries and the Omnibus Tour: *Manchild in the Promised Land*

It was as though I had found my place and Harlem
had found its place. We were suited for each other
now.

      Claude Brown, *Manchild in the Promised Land*

Around the New York offices of the Macmillan publishing company in the early
1960s, the towering 1,500-page draft of *Manchild in the Promised Land* was
known as "Claude Brown's box of groceries." Brown, a novice author, was worried that Macmillan would demand return of its advance payments to him if he
did not get the book done on time, so he had rushed to New York from Howard
University (where he was enrolled) to deliver a large box containing the manuscript. Macmillan's editors were mystified by the manuscript's diffuse narrative,
rough language, and digressive wanderings through the inner city. *Manchild*
meandered through flashbacks and flashbacks within flashbacks, seemingly
uninterested in driving toward a clear ending from its dramatic opening
episode, in which the thirteen-year-old Claude Brown is shot down in the street
near his home. Brown's narrating voice often tended toward conversational
imprecision and repetition—in three short paragraphs in *Manchild* describing
a woman's kindness to him, "nice" or a variant of it appears six times and "real"
or a variant of it appears four times[1]—and, unlike even the most hard-boiled
inner-city writers published by major houses to that time, he used words like

"cunt" and "fuck" not only when representing the speech of his characters but also when speaking directly as narrator. Macmillan asked Brown to cut the manuscript to one-third its original length (which he did), suggested he limit the profanity and clarify the "dialect" usages (which he did not do) so that the Book-of-the-Month Club and *Reader's Digest* might take an interest in his story, and found a young editor eager to assume responsibility for the book.[2]

Manchild became an instant bestseller upon its publication in late summer, 1965, when the riots in Watts and efforts to interpret them marked the arrival of the full-blown urban crisis. Also published that year were *Dark Ghetto* and *The Autobiography of Malcolm X*. These books appeared at—and helped to shape— the moment the urban crisis achieved general reception in its canonical form, as a ghetto-centered social and cultural upheaval organized under the rubric of race and its semi-synonymous subtopics of poverty, crime, riots, and urban renewal. The institutions that produced representations of inner cities—not only book publishers but also television networks and stations, magazines and scholarly journals, newspapers, universities—very rapidly adapted themselves to manage the prodigious flow of representations out of the second ghettos that would dominate thinking about cities during the 1960s (and to this day). Publishing houses, caught off guard as Macmillan had been, rushed to develop an editorial apparatus suited to evaluating and processing the writing of the new order of urban intellectuals like Brown and Malcolm X. These new-model black urban intellectuals presented themselves as speaking from behind the second ghetto's increasingly forbidding "invisible walls": they drew a new set of maps and provided a new set of appropriate voices and characters through which American culture undertook to know the ghetto by the testimony of its inhabitants.

Brown's "class of 1965" also demonstrates how the ghetto-centered logic of urban crisis incorporated previously freestanding problems, like that of juvenile delinquency. As the ghetto became the definitive inner-city terrain in which to pursue the definitive urban subject of race, the ex-delinquent authors of first-person ghetto narratives became powerfully authoritative urban intellectuals. Claude Brown, traveling in the vanguard of this group, wrote from the postwar inner city's most crisis-infused subject position. Delinquency took on a new accrediting function for writers of Harlem like Brown, Malcolm X, and Piri Thomas, who cited their own delinquent careers (or, in Kenneth Clark's case, his extensive work with Harlem delinquents) as markers of their intimate experience of ghetto pathology and its root causes.[3] The effusion of prison writing during the urban crisis—by, for example, inmates of the California prison system like Eldridge Cleaver and George Jackson—demonstrated how influential commentators presented their delinquency as a credential, establishing street-level authority to represent the second ghetto and thus to speak for and about "black America." Tracing Brown's movements in and out of Harlem, reform school, and Greenwich Village, *Manchild* outlines and contains a whole complex of ghetto narratives that developed in the 1950s and 1960s; the delinquent's story becomes merely the authenticating first act of this omnibus narrative. In *Manchild*, as in the literature of urban crisis, delinquent narrative became incorporated as a standard opening procedure to establish street credibility for a new kind of urban intellectual.

Reading *Manchild* as *about* the making of a new-model urban intellectual equipped to engage with the urban crisis—a reading the following pages will pursue—offers ways to account for precisely those aspects of the book that mystified Brown's editors at Macmillan. Like its bruising and untrained language, *Manchild*'s fragmentary narrative and its map of the inner city take form around the project of constructing a literary persona equipped to represent the ghetto in a moment of urban crisis. The narrative and spatial plots of *Manchild* survey the ground on which Brown places himself as a representative member of what he calls the "first Northern urban generation of Negroes." This claim of social representativeness constitutes an important element of Brown's credentials to represent the ghetto's inner life in prose: his delinquency, like the blood he sheds on the pavements of Harlem, marks Brown's rough grammar and hipster locutions as authoritative language. If Brown's persona was a product of the signature pathologies of ghetto life, then his voice had special authority to address the subject of urban crisis, and people who regarded the second ghetto as a separate world were obliged to rely on experts like him for their maps of that world.

Brown's language and credentials were both on display on 29 August 1966, a year after *Manchild's* publication, when he and Arthur Dunmeyer, a childhood friend who appears as "Dunny" in *Manchild*, testified before a U.S. Senate subcommittee examining the "Federal Role in Urban Problems."[4] Senator Abraham Ribicoff, the subcommittee's chairman, explained that Brown was there as "author of *Manchild in the Promised Land*"; Dunmeyer was there as a character from the book, "even more of a 'manchild' " because he had followed the route Brown avoided, graduating from reform school to a serious criminal career and thus to Sing Sing, Dannemora, and Attica. Senator Ribicoff asked them to "just talk as you will," and Brown and Dunmeyer obliged by expounding in free form on violent crime in particular and life in America's urban ghettos in general. Brown told stories about street life and his family, read excerpts from *Manchild*, attacked Daniel Patrick Moynihan's study of the Negro family, and concluded his testimony by telling Ribicoff, "I think you are beautiful, baby." Ribicoff responded, "I think I understand what you are saying, and I take it as a compliment. . . . I read your book and it was sensitive and I was deeply touched."[5] Brown and Dunny, characters from the book in the flesh, were there to do the cultural work of mapping an inner life onto the spaces of the second ghetto, to give the senators insight into the minds of violent young men in whom were concentrated a set of social pathologies understood to drive the urban crisis. In at least one case, they were preaching to the converted: among the committee members was New York's Democratic senator, Robert Kennedy, who as attorney general had helped lead the move to treat juvenile delinquency as an aspect of racial conflict.

Brown, therefore, arrived upon one of the nation's most exclusive ritual grounds of political representation because he had in *Manchild* established himself as both representative of ghetto dwellers and equipped to represent the ghetto in the appropriate language: "just talk as you will," Ribicoff told him.[6] The resonance between political and literary representation takes on added meaning in light of Brown's own ambitions of the time, unstated in *Manchild* but developed in interviews, to hold public office. Several reviewers of *Manchild* noted this ambition; one, writing in the *New Republic*, suggested that if Martin Luther King ever became president "he might do worse than to appoint Claude Brown as Attorney-General."[7] Brown, developing Norman Podhoretz's assertion that "nobody really represents . . . the lower-class Negro of Harlem, the kind of people [Brown] came up with," explained,

> There was not one Negro anywhere in the country whom the white power structure could turn to and say: Look, go down there [in Watts] and reason with those Negroes, who—who are running havoc in the streets. . . . It should have shown the white power structure that Negro masses are not represented. . . . They weren't going to listen to any comedians. They weren't going to listen to any Roy Wilkenses, Martin Luther Kings, Whitney Youngs.[8]

Brown, credentialed by *Manchild* to represent the ghetto and the "Negro masses" in prose and further credentialing himself in law school for a political career (which, finally, he never pursued), imagined himself to be uniquely equipped to shuttle back and forth across the boundaries of the ghetto in doing the work of representation. *Manchild* treats the urban crisis centering on "black America" as a set of social conditions giving rise to urban unrest and as a set of intellectual and political conditions giving rise to a new order of urban intellectual. In that sense, *Manchild* is ordered by its consideration of the fit between the changing inner city and the need to represent it.

"The Cry of the Ghetto"

In his introduction to a collection of excerpts from the autobiographies of black Americans, Henry Louis Gates Jr. remembers that during the urban crisis he and and his family, far away from Claude Brown's "urban world" in a "village in the hills of West Virginia," read *Manchild* as part of their search "for a key to unlock the madness of American racism." That is, Gates turned to Brown for an explanation of what it meant to live in the urban capitals of "black America," the demographic and representational center of which had shifted after midcentury from the rural "village" to the Northern inner city. In that introduction, Gates also observes that "the autobiographical act" as a strategy for establishing a literary persona has made autobiography the central genre of "the African-American literary tradition." In many cases, black authors run counter to the norm in publishing an autobiography as a first book that establishes a literary persona to do further work rather than publishing an autobiography after first establishing a literary name and oeuvre.[9] Claude Brown's career supports Gates's contention: he made his debut with an autobiography, *Manchild in the Promised Land;* followed it a decade later with a second book, *The Children of Ham*, which examines the lives of a group of young runaways; wrote articles on a number of related issues; and has been working for some time on nonautobiographical studies of violence and the social effects of the illegal drug trade. *Manchild*, which has been by far Brown's best-read and most-discussed writing, illustrates as well the particular importance accorded during the urban crisis to first-person ghetto narrative—one of the postwar inner city's principal contributions to the literary tradition built around the mapping of that mental-social-geographical complex called "black America."

Much of what *Manchild* has to tell its readers about the second ghetto comes in the form of expletive-laced dialogue with other characters, and Brown's own authorial persona speaks in a similar register even in the absence of quotation marks. *Manchild's*, and not just its characters', analysis of ghetto life proceeds from such assertions as "Harlem was getting fucked over by everybody" (198). *Manchild's* self-presentation of first-person speech from the ghetto—so shocking to the editors at Macmillan—took special force from a belief central to the canonical urban crisis: that whites and others outside the ghetto, having no understanding or experience of the separate black inner city and therefore unable to understand what it was like to be black in America, had to rely on black insiders for firsthand descriptions of ghetto life. These descriptions were marked as firsthand by authenticating language and by story lines that plotted the formation of narrators—who spoke that language—on the map of the second ghetto.

Kenneth Clark's *Dark Ghetto* also suggests the logic by which the first-person narrator claimed a special authority to map the second ghetto from within. *Dark Ghetto's* first chapter, entitled "Prologue: The Cry of the Ghetto," consists entirely of fragments of testimony from residents of Harlem, identified by gender and age (and, in two cases, as drug addicts), describing their lives and their sense of what it means to be black in America. No analytical framework accompanies these quotations, the implication being that the rest of the book will elucidate their meaning. Clark further weds the analysis to the testimony in asserting that *Dark Ghetto* "is, in a sense, no report at all, but rather the anguished cry of its author," thus presenting his own expert testimony as continuous with the unvarnished speech of ghetto people. The sociological study derives important authority from this identity between "the anguished cry of its author" and the cries of Harlemites that form the prologue. Clark therefore lists his own racial credentials ahead of his scholarly credentials—"the reader should know that the author is a Negro, a social psychologist, a college professor"—and plots his authorial persona on the terrain of the ghetto: "*Dark Ghetto* is a summation of my personal and lifelong experiences and observations as a prisoner within the ghetto."[10]

Clark's rhetorical strategy illustrates the ways in which the figure of first-person speech formed a vital center of a boom in writing the ghetto, a kind of writing that accompanied and helped to constitute the urban crisis. During that boom, a great deal of writing in a variety of genres revised the composite ghetto imagined by American letters. *Dark Ghetto*, a seminal work in the rapidly expanding and ghetto-obsessed field of urban studies, and *Manchild*, one of the more widely read first-person ghetto narratives, were part of that revision. The question of what kinds of urban intellectuals would execute the revision and in what form—the calculus of authorship—was conditioned by a growing assumption (both lampooned and seconded in Miller's *Siege of Harlem*) that the physical separation of the races in cities, and the violent encounters between them, expressed and reinforced a concomitant, essential difference in how blacks and whites understood themselves, one another, and the world around them.

Those voices that positioned themselves as coming from within the physical and experiential boundaries of the ghetto therefore claimed a special authority in mapping it. During the urban crisis, conceptual movement through the city of feeling encountered new and more difficult obstacles at the boundaries of the ghetto—as one can tell from the formal and thematic grinding of gears that attends such crossings in Miller's *Siege of Harlem* and others' evaluations of it. As one of the period's typical cases for restricting whites and blacks to separate cultural spaces put it,

> The white person, no matter how liberal he may be, exists in the cocoon of a white-dominated society. Living in a white residential area, sending his children to white schools, moving in exclusively white social circles, he must exert a special effort to expose himself to the actual conditions under which large numbers of Negroes live. Even when such exposure occurs, his perception is likely to be superficial and distorted.[11]

The notion of essential differences between white and black identities extended the principle of separation through both the city of fact, the "actual conditions under which large numbers of Negroes live," and the city of feeling as described and written by blacks. The widely received creed of radical separation, appearing in various forms and in remarkably various ideological circumstances, fueled the need for clearly accredited black first-person narrators to describe the ghetto from within, to explain Claude Brown's world to an increasingly suburbanized and predominantly white national audience.

A growing number of experts and analysts, especially journalists and social scientists, positioned themselves as authoritative investigators with credentials to cross into the ghetto and report back to the world beyond, but for the most part they did not presume to speak from within the ghetto in the voices of its residents. Kenneth Clark did presume to speak in such a voice, but only after making clear that he spoke as *both* Harlemite and social scientist, thus locating the sources of his authority on both sides of the imaginary barricades. *Siege of Harlem*'s convoluted dialect strategy showed that Warren Miller felt the lack of a similar double credential. Miller discovered that during the urban crisis the ideal of the well-wrought novel was a weak basis for claiming authority in representing the inner city, while stronger claims were based in ostentatiously rough documentary prose and the ideal of testimony and analysis direct from the street (or prison). The climate of urban crisis seemed to demand representations of the inner city that trumpeted their own veneer of factuality rather than technique, the better to speak to the day's headlines. Recall that in choosing *Manchild* as one of the most important books of 1965 ("The Year of the Fact"), *Newsweek* suggested that Brown would do more to account for the causes and meanings of the Watts riot than the McCone Commission appointed for that purpose. Claude Brown's inelegant, profane prose scratched an itch for what felt like—what *read* as—fact. This hunger for the feel of documentary did not eliminate the novel as a form that mapped the ghetto, but it led to a new valuation of documentary styles and a significant expansion of ghetto literature in the crucial area of overlap among literary formulas, social science, and journalism where the popular autobiographies of reformed criminals tend to fall. Looking back, Brown says, "It would have been easier to write *Manchild* as a novel," but the moment and the public demanded testimony that advertised its factuality in the form of autobiography.[12]

As the rhetorical assumptions behind Clark's "Cry of the Ghetto" demonstrate, there arose a powerful expectation during the urban crisis that black people marked as ghetto dwellers by their speech and their intimacy with social "pathology" might speak the answers to urban questions of the day. Urban blacks, as Robert Beauregard points out, functioned in the logic of urban crisis as personifications of urban decline, and it therefore stood to reason that in describing their supposedly inaccessible inner lives and social being they articulated the essence of what was wrong with cities. Introducing a book of verbatim testimony collected from residents of American ghettos at public hearings, a "Cry of the Ghetto" at book length, the United States Commission on Civil Rights summarized the needs of anxious and confused white readers encountering such testimony: outsiders needed "a picture of ghetto life which affords possible answers to questions sometimes asked by white people about minority groups, i.e., What do they want? Why don't they work? Why can't they, like early immigrant groups, simply better their condition and move out of slum areas through personal effort?"[13] Placing ostentatiously unedited blocks of authentic ghetto speech in the formal foreground, the commission's report and Clark's "Cry of the Ghetto" acknowledged readers' expectation that black voices speaking from the ghetto might answer these questions. Those generic readers might similarly expect to find such answers somewhere within Claude Brown's rambling, profane, conversational, ostensibly unpolished book, which had the quotidian heft of a "box of groceries."

Manchild as Omnibus Narrative

Manchild in the Promised Land is, of course, anything but free-form unedited testimony: its narrative structure, most crucially, reveals a deep, ordering impulse to show how the second ghetto produced Claude Brown, urban intellectual. We might read the book in three conceptual "acts" abstracted from its meandering and often diffuse narrative. These acts overlap, intertwine, and succeed one another; together, they survey the various narrative possibilities in Brown's changing engagement with Harlem and the world beyond it. In its first act, *Manchild* tells a familiar story of juvenile delinquency and reform; in its second act, it samples narratives of the making of an artist, bohemian, athlete, professional, politician, or entrepreneur; in its third act, it invokes but rejects stories of conversion: Protestant conversion leading to reformist social work; Coptic or Black Muslim conversions leading to political radicalization. *Manchild* samples these standard narrative lines as it surveys a set of possibilities, touching upon them in fragmentary and glancing ways but never pursuing any one line to its conclusion or to the exclusion of the others. The resulting omnibus narrative accounts for the making of an urban intellectual, and Brown's sampling of narrative lines serves to generalize his own experience. He pursues his stated purpose of representing a people, and substantiates his authority to do so, by showing how the story of his life intersects with some standard stories by which black males of his generation became known to other Americans during the urban crisis.

Brown plots through the example of his life a conjunction of people and place—how black people live in the second ghetto and in the postindustrial city that contains it. In the last paragraph of his foreword, Brown discusses the children of black Southerners come North, ending with these much-quoted lines: "To add to their misery, they had little hope of deliverance. For where does one run to when he's already in the promised land?" Chapter 1 then begins with a voice shouting "'Run'" and Claude running and yelling "'I'm shot'" (viii–9). That progression from a people running to a single boy running, from "they" to "one" to "he" to "I," delivers the reader from the generational frame of the fore-

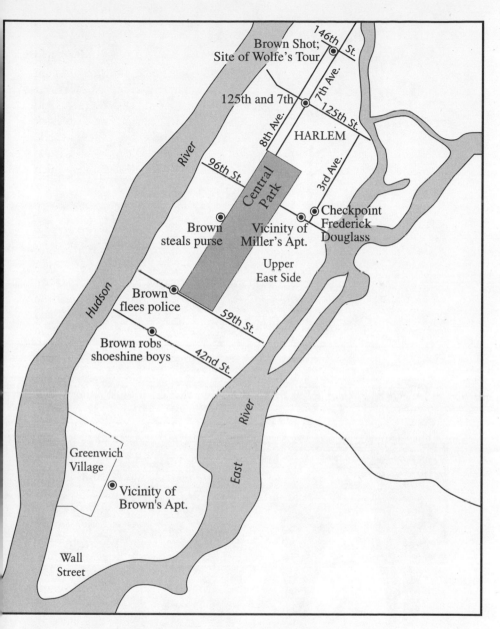

Figure 9. Manhattan. University of Wisconsin Cartographic Laboratory.

Figure 10. Cover of *Manchild in the Promised Land*. Photograph by Leroy McLucas.

Figure 11. Claude Brown. (*Newsweek*, 16 August 1965, p. 81.) Newsweek-Robert McElroy. © 1965, Newsweek, Inc. All rights reserved. Reprinted by permission.

Figure 12. Nelson Algren. (*Newsweek*, 16 August 1965, p. 82.) Newsweek-Jeff Lowenthal. © 1965, Newsweek, Inc. All rights reserved. Reprinted by permission.

word into chapter 1 of a life that will be exemplary of his generation's. The authority of his "I" as producer of a social document rests on that representative status. The story of his delinquency (which begins to end when he is shot and realizes he might die young) positions him to tell readers trained by the logic of the urban crisis what they most want to know: first, the inside details of a genuinely pathological ghetto life and, second, how Brown "survived" to tell about his youth.

In its first act, then, *Manchild* tells the story of juvenile delinquency and reform, refitting the delinquent genre's formulas and priorities to serve the purposes of ghetto narrative engaged with the urban crisis. Brown exhaustively describes his various delinquent activities, making the case for his intimate and expert encounter with the ghetto's defining pathologies by making it clear that he was on the way to being dead or locked up for good by the age of twenty-one. However, he transforms the traditional teen gang material to make of it an introduction enabling *Manchild*'s piecing together of many narrative lines. In *Manchild*, delinquency becomes the path by which Brown acquires the information and expertise that equip him to talk (as the foreword's first sentence puts it) about the ghetto.

Brown notes that he was in the "Forty Thieves" branch of the Harlem Buccaneers gang, and he discusses the "bopping" gang culture that flourished in the 1940s and 1950s until the growth of the street trade in heroin, but he uses the teen gang keywords only in passing as he moves to other emphases. "Rumble" and "gang" do not carry the generic charge pointed up by the delinquent literature's glossaries. (*Manchild* does not have a glossary, and Brown rejected his publisher's suggestions that he include one.)[14] *Manchild* does use the keywords, for instance, to describe Brown's worries about being sent upstate to the reform school at Warwick while still weak from his stomach wound—"Bumpy from 144th Street was up there," and Brown "had shot him in the leg with a zip gun in a rumble only a few months earlier" (16)—yet *Manchild* affords not a single glimpse of the formalized gang initiations, rumbles, meetings, and ceremonies that structure teen gang narratives like *Cool World*. Brown makes no mention of uniform dress or turf and completely eschews the pseudo-military rhetoric of generalship so prevalent in accounts by ex-gang leaders. Although he consistently notes that other delinquents looked up to him and followed his example, Brown makes clear that they did so without encouragement or formal command from him.

Brown understands juvenile delinquency as an entrepreneurial, fiercely individualistic enterprise that reveals what Albert Cohen would call the subcultural structure of the ghetto rather than the secret world of the gang. Brown sees himself and his fellow delinquents not as punks who will become outcasts but as novices in training to become typical Harlemites, who as adults must hustle to get ahead against the long odds of ghettoization. Those of Brown's childhood associates who survive to adulthood, skirting between prison and violent death, will become the types populating such a community: a handful will be conventional hard-working family men and women; others will be preachers, political operators, numbers runners, drug dealers, sexual hustlers of one kind or another, artists, athletes, even minor celebrities. Brown understands delinquency, rather than reform, to provide their primary training into citizenship.

With the traditional delinquent material subsumed and transformed into a device for establishing Brown's credentials to represent the ghetto, the conventional delinquent's reform becomes instead a process in which he comes to understand the ghetto and bend its lessons to his advantage. Brown dedicated *Manchild* to "the late Eleanor Roosevelt, who founded the Wiltwyck School for Boys [another reform school], and to the Wiltwyck School, which is still finding Claude Browns," but his long stays in reform schools do not change him in the way they were intended to. The conventional pattern of the delinquent's reform, found in *Cool World*, for instance, has the delinquent tending to his flower beds and declaring his rejection of the inner city from his pastoral remove. Brown, on the other hand, becomes a better criminal and street fighter in reform school, and upon returning to the streets he deals drugs, associates with a more accomplished class of criminals, and masters the Murphy game and other confidence hustles.

In reform school, Brown (and, therefore, his reader) undergoes a concentrated course in the ghetto's street life, learning about jazz, homosexuality, the Black Muslims, details of criminal technique, how to do time in prison, how to live in the ghetto, and how to make a way for himself in the world—"When they came down on me, I was just going to hit the biggest cat and pray" (135). He also opens avenues out of the ghetto when he enters into the republic of letters. From the moment that the "real" "nice" Mrs. Cohen, a counselor at Warwick, gives him a biography of Mary McLeod Bethune, he begins to understand himself anew as a reader, the first step toward becoming a writer and eventually an urban intellectual. Like Duke Custis, who comes to believe Doc Levine's claim that "when you can read an write why you can do any thing," the adolescent Claude Brown arrives early at an understanding that reading and writing might offer alternatives to the fate mapped out for him along the ghetto-prison axis. Biographies of Bethune and black athletes Jackie Robinson and Sugar Ray Robinson, as well as of Albert Einstein and Albert Schweitzer, lead him to consider for the first time in his life "what might happen if I got out of Warwick and didn't go back to Harlem" (157).[15] Unlike Duke, Brown does not imagine separating himself from the city, and he does, in fact, return to Harlem and prepare to embark upon an adult criminal career, but *Manchild* presents his jailhouse encounter with his future métier of biography and autobiography as planting in him the notion of a larger narrative and geography extending beyond the limits of the ghetto.

Manchild invests great importance in Brown's reading and writing his way across the boundaries of the ghetto: it will become his cultural role to make such crossings in prose for the reader. Reform school, a condensed version of the ghetto and the place where Brown acquires language in a new and potent way, becomes a cradle of urban intellectuals, where Brown encounters in their nascent stages young jazz musicians, athletes, Black Muslims, political activists, and other future spokesmen for his postwar generation. He treats the first steps he takes in prison toward discovering his own cultural role as the very process that opens up a world beyond the ghetto for him. Like Frederick Douglass and many others in the black literary tradition, he shows himself reading and writing his way out of confinement—not out of Harlem entirely but out of the Harlem-Warwick axis that stands for the interchangeability of jail and street, limited opportunity, and a desolate future.

Mentors like Mrs. Cohen and her husband, Alfred (at Warwick), and Ernst Papanek (director of Wiltwyck) show Brown a whole new way to carry himself in the world by trading in words rather than violence. Papanek, a student of Freud and a survivor of Nazi concentration camps, "never got mad, . . . was always telling the truth," and proves to be "slick . . . real slick" as he "just took over everything with a few words that we couldn't even understand too well" (86). This is the model for Brown's authorial persona: dispassionate, never moralizing, deceptively slippery even when blandly factual. Reform school, then, becomes the place where Brown begins to assemble the tools that will allow him to bend to his advantage the intimate knowledge of ghetto pathologies he gains as a delinquent. The connections he makes there among reading, writing, and the crossing of ghetto boundaries define his role as an intellectual during the urban crisis, which is to write his way back *into* the ghetto with the reader in tow, in order to show where he lived, what he lived for, and how he "got out."

The premises for "getting out" having been established in act one, *Manchild*'s act two reviews Brown's options with a survey of conventional avenues leading out of the ghetto. Act one grounds his project and credentials in his connection to the "victims"—career criminals, convicts, junkies, those who die young. In act two, moving back and forth between the street life of Harlem and other possibilities—jobs in the garment district, at a fast food place, and elsewhere, as well as the bohemian subcultures of Greenwich Village—Brown touches upon standard narrative models for male delinquents who got clear of the ghetto's street life. In so doing, he adapts the street-derived authority of stock male heroes of deghettoization narratives, positioning himself as an urban intellectual to tell the ghetto's stories.[16]

Brown's associates go down the roads he could have taken. Most of them do not get far: they overdose on heroin, fall from rooftops, are shot or stabbed, go to jail for long terms, or remain on the streets as hookers, petty hustlers, or junkies. Some of them make a niche for themselves within the orders of

Harlem: Turk becomes a professional boxer; Alley Bush, renamed Bashi, becomes a political activist, winning notoriety when he starts an altercation at the United Nations; Danny kicks his heroin habit, has a Protestant conversion experience, and raises a family. During the course of his education in the street life and his forays into the world beyond its limits, Brown lives a part of each possible life. Moving through the stories of the victims, he tries heroin with the junkies, does time with the future jailbirds, gets shot like those who die young, and deals drugs and runs petty cons like those who will become career criminals. Moving through the success stories, he fights with the future boxer; plays the piano with a new generation of jazz musicians; dabbles in paints; discovers the women of Harlem as a consumer market during his stint as a budding cosmetics entrepreneur; and talks politics, rebellion, and black consciousness with reformers, Black Muslims, and other activists wrestling with the conditions that underlie the developing urban crisis.

Each sampled narrative line supplies a piece to his composite story and contributes its authority to his formation as an urban intellectual. For instance, Brown rehearses classic moments in the making of a street fighter, the first step in one standard version of the making of a boxer. The most important moment is a scene in which his father sends him back out to the street to fight the Morris brothers: "I said, 'Dad, these boys are out there, and they messin' with me.' He said, 'Well, if you come in here, I'm gon mess with you too. You ain't got no business runnin' from nobody' " (267).[17] Brown not only attends the same reform school (Wiltwyck) as did two-time heavyweight champion Floyd Patterson, he passes through the narrative "school" of black boxers like Patterson, Sugar Ray Robinson, and, especially, Archie Moore: a delinquent learns to fight in the streets, goes straight (often in reform school), studies the sweet science of boxing, learns to discipline the burning impulse to violence, turns pro, wins the title, and devotes himself to steering a new generation of street fighters toward productive citizenship.[18]

But Brown tells only a piece of that story, and he becomes a writer instead; it is, rather, his friend Turk who succeeds as a professional boxer. Brown identifies Turk, who has pursued one of Brown's possible destinies, as a double of himself: "He was living proof that we could make it—the cats who had come up our way in Harlem . . . We weren't all cursed or destined to end up in jail. I suppose that I was the living proof of it to him too" (303). The sampled story of the doomed street fighter turned athletic celebrity helps Brown to position himself alongside those who, in the popular phrase, "fought their way out of the ghetto" against long odds favoring an early death or a wasted life. The identity between Turk and Brown adapts the familiar steps of the fighter's story to the urban intellectual's. Like the boxer, in this formulation, the intellectual emerges from the ghetto as, in the Old Testament phrase, "a firebrand plucked from out of the burning." He carries within himself the violent destructive force of "the burning," but he uses its heat to forge rather than destroy himself, and he uses its light to illuminate. In order to keep these two properties in balance, he learns discipline via technique (boxing, writing), turning the generalized conflagration of "the burning" into a useful and controlled "fire in the belly" that on the one hand gives him the strength to leave the ghetto and on the other hand makes him hungrier, wiser, and tougher than those who did not grow up in the ghetto. The imputation of this model of an intellectual's relation to place is that Brown's language, like Turk's punches, contains and controls all the raw anger and unschooled power typically assumed to constitute the ghetto "survivor's" edge. In drawing the lines between Turk's narrative and his own, then, Brown tells a story about his own formation as an intellectual that taps into a familiar ghetto narrative.[19] As suggested above, *Manchild* touches upon other stock success stories in this manner, but Turk enjoys a special status as Brown's principal alter ego that places him above the artists, social workers, political activists, salesmen, strivers, and ex-junkies made good. Turk frames Brown in Brown's chosen persona—an authentically violent man who fought his way up from the street but sustained his connection to it.[20]

The entry into a larger narrative and geographical terrain effected in acts one and two requires a complementary movement back into the ghetto: "When I went uptown now, I always had a definite purpose" (279). In act three, Brown narrates his reengagement with Harlem, the ways in which he mediates between possible passages into a larger world—represented above all by his Greenwich Village apartment—and returns to his home ground. (Again, these conceptual acts overlap one another as he constantly shuttles in and out of Harlem.) As in his departure, he has multiple models for that return, and he again samples each of his options in constructing his position as an urban intellectual. The problem in act three derives from the central problem of the canonical urban crisis: what to do about the ghetto in general and its violent criminal delinquents in particular. Two principal groups offer competing narrative lines, and competing religious conversions, to propel Brown toward one of two outcomes commonly found in ghetto narratives of the urban crisis: a mainstream Protestant (or, given the influence of the Cohens and Papanek, a "Judeo-Christian") conversion leading to social work, the objective of which is to produce future Claude Browns one by one; or conversions offered first by the African Christian Coptic sect and then by the Black Muslims to a self-consciously "black" religion and political radicalization, the objective being to fight for blacks as a class by directing the resources of a generation made strong in street life against the very roots of ghettoization. Predictably, *Manchild*'s composite narrative evaluates both lines of narrative and religious possibility— and draws upon their authority in mapping both the ghetto and its protagonist's cultural role—but pursues neither line to its conclusion.

Brown's most important "definite purpose" in Harlem, more often than not, involves his younger brother, Pimp, whose first steps into crime, drug use, and the street life cause Brown to consider how he might put his own experience to use in helping others. Brown's encounters with a number of people dedicated to saving junkies and delinquents offer models of such familial social work. Ernst Papanek, for instance, shows the young Claude Brown an efficacious blend of social responsibility and streetwise operator's technique, communicated in smooth, manipulative, politic talk. Similarly, the resonantly named Reverend William James, whose Metropolitan Community Methodist Church administers programs for young people in Harlem, models a knowing distance from street life. "Reverend James seemed to know a lot about street life that I never expected any minister to know" (394), Brown finds, but the reverend is no hustler: "'The cat's a minister, man'" (401), who tends to a community of believers, as opposed to a preacher who hustles a collection of marks. James's simultaneous intimacy with and distance from the street life afford him an analytical insight into Harlem that attracts Brown—not only because he feels James might be able to save Pimp but because James offers a model for a budding urban intellectual looking for ways to engage with his subject matter.

As the dedicatory note prefacing *Manchild* suggests, patrons like Eleanor Roosevelt and characters like Reverend James and Papanek represent a system of exemplary individuals and at least partially efficacious institutions (reform schools, churches, youth programs) designed to find and save Claude Browns. On his way to becoming a writer, Brown passes through the story of social work offered by this mix of post-Progressives, center-leftists, and Great Society liberals. *Manchild* thus builds into Brown's own project the authority conferred upon Papanek and Reverend James—and upon social workers like the great light-heavyweight Archie Moore—by the urban crisis, when delinquency in the second ghetto was a central element of the urgent problem posed by the inner city. The engagement of such exemplary social workers with delinquents helps Brown to produce himself as an urban intellectual, and in turn he presents his own example, codified in the book itself, as a form of social work. Thus, walking up 145th Street as an adult, speculating on the strength imparted by the ghetto to the children who survive its hard lessons, he remembers an episode from his youth in which a little boy towing a dog with a black spot over one eye accosted him on 145th Street, saying "'I want to be like you'" (421). At the time of the original encounter, he had been embarrassed because he was a well-known criminal widely expected to die young; now, in the retrospect afforded by the third act of his narrative, he likes the idea of himself as a model of behavior.

However, Brown's second thoughts about this grossly improbable little boy and his dog do not cancel the original encounter. The omnibus narrative Brown patches together in *Manchild* from his sampling of narrative lines, including the one offered by social workers, fits him to write the ghetto, not to save boys from delinquency. He does not undergo a religious conversion, he does not enter into the institutional structures offered by social workers, and he cannot save his brother Pimp, who dabbles in heroin, commits armed robbery, and goes to jail. The narrative of social work is subsidiary to Brown's commitment to a larger, composite narrative in which strong individuals sink deep into the street life, learn from it, and emerge with special cultural potential—expressed in the authenticating language of urban insiders—derived from the second ghetto.

Brown's self-construction as an urban intellectual proceeds on that model, and his training in the street teaches serious doubts both about the uses of religious belief and about the efficacy of social work, except by way of example. Brown, therefore, comes to terms with his inability to keep Pimp out of jail by suggesting that Pimp might pursue his older brother's self-reliant route through prison, out of the street life, and into the writing life. "'Pimp's changin', man,'" he tells Danny. "'Or at least I think he is. The cat finished high school in the joint, got a diploma, and he's talkin' some good stuff. He writes a lot of poetry in the joint.'" Danny responds, "'The joint could make a cat deep sometimes, sometimes it'll make him real deep'" (420). Brown and Danny laugh at this cliché, but *Manchild* nevertheless argues very clearly that "prison" (that is, reform school, which is "jail in disguise"), and not the social workers he encountered there, did in fact make Claude Brown "deep"—and worth reading.

The Black Muslims emerge from the same crucible that produces Brown: they get "deep" in prison as well. As a recent jailhouse convert to the Muslim faith tells Brown, "'A lot of cats are finding out where it's at in the joint'" (330). Prison serves as a social microcosm that provides educational perspective on the inner city for such converts. Working from that perspective, the Muslims (and before them the Coptics) offer Brown a systematic analysis of second ghetto pathologies and various plans to "get Harlem out of Goldberg's pocket," as Brown's old crony Bashi puts it—from economic self-determination to armed revolt, "'even if most of us have to die'" (337).

The Muslims thus offer Brown another ready-made third act, one that would become standard during the urban crisis (and after): the delinquent, recognizing that his criminality proceeds from his encounter with city- and nation-structuring arrangements of power and capital, returns to the ghetto to contribute his hard-won strength and insight to the dirty work of altering those arrangements. This is the story told by Malcolm X, the Black Panthers, Sonny Carson, the Soledad Prison writers, and gang members who turned to politics, among others.[21] Brown recognizes the Muslims' authority to offer this conclusion: "The Muslims were the home team," having won the right to represent Harlem by passing through an act one similar to Brown's in their own delinquent careers. As opposed to the NAACP or the Urban League, the Muslims "were the people who were right out there in the street with you. They had on suits, but their grammar wasn't something that would make the average Negro on the street feel ill at ease. The words that they used were the same words that the people on the street used. You could associate these people with yourself" (348). The Muslims share a formative experience with Brown and thus present a similar linguistic credential: they know the things he knows about the ghetto, and they speak with his authoritative grammar.

Although the Muslims share a first act and delinquent credentials with Brown, and offer him a possible third act, he only samples that narrative option without pursuing it. Such was the Muslims' cachet as quintessential second ghetto types in the 1960s that *Manchild* seems obliged to go out of its way to show how refusing the Muslims' third act is consistent with the behavior of a genuinely ghetto-trained urban intellectual. Despite acknowledging the attraction of conversion to Islam, and despite concluding that the "Muslim movement is a good thing" because it encourages black entrepreneurship and lets "the nation know that there are black people in this country who are dangerously angry" (349), *Manchild* dismisses the Muslims' proposed third act as a false ending. Brown's critique takes root in act one of his story and follows two principal lines, both of which solve his problem: he undermines the Muslims' street credentials, and he reduces them to ghetto types, unequipped to attain the analytical perspective on Harlem that he enjoys.

First, he holds that the Muslims provide a crutch, an easy way out, for the weakest survivors of street life: "There was one common thing I noticed about all the cats in the Muslim movement. They seemed to be the cats who were very uncertain about where they were, who they were, or what they were going to do, the cats who had never been able to find their groove" (342). This argument holds, in essence, that in shedding their "slave" names and taking new ones, Black Muslims have failed the essential test of act one: "'when those niggers start coming down on you,'" explains a seasoned veteran of Warwick to the newly arrived Claude Brown, "'you just run out there as soon as somebody call your name and say, "Who is Claude Brown?" Like, you say, "I am," and run up and hit the biggest nigger first. Hit him first, and hit him as hard as you can'" (134–35). Brown thus undercuts the Muslims' act one–derived delinquent authority, in effect pulling street rank on them by characterizing them as incompletely tempered by the crucible of street life. In the mid-1960s, when the Muslims' claim to represent the second ghetto enjoyed blue-chip status among urban intellectuals, Brown was almost alone in questioning the grounding of their political persona in the street.

Second, *Manchild* understands the Muslims to offer the wrong act three because they have not outgrown the impulses that motivated Brown in act one. Brown takes the enormous liberty of collapsing Muslims and Coptics together with political radicals, emphasizing the language of violent racial conflict spoken by some Muslims and by many whose rhetoric and self-presentation superficially resembled those of the Muslims. Having achieved that simplifying compression of religious and political dissenters, creating an extremist foil for the Protestant and Jewish social reformers occupying the vital center, Brown belabors the extremists for their immaturity. "'The revolution you're talking about,'" he tells Bashi, "'I've had it. I've had that revolution since I was six years old. And I fought it every day—in the streets of Harlem . . . —when I was there stealing, raising hell out there, playing hookey.'" As Brown tells it this time, he "'rebelled against school,'" robbed stores downtown, and sneaked onto the subways because all of them were owned and operated by white people. In youth homes and reform schools, he met a generation of "'young, rebellious cats who couldn't take it either,'" some of whom went on to preach Bashi's brand of violent revolt. Act one ended, however, when Brown realized that "'nobody was winning. That revolution was hopeless. The cats who had something on the ball and they could dig it in time, they stopped. They stopped. They didn't stop being angry. They just stopped cutting their own throats, you know?'" (340). In *Manchild*, the Muslims remain trapped in act one, either as a new breed of Harlem street operators (like Alley Bush/Bashi, who preaches abstention and then sneaks a drink with Brown in a secluded bar) or as angry delinquents who have not woken up to the fact that violent rebellion is suicide. "'Look, Alley,'" Brown tells his old running partner at last, "'if you just want to die, why bother to go out there and do it in the name of freedom?'" (341).

These conversations, reported in *Manchild*, took place in the 1950s and early 1960s. In 1965, *Manchild* was arguing, in short, that Brown had outgrown the Muslim movement well before the Muslims—and Malcolm X in particular, whose narrative shares an act one with Brown's and goes on to accept the subsequent acts offered by the Muslims—became a prominent set of characters in the canonical dramas of the urban crisis. The notion of outgrowing the kind of hopeless, self-destructive anger Brown associates with the Muslims and "Harlem radicals" runs through *Manchild* from a formative moment in Brown's life, the Harlem riot of 1943. Despite the lessons he learns about his generation's special frustration, Brown never arrives at an explanation for the riot to refute his resolutely Southern father's description of it: "'just a whole lotta niggers gone fool'" (13). The riot is the apotheosis of the street life, not a political struggle, as the six-year-old Brown and his friends loot and destroy the neighborhood's businesses. Brown has sympathy with the Muslims to the extent that they offer the opposite of the riot—black-owned business, economic self-determination. However, all talk of revolt and separatist violence strikes him as either weak posturing or a case of "niggers gone fool": "'Now, look at it realistically, Alley. How the hell are you gonna come in here and say, "Look, white man, we're living in your world, but I want you to let us have a revolution?" This is what it would amount to, because the black man's just in no position to revolt against anything here'" (340).

Manchild's omnibus narrative appropriates the Muslims' widely recognized anger and cultural currency in showing that Brown has the experience of act one in common with them, but it stops well short of accepting the change of name and the understanding of the ghetto—in short, the succeeding acts—they offer him. *Manchild*'s gathering of narrative lines runs to a different conclusion, in which the concatenation of those narratives and his intimacy with them equip Brown to represent the ghetto. The assembled narratives of his generation form a portrait of the ghetto in crisis, and his sampling of them credentials him to speak of and for "black America." *Manchild* is, among other things, about equipping Brown to write with authority about the very conditions that motivate the Muslims to what he presents as their misguided militancy.

In *Manchild*, Brown positions himself to broker the traffic of representations flowing out of the ghetto to an increasingly anxious reading audience peering through the peepholes made by genre in its walls. It follows, then, that he has no sustained interest in learning Amharic. "The true black man's language," offered by the Coptics, does not equip him to speak to that larger, predominantly white audience outside the ghetto. The Coptics and the Muslims, like the junkies and the criminals, serve instead to provide the structuring "why" of the omnibus narrative: why Brown's generation demands attention, why Brown must write its stories, why the reader must read this book in a climate of urban crisis. During his encounter with the boy and his dog, Brown says "All my life, I've been looking for a dog to walk," an ordering sense of mission. *Manchild*'s composite narrative proposes that Brown discovers that mission in doing the cultural work of representing the second ghetto in prose.

The Best Way to Look at Harlem

Manchild samples, surveys, cuts, and pastes a variety of narratives in assembling its account of Claude Brown's emergence from the second ghetto. They add up to a larger plot: the formation of a new kind of urban intellectual native to the postindustrial inner city. *Manchild* also plots that character's formation in the spatial sense: the book's map of the inner city establishes Brown's special relationship to the social landscape. In 1965, that landscape already spoke of urban crisis to even (or perhaps especially) the most casual observer. The cover of *Newsweek*'s issue of 30 August 1965, appearing two weeks after the magazine had run a glowing review of *Manchild in the Promised Land*, showed a motorized National Guard patrol moving past gutted businesses through the rubble-strewn landscape of Watts after the riots. The photograph was captioned with a concise formulation of the urban question of the day: "Los Angeles: Why?" Part of Claude Brown's authority to address that question proceeded from the identity between the landscape in which his authorial persona took form and the landscape of the postriot ghetto. Brown provides images of Harlem's looted businesses during the riot of 1943, when he was six years old:

"None of the stores had any windows left, and glass was everywhere. . . . Everything I picked up was broken or burned or both. My feet kept sinking into wet furs that had been burned and drenched. The whole place smelled of smoke and was as dirty as a Harlem gutter on a rainy day" (13–14). The extraordinary urban cataclysm of the riot collapses into the most everyday of images, a rainy day in Harlem, suggesting that the day-to-day plot of Brown's movements in space will reveal a world that houses the answers—that, with Brown's first-person help, will *speak* the answers—to *Newsweek*'s "Why?"

Manchild's mapping of Brown's world begins in the foreword's delineation of the "slum ghetto" as "a dirty, stinky, uncared-for, closet-size section" of the metropolis in which "the first Northern urban generation of Negroes" engages in an "endless battle to establish their own place . . . in America itself" (vii–viii). As the reader passes from the general to the specific at the end of the foreword, as the generational "they" flows into the "I" of "'I'm shot!'" that opens Brown's personal narrative, the reader enters the landscape of Harlem as Brown inhabits it. A series of violent events introduce and etch in his memory the features of that geography: the thirteen-year-old Brown, thieving as usual, is shot through the belly in an alley and collapses on the floor of a fish-and-chips joint; his mother's screams flow into the remembered scream of a boy he saw thrown from a roof on 149th Street. Continuing what will become a long flashback as he dreams in his hospital bed, he travels in memory to "the dilapidated old tenement building that I lived in," in which the super had beaten a man to death "for peeing in the hall" (12); he passes through the wreckage-strewn streets of Harlem as a six-year-old looter during the riot of 1943; he relives his budding career of violence in the park, in the street, and in the Youth House. This opening movement ends with Brown's memory of being sent to visit his grandparents in the South. When he returns a year later, each stop on the subway ride uptown triggers a memory that makes a violent coda to the initial movement— shaking down white shoe shine boys at Forty-second Street, dodging the police at Fifty-ninth, a purse-snatching at Eighty-first—until he arrives once more in a Harlem awash in vomit, blood, and urine: "vomit was all over the street near the beer gardens" and "there was a lot of blood near the beer gardens and all over the sidewalk at Eighth Avenue." In the hallway of his tenement building, "somebody had got cut the night before, and blood was still in the hall. And somebody had pissed on the stairs, and it was still there, just like it should have been" (53).

The opening movement, then, introduces the landscape on which *Manchild* plots its omnibus narrative. In describing episodes of drug use and gang rape on the roof of his building, murder and near-murder in its hallways, and Brown's home life, *Manchild* maps on the blood- and graffiti-spattered form of his tenement building a way of life built by transplanted rural black Southerners and their seemingly unmanageable Northern urban children. Following the young

Claude Brown as he slips easily from his parents' control into the streets, *Manchild* extends that map across the terrain of Harlem, plotting the content of life as lived by Brown's generation on a landscape of crowded, violence-filled streets, ineffectual schools, and the bars, alleys, storefront churches, and back rooms in which hustlers do their business.

Brown's engagement with this world, and especially with elements of its landscape, produces impeccably pathological credentials to represent Harlem: "By the time I was nine years old, I had been hit by a bus, thrown into the Harlem River (intentionally), hit by a car, severely beaten with a chain. And I had set the house afire" (21). The last item, set off from the others in a melodramatic sentence fragment, suggests that Brown had by the age of nine developed a capacity for destroying a world that was trying to destroy him, a suggestion supported by Brown's unquestioning participation in the riot of 1943. Many of Brown's initial readers bought the book to find out the same thing his mother wants to know: "'Boy, why you so bad?'" (21). Like the gang member Duke, mapping his three-block world for Doc Levine in *Cool World*, the young rioter Claude Brown accounts for himself by mapping the terrain occupied by his troublesome generation.

Manchild uses this landscape to make and reinforce its arguments. For instance, Brown's contention that the Coptics, Muslims, and others who have pursued similar third acts are "weak cats" finds support in an anecdote about a gang fight in a tenement hallway. Brown remembers that a friend named Lonnie, now a Coptic priest, had in their childhood been a fellow gang member (of the Buccaneers) but had always been "a good boy" who "didn't steal and stuff like that." Cornered in a gang fight with the Chancellors in a hallway on 148th Street, Lonnie let down his partners by failing to gun down the attacking enemy. "This was the sort of cat he was," concludes Brown: "He had no business gang fighting anyway" (236). A boy named Rock, a genuine delinquent, had to save them all by snatching the gun away from the future Coptic holy man and shooting one of the most notorious Chancellors. Lonnie's failure to fill the hallways of that tenement on 148th Street with pools of blood—a failure to establish himself as expertly trained by his environment in authenticating violence—marks the third act he later pursues as an avenue for the weak. Brown's narrating persona can and must absorb Lonnie's talk of the black man's true religion and of white devils and black science, that being some of the most dramatic language of urban crisis on display in the ghetto, but Lonnie's insufficiently consummated engagement with the landscape of Harlem reveals him as a weak vessel. In *Manchild*, Lonnie is not an urban intellectual equipped to represent Harlem; he is *material* for such a writer to work with.

The Muslims, despite being "uncertain cats" like Lonnie, fare better. They stake their claim as second ghetto exemplars by taking over the intersection of 125th Street and 7th Avenue, and Brown accepts that claim to the extent that the

Muslims speak the language of Harlem. "The Muslims had become a part of the community," he concedes. "They became the Seventh Avenue speakers" (347). Emerging from jail and the streets of Harlem, they develop a self-presentation—part con and part social critique, in Brown's rendering—that constitutes valid credentials for their claim to represent Harlem. However, as he does in rejecting the Coptics and their offer to teach him Amharic, Brown draws the line at according the Muslims the right to speak beyond the boundaries of Harlem. If Lonnie is too much the good boy, then Bashi (with his big talk of armed revolt and his illicit drinking) is too much the Harlem operator to establish himself as an analyst of the street life and all it might mean. Bashi and the Muslims are Harlem types, representative of the place but not equipped to represent it. Like the prostitutes on 125th between Third Avenue and St. Nicholas Avenue, the Muslims inhabit the grid of Harlem but do not share Brown's credentials—established in his survey of narrative options that includes and subsumes both Muslims and prostitutes—for moving beyond Harlem and returning to it with a hard-won analytical perspective.

Brown's acquisition of that perspective, incorporating but transcending the localisms of ghetto operators and other aspirants to the work of representing Harlem, organizes the spatial plot of *Manchild* as well as the narrative. Brown moves back and forth across the borders of Harlem: he constantly shuttles in and out of Harlem in his daily movements, and his residence shifts from his parents' home to various reform schools and back, then to his own apartment in Harlem, down to the Village (off Cooper Square), and finally back uptown (in a movement similar to Warren Miller's in the 1950s) to an apartment on Ninetieth Street near the edge of Harlem. These movements combine to establish the proper relation to Harlem and to the rest of the metropolis. *Manchild* balances the movement of the narrator's emergence from the ghetto (and his continuing rootedness in it) with the movement of crossing into the ghetto from the outside—the journey upon which Brown's readers wish to accompany him.

The spatial drama of *Manchild*, therefore, has to do with Brown's effort to find the appropriate relation to his subject and credentialing terrain, the second ghetto. He presents his initial move to the Village as the only alternative to an eventual move to Sing Sing. That move to the Village therefore raises the possibility of severing his ties to the ghetto and an appropriately pathologized life story. Brown, however, assures us that "even though I lived downtown and worked and went to school at night, Harlem was still my point of relating to life and events and putting them together, my point of reference" (206). That is, "the ghetto" exists as a mental-spatial complex from which Brown's persona cannot be uprooted, even as he explores a wider world.

The point of moving to the Village, then, is to move back into Harlem, developing the outsider's perspective on Harlem he will need in order to deliver his insider's wisdom to naive readers: "It seemed that every time I came uptown, I learned something. The best way to look at Harlem was to be on the outside and have some kind of in" (253). The Village serves as a kind of staging ground appropriate for an observer and writer interested in encountering a variety of urban types. Based there, he can sustain access to his accrediting terrain while developing connections to artists, writers, and the larger metropolitan audience he will address. Similarly, Brown comes into contact with a new repertoire of metropolitan subjectivities—white and black bohemians, young blacks raised in Harlem and intent on upward mobility into the middle class, people who plan to go to college—without losing contact with the dead-before-twenty-one way of life practiced by many of his Harlem associates. *Manchild* does not map the Village in detail, therefore, because the Village's sole function is to change his relation to Harlem. His loft apartment near Cooper Square, like the Invisible Man's "hole in the ground" under a building full of white residents on the edge of Harlem, establishes Brown in a liminal position from which he crosses at will the increasingly forbidding boundaries dividing the inner city.

If in the Village Brown encounters the wider world outside the ghetto generically opened to the reforming delinquent, he makes it clear that he can also find his way back to Harlem. This condition of extraordinary access takes spatial form in Brown's returns to the grid of Harlem's streets. In mapping the ghetto, *Manchild* orders a vast profusion of details in a series of narrative digressions plotted on a grid of streets. Chapters and episodes tend to begin with a time coordinate pegged to an intersection or landmark: "I came uptown one night and met Danny on the corner of Seventh Avenue and 145th Street" (212); "One night in the fall of 1956, I was walking down Lenox Avenue" (234); "I first heard about the Black Muslims in 1955. They had started talking at night down on 125th Street and Seventh Avenue" (327). The grid organizes both Brown's understanding of social order and his memory. Plotted with personal landmarks where conversations, fights, and other encounters taught him particular lessons about his life and the ghetto, the grid of Harlem holds Brown's living past like a trellis overhung with vines.

Brown treats his many returns to Harlem as providing instant access to this past. If *Manchild* does not plot the Village on this grid, thus firmly separating the Village from the ghetto, the subway does provide access to the grid uptown (like the El in Stuart Dybek's "Blight," connecting the classroom to the old neighborhood and the present to the past). *Manchild* establishes this principle of access in the coda to the book's opening movement, already discussed, in which the young Claude Brown rides the subway uptown upon his return from the South. Entering the numbered grid as he approaches Harlem, Brown enters as well into the realm of violent memories that mark him as an ex-delinquent: every numbered station triggers the appropriate memory of rotten behavior. The reader, tagging along as Brown crosses and recrosses with impunity beneath the cultural barbed wire and barricades at the boundaries of the ghetto of feeling, enjoys the privilege of Brown's intimate access to the inner city's forbidden districts. Brown's impeccable credentials as a child of the ghetto, credentials plotted on the grid of Harlem's streets, give his readers outside the ghetto the sense of sailing past Checkpoint Frederick Douglass into the place where the answers to the "Why?" of urban crisis can be discovered in the landscape's form and the speech of the people.

If, having finished *Manchild*, such readers felt no closer to an answer to the "Why's?" of urban crisis, that was because *Manchild* was about "Who?" The book's narrative collage and its spatial survey, dramas of movement in and out of the ghetto, reach closure with Brown and Harlem finding their positions in relation to one another: "It was as though I had found my place and Harlem had found its place. We were suited for each other now" (372). Brown has found the right relation to his subject matter, placing Harlem and himself in their respective metropolitan contexts. Harlem has found in Brown—has *made* Brown, *Manchild* argues—an urban intellectual suited to the task of representing it.

The Claude Brown invited to talk about the ghetto by Senators Ribicoff and Kennedy was an amalgam of two characters: Claude Brown the narrating protagonist of the story and Claude Brown the authorial persona responsible for crafting it. The former had the authority of experience that Dunny, also invited to speak, represented; the latter had credentials as a writer, an urban intellectual, akin to those of the novelist Ralph Ellison, who appeared before the senators the day after Brown and Dunny did. *Manchild* offered a composite narrative in which the delinquent protagonist grew into the author, establishing a two-way flow of identity between them that posited unmediated access between the urban intellectual and the six-year-old rioter he had been. *Manchild*'s occasional gestures at distinguishing between the two are manifestly inadequate, which tends to narrow the distinction between them to nothing: in *Manchild*, Brown sometimes calls himself "Sonny," but reverts most of the time to "Claude Brown," as if to admit that there is no point in trying to do anything but let the two become one. *Manchild*'s surveys of ghetto narrative and space argue for the expansive reach enjoyed by this composite mind that embraces both "the problem" and imaginative representation of it.

Manchild ends with an image of Brown when he was a little boy, coming in from the streets of Harlem to talk about the violent things he had seen: "You might see somebody get cut or killed. I could go out in the street for an afternoon, and I would see so much that when I came in the house, I'd be talking and talking for what seemed like hours" (429). In *Manchild*, Brown presents himself as coming in from the street to tell his readers what Saturday night in Harlem is like, what happens in storefront churches, what kids do when they play hookey and stay out all night, how street reputation works, how to do time in prison, how the coming of heroin changed the inner city forever, why and how to call men "baby," what Black Muslims and Harlem activists meant to what he calls "the era of black self-reflection," how he "got out" when so many others did not. In so doing, *Manchild* presented to its readers not only an omnibus survey of the second ghetto and its stories but also a model of the urban intellectual's role in crafting the fit between the city of fact and the city of feeling when both were in violent motion.

The War of Position

"Motherfucking right, it's confusing; it's a gas, baby,
you dig."
          "A Harlem intellectual" in Chester Himes,
                    Blind Man with a Pistol

As Warren Miller put it in opening his review of *Manchild in the Promised Land*, during the urban crisis the second ghetto was under scrutiny "by all disciplines, all sorts of people, and for an enormous variety of purposes." In the late summer and fall of 1965, all sorts of people were scrutinizing *Manchild*'s rendering of Harlem and evaluating it according to their various interests in the urban crisis. A poet, fiction writer, and translator named Guy Daniels, who reviewed *Manchild* for the *New Republic* on the strength of his own personal familiarity with Harlem, mock-confessed to being intimidated by the massive convergence on the book of intellectuals accredited to address inner-city subjects: "By this time both Claude Brown and his book have been analyzed by so many experts — in sociology, education, child psychology, juvenile delinquency, etc. — that the mere lay reviewer is intimidated into a cold sweat."[1]

A pack of reviewers and blurb writers constituting a cross-section of New York City's and the nation's leading urban intellectuals weighed *Manchild*'s virtues and failings in the public forum. In addition to Miller, Daniels, and the many experts in education, social science, social work, and public policy, the critics included novelists Norman Mailer and James Baldwin; New York intellectuals Irving Howe, Norman Podhoretz, Nat Hentoff, and Paul Goodman; Garry Wills, who defended Brown in *Commonweal* against Miller, Hentoff, and Goodman; Tom Wolfe, who introduced excerpts from *Manchild* in the *New York*

Herald-Tribune; Albert Murray, who lumped Brown with Warren Miller as purveyors of clichéd "social science fiction"; columnist Dick Schaap, known primarily as a sportswriter; playwright and novelist Romulus Linney, who compared *Manchild* to *Pilgrim's Progress* in a glowing review on page one of the
New York Times Book Review; literary critic and historian Daniel Aaron, author
of *Writers on the Left;* jazz critic Whitney Balliett, for the *New Yorker;* and various reviewers in *Time, Newsweek,* other magazines, and newspapers across the
country.[2]

These reviewers held Brown to a twofold standard set up on the one hand by
a pressing social dilemma—as delineated in *Dark Ghetto,* interpretations of
ghetto riots, and the news of the day—and on the other hand by literary precedents for writing the postwar inner city. In the matter of literary precedents,
Brown was compared not only to writers of Harlem like Ellison, Baldwin,
Hughes, and Jones but also to the poet of upward social mobility Horatio Alger
and to his opposite numbers, prewar social critics like John Steinbeck and the
Chicago realists (especially Wright and Farrell); to model autobiographers
Benjamin Franklin, Samuel Pepys, and St. Augustine; and to the vast literature
of youth and delinquency that had developed in the 1950s, a generic field in
which *Cool World* had staked out high ground for Warren Miller.

As a politically engaged writer and an expert on the literature of delinquency, Miller was therefore, even as late as 1965, a logical choice to review a
reformed delinquent's narrative of life in Harlem. His current status as a writer
of Harlem may have been shaky, but he could certainly help readers outside the
ghetto receive voices from inside it. Miller saw the literature of delinquency as
documenting a powerful source of "social discontent," drawing to the troubled
inner cities a readership that might generate the political will needed to transform them. Five years before *Manchild*'s publication, reviewing another
reformed black delinquent's story as rendered by *New York Times* reporter Ira
Henry Freeman in *Out of the Burning* (1960), Miller had argued that "lacking
an 'Uncle Tom's Cabin,' one book that will arouse us all, there is a need for stories like this, for books that present us with a life rather than with statistics
(which are hard to read and easy to ignore)." In the early 1960s, as Miller took
up the notion of urban crisis and turned from delinquency to race, he continued
to look for "a view that is new and that matters," one that could mobilize the
will of a large and constructively horrified readership.[3]

One would think that *Manchild* was the kind of book Miller had in mind, but
he was quick to say that Brown's view was not new and did not matter. Given
that the conjunction of delinquency, race, and the inner city formed the ground
of Miller's passionate engagement with pressing social issues, his categorical
effort to remove *Manchild* from the then-formative literary canon of urban crisis comes at first blush as a surprise. Although *Manchild* was generally received
with great fanfare as a timely and indispensable treatment of ghetto life written

by a major new voice in the urban conversation, Miller's review argued that "Brown has nothing to say that has not already been said better by James Baldwin and John Killens; indeed, it has been put more accurately and succinctly by Dr. Kenneth Clark's teams of sociologists in their statistical tables." Having dismissed Brown's value as a reporter of raw experience (Clark, the social psychologist, had done a better job in that regard), Miller then let him have the other barrel: Brown's "vocabulary of a couple of hundred words and phrases" was "not a language at all but an impoverished patois," producing a "shapeless" and repetitive "literary disaster." That is, Brown was not a *writer*, as opposed to Baldwin (who had ratified Miller's authorial access to Harlem in 1959) and Killens (who had just as authoritatively closed his gate to Miller in 1964). Even so, Miller reported with bitterness, *Manchild* had been sold for a large advance to a reprint house, book clubs were disseminating it, and, worst of all, "people who ought to know better" were reading it. "All of which," he concluded, "leaves one with the suspicion that we cheer this unnecessary book in order to permit ourselves, with a little better conscience, to turn our backs on the Problem."[4]

Miller's dismissal of *Manchild* on the grounds of its generic redundancy and lack of literary merit seems especially surprising when we compare it to his enthusiastic review of *Out of the Burning*. Miller had found value in the formulaic predictability of *Out of the Burning*, allowing this case study to hang together with others:

> Inevitably, such a book will repeat, in part, aspects of others that have been done before. It is not because the author has borrowed from other writers, but because there is an almost ritualistic quality about the gangs—and the boys offer of themselves to the life of the gangs. . . . Indeed, part of the compelling horror of this tale is its sense of the basic sameness of situation of so many thousands of children.

Why, then, identify *Manchild* as "unnecessary" because it has "nothing to say that has not been said better" by others, especially when so many other readers were exalting Brown as the first insider to map in narrative form the street life of the second ghetto? Why throw out *Manchild*'s wealth of powerful testimony on the grounds that Brown could not write, when Miller overlooked *Out of the Burning*'s lack of "linguistic adventurousness" and even suggested that "the material imposes itself so effectively" that the writing receded to insignificance? Why claim that Clark's research supersedes Brown's memoir when Miller himself saw "a need for" ex-delinquent's stories, "for books that present us with a life rather than with statistics"?[5]

In answering these questions, I will engage with a relatively cohesive critique of *Manchild* delivered in particular by urban intellectuals who, like Miller, aligned themselves in the left and liberal preserves of the period's political spectrum. Like the many ringing endorsements of Brown in the role of pioneering cultural cartographer (exemplified by Tom Wolfe's introduction to excerpts from *Manchild*, discussed below), the attack on *Manchild* proceeded along lines suggested by the book's principal strategies—the survey of ghetto narratives, the mapping of the inner city, the use of street language—to account for the making of an urban intellectual. The readers' responses, pro and con, demonstrate the stakes and the terms of a messy war of position being fought in 1965 among urban intellectuals, as they scrambled to sort out their hierarchies of influence and expertise in relation to what struck them as a new urban order requiring new imaginative explorations. In *Manchild*, Brown represented the second ghetto, and presented special credentials for doing that cultural work, in ways that seemed to refuse the offers of alliance extended by downtown social critics like Miller and, further, to shut whites entirely out of the work of writing Harlem from within. Downtown critics, especially those on the left who regarded the urban crisis as an opportunity to launch a persuasive critique of American social order, therefore responded to Brown's failure to ally himself with them as they would to an assault on their own authority to engage with the urban crisis on its most important ground.

The urgency of these considerations in the early moments of urban crisis raised the stakes in determining access to the city's inner spaces and workings and continued to do so as the crisis built toward a peak at the end of the decade. With the further development and then the waning of the crisis in the early 1970s, when the rioting came to an end and the far less incendiary problem of fiscal crisis briefly rivaled that of racial conflict, *Manchild*'s, and Brown's, historical moment seemed to have passed. *Manchild* is in many ways an initiatory text and was read as such in the mid-1960s. Its form and argument bear the marks of precisely the historical moment when a large readership turned its attention to a new space opening up on the maps that American culture continuously draws and redraws of the nation and of itself.

A Guided Tour

"Most of us who did not grow up in Harlem rely on novelists and journalists to have our experiences for us and pass them on, painlessly, into our lives," wrote Raymond Schroth, a Jesuit commentator on "socio-literary matters" for the magazine *America*, in his review of *Manchild*. (If Schroth's observation seems quaintly print-oriented in an age when television and movies dominate the representation of "black America," his larger point about the secondhand quality of most Americans' engagement with places like Harlem still stands up.) Whatever pleasures and lessons Claude Brown as autobiographer might have to offer—for instance, Schroth suggests that "*Manchild* enunciates a vulgar proof for the immortality of the soul"—his cultural role resembled that of a tour guide for concerned outsiders. In addition to "drink[ing] beer with Negro friends" and physically entering the spaces of "black America" by wandering "wide-eyed up Lenox Avenue," Schroth continued, people like himself who were concerned about the urban crisis moved through the spaces of "black America" as they were rendered in prose. He read Baldwin, Ralph Ellison, *Ebony*, and even *Black Like Me*—in which, Schroth explained via a continuing spatial metaphor, a white man darkened his skin with pigments to manage "a fleeting invasion of forbidden territory."[6] *Manchild* was an important book because, by guiding the reader through the physical and especially the mental geography of a violent young black man's neighborhood, it guided that reader into what almost everybody agreed was the heart of America's thoroughly intertwined racial and urban crises.

Schroth, whose review manifested an evocative period balance between seeking out juicy representations of ghetto "pathology" and reminding himself that there was more at stake than his own desire for sensation, found himself divided in his response to Brown's story. On the one hand, the book would "survive as a social document" rendering a desperately needed point of view: "At last a plain and primitive voice has tried to speak from the streets." On the other hand, *Manchild* could only be a substitute for "real experience, while the Negro next to us in the subway stays a million miles away." *Manchild* tells us, Schroth concluded, "about what it is like to be black in Harlem on Saturday night" but nevertheless "leaves most of us still tourists, slummers, spectators."[7] Whether their interest amounted to social concern or tourism, or the combination of the two that characterized the mentality of urban crisis for many Americans, readers motivated to explore the inner city had in Brown a new and compelling order of guide. He could take them through a landscape that afforded unique and spectacular access to the materials of contemporary urbanism.

Introducing an excerpt of *Manchild* in the *New York Herald-Tribune* prior to the book's publication in 1965, Tom Wolfe undertook to show through the metaphor of tourism that Claude Brown's arrival on the literary scene constituted a stirring new development in the writing of American cities. Writing in his patented New Journalistic style—his introduction begins "Fish and Chips; mouldy!"—Wolfe explains *Manchild*'s importance by foregrounding the unique depth of access to Harlem afforded by Brown's street-derived authority. As "the only man who ever grew up in 'the street thing' . . . in Harlem and came out of it and wrote about it," Brown eclipses previously authoritative Harlem writers, especially James Baldwin, who is demoted from tour guide in his own right to "some Moral Rearmament tourist from Toronto come to visit the poor." Brown has new and privileged information to impart to Baldwin, literary critics, students of the urban crisis, and readers of the daily newspaper (who were, in the case of *Herald-Tribune* readers, probably still reeling from the "New York City in Crisis" series of the previous winter and spring). Wolfe therefore introduces Brown by describing an actual tour, in which Brown takes Wolfe and a photographer to the figurative heart of Harlem. Moving along a narrow alley to the place where Brown was shot when he was thirteen, Wolfe finds himself in "the middle of a Harlem block," a secret inner terrain to which only a man like Brown can conduct him. "Suddenly," Wolfe finds, "we are into some kind of incredible scene from Hogarth," a vast garbage heap in which junkies and drunks accost him: "'What do you want back here?'" a woman asks them. "'You tourists?'"[8]

This journey to the center of a Harlem block neatly figures Brown's cultural role. His engagement with the street cannot be questioned, since he can show Wolfe the spot on the pavement where he almost died with a bullet in his guts, and Brown's access to street life allows even an outsider like Wolfe to play Hogarth by describing the landscape of Harlem. Brown, then, leads Wolfe in two complementary movements: the first begins outside the ghetto and moves into its darkest interior spaces, carrying Wolfe as tourist into the inner city's most restricted landscape; the second begins where *Manchild* begins, at the fish and chips joint where Brown was shot (thus the "Fish and Chips; mouldy!"), allowing Wolfe to imagine the journey that Brown made out of the ghetto from the inside. In Wolfe's account, Brown grants access to the space, narrative, and language that together make up "the ghetto" as Wolfe understands it; the tour makes Wolfe a better urban intellectual, a Hogarth for his time and place.

Rising out of the ghetto and establishing analytical access to it were narrative and spatial movements that obsessed all manner of readers and writers during the urban crisis. The scope of Brown's cultural work, as Wolfe presents it, therefore extends far beyond Harlem. Wolfe generalizes the block in question, 145th Street between Seventh and Eighth Avenues, as the generic type of the black inner city: everything about it "has American City Colored-Section written all over it." Carrying outsiders into hidden layers of ghetto life in ways that Baldwin and other writers with insufficient street credentials cannot, Brown's close engagement with criminality, violence, and other defining "pathologies" of the second ghetto promises access to a deeper understanding of the "American City Colored-Section" and thus of the American city in crisis. Wolfe sees this deeper understanding as enacting an unfulfilled promise held out by genres that have dominated the literature of the second ghetto and its prewar predecessor, the ethnic slum:

> At all the conferences and seminars on Negro Writing in America they all get up and put their hands up on their brows like an eyeshade and look out over the horizon for the battalion of Negro writers who are going to tell them what that Harlem scene is, you know, like, but they never come. It is just like the way everybody in the 1930s kept waiting for some Proletarian Prometheus to rise up from the working class and write the saga of America, but that horse never came in, either.

Incredible! No Negro writer ever lived in and told about the whole street thing in Harlem until Claude Brown.[9]

Whether or not Brown was in fact "the first" or "the only one" to provide such a perspective on Harlem, Wolfe deploys the hyperbole to show how the urban stage has been cleared for Brown as both reporter and literary figure. Wolfe goes so far as to invoke and then dismiss the Chicago neighborhood novelists, who were often typed as aspirants to the title of "Proletarian Prometheus," establishing Brown's literary role as their successor. Wolfe is proposing, with his usual needling breeziness, that Brown and the writers to follow will imagine the postindustrial city for us in the same definitive way in which the Chicago realists managed the encounter of the American literary imagination and the industrial city. In a climate of urban crisis occasioned by the violent emergence of the postindustrial city, a large audience of readers with hands figuratively to their brows anxiously awaited Brown's entrance.

Warren Miller was no aspirant to the title of Proletarian Prometheus or Negro writer (although his two Harlem novels, use of dialect, and ethnically polysemous name seem to have earned him listings in reference works as a black writer),[10] but he did write "about the whole street thing in Harlem" as lived by *Cool World*'s juvenile delinquents and by the various hipsters, civil rights activists, and humble citizens who populate *Siege of Harlem*. Both of his Harlem novels meditate explicitly on the relation between the outsider's movement into the "American City Colored-Section" incarnated in Harlem and the problem of establishing analytical access to that barricaded piece of the social landscape. The novels, finding in the ghetto a system of answers to the question of what is wrong with the postwar city, make secondary drama out of the author's movement into the narrating voices that speak those answers from within the ghetto. As Brown does, then, Miller offers to reader-tourists like Wolfe and Schroth a set of "experiences" that novels and journalism can have for us and pass on, "painlessly, into our lives." Miller's two Harlem novels played their incremental parts in developing the racial logic of urban crisis and constructing the second ghetto of feeling—thus helping to prepare the literary stage for Brown's grand appearance on it. That probably made it all the more galling for Miller to conclude that Brown, whose credentials as a tour guide came in time to eclipse Miller's own, was throwing away his chance to say something meaningful about the urban crisis.

The Worst Boy in the Neighborhood

Miller had no use for *Manchild*, but plenty of other people did. The people who thought *Manchild* was an important book made a curious bunch of bedfellows. Leftists like Irving Howe, liberals like Garry Wills, and Hollywood centrists like Budd Schulberg (discussed in the next chapter) all thought it was a great book and said so in writing. So did readers from the center to the right like Tom Wolfe, who made it his business to lampoon leftist and liberal intellectuals' responses to "authentic" proletarian voices; Lyndon Johnson's Attorney General Nicholas Katzenbach, chair of the President's Commission on Law Enforcement and Administration of Justice, whose report quoted Brown on ghetto life; and the social scientist Edward Banfield, vilified by left intellectuals for writing essays with titles like "Rioting Mainly for Fun and Profit," who was enthusiastic about the "direct evidence" of ghetto life that Brown could provide.[11] Wolfe, Katzenbach, and Banfield read *Manchild* as a record of ghetto life, a much-needed tour of black America; readers on the left welcomed the tour, as well, but they also read *Manchild* as a lost opportunity to deliver a particularly effective, organically "street" version of the kind of social critique one could find in, for instance, the Harlem novels of Warren Miller.

One of the curious aspects of *Manchild*'s literary-historical fate is that the most damaging critical responses to it came from readers on the left, who anticipated a more general consensus in choosing *Autobiography of Malcolm X* (initially overshadowed by *Manchild*) as the canonical autobiography of the urban crisis. It was precisely the role of tour guide that *Manchild* constructed for Brown, the role in which Wolfe confirmed him, that served as the jumping-off point for the attack on *Manchild*. Miller's review of *Manchild* advances that attack's two principal and interrelated lines: that *Manchild* was flawed in its relation to the city of fact by Brown's inability or unwillingness to deliver a systematic social critique; and that Brown was a mediocre writer, a hustler playing at urban intellectual who, although underequipped to build the city of feeling, took advantage of the urban crisis to somehow "con" eager white middle-class readers. The thematic link binding these lines together was a reading of *Manchild*'s survey of narrative possibilities as failing to script an engagement with the downtown community of urban intellectuals.

The historical link between Brown and this community went back at least as far as Ernst Papanek and the reform school at Wiltwyck. In 1961, four years before *Manchild* appeared, Brown had his first publication in a special issue of *Dissent* devoted to making a portrait of New York City. The way Tom Wolfe tells it in the *Herald-Tribune*, the editors of *Dissent* had asked Ernst Papanek, Brown's mentor at the Wiltwyck School, to contribute an article on Harlem, but Papanek referred them to Brown, who wrote what amounted to a sketch study for *Manchild* entitled "Harlem, My Harlem." Brown contests Wolfe's version: he acknowledges that the editors of *Dissent* knew Papanek but claims that his first contact with *Dissent* was a letter he wrote in response to Norman Mailer's maunderings on "the White Negro."[12] In either case, Brown's "Harlem, My Harlem" was published among articles by a number of prominent left and liberal intellectuals who moved in the ideological orbit of *Dissent*, a journal founded in 1954 by socialists and other anti-Stalinist leftists opposed on the one hand to totalitarian ideologies and on the other to the Cold War liberalism of ex-leftists. Among the contributors to the special issue on New York were Daniel Bell, Dorothy Day, Herbert Gans, Michael Harrington, and others whose paths Brown would cross again in print—Irving Howe, Nat Hentoff, Norman Mailer, Paul Goodman. To the extent that the issue manifested a unifying theme, it was the various contributors' "common sadness over [New York City's] decline and its difficulties" in the post–World War II period, a close cousin to the narrative of industrial Chicago's decline examined in part 1 of this study.[13] The industrial New York of the 1930s, wistfully described by Howe as alive with the faith and political conviction of immigrant ethnics, had receded into the past; the romantically energetic immigrant slums and prewar Black Metropolis of Harlem had given way to the second ghetto and its baffling pathologies; the growing suburban areas of a three-state metropolitan region enveloped the relic of what now felt like a cozily knowable prewar New York.

In 1961, juvenile delinquency persisted as a defining urban problem, but the second ghetto was already showing signs of succeeding delinquency in that role. Given *Dissent*'s emphasis on New York's postwar transformation and decline, especially, it is no surprise that both juvenile delinquency and the ghetto played important roles in *Dissent*'s portrait of New York in 1961. Dry little swatches of social science, in the form of excerpts from a report of the Juvenile Delinquency Evaluation Project of the City of New York, were scattered throughout the special issue, as if to suggest that delinquency pervaded the landscape of postwar New York City because it proceeded from the dislocations treated elsewhere in the issue—black and Puerto Rican migrations, the decline of white-ethnic slums, urban renewal. Norman Mailer supported this impression with an account of his movement through the inner city to visit with a Brooklyn street gang, following the well-beaten generic path of teen gang reportage made familiar by journalists like Harrison Salisbury. Even Herbert Slochower's gaseous critical essay, "The Juvenile Delinquent and the Mythic Hero," gestured sketchily at the context of urban change—"the dislocations in the contemporary scene"—in developing its case for the delinquent as a kind of "mythopoeic hero" on the order of Hamlet, Don Quixote, and Ahab.[14] A number of reminiscences, like Irving Howe's, described the prewar immigrant-ethnic neighborhoods of the Lower East Side and Brooklyn, but Harlem and Greenwich Village were clearly the present-day city's most charged terrains. Michael Harrington, writing about Harlem rather than delinquency, opened with a long epigraph from Miller's *Cool World*, suggesting that "like the young Negroes of *The Cool World*, Harlem watches all the wonderful movies about America with a certain bitter cynicism."[15] Brown, of course, also wrote about Harlem, followed by Eileen Diaz on Puerto Rican New York. Separate articles on "The Village," "The Village Beat Scene," and the politics of housing and renewal in the West Village covered Greenwich Village, the center of the city's thriving countercultural scene and the place where intellectuals could rub elbows with representatives of various subcultures—including black artists and bohemians.

Dissent, then, mapped a city very similar to the one Claude Brown would traverse four years later in *Manchild in the Promised Land*, and Brown's article in *Dissent* suggested how the map he had to offer would complement those of the other contributors in covering much the same terrain. Brown begins his piece by offering a rough draft of the credentials he would develop in greater detail in *Manchild:* "At the age of nine I had already acquired the reputation of being the worst boy in the neighborhood."[16] Brown's language contrasts sharply with that of the other contributors, who tend toward Whitmanian stylings (Robert Nichols's poem "The City" begins "I sing of the city revived"), participant-observer and case-history framings of poor people's and delinquents' stories (Day on poverty, Mailer on teen gangs), and grand overviews of urban process, which predominated. Compare Brown's homely opening to that of, for instance, Percival Goodman and Paul Goodman—"We propose the banning of all cars from Manhattan Island"—or to Daniel Bell's: "In 1956, the Regional Plan Association . . . asked the Harvard School of Public Administration to conduct an economic and demographic survey of the New York metropolitan region."[17] A few first-person forays like those by Diaz, Day, and Mailer tried to capture ground-level perspectives, but most of the contributors came at their subject from Bell's bird's-eye view, pursuing understandings of vast processes like the expansion of service industries and the city's physical transformation in an age of redevelopment, highway building, and suburbanization.

This was a community of concerned intellectuals prepared to value Brown's testimony, as were others across the political spectrum who understood themselves to have little else in common with Irving Howe and company. As respected writers and scholars, the editors of *Dissent* had access to the forum of printed opinion and could facilitate Brown's entry into it, but they also stood for countless other readers who lacked such access but just as eagerly awaited —hands to brows, in Wolfe's image—the advent of an authentically "street" first-person voice from the second ghetto. Headquartered in the city that enjoyed the status of American urbanism's chief ground and icon, the *Dissent* intellectuals were also particularly well situated to move Brown to the center of the national urban conversation. Howe, Alfred Kazin, and many others had already mapped the motherland of the prewar urban village to this community's satisfaction, and *Dissent's* contributors could of course provide the global views of urban changes that were producing a new, troubling inner city, but they understood themselves to need people like Brown to explain the new order of troubles as a way of life for the people of Harlem and places like it.

Four years later, in *Manchild*, moving through *Dissent*'s schematic Manhattan landscape of Harlem and the Village, Brown both disappointed writers on the left and became a major broker in the traffic in representations of the inner city. In *Manchild*, he touched with singular authority upon many of the *Dissent* special issue's subject matters as seen from street level—delinquency, ghetto life, crime, jazz, drug abuse, and the divide between the races that became *the* urban issue in the years between Brown's first appearance in print and the publication of *Manchild*. That was the promise of Brown's initial publication in *Dissent*, and if that promise was realized in many ways for many readers, *Manchild* turned out to be a disappointment for precisely those who gave Brown his first break—intellectuals who had been scanning the horizon for a writer like Brown to emerge from the ghetto with a book in hand that substantiated their response to American urbanism in transition. Brown, looking back from the vantage point of the early 1990s, observes that *Manchild* disappointed these readers because "they were expecting a book saying what was wrong with capitalism."[18]

Brown's comment offers a way to specify amorphous terms like "left" and "liberal," at least in this context, by defining them in relation to the postwar transformation of American cities that culminated in the urban crisis. Brown's most disappointed readers understood that transformation to be a crisis brought about not by the moral failure of the welfare state or by a societywide failure to get tough with punks but by the workings of capital. By "capital," they meant that composite of dynamic private interest and acquiescent public authority metaphorically suggested by the American flags and Wall Street locale framing *Cool World*'s model of the City of the Future. For urbanists, the clearest institutional examples of that alliance of private and public elites were the progrowth coalitions of business and government that managed the titanic reconfiguration of inner cities for a postindustrial age in the 1950s and 1960s. We might (with brutal simplicity) divide this basic position into "left" and "liberal" polarities. On the left, where *Dissent* placed itself, voices argued that the urban crisis demanded and enabled a root-and-branch critique of American capitalism, a system of economic and social organization that was breaking down under the pressure of its internal contradictions. Those voices clustered around the "liberal" polarity tended toward a view of the urban crisis as demonstrating that American capitalism, while sound in principle as the basis for liberal democracy, was not sufficiently humane or efficient and required extensive reform. (Warren Miller was something of a socialist, but his habit of expressing his politics through ironic baffles made him acceptable in liberal venues like the *Saturday Review*.) Both groups regarded Brown, an ex-delinquent with a violent story to tell, as a natural witness who might testify to the effect that the workings of capital had on people in the streets of the transformed inner city.

If the course of postwar urban change had to do with the workings of capital, and if this structuring process moved beneath the racial ordering principle of urban crisis, then *Manchild*'s failure to be about what was wrong with capitalism indicated Brown's inadequacy as an urban intellectual. Thus, in the negative reviews, Brown becomes a naif out of his depth. Miller finds that "politically (whatever happened to that School of Hard Knocks we used to hear so much about?) Brown is a baby." Miller finds evidence of Brown's political immaturity in *Manchild*'s lack of references to even the most moderate political organizations (the NAACP, the Urban League, CORE, and SNCC); in Brown's obsolete 1950s-vintage vocabulary of "rebellion" against parental authority, when what the moment requires is a recognition of ghetto people's relation to the authority of the state; and in Brown's weak grasp of the meaning of representation in the political sense. Miller found it significant that Brown, who suggests that Harlem's black congressman Adam Clayton Powell "stays in office . . . because all the women vote for him," does not understand that Powell "holds power because he is useful, in his own way, to the white man; nor does Brown perceive that Powell's true and awful culpability is . . . his utter failure to politicize his people."[19]

Nat Hentoff, who had contributed a piece on jazz to the 1961 issue of *Dissent*, understood *Manchild* to be at least partially conscious of allowing "society to cop out" by restricting its treatment of "the whole ghetto pathology" to one individual's successful travail rather than attempting a systemic critique of "those social forces that maintain the ghetto." In the end, "none of the fragmentary indictments nor the rising motif in *Manchild* of a growing collective pride in being black brings Brown to a recognition of the need for counter-power in the ghetto if the beautiful cats who make it are not to continue to be small in number." Thus, Hentoff argues, *Manchild* reassures even as it disturbs "white America" (the necessary corollary to the idea of "black America"), suggesting that ameliorative programs like Operation Head Start and the "'War on Poverty' (with its wooden bullets)" can help others to "make it" and obscuring the deeper need for economic transformation that can be won only through black political "counter-power." In Hentoff's view, Brown falls far short of a comprehensive assessment of "today's under-class" in concentrating on the superficial and highly marketable details of his own story.[20]

Paul Goodman, another contributor to the *Dissent* issue of 1961, identified *Manchild* as part of the problem to which Goodman and his allies were seeking solutions. Brown, "as stupid as most others of his age," did not strike the frankly self-important Goodman as "a young ally in making the world I want." Writing as a controversial critic of public education, Goodman predictably takes the contrarian position that Brown's childhood experiences in criminal delinquency and lively sexual experimentation amounted to a "progressive" street education in many ways "superior to the average middle-class or lower-class schooling." However, "getting out of Harlem, [Brown] falls into America," by which

Goodman means that Brown betrays this promising start and the world that formed him by treating Harlem with the spurious detachment typical of American public life and education. Brown treats Harlem as a "'scene,' in a series of reports on heroin, the Muslims, etc., the genre of the New York *Post*. Instead of groping for universality, self-recognition, and commitment, the young man settles, as a detached observer, for sociological abstractions, and so he legislates himself right out of humanity." The crux of such abdication of humanistic responsibilities is a "total silence about politics." In addition to the predictable list of subjects pertaining to the ghetto—the civil rights movement, economic institutions—Goodman demands to know Brown's views on Cuba and the atom bomb. Goodman discovers in this silence on politics a basic failure to grapple with the meaning of Harlem and thus dismisses Brown as unprepared to pursue the transformation of consciousness to which Goodman would like him to aspire.[21]

For Miller, Hentoff, and Goodman, Brown was too much the victim of capital—inadequately educated, unable to see the larger urban picture, a ghetto operator eager to sell his persona to slumming white tourists—to do the cultural work of analysis thrust upon him by his privileged vantage point on the metropolis. The critique of *Manchild* tellingly located Brown's inadequacy as an urban intellectual in the overly narrow angle of difference between Brown's authorial persona and Brown's narrating protagonist. This collapse of authorial persona with protagonist was the key to *Manchild*'s success in plotting Brown's persona on the map of Harlem, and it was the central effect of *Manchild*'s linguistic strategies (the language of narrator and protagonist running seamlessly together), its survey of narrative options (yielding a metanarrative in which Claude Brown the urban intellectual and Claude Brown the six-year-old rioter have unlimited access to one another), and its mapping routine (creating a sharply divided city that only Brown's persona can traverse at will). For Miller, it is precisely the success of these strategies, showing that Harlem in all its pathological force has shaped Brown's authorial persona, that unfits Brown for the work of analyzing as opposed to exemplifying ghetto life.

Miller's frustration carried into his reading of *Manchild* as a literary artifact. Miller was perhaps most extreme in pronouncing Brown's prose "an impoverished patois," but several others also suggested that Brown was not a writer. Rather than providing an efficacious vocabulary peculiarly suited to addressing the urban crisis, Brown was in Miller's view giving readers a touristic taste of local color that obscured, rather than exposed, meaning. Brown thus stood accused of replicating the slippery manipulations he admired in Ernst Papanek's command of language: "If you asked him the hard Wiltwyck questions like, 'When am I going home?' or, 'Why are you keeping me here so long?' and Papanek couldn't tell you, he wouldn't lie about it. He would tell you something that left you knowing no more than before you asked him the question, but you would feel kind of satisfied about it."[22] Miller and other critics were frustrated by what they saw as Brown's parallel refusal to answer the hard Harlem questions: Why had he been so bad? What was the future of American urbanism? What should we do about the second ghetto? *Manchild* left these readers feeling that they knew no more about the answers to these questions than they had before they read it but ashamed of the thrill they got from learning intimate, sensational details of ghetto life. For Miller, Brown's authenticating language marked him as a victim of ghetto life rather than as an urban intellectual with valuable material to contribute. It was as if Duke Custis, sensing a chance to make a big score, had wrested control of *Cool World* away from Warren Miller and rambled on for hundreds of pages, diffusing Miller's well-crafted social critique in a welter of exciting detail.

Brown's Credentials and Miller's Problem

The critique of *Manchild* advanced by Miller and others, then, is that Brown did not respond to the analytical responsibilities placed upon him by the city of fact in crisis. However, we should also recognize a second, equally important source of friction between Miller and Brown, a source that points to a drama played out entirely within the city of feeling. Miller worried that "people who ought to know better" were reading and accepting what amounted to an urban intellectual's campaign biography, which ended by producing Claude Brown as uniquely equipped to represent Harlem in ways that shunted writers like Miller to the margins of the urban conversation.

To the extent that it was not about what was wrong with capitalism, *Manchild* posed a significant threat to downtown intellectuals' imaginative access to Harlem. Brown definitively introduced a powerful set of authorial credentials that put university-trained subscribers to the logic of urban crisis, especially white ones, on the defensive: "The credentials needed to write about life as an American Negro are getting tougher," observed a reviewer of *Manchild* in the *Economist*. "Soon, perhaps even now, the Negro who has never been a juvenile delinquent will find no listeners for his story of what it is like to have a dark skin in a white society. Mr Claude Brown is an impressive product of the new school."[23] Brown's authoritative mapping of his persona in the violent streets of the ghetto tended to clear those streets of all those who could not demonstrate a similarly intimate knowledge of ghetto pathology. White mavericks like Ed Banfield, who claimed that the urban crisis was not a racial crisis (or a crisis at all), still assumed themselves to have access to the subjectivities of ghetto residents, but most white intellectuals did not. Texts as different as *Dissent*'s special issue on New York, *Siege of Harlem*, and Tom Wolfe's profile of Brown suggest the parameters of a hegemonic conventional wisdom: those without appropriate credentials who subscribed to the notion of urban crisis were obliged to regard themselves as waiting for black urban intellectuals to tell them about the future as it took form on the streets of the second ghetto.

Miller therefore needed Brown to make some gesture of alliance to any analytical precedents that Miller could recognize: the kinds of gestures toward Marx and a Marxist pantheon of heroes made by the Black Panthers, the kinds of gestures toward a postcolonial or Third World reading of the ghetto made by William Gardner Smith, or even the kinds of gestures toward reformist social science made by ex-delinquents turned social workers like Piri Thomas. Without such acknowledgments of an ideological and linguistic architecture shared by Brown's city of feeling and those built by his critics, the logic of urban crisis argued that there could be no sustaining connection between Brown's local-scale rendering of ghetto life and the grand-scale critiques of capital (the City of the Future; New York City in decline) purveyed by Miller and the *Dissent* intellectuals. Failing to import their critique into his textual Harlem in order to endorse it at street level, Brown thus offered downtown intellectuals no conceptual gateways through the barricades around "black America"; rather, his credentials simply trumped theirs. Miller thus found himself at the boundaries of the ghetto of feeling with outdated working papers ("expert on delinquency" was no longer good enough), peering over conceptual barricades that he had enthusiastically helped to construct by promulgating the notion of a city radically divided into two separate nations.

Manchild's authoritative survey of narratives similarly put off the *Dissent* intellectuals because *Manchild* refused to invest in any of its sampled narrative fragments, let alone a third act of conversion to their ways of thinking. The narrating protagonist thus failed to "grow" and "change" on the way to what Goodman called "commitment" (as opposed to "sociological" detachment). A narrative that chose one of the many sampled lines and developed it—Claude Brown as organic radical or reformer, jazz musician, fighter, Black Muslim, social worker, or even (especially) doomed career criminal—would have provided satisfaction in a way that the omnibus narrative's "conclusion" did not. The omnibus narrative ended, instead, with Claude Brown's arrival on the scene as an urban intellectual, deploying an intimidating set of credentials but showing no genuine interest in pursuing an alliance with critics of capital. *Manchild* predicated Brown's singular freedom of movement through the inner city of feeling on his independence from the entangling social, political, and cultural alliances offered to him as a series of narrative options. The *Dissent* intellectuals had offered him one: ex-delinquent emerges from the ghetto, steeps himself in the language and ideology of political dissent, returns to the ghetto equipped to critique capital in ways that open a two-way flow of access between him and his downtown allies. He had sampled that narrative, turned the encounter to his advantage, and moved on, leaving *Dissent* in his wake as one more New York scene to be explored but not invested in.

Miller's review of *Manchild* thus becomes an evaluation of new rules for writing the ghetto, complicated by the friction between Miller's efforts to de-authorize Brown and Miller's acquiescence to a logic of urban crisis that called for a Claude Brown to write Harlem. Miller's review recognizes Brown's importance as a threat and sets out to deny him the command over representations of the ghetto that *Manchild* proposes to establish for him. The review thus argues for severing the ties binding *Manchild* to the Harlem of fact—since, in Miller's estimation, Kenneth Clark's research supersedes Brown's anecdotes—and for severing the ties binding Brown to the community of urban intellectuals that helped to get him published. This comprehensive assault on Brown is not merely some mean-spirited pique on Miller's part; rather, Miller struggled mightily to preserve a line of entry into the ghetto for the authorial personas of socially engaged literary intellectuals like himself. The bitterness of the struggle came in great part from the self-contradiction that made it necessary. Miller's antagonist was not Brown; Miller was up against a received wisdom of racial separation in which he deeply believed. One can hear the torment of a passionately conventional student of urban crisis in Miller's plaintive reminder to readers of *Manchild* "that to be born black does not mean being born with the answers."[24]

Claude Brown and his initial readers, Warren Miller prominently among them, occupied a historical moment of urban crisis that defined them as much as they defined it. Miller's novels and Brown's autobiography are in important ways about that mutual process of definition, which gives them their period feel. There is something powerfully, poignantly dated about these books; they have the charge of combined familiarity and strangeness we find in old maps. In 1960, Miller himself described one of his novels of the 1950s, a satire of McCarthyism entitled *The Sleep of Reason* that no American publisher would touch until well after McCarthy's fall, as having "a period quality; one almost hears the rustle of the crinolines. It has become a historical novel; it lacks only bosoms, unbridled passion, and smooth-bore cannon."[25] Read now, *Cool World*'s teen gang sensationalism and *Siege of Harlem*'s hep apocalypticism feel "historical" as well. *Manchild* also seems dated: massive and diffuse because it enjoys the editorial leeway accorded to a hot "problem" book; archaic in its talk of young men "good with their hands" that predates the great inner-city arms race of the 1970s and 1980s, in its earnest explanations of why black men call one another "baby," in its beautiful cats.

As dated as Brown's and Miller's books can seem, they can also seem remarkably fresh when some later book or movie raises echoes of them. They are part of the foundations of many of our contemporary cities of feeling, but they have been silted over by three decades of postindustrial urbanism that they now seem to anticipate.[26] Miller has almost completely disappeared, remembered only by a few aficionados and some veterans of the *Nation* and the *New Yorker*, but one can still find resonances of his writing—of the ideas and social conditions that inflected it—in the urban literature. Readers of the performance artist Sapphire's celebrated first novel *Push* will recognize a close relative of Duke Custis and *Cool World*'s dialect strategy in the character and voice of the narrating protagonist Claireece Precious Jones. Like Duke's, Claireece's life in Harlem is an index of social pathologies, her possible salvation is a testament to concerned professional help, and her halting but eloquent voice tells a story that codes the author's journey in the protagonist's: Miller-as-Duke writes, "When you can read an write why you can do any thing. Do any thing. Be any thing"; Sapphire-as-Claireece writes, "Sure you can do anything when you talking or writing, its not like living when you can only do what you doing."[27] Like Miller in 1959, Sapphire has made a dramatic entry into an extensive literature that seeks to explore the mental and physical worlds of baffling ghetto teenagers: Claireece is an unwed mother, a type who, with the help of Daniel Patrick Moynihan and countless other policymakers and commentators, has joined the male delinquent at the center of debates over urban poverty. The fact that Sapphire is black should remind us that almost everyone who writes about Harlem or the postindustrial ghetto feels obliged to pass through Checkpoint Frederick Douglass. One can read the subtextual drama of the author's and reader's difficult crossings of the line—and such crossings must, according to standard notions of inner-city life, be marked as difficult—in the language and form of the text. (Miller was nothing if not versatile, and one can read that versatility in another genre that raises echoes of his work. Even more than *Catcher in the Rye*, Warren Miller's Amanda Vail novels of the 1950s anticipate the postcollegiate angst, backward-looking Gotham romanticism, and breathless self-importance of Jay McInerney's *Bright Lights, Big City* and so many other tales of bohemian and service-professional life in postindustrial New York City.)

Manchild has not disappeared, remaining in print and continuing in its perennial role as a rough minor classic of street sensibility by a man present at the creation of social and textual cities we recognize as "ours." It surfaces regularly in the curricula of high schools, colleges, and prisons, less often in graduate courses and academic scholarship. It also surfaces all over popular culture. One might see *Manchild*—the movie rights to which, Brown says, "have been sold a dozen times over"[28]—as an ur-text lurking at the base of the genre of black gangster narratives that played such a large role in imagining the inner city in the 1970s and then again in the late 1980s and 1990s. *Manchild* adds to the black autobiographical tradition and the delinquent literature that precede it, but it also suggests within its purposeful wanderings a whole literature of the inner city that developed after it. Countless works of fiction and memoir appearing in the 1960s and the three decades that followed would retell *Manchild*'s first act, often in the terminal form of the dead-before-twenty-one story, and countless others would follow to their conclusions the sampled but refused possibilities of *Manchild*'s second and third acts. The movie of *Manchild* has not been made, but movies and books that cover essentially the same narrative and social ground remain a cultural staple—and form an avenue for the emergence of black artists and urban intellectuals.

Warren Miller and Claude Brown are two among many founding architects of the generic ghetto that emerged in the mid-1960s and has developed since then into a kind of mythic space in which all manner of social and cultural dramas are rehearsed. The authorial personas of Miller and Brown, passing like ships in the night (Miller firing one broadside at Brown) as they trundled back and forth with their cargos of representations between Harlem and the Village, played their parts in the imaginative mapping of the second ghetto in the moment of its arrival at the center of postindustrial urbanism.

Conclusion: Notes from a Cultural Sea Change

Budd Schulberg, novelist and Hollywood screenwriter, felt that the Watts riots of 1965 required a response of him. Schulberg, who had gained his greatest renown for his boxing novel *The Harder They Fall* (1947) and his screenplay of *On the Waterfront*, thought of himself as a 1930s- and 1940s-vintage realist. Like Nelson Algren, Schulberg credentialed his authorial persona to deliver social critique at street level with an urban insider's knowledge of the manly pastimes (boxing, horse racing, gambling) and inner lives of petty criminals, laborers, and workers in the industrial trades.[1] "As an American writer, still oriented toward social fiction," Schulberg made it a point to uphold, as Algren did, "the old-fashioned notion that an author has a special obligation to his society, an obligation to understand it and to serve as its conscience." The use of "still" and "old-fashioned," like the white-ethnic neighborhood voices of New York and New Jersey in his books and movies ("I coulda been a contender," etc.), invoked resonances of the industrial city and the literatures of social criticism and decline that mapped it, including the work of Chicago realists like Algren. But in 1965 the postindustrial inner city, wracked by rioting, suddenly demanded the attention of a writer who claimed those antecedents and interests— and who, like Warren Miller, prided himself on staying on the developing forward edge of the day's most compelling social issues. Schulberg therefore "felt an itch, an irresistible urge" to fashion a literary response to the Watts riots, which he understood to have blossomed into something far more cataclysmic than mere rioting: "a genuine, full scale Revolt, a rebellion that had been years in the making in the festering black ghettos of Los Angeles," a civil war between blacks and whites. This struggle was happening close enough to

Hollywood, Schulberg's particular "corner of the nation," that he, who was handsomely paid as one of Hollywood's in-house purveyors of "social fiction," felt obliged to do something about it.[2]

Despite having the kind of insider knowledge of Watts expected of his generation of urban intellectual—"I had gone to Watts in my youth to hear T-Bone Walker and other local jazzmen in the honky-tonks"—Schulberg found himself unequipped to represent to his own satisfaction the ghettos of Los Angeles, which he regarded as part of his literary beat. "If I were to understand this urban tragedy, it would require not merely a look but a lot of looks, and not merely superficial looks but finally, somehow, from the inside looking out."[3] Schulberg wholeheartedly accepted the racial logic of urban crisis: he felt impelled to produce representations of Watts that allowed him (and, therefore, his readers) to "understand" the ghetto from the inside, but he assumed the existence of invisible walls dividing the city of feeling that prevented him from executing such an imagined entry into ghetto life in his own, improperly authenticated "outsider's" hand and voice. Since he deemed himself unequipped as a writer to get "inside" enough to scratch the representational itch inspired in him by the principal social crisis of his time, he went to Watts to find those who could.

Schulberg founded the Watts Writers' Workshop in the aftermath of the riots. "Stories aren't fancy things," Schulberg told the workshop's first serious participant, nineteen-year-old Charles Johnson. "They're the things you've been doing, what you did in the uprising last month, what you're thinking about now."[4] As a well-connected professional writer leading a workshop filled with novices, Schulberg would help to organize and polish the untrained language with which they turned the materials and events of ghetto life into literature. He would also provide a forum in which rough work could be aired, brought to the attention of experts, and eventually published.

Schulberg saw himself as a teacher; he therefore needed a textbook. He had read in the canon of ghetto narrative and its accepted antecedents, "from the autobiography of Frederick Douglass, to Dr. Clark's *Dark Ghetto*, the angry essays of Baldwin, and the abrasive *Autobiography of Malcolm X*," but he made *Manchild in the Promised Land* "our first textbook." That is, Schulberg aspired to make *Manchild*—its comprehensive survey of ghetto narrative and language, its spatial plot of the ghetto, its account of the development of Claude Brown as an urban intellectual—the template for the writing of a new cohort of urban intellectuals emerging from the damaged terrain of Watts with a body of new urban literature in hand. This new corpus of poetry, fiction, and autobiography would do the work of representing the inner city in crisis. Charles Johnson, at least, endorsed Schulberg's choice of *Manchild*. Brown spoke the right language and told the right stories: "'That's a real tough book. I didn't know you could put words like that in a book. Sounds just like we talk on a Hundred and Third Street. Everything he puts in that book, that's just like

what's going on here in Watts. I could tell a hundred stories just like it.'"
Schulberg felt obliged by the responsibilities of his cultural role to find and
develop "a hundred stories just like it," a body of literature schematically outlined by *Manchild*.[5]

Succession: New Orders and Old Orders

Schulberg's response to the Watts riots suggests some of the literary repercussions of the urban crisis. On the one hand, Schulberg concluded that his own
training as an urban intellectual was in some ways still of great value in a
moment of crisis. He could be a mentor to ghetto writers, linking them to a
great tradition of writers of "social fiction" who fulfilled their "special obligation" to produce social critique. In his introduction to *From the Ashes*, a collection of writing by participants in the Watts Writers' Workshop, he includes
among his honor roll of such literary antecedents several—Melville, Whitman,
Norris, London, Sandburg, Sinclair, Dos Passos, the Chicago realist Richard
Wright—who drew observantly upon industrial cities of fact, especially on the
lives and milieux of the wage-earning classes and underclasses, in shaping
American literary realism. On the other hand, Schulberg concluded that the particular set of qualities and credentials he presented as an urban intellectual was
obsolescent, unfitted to the vitally important work of recognizing and figuring
the postindustrial inner city in crisis. Other writers better suited to the task
would have to take up his duties. These two conclusions and the tension between them drive Schulberg's account of how he participated in one local
instance of *Manchild*'s canonization. That account tells a quintessentially postwar narrative of succession, in this case within the community of urban intellectuals. As in the neighborhoods of American cities, the succession is made up
of persistences as well as drastic change: the older order, incarnate in Schulberg, provides a substructure shaping the new; younger black writers, supplanting aging white ethnics, remake the literary landscape.

In passing from Nelson Algren to Claude Brown, I have offered a similar
succession—not a simple matter of younger writers supplanting older ones or
blacks replacing whites but rather a complex of overlapping persistences and
changes that has layered new orders of urban intellectuals and new ways of
writing on preexisting ones. The emergence of the postindustrial inner city was
accompanied by the emergence of newly rearranged groups of urban intellectuals telling the stories and drawing the maps of postindustrial urbanism.
Among the writers who command most of my attention in this study,
Gwendolyn Brooks, William Gardner Smith, David Bradley, Diane McKinney-
Whetstone, Warren Miller, and Claude Brown do the work of representing the
second ghetto as it takes lasting shape. Nelson Algren and Jack Dunphy imagine the industrial white-ethnic neighborhood order in decline, while Mike

Royko, Stuart Dybek, and Pete Dexter trace the changing relation of the urban village's enclaved survivals to the postindustrial inner city. Finally, Smith, Bradley, McKinney-Whetstone, Royko, and a host of developers, political leaders, city planners, and their critics (Jane Jacobs, Denise Scott Brown) map the expanding preserves of the service-professional classes—office workers, managers, so-called urban pioneers, and all the rest who have since fallen under the loose rubric of "yuppies."

I have, then, described in case-study form a cultural and social sea change, the transformation of literary urbanism tied to the transformation of American cities in the decades after World War II. If that sea change and the successions and overlaps it entailed were extended, even diffuse, we can make out signs of them in a variety of texts, and not just in the novels and poems typically regarded as literary texts. The succession narrative and its historical contexts move beneath the surface of everyday artifacts: for example, *Newsweek*'s issue of 16 August 1965 charts the sea change in three seemingly unrelated articles.

The issue of 16 August 1965 gives a sense of what the parallel transformations of the city of feeling and the city of fact might look like to a reader flipping through *Newsweek* while waiting in a dentist's office, eating a meal, or riding a bus in late summer 1965. The particular issue in question is in itself of no special historical significance, but one can read in this everyday text signs of significant social and cultural change over time, and one can make out a logic driving that change.

The issue's cover shows the forms of men, caught in searchlights, lined against a wall to be frisked by police, with the caption "CRIME in the streets." The cover story explains that, according to the FBI's Uniform Crime Reports, "every category of crime was on the increase" and that since 1958 "serious crime has spiraled upward at a rate of five times that of the population."[6] The story devotes a single paragraph to noting that the statistics are open to further interpretation and quotes some experts who feel the statistical rise greatly exaggerates the actual problem, but the thrust of the story overwhelms the caveat. The reader is obliged to conclude that there is much more crime than before in America, especially in urban America, and that this "crime wave" is part of a significant rise in urban violence and fear.

In sketching the causes of the rise in crime and popular anxiety over crime, the cover story makes a thumbnail sketch of postwar urban development. Concentrating upon "social, economic and psychic conditions under which crime seems to occur more often," *Newsweek* describes increasing "anonymity" and other strains on the social fabric attendant upon continuing urbanization, a large postwar cohort of young people violently at odds with the ways of life accepted by their parents, the intractability of poverty in an increasingly affluent society.[7] These complex, bewildering lines of analysis, all of which skim the surface of the postindustrial transformation of urban economies and populations, lead the cover story's argument toward the organizing principle of race, which subsumes the others in sharply representable form.

Newsweek's cover story, then, hits upon one narrative line—the black migration from South to urban North—that organizes the others. At the heart of the problem of crime, the cover story finds, are poverty and the inner city, two terms that, like the word "urban" itself, threatened in the urban discourse of the mid-1960s to collapse into semi-synonyms of the word "Negro." Attorney General Nicholas Katzenbach tells *Newsweek*, "the bigger the city, the harder it is to deter crime." In Katzenbach's and *Newsweek*'s accounts, "the high rate of juvenile crime," the panic button of the 1950s, converges with "the high rate of Negro crime," the panic button of the 1960s, and these "two harsh facts" flow together as functions of Problem Number One, racial segregation. *Newsweek* concludes that "all too often, to speak of the slum today is to speak of the Negro" and quotes the blunt summation of this line of thinking by an anonymous "former high-ranking Administration official": "'to speak of crime today is to speak of Negro crime.'"[8]

To speak of the violent, young, male Negro criminal was therefore to speak of postwar urban development in condensed form. He was the text in which the postwar period's most important urban stories could be read: to somehow figure out the criminal violence was to figure out the ghetto was to figure out the city-structuring effect of racial difference expressed as social cleavage. It follows that informants who could provide firsthand information on crime among youth in the ghetto were positioned to address issues at the top of the national agenda. Attorney General Katzenbach, like Senator Ribicoff's Senate subcommittee, turned to Claude Brown for testimony on the formation of young black male criminals. Katzenbach chaired the Commission on Law Enforcement and Administration of Justice, appointed in 1965 by President Johnson to respond to the widespread worry over the increase in crime. Among the many sources of information on life in the black lower class cited by the commission's report, published in 1967, were the final lines of *Manchild in the Promised Land*'s foreword: "For where does one run to when he is already in the promised land?"[9]

Newsweek also looked to Brown, and directed its readers to look to Brown, for direct evidence of ghetto life and for imaginative literary exploitation of it. On page 81 of the 16 August issue, in the Books section, appears a respectful and enthusiastic review of *Manchild*, endorsing Brown in the role of exemplary child of the postwar inner city: "a man who was singled out by his voiceless generation—the 'plague generation,' he calls it—to be their tribune unto the nations, their witness and tongue, to tell how it was and what happened, and to count the appalling losses." The mock-biblical language here earnestly underscores, rather than ironizes, both the sense of crisis (often couched in language appropriate to a biblical plague) and Brown's role as spokesman for black Americans. If Brown's credentials as an ex-delinquent—"a battle scarred veteran of a 'bebopping' gang" and the Harlem riot of 1943—position him to speak for an increasingly urbanized and Northern people, they also equip him with novel and efficacious resources of language: he speaks "the violent argot of the streets." The ex-delinquent Brown promises to be just the man to explain and make literature from the complex of pathologies identified and located in the second ghetto by the cover story, the "harsh facts" driving the wave of criminal violence and political disorder.[10]

Newsweek's review of *Manchild* saw Claude Brown, a new-model urban intellectual, emerging out of the rubble of what many were calling urban decline and the failure of urban renewal. The picture of Brown accompanying *Newsweek*'s review literalizes that cultural role (fig. 11). Brown, looking young and powerful in a blocky suit, tieless, stands hand on hip (producing the effect to which Walt Whitman seems to aspire in the portrait in *Leaves of Grass*) against a backdrop of inner-city textures: weathered brick walls, rubble, garbage. The caption reads "Brown: 'The plague generation.'" A similar photograph accompanied an enthusiastic page 1 review in the *New York Times Book Review*, an almost identical shot in what appears to be the same location, with two children framed in the window to Brown's right—suggesting that Brown speaks as well for the next generation being formed in the crucible of the second ghetto. The reader sees in *Newsweek* and the *Times* a literal mapping of authorial persona on the urban landscape. Brown emerges from this postwar landscape to map it in prose, to write the key terrain of urban crisis from the inside out, to play the role Budd Schulberg's succession narrative cast him in.

The 16 August issue of *Newsweek* offers a version of that succession narrative, suggesting the writers of the postindustrial ghetto as literary successors to the writers of the urban village by juxtaposing Brown's arrival on the urban scene with Nelson Algren's departure from it. Page 81 also features a review of Nelson Algren's latest book, a mélange of journalism and criticism entitled *Notes from a Sea Diary: Hemingway All the Way*. The review runs onto page 82, where a shirt-sleeved Nelson Algren, in his fifties and looking weathered, smiles or grimaces in some unidentifiable sunny locale above the caption, "Algren: 'O chasmed love'" (fig. 12). As Brown appears to claim a place at center stage in representing the inner city, Algren sails off on a sea journey, entirely leaving the American urban literary scene that he had seemed poised to dominate at midcentury. The juxtaposition of Brown's arrival and Algren's departure is probably unintentional, but the logic of urban crisis gives it a powerful charge.

Persistence: Departure and Return

Sea Diary is a retrospective and disappointed book: a diminished writer's account of retreat from his literary turf resonates with his embittered defense of the legacy of a dead contemporary (Hemingway) against hyenalike critics come to pick at the corpse. Algren had by the 1960s departed from the model of the practicing urban intellectual invoked by Schulberg. Algren had stopped writing novels and what Schulberg called "social fiction," his original stock in trade, and now cast himself in *Sea Diary* as "a free-lance journalist out of Chicago" who reviewed other people's city books, covered the offbeat and lowlife, and wrote travel pieces.[11] The "*out of* Chicago" (my italics) is telling. Although still based in Chicago, Algren considered himself to be alienated from his old beat, and *Sea Diary* explores the theme of exile both as travel and as a conflict between Algren and the literary standard-makers of the day, who had turned on Hemingway as well as Algren. "What was I doing in Asia?" he asks himself upon awakening in a prostitute's bed in Pusan. "This time I could find no other reason than that I didn't want to be at home" (55–56). *Newsweek*'s reviewer therefore values Algren as "Chicago's own flying Dutchman," a rootless, tale-spinning old curmudgeon: a producer not of contemporary "social fiction" but of a pleasingly nostalgic, curious body of light "Algreniana"; "an old hand" whose oeuvre always finds its way down well-grooved paths to the fixed poker games and whores-with-hearts-of-gold he first made it his business to write in the 1930s.[12]

By 1965, Algren imagined as complete the story of the industrial city's decline, and the concomitant decline of the Chicago realists who were that city's leading students, in which he saw himself caught up at midcentury. Developing the implications of the great urban crisis of the late nineteenth century and early twentieth century built around industrialization, urbanization, and immigration, Algren and his literary ancestors had created an influential, integrated set of representations, models, and critiques of the prewar city. By midcentury, narratives of decline detailing the breakup of this industrial city's orders, including the representational, could be found throughout American culture and, of course, in literary culture. After *Golden Arm*, Algren gradually removed his authorial persona from the terrain of the contemporary inner city. By the 1960s, he was imagining the final foreclosure of the landscape onto which he mapped his writing persona: "the day that the double-tiered causeway is merged with the expressway that merges with the coast-to-coast thruway making right-hand turns every mile into a hundred solid miles of mile-high skyscrapers."[13] Algren, who was in 1949 still the next big thing in urban literature, was shuffled off the urban stage as it changed around him into the signature landscape of postindustrial urbanism.

Sixteen years after *Golden Arm, Sea Diary* removes itself from the urban scene and from the present. In it Algren makes a tour of Asian ports and considers his past, inventories the prostitutes of the Orient, dabbles in poetry (the "O chasmed love" part), and defends Ernest Hemingway against critics like Dwight Macdonald, Leslie Fiedler, and Norman Podhoretz. Algren dismisses these effete characters as "mere nose drops in the nostrils of literature" (245) and mounts a comprehensively revisionist defense of Hemingway as a social realist and literary "dissenter" against their accounts of his technical and psychological "failures." If Algren does seem genuinely motivated by these critics' shabby treatment of a literary hero, there is as well a second source of his animus against them. His defense of Hemingway (who enthusiastically admired Algren's writing) serves as an excuse to attack an influential group of critics who also played active roles in the decline of Algren's literary reputation and in pronouncing his brand of "social fiction," Chicago realism, passé. When Algren defends Hemingway from Dwight Macdonald's parodic assaults— Hemingway never learned new tricks, "and nothing is worse than a trick that has gone stale," or "his legs began to go and his syntax became boring. . . . But the bartenders still liked him" (89)—Algren is also counterattacking against critics like Macdonald who have been saying the same about him.

In recasting Hemingway as an (improbable) ally of the Chicago realists, as a literary reporter or social realist wronged by critics, *Sea Diary* mounts as well a defense of Algren's notion of literature. Algren contends sweepingly throughout *Sea Diary* that critical and literary life has declined in the postwar era in growing apart from the fundamental purposes of literature as defined by people like Algren (and Schulberg), which is to observe social reality and to make poetry out of questioning its orders and the meanings they make available.

Enacting this vision of literary work, Algren's journey to the ports of the East leads him to a familiar set of social materials—crooked card games, petty criminal schemes, legions of prostitutes—that figure the entrapment of desperate marginal characters in the workings of vast urban machines organized and powered by the imperatives of commerce. He plots this familiar world in familiar ways. Constricted streetscapes like the "fogbound warren" of Pusan's red-light district or Bombay's Street of the Hundred Cages, in which prostitutes ply their trade, recall the narrow vistas of Chicago's urban villages. In shabby dwellings like Calcutta's Kanani Mansions, an "ominous tenement" akin to Jailer Schwabatski's rooming house in *Golden Arm*, hustlers and loiterers forming cross-sections of the underlife are always figuratively in the street. Algren finds the same building blocks of literature in the Far East that he found on the Near Northwest Side of Chicago. Faced with the criminality and indigence of Bombay, he concludes, "I couldn't be sure that I wasn't still in Chicago" (120).

But *Sea Diary* is not a novel of the city disguised as an essay; its deepest impulses are secondary and critical. When *Sea Diary* returns in flashback to the familiar landscape of Chicago's neighborhood order, pushing the identity between the port cities of the Orient and the Chicago Algren wrote in the past, it reveals the central purpose of the narrative's grand movement through space: not to imagine a way of life but to launch a wholesale attack on the intellectual and critical consensus that has excluded Algren. The prelude to Algren's discussion of Hemingway is an anecdote about the decline and fall of an amateur tightrope walker, an immigrant "greenhorn" who lived next door to Algren during a "lost summer" in Algren's childhood. That story traverses the low-rise landscape and downward-tilted narrative line of *Golden Arm* and *City on the Make:* a constricted autumnal vista bounded by wires and fire escapes where "washing was whipping whitely" (a central image in *City on the Make*); a "Room without Corners" (like the one in *Golden Arm* where Sophie goes irretrievably mad) where police bring the tightrope walker in order to break his nonconformist will; a "neighborhood factory that manufactured endless belting for other factories" (like the Endless Belt and Leather works in *Golden Arm*) where the fallen dissenter is refitted as a cog in the city machine; old-style taverns (like Antek's in *Golden Arm*) where he sinks into the grotesque half-life of the terminal drunk (97–101). The story of the tightrope walker serves as prologue to a story of great writers, among them Hemingway, dragged down and disciplined by the machine of criticism, which Algren understands to be implacably alienated from the lives of his subjects, the "people who don't read" (105). In Algren's telling, this intellectual decline explains how the critics could have turned on him and celebrated instead a writer like Saul Bellow, a putative Chcago writer with a very different authorial self-conception: "How else to explain that a compilation of literary allusions such as *Herzog*, possessing no value beyond cuteness, can be mistaken for a living book?" (103 4). The tightrope walker, unsurprisingly, is supposed to be Algren too, dragged down and disciplined by a critical consensus that has devalued Chicago realism on the prewar model.

Sea Diary, then, wants to explain Algren's yoked departures from the American city of feeling and from the first rank of postwar writers as the result of a critical conspiracy. *Newsweek*'s review accepts and is amused by this story, but at the same time the reviews of Algren and Brown together posit a different context for that departure: a narrative of succession in which some of the primary work of observing and questioning contemporary urbanism now fell to writers, like Claude Brown, who engaged with the postindustrial city. The most important representational materials for that work were to be found in the second ghetto landscape of "black America," positioned at the center of a metropolis from which Algren, an elder statesman among industrial urbanism's literary figures, was for reasons of his own in a kind of exile or diasporic flight. The irony of Algren's flight, readable in *Sea Diary*, was that it led him to familiar materials that were resonant with Brown's—poverty, criminality, entrapment, all inflected by questions of race (arising in the interaction of white Americans with indigent Asians).

The exile, as exiles will, returned. When the urban crisis was over, and the postindustrial city of feeling had achieved a measure of generic stability, Algren came back to his subject. Algren's eventual return in the 1970s to the literary work of the urban intellectual, as he originally conceived of that work, fittingly entailed a turn to the materials of ghetto narrative. Algren nursed his grudge against the literary and critical worlds for the rest of his years, and he finally left Chicago for good in 1975, moving to Paterson, New Jersey, and eventually to a writers' preserve at Sag Harbor on Long Island, but before his death in 1981 he made a return to the social realist novel, the genre he had abandoned in the 1950s. Algren's last novel, *The Devil's Stocking* (published posthumously in 1983),[14] fictionalizes the story of black middleweight boxer Rubin "Hurricane" Carter, imprisoned for a triple murder that some people believed he did not commit. Among Carter's supporters were some famous people, like Muhammad Ali and Bob Dylan, who made him a minor cause célèbre. Algren, drawn to the sense of constriction and thwarted aspiration in Carter's story, effected his return as novelist to the inner city by telling that story, by moving through "black America" and through a set of narrative patterns definitively surveyed by *Manchild*.

Algren had not written a novel since *A Walk on the Wild Side* (1955), a comprehensive rewrite of his earlier novel *Somebody in Boots* (1935), and he had abandoned his last serious attempt at a new one—the Chicago drug novel *Entrapment*—in the 1950s. *Devil's Stocking* started out as reportage, but Algren came to believe that the story of Hurricane Carter's encounter with the legal, economic, and racial machinery of urban order had the makings of a novel. The materials of the story circulated ready to hand in the form of Carter's autobiography, *The Sixteenth Round*, which Algren reviewed for the *Los Angeles Times* in 1974.[15] In the review, Algren has almost nothing to say about Carter's writing, or about the book itself at all, but he outlines the narrative as a set of raw materials: a promising black boxer with a long criminal history convicted of killing three whites in a bar, inconsistencies and signs of a possible frame-up in the government's case against him, a context of heightened racial tension (the murders took place in 1966, the first trial in 1967) that gave the events greater significance. Carter offered ready-made a story of "entrapment" that spoke to the organizing urban issues of the day.

Carter's *Sixteenth Round* touches upon some of Algren's favorite themes and subjects—Algren had written about boxers and barroom murders before[16]— but it also develops narrative lines sketched out in *Manchild*'s survey of first-person ghetto narrative. Claude Brown accordingly identified *Sixteenth Round*, in a blurb appearing on the back cover of the paperback edition just above a blurb extracted from Algren's review, as the "most powerful book I've read to date—eloquently written and extremely revealing." There was much in *Sixteenth Round* to remind a reader of *Manchild:* profanely colorful and authenticatingly stiff by turns, Carter's jailhouse memoir offers the story of a "manchild" (born, like Brown, in 1937) who "has heart" and is "good with his hands," becomes "war counselor" of a delinquent gang, gets into trouble with the law, and finally finds his calling as a fighter and writer.

Hurricane Carter thus pursues the specific career path taken by Brown's friend Turk, but at the same time he follows Brown's career path in detailing his own formation as an intellectual. In the army, he learns the discipline of boxing and finds a mentor who encourages him not only toward a Muslim conversion (one of the third acts that Brown considers and rejects) but also toward conquering his stutter and developing himself in Brown's métier, the discipline of facility with language that parallels the fighter's facility with his hands: "As I began learning how to talk with some clarity, all the knowledge that I had picked up in the course of my life . . . began to pour from my mouth like the unbridled Niagara. . . . I developed a special feeling for verbal expression. . . . My whole life changed. My attitude, even my boxing ability, greatly improved."[17] These parallel developments continue as Carter leaves the army and rises to the rank of leading contender for the middleweight title, but Carter finds himself imprisoned for a number of minor offenses and finally for life after being convicted of the triple murder. *Sixteenth Round* ends with Carter in prison and working on his latest appeal, the boxer as urban intellectual equipped by street life and his time in prison to analyze, fight against, and write about a social order that he sees as bent on the destruction of young black men.

Algren's *Devil's Stocking* found the same materials in Carter's story and in Paterson and New York that Algren had earlier found in Chicago's neighborhoods and in Pusan, Bombay, and Calcutta. *Devil's Stocking* entraps its characters in a narrow landscape: the male lead, Ruby Calhoun, a revitalized version of Frankie Machine, finds himself penned in by crooked police and the politics of race; his mistress Dovie-Jean, the female lead and a similar gloss on Molly Novotny, ends up marooned in a Times Square whorehouse. Ruby, the fictionalized Rubin Carter, is a naturalist brute rather than a formative urban intellectual. Loutish and vigorous, he moves almost blindly through an annihilating inner city and the prisons that express in purest form its constricting logic. *Devil's Stocking*, detailing the destruction of a regular guy rather than the formation of an urban intellectual, is in that sense closer to *Golden Arm* than to *Sixteenth Round* or *Manchild*. Returning to the novel form after a long hiatus, during which other writers developed generic formulae for representing the postindustrial city, Algren produced a novel that reads like a New Journalist's rewrite of *Native Son* (complete with extended trial scenes). He slots black inner-city types into the well-worn positions occupied by his old Polish subjects, positions nakedly exposed to the structuring forces of urban order. This generic compromise makes sense: Algren's standing interest in the theme of entrapment fit closely with canonical understandings of the second ghetto that had been formulated in the 1960s and developed into a large and various literature. In the end, the urban intellectual who emerges in *Devil's Stocking* is Algren, not Ruby Calhoun: Ruby's life might have been an exercise in constriction and futility, but the old urbanist was back to work.

Plenty of Algren's faithful readers regard *Devil's Stocking* as an embarrassing last spasm, but there were critical voices to endorse his return to the novel of the city. For instance, John Aldridge, writing in the *New York Times Book Review* in 1983, uses *Devil's Stocking* to elevate Algren above fellow Chicago realist James T. Farrell.[18] Both Algren and Farrell were recently deceased in 1983, and both had last novels in the bookstores. "[N]either gained significantly in reputation after the success of his early work," but Aldridge argued that Algren had adjusted his talents to the changing times with more success than Farrell, whose final novel, *Sam Holman*, is "a product of played-out energies, decrepit ideas and an evidently compulsive desire to perform the act of writing long after there existed anything authentic to be said." This sounds like a critical requiem for a "played-out," "decrepit" city of feeling built by Chicago neighborhood novelists in the 1930s and 1940s, in which Farrell apparently entombed himself and which Algren finally managed to depart, confirming "one's impression that Algren remained to the end the better writer" with "far richer verbal gifts . . . a much more vital relation with his materials . . . a larger and freer range of imaginative inventiveness." Aldridge reads *Devil's Stocking*, Algren's move into the narratives associated with "black America," as giving Algren's literary persona greater scope and continuing life. It makes Algren's imagination "more vital," "larger and freer." Algren becomes the more significant writer because his imagined city manifested both a richer historical life (from prewar slum to postwar ghetto) and a richer architecture of language than did Farrell's.

As Budd Schulberg did so swiftly in founding the Watts Writers' Workshop, the much less flexible and enterprising Algren eventually found a way to do what he had always done that also allowed for engagement with "black America," which became *the* urban subject in the mid-1960s and has enjoyed that status ever since. Algren, then, finally evolved a way to move in his original manner—via the novel—through the postindustrial city of feeling from which he had understood himself to be excluded in the 1960s. Like the Eastern European neighborhoods of the Milwaukee Avenue corridor, persistent relics of the industrial city that sustain the old ways even as they recede under newer urban orders and change through their interaction with those orders, Algren's writing entered the zone of overlap in which older and newer orders of urban literature engage with one another. *Devil's Stocking* descends on the one hand from *Golden Arm* and the Chicago realist tradition but on the other from

Sixteenth Round and the literature of the ghetto that developed *Manchild*'s generic outline.

In turn, *Manchild*, and the literature of urban crisis it surveys and anticipates, owes a debt to the Chicago neighborhood novelists, whose representational project it extends into the terrain of the postindustrial inner city. Claude Brown identifies Algren's old friend and fellow Chicago realist Richard Wright as his "literary idol," and Brown encapsulates Wright's influence on him in a story of *Manchild*'s genesis. Brown says that for six months after signing a contract with Macmillan he could not write a word but that he finally broke through the initial block and began to draft *Manchild* after happening across a copy of Wright's *Eight Men* in a Trailways bus station in Washington, D.C.:

> Wright was my literary idol, and I couldn't understand how I had missed that one [book by him]. I wanted to write like him, with the emotional impact, the force, the captivating impact. It's like, if I play a trumpet and I admire so and so; I don't want to play just *like* him, but I want my playing to have that same *effect*. . . . So, anyway, I couldn't understand how I had missed that one. I read it that night, and at 4:00 in the morning I put a clean sheet of paper in the typewriter and started writing *Manchild*.[19]

In Brown's story of literary succession, as in Stuart Dybek's nod to the possibilities for urban literature suggested by Algren, a Chicago realist provides a model for writers of the inner city to follow. Brown's work starts where Wright's work stops, the two oeuvres flowing together into one continuous effort to write the city. And if Brown's Harlem was part of an emergent urban world that Algren regarded as new and strange in the 1960s, Algren would probably find much that was familiar in the portrait of Harlem in decline that Brown has drawn in latter years.[20]

Algren, Brown, and the other writers of Chicago, Philadelphia, and New York I have discussed form an overlapping complex of persistences and successions. They wrote and rewrote the city of feeling as the postindustrial city of fact took new and compelling shape around them. When Algren described Chicago as "an October sort of city even in spring," he described the process of layering we can trace in the material cities the writers observed and the textual cities they created. When one set of urban orders declines, entering its autumnal or "October" phase, signs of the next round of urban orders begin to appear; one can see signs of the coming "spring." As these new orders mature into a new layer of urban development, survivals of the October city can be seen among the roots and in the interstices of the new, dominant orders. And, if one knows what to look for or enjoys the benefit of hindsight, one can see signs of an inevitable autumn to come, of a future decline, in even the most vigorous, expansive, permanent-seeming urban orders when they are in their springtime vigor. Despite Algren's choice of a natural metaphor, this figurative round of seasons is not an "ecological" process. Rather, the redevelopment of material and textual cities is the result of choices made by individuals, groups, and institutions: how to invest money and effort, what to build and what to publish, how to live and what to write, social policy and word choice. There is a literature of city life, and a history of it, in the shifting overlap of urban orders shaped by those choices.

Notes

Introduction

1. Nelson Algren, quoted in Bettina Drew, *Nelson Algren: A Life on the Wild Side* (Austin: University of Texas Press, 1989), 132.

2. Both "postindustrial" and "inner city" require further explanation. First, as opposed to the "post" in "postwar," which does describe the clear end of hostilities, the "post" in "postindustrial" does not imply that there are few or no manufacturers left in a city. It means, rather, that a city is in important ways no longer arranged primarily, as it once was, around manufacturing concerns and the kinds of social and spatial arrangements that tend to accompany them. The "post-" suggests a layering of new orders—a primary service economy, a revised structure of neighborhoods, a new political arrangement, and so on—over, rather than the eradication of, the industrial order. Second, the term "inner city" has an involved history of declining precision. Robert Park and other sociologists of the Chicago School were already using it in the 1920s to describe the oldest and most central parts of the industrial city, but it has since about 1960 taken on a number of indirect meanings: like the word "urban," it often serves as a vague semi-synonym of "ghetto," as well as of "black." I will use "inner city" to describe a particular social landscape that took shape in the postwar period at the center of the metropolis. Defined positively (and extremely oversimplified), "inner city" describes a complex of redeveloped downtowns, white ethnic and professional districts, black and Hispanic districts (further oversimplified as "ghettos" and "barrios"), and new immigrant districts typical of the postwar inner city and representations of it. That landscape tends to develop within the boundaries of the prewar industrial city, although at times it does extend to the inner ring of older suburbs. Defined negatively, then, the term "inner city" describes the part of the suburbanized metropolis that is not the suburbs: the inner city

is typically the part of this metropolis that falls within the political boundaries of the older industrial city.

3. I use "redevelopment" to describe a general process: the managed physical reshaping of cities designed to produce financial gain, political leverage, social change or stability, or other outcomes. I use "urban renewal" to describe a particular movement to redevelop the inner city: the national agenda emphasizing slum clearance, expanded transportation networks, and the revitalization of downtown business districts that dominated governmental conceptions and funding of redevelopment projects between the 1950s and early 1970s. Urban renewal was characterized by two deeply intertwined but ultimately opposed impulses: the drive, which eventually predominated, to encourage economic growth and stimulate business activity through reconfiguring the inner city; and the drive, powerfully discredited in public discourse by the early 1970s as a component of the Great Society agenda, to house people (especially poor people) and otherwise shape the inner city as a place of residence and community.

4. Hubert Saul, "Deep Down, Out of the Sun," review of *The Cool World* in *Saturday Review*, 13 June 1959, 40. For the analogy to *Uncle Tom's Cabin*, see Jeanette Wakin's interview with Warren Miller, which accompanied Saul's review in the *Saturday Review*, 18.

5. Robert Beauregard and Sharon Zukin have helped lead the way in studying the effect of discourse (Beauregard) and the symbolic economy (Zukin) on American cities in the postwar period. See, e.g., Beauregard, *Voices of Decline: The Postwar Fate of US Cities* (Cambridge: Blackwell, 1993), and Zukin, *The Cultures of Cities* (Cambridge: Blackwell, 1995).

6. The exclusion of Los Angeles by my focus on the Rust Belt requires at least a brief further acknowledgment of that city's importance in shaping postwar cities of feeling. Not only do many of the postwar period's most important urban narratives have special meaning for Los Angeles—black migration from the South and Southwest, the redeployment of government funds in the form of defense spending and subsidized suburbanization, the emergence of the service city, civil disorders large and small—but Los Angeles is a principal home terrain for both the movie industry and the hard-boiled detective tradition. Both the movies and the detective tradition (written and filmed) have provided some of the most important cultural equipment for creating the city of feeling.

7. I use terms like "black" and "white"—and within the category of "white" I use "white ethnic" and within that "Irish," "Polish," and so on—because these terms and others like them are used by the literature I study, and the people who read it, to organize their understandings of urbanism. I do this with the knowledge that such conventional labels, describing urban peoples in constant cultural and social motion, are in common usage because they elide more than they clarify. Applied to residents and neighborhoods of American inner cities, "Irish" is in some ways as reductive a fiction as "black" or "Southern black," but that is precisely why the terms have traditionally been of use in simplifying complexity, for good or ill (usually ill). I have not appended the suffix "American" to these terms, and I have not used "African American," for two reasons. First, the cumbersome suffix aspires to greater precision but does almost nothing to impart it. ("Black" and "Irish" strike me as more forthright and clean-edged fictions than "African American" and "Irish American.") Second, most of the people who wrote, read, and lived in the texts I analyze did not as a rule bother to append the suffix,

even when they bothered at all to use the more polite ethnic and racial labels made available to them.

Chapter 1

1. Nelson Algren, introduction to *The Neon Wilderness* (1947; reprint, New York: Hill and Wang, 1960), cited in Drew, *Nelson Algren*, 171.

2. The Doubleday advertisement appeared in the *New York Times Book Review*, 2 October 1949, 11.

3. Nelson Algren, *The Man with the Golden Arm* (1949; reprint, New York: Four Walls Eight Windows, 1990), 96. Subsequent references in the text.

4. Nelson Algren, *Chicago: City on the Make* (1951; reprint, Chicago: University of Chicago Press, 1983), 25–26. Subsequent references in the text.

5. Beauregard, *Voices of Decline*, 3, 109. In *Voices*, Beauregard definitively collects and analyzes the journalistic and policy literature of decline.

6. A. J. Liebling, *Chicago: The Second City* (New York: Knopf, 1952), 12.

7. Jack Lait and Lee Mortimer, *Chicago Confidential* (New York: Crown, 1950), 9.

8. Carl Sandburg, "Introduction, to Chicago," *Holiday*, October 1951, 33. *Holiday*, a handsome large-format travel magazine, devoted most of its October 1951 issue to a series of articles that together made a portrait of Chicago at midcentury. Noted contributors to the issue included Gwendolyn Brooks, the neighborhood novelist Albert Halper, Colonel McCormick (publisher of the *Tribune*), gossip columnist Irv Kupcinet, Robert Hutchins (president of the University of Chicago), and Nelson Algren. That Sandburg asked his "question that occurs" about the city's decline in his introduction to this issue made it clear that decline would be a principal theme, sometimes explicit and always implicit, of the articles that followed. The subtext of decline grated against a competing narrative of the city's continuing growth and physical vigor that took form around the monumental development of the Loop and North Side. The central figure of this story of growth was the skyline of skyscrapers. The troubled co-existence of these two narratives—one about the city of neighborhoods and the decrepitude of Sandburg's "tall bold slugger," one about the enduring vitality of the increasingly service-oriented urban core in a suburbanizing age—gave *Holiday*'s portrait of Chicago an edgier inner life than is typical of travel magazine features. A train of regrets and grievances cuts across the powerful generic tendency of the magazine toward a determinedly sunny tone and upward-curving narrative lines.

9. Carl Sandburg, "Chicago," in *Chicago Poems* (New York: Henry Holt, 1916), 3–4.

10. James T. Farrell, quoted in Lewis Fried, *Makers of the City* (Amherst: University of Massachusetts Press, 1990), 121.

11. Liebling, *Chicago*, 143.

12. This periodization acquired a continuing discursive life. A popular history of Chicago written in the 1970s, for instance, contains a chapter entitled "Golden Age" that deals in large part with "those twenty years following the fair" (1893–1913) that constituted "a golden age for the cultivated people of Chicago" in which great writers and other artists converged on the city in waves. The history, Finis Farr's *Chicago* (New Rochelle, N.Y.: Arlington House, 1973), closes with an Atlantean passage extending the logic of decline from the end of the golden age through the troubled present—all he

could say for the city of 1968 was that "one hoped it might survive"—to the very end: "All we can now write with certainty is that Chicago was wonderful in its time, and its story will be often repeated, until Lake Chicago comes back to cover the ruins, and the land falls silent under the sky" (400–401). Farr's history, like *City on the Make*, moves from consideration of larger-than-life characters in the golden age to an image of depopulated ruin.

13. Lait and Mortimer, *Chicago Confidential*, 8.

14. Ibid., 39–40.

15. Ibid., 50–51.

16. Liebling, *Chicago*, 12–13.

17. Ibid., 13.

18. There were dissenting midcentury arguments for the continuing vitality of postwar Chicago's literary culture. See, e.g., Albert Halper's foreword to *This Is Chicago: An Anthology*, ed. Albert Halper (New York: Henry Holt, 1952), vi; and Alson J. Smith, *Chicago's Left Bank* (Chicago: Henry Regnery, 1953). Smith argues that midcentury Chicago is entering a period of literary revival he dubs "the Algren Age."

19. Lait and Mortimer, *Chicago Confidential*, 8–9.

20. Liebling, *Chicago*, 81.

21. Some versions of this list, like that made by Doubleday advertisements for *Golden Arm* or by the novelist Albert Halper in his contribution to *Holiday*'s Chicago issue of October 1951 (53), stretched the definition of Chicago writer to near-meaninglessness by including Hemingway, who grew up in the suburb of Oak Park but did not work in Chicago or write about it. By contrast, the canonical list cited by Liebling, Lait and Mortimer, and Algren—among others—rarely included Gwendolyn Brooks, indisputably a "Chicago" writer (a matter taken up in chapter 4).

22. Liebling, *Chicago*, 81.

23. Nelson Algren, "The People of These Parts: A Survey of Modern Mid-American Letters," in *City on the Make*, 81. This essay was first published as an afterword to the two 1961 editions of *City on the Make* (Sausalito, Calif.: Contact Editions; and Oakland, Calif.: Angel Island Publications).

Chapter 2

1. Arthur Shay, *Nelson Algren's Chicago* (Urbana: University of Illinois Press, 1988), ix.

2. Saul Bellow, "The City That Was, the City That Is," *Life*, October 1983, 21.

3. Shay, *Nelson Algren's Chicago*, ix.

4. Ibid., xxi.

5. Gregory D. Squires, Larry Bennett, Kathleen McCourt, and Philip Nyden, *Chicago: Race, Class, and the Response to Urban Decline* (Philadelphia: Temple University Press, 1987), 98.

6. Carl S. Smith devotes a chapter to the railroad in the literature of industrial Chicago in *Chicago and the American Literary Imagination* (Chicago: University of Chicago Press, 1984), 101–20.

7. Squires et al., *Chicago*, 25–26.

8. For two very different and very thorough accounts of the growth of nineteenth-century Chicago, see William Cronon, *Nature's Metropolis: Chicago and the Great West*

(New York: Norton, 1991), and Donald Miller, *City of the Century: The Epic of Chicago and the Making of America* (New York: Simon and Schuster, 1996).

9. For an extended discussion of the post–Civil War effort to determine America's prototypical industrial city, from which Chicago emerged after 1893 as the consensus choice, see Sidney H. Bremer, *Urban Intersections: Meetings of Life and Literature in United States Cities* (Urbana: University of Illinois Press, 1992), 36–65.

10. Henry Claridge, "Chicago: 'The Classical Center of American Materialism,'" in *The American City: Literary and Cultural Perspectives*, ed. Graham Clarke (New York: St. Martin's Press, 1988), 86. The title of the essay is drawn from a remark made by Saul Bellow ("Interview with Saul Bellow," *TriQuarterly* 60 [Spring/Summer 1984]: 12).

11. Harold M. Meyer and Richard C. Wade, *Chicago: Growth of a Metropolis* (Chicago: University of Chicago Press, 1969), 30.

12. Bremer, *Urban Intersections*, 63.

13. Felix M. Padilla, *Puerto Rican Chicago* (Notre Dame, Ind.: University of Notre Dame Press, 1987), 100–101.

14. Squires et al., *Chicago*, 97.

15. Mike Royko, *Boss: Richard J. Daley of Chicago* (New York: New American Library, 1971), 30.

16. Ibid., 30–31.

17. Ibid., 31–32.

18. In *Chicago and the American Literary Imagination*, Carl S. Smith explores efforts by writers in the late nineteenth and early twentieth centuries to condense the form and meaning of the city into descriptions of the railroad, the large building, and the stockyards.

19. Squires et al., *Chicago*, 153.

20. Bremer's *Urban Intersections* and Smith's *Chicago and the American Literary Imagination* explore this process of establishing the terms for representing the industrial city. See also Carla Cappetti, *Writing Chicago: Modernism, Ethnography, and the Novel* (New York: Columbia University Press, 1993), which examines the cross-influences of literary and sociological representations.

21. H. L. Mencken, quoted in Hugh Dalziell Duncan, *The Rise of Chicago as a Literary Center from 1885 to 1920: A Sociological Essay in American Culture* (Totowa, N.J.: Bedminster Press, 1964), viii.

22. H. L. Mencken, quoted in Duncan, *Rise of Chicago*, viii.

23. Malcolm Cowley and Maxwell Geismar were particularly keen on Algren's prewar work. For more on critical reception of Algren, see Drew, *Nelson Algren*, esp. 142–43; and Martha Heasley Cox and Wayne Chatterton, *Nelson Algren* (Boston: Twayne, 1975).

24. Other Chicago neighborhood novelists of the period include Albert Halper, Meyer Levin, McKinlay Kantor, and Willard Motley.

25. Richard Wright, introduction to Nelson Algren, *Never Come Morning* (New York: Harper and Brothers, 1942), ix–x.

26. Each of these domestic, urban crises was also linked by various commentators to a parallel crisis in global relations. The domestic upheavals surrounding the juvenile delinquency panic of the 1950s were often traced to the anxieties of the Cold War, and more than one student of delinquency saw in the gang an instructive echo of fascist social dynamics. Similarly, the domestic upheavals of the urban crisis of the 1960s,

especially riots and street crime in Northern cities, were often linked to the Vietnam War as two facets of a general crisis in America's, or the world's, political and cultural order. One reason for Wright's continuing "relevancy" in the 1960s was his willingness to link his characters' anger to their historical situation.

27. Nelson Algren, quoted in H. E. F. Donohue, *Conversations with Nelson Algren* (New York: Hill and Wang, 1964), 154. I am indebted to Carla Cappetti's *Writing Chicago* for directing my attention to this quotation.

28. Nelson Algren, quoted in Drew, *Nelson Algren*, 117.

29. Farrell studied with Park, contributed minor studies to the Chicago School project (on dance marathons, for example), and wrote Chicago School figures into his novels: e.g., a public speaker offering sociological analysis of the slum appears on a street-corner in Studs Lonigan's neighborhood. See Farrell, *The Young Manhood of Studs Lonigan* (1934), in *Studs Lonigan* (Urbana: University of Illinois Press, 1993), 407–9. Wright stated unequivocally that his reading of sociology had enlarged and enriched his understanding of the position of black migrants like himself to the big city. Wright points out the convergences in the novelistic and sociological impulses to map black Chicago in his introduction to St. Clair Drake and Horace Cayton's *Black Metropolis: A Study of Negro Life in a Northern City* (1945; reprint, New York: Harper and Row, 1961), 1:xvii–xix. Beyond his professional and personal dealings with Wright, Farrell, and faculty of the University of Chicago like Louis Wirth, Algren studied sociology at the University of Illinois (before switching to journalism) and often described himself as pursuing a broadly "sociological" project.

30. Robert Park, "The City: Suggestions for the Investigation of Human Behavior in the Urban Environment," in *The City*, ed. Robert E. Park, Ernest W. Burgess, and Roderick D. McKenzie (Chicago: University of Chicago Press, 1925), 3.

31. Algren was trained as a journalist and in the 1960s took to calling himself a journalist. He did not write a novel between 1956 and the late 1970s, and that final novel, *The Devil's Stocking* (1983), originated as a nonfiction account of the travails of the boxer Rubin "Hurricane" Carter. See the conclusion of this study for more on *The Devil's Stocking*.

32. Squires et al., *Chicago*, 26–28. My portrait of postindustrial Chicago owes a good deal to this book, which, like the other volumes in Temple University Press's Comparative American Cities series, provides an excellent account of urban economics, politics, and social history after World War II.

33. John Mollenkopf, *The Contested City* (Princeton: Princeton University Press, 1983), 13.

34. Squires et al., *Chicago*, 26.

35. The population of the city proper grew 6.6% in the 1940s and declined 1.9% in the 1950s, while the population of the suburbs grew 32.7% in the 1940s and 71.5% in the 1950s. Between 1945 and 1960, 688,000 new houses were built in the Chicago area: 76% of them were single-family homes and 77% of them in the suburbs. These statistics are drawn from Squires et al., *Chicago*, 104.

36. Ibid., 26–27.

37. Ibid., 26.

38. Ibid., 158.

39. Ibid., 157.

40. Liebling, *Chicago*, 15.

41. Squires et al., *Chicago*, 105.

42. Martin Meyerson and Edward Banfield, *Politics, Planning, and the Public Interest: The Case of Public Housing in Chicago* (Glencoe, Ill.: Free Press, 1955), 30. Meyerson served as head of planning for the plan commission; Banfield became one of the most prominent urbanists of the postwar period.

43. Ibid., 19–20.

44. Meyer and Wade, *Chicago*, 406.

45. The definitive account of this process is in Arnold R. Hirsch, *Making the Second Ghetto: Race and Housing in Chicago, 1940–1960* (New York: Cambridge University Press, 1983).

46. It bears emphasizing that most of Chicago does not look like the area around the core. As one moves away from the Loop and the lakefront and into the neighborhoods, the lines and patches of monumental postwar development are fewer and further between in what remains a low-rise landscape, either of prewar vintage or on the prewar model. The high-rise projects, most of which were built between 1955 and 1965, were both a response to social change in the inner city and concrete examples, even causes, of that change. Driving south away from the Loop on the Dan Ryan Expressway, along which march for block after block the towers of the Robert Taylor Homes, one can see the landscape of the second ghetto in its pure form. As one moves out of the wide band of postwar construction concentrated in a semicircle around the Loop, however, it becomes apparent that much of the city has not been reconfigured so thoroughly. Farther out on the South Side and West Side, the concerns embodied in the Dan Ryan and the Robert Taylor Homes commanded less political leverage and less influence over funds in the downtown-centered politics and planning of the 1950s and 1960s.

47. On the popular and critical success of *Golden Arm*, see Drew, *Nelson Algren*, 209.

48. Leslie Fiedler argued that during the 1950s American literary culture moved from a prewar "Cult of Social Consciousness" to a more apolitical "New Personalism." See Leslie Fiedler, *Waiting for the End* (New York: Stein and Day, 1964), 36–42. For a second, sympathetic account of this shift, using Chicago realist Theodore Dreiser as an example, see Lionel Trilling, "Reality in America," in *The Liberal Imagination* (Garden City, N.Y.: Doubleday, 1953), 1–19. For later analyses of the turn away from "politics" in literary culture in the 1950s, see, e.g., Richard Ohmann with Carol Ohmann, "A Case Study in Canon Formation: Reviewers, Critics, and *The Catcher in the Rye*," in Richard Ohmann, *Politics of Letters* (Middletown, Conn.: Wesleyan University Press, 1987), 45–67; David Van Leer, "Society and Identity" in *The Columbia History of the American Novel*, ed. Emory Elliott (New York: Columbia University Press, 1991), 485–509. For parallel arguments about painting and music, see Erica Doss, "The Art of Cultural Politics: From Regionalism to Abstract Expressionism," and Lewis Erenburg, "Things to Come: Swing Bands, Bebop, and the Rise of the Postwar Jazz Scene," both in *Recasting America: Culture and Politics in the Age of Cold War*, ed. Lary May (Chicago: University of Chicago Press, 1989).

49. Nelson Algren, introduction to *Neon Wilderness*, quoted in Drew, *Nelson Algren*, 294–95.

50. Drew, *Nelson Algren*, 275. For a review of Algren's critical fortunes less sympa-

thetic to his self-conception but still largely sympathetic to Drew's argument, see Cappetti, *Writing Chicago*, 144–55.

51. Conrad Knickerbocker, "Scraping the Barnacles off Papa," review of *Notes from a Sea Diary*, by Nelson Algren, *Book Week*, 15 August 1965, 3. Knickerbocker lists "Norman [Mailer], Saul [Bellow], Jimmy [Jones], and Terry [Southern]" as current leading novelists, the idea being that these writers had usurped Algren's role as purveyor of antic representations of low life. The fact that this list includes Saul Bellow, who had lived in Chicago and set novels there, points to the extent to which Bellow, Chicago's most critically successful postwar novelist, was not generally identified with the Chicago tradition of "up-close" realism that Algren constructed for himself. Algren also argued that Bellow was not a Chicago writer in the sense that Algren was (see chapter 4 and the conclusion of this study).

52. Quoted in Nelson Algren, *Who Lost an American?* (New York: Macmillan, 1963), 252.

53. Drew, *Nelson Algren*, 253.

54. See, for instance, Charles Bowden and Lew Kreinberg, *Street Signs Chicago: Neighborhood and Other Illusions of Big-City Life* (Chicago: Chicago Review Press, 1981), an attack by two urbanists on various pieces of received Chicago myth that underlie the narrative of decline. "The city of neighborhoods was never about neighborhoods," they assert. "The city that worked was a bad place to work" (19).

55. For more on the decline and subsequent resurgences of the Chicago School, see M. Gottdiener, *The Social Production of Urban Space* (Austin: University of Texas Press, 1985), 27–41; Fred Matthews, *Quest for an American Sociology: Robert E. Park and the Chicago School* (Montreal: McGill-Queen's University Press, 1977), 179–89; and Harold Finestone, *Victims of Change: Juvenile Delinquents in American Society* (Westport, Conn.: Greenwood Press, 1976). Finestone also traces the Chicago School's continuing influence in the postwar study of delinquency.

56. See Studs Terkel, foreword to Algren, *City on the Make*, 5; and Rick Hornung, "The Hustler," *Village Voice Literary Supplement*, December 1990, 34. Terkel argues that Algren gave American literature early inklings of the suburban high school junkie and the "young black mugger"; Hornung argues that "forty years after Algren wrote his last Chicago novel, his characters still walk the streets" as "panhandlers or crackheads, homeless drifters or the 'hardcore unemployed.' . . . Years ago, when city life was supposed to be simpler, Algren warned us of the society we'd created."

57. Richard Brautigan, *Trout Fishing in America* (New York: Dell, 1967), 45–47.

58. Henry Louis Gates Jr., "Canon Confidential: A Sam Slade Caper," *New York Times Book Review*, 25 March 1990, 1, 36–38.

59. Padilla, *Puerto Rican Chicago*, 85–86.

60. Ibid., 144.

61. Connie Lauerman, "Growing Pains," *Chicago Tribune Magazine*, 18 October 1992, 13.

62. Ibid.

Chapter 3

1. Theodore Dreiser, *Sister Carrie* (1900; reprint, New York: Oxford University Press, 1991), 13.

2. Algren, *Man with the Golden Arm*, 96. Subsequent references in the text.

3. Liebling, *Chicago*, 143.

4. One of the most arresting of these laments, a particularly anguished version of white-ethnic decline in which prosperity and WASPs are the villains, is Michael Novak, *The Rise of the Unmeltable Ethnics* (New York: Macmillan, 1972).

5. Bettina Drew, *Nelson Algren*, 152, reaches a similar conclusion about the development of Algren's character system from text to text, tracing a progression from concern with "adolescence, juvenile delinquency, and the forming of personality" toward more adult characters and social environments.

6. One black character does appear north of the Lake Street ghetto. He is a bouncer in a Jewish gambling house and has no contact with Frankie's Polish neighborhood except in that capacity.

7. For an account of fear, violence, and other upheavals in the white-ethnic neighborhood order occasioned by the expansion of black Chicago, see Hirsch, *Making the Second Ghetto*, esp. 45–47.

8. Robert Herrick's *The Web of Life* (New York: Macmillan, 1900) and Alexander Saxton's *The Great Midland* (New York: Appleton-Century-Crofts, 1948) form another such complementary pair, although less obviously. *Web of Life* narrates the disillusionments and growth of a young, University of Chicago–trained doctor and is set against the backdrop of a railroad strike. *Great Midland* reverses the main narrative line and subplot, moving its University of Chicago story to the background and its railroad story to the foreground. Both novels use railroad imagery to schematize Chicago, and Saxton's railroad is similar to Algren's El in that it contains Chicago's geography and intimidates the novel's characters; finally, two cars couple through the body of one character, making literal the kinds of impalements and crucifixions Algren's El figuratively threatens.

9. Dreiser, *Sister Carrie*, 7. Subsequent references in the text.

10. Philip Fisher, *Hard Facts: Setting and Form in the American Novel* (New York. Oxford University Press, 1985), 129.

11. Wright, introduction to Algren, *Never Come Morning*, x.

12. See, e.g., Farrell, *Studs Lonigan*, 538–46; and Richard Wright, *Lawd Today* (1963; reprint, Boston: Northeastern University Press, 1986), 48–50.

13. Algren, *City on the Make*, 67, 75.

14. The prose poem has become a form used to position a literary persona in the inmost ring of the Chicago canon. Studs Terkel's bid for such inclusion takes the form of a slim volume clearly and admittedly derived from Algren's *City on the Make*. Terkel urges us to consider his *Chicago* (New York: Pantheon, 1986) as "a long epilogue to what is still the classic tribute to a city, Nelson Algren's *Chicago: City on the Make*" (131) and includes as an afterword to his own *Chicago* the foreword he wrote for the 1983 edition of *City on the Make* cited throughout this book. For a commentary on the prose poem form (itself in the form of a prose poem), see Dave Etter, "Chicago," in *TriQuarterly* 60 (Spring/Summer 1984): 319–21.

Chapter 4

1. Gerald D. Suttles, *The Man-Made City: The Land-Use Confidence Game in Chicago* (Chicago: University of Chicago Press, 1990), 250.

2. Algren, *Who Lost an American?* 278.

3. Ibid., 285.
4. Suttles, *Man-Made City*, 249.
5. Algren, *City on the Make*, 54.
6. Algren, *Who Lost an American?* 275.
7. "What about Saul Bellow?" one might also ask. He might seem a likely candidate for Algren to recognize as a Chicago writer at midcentury. Only a few years younger than Algren, Bellow had grown up in an urban village near Humboldt Park, within walking distance of the Polish Triangle. (He and Algren "grew up in the same Division Street neighborhood," Bellow told an interviewer [John Blades, "Bellow's Last Chapter," *Chicago Tribune Sunday Magazine*, 19 June 1994, 8], despite the fact that Algren did not grow up there.) By midcentury, Bellow had published two well-received novels, *Dangling Man* (1944) and *The Victim* (1947), and excerpts from a third, *The Adventures of Augie March*. In 1951, when Algren argued in *City on the Make* that there were no more Chicago writers left, Algren had known of Bellow for a decade, having worked with him for the Illinois Writers' Project. Yet Algren does not see Bellow as breaking the monotony of the cultural desert he envisions in *City on the Make*.

When Algren passed him over in *City on the Make*, Bellow did not yet have the reputation of a "Chicago" writer. He had not yet published *The Adventures of Augie March* (1953), the big book about a picaro from Chicago's urban villages that gained him widespread recognition as an important postwar writer. More important, Bellow did not necessarily fit Algren's model of a Chicago writer. Bellow's first two books, closely observed little novels of ideas, seemed to show as much affinity for Henry James as they might for Dreiser. Also, Bellow was already launched as a university-based intellectual on the postwar model, willing and able to engage literary critics and scholars on their own terms, and he was on the way to becoming a favorite of the same critics who were losing patience with Algren—which meant to Algren that something had to be wrong with him.

When Algren did begin writing about Bellow in later years, it was to dismiss him as a precious, derivative academician (see the conclusion of this study). That makes sense, because after the publication of *Augie March* in 1953 Bellow was widely celebrated as a Chicago writer, but his achievement was generally supposed to be that he and his characters transcended the urban village, surviving its dissolution while partaking of its essence. They are, in Gerald Suttles's paraphrase of Alfred Kazin, "modern men who have escaped the tribalism of Chicago" (Suttles, *Man-Made City*, 250). *Augie March* starts with all the elements of a neighborhood decline—a poor family, hard times, a narrow landscape—but parlays them into a wildly expansive account that takes flight from the neighborhood on its way to the suburbs, New York, Mexico, Paris, and encounters with the rich, famous, and educated. *Augie March* is not a neighborhood novel, and it is not about decline: it is about what comes after, and beyond, the old neighborhood.

Bellow *has* over the years told his own version of Chicago's literary decline, but the point is always to identify the Chicago realist tradition as one influence among several, not to portray himself as the last of a dying breed. Bellow therefore concedes to Algren the status of the last of the prewar writers: "There used to be, in the old days, something called a 'Chicago school,'" he told an interviewer in 1973, then recited the familiar story of a mass exodus to Hollywood and New York, leaving Chicago a literary backwater by midcentury. Having decided that Chicago is "lacking in culture fundamentally," he quoted Algren on the writer's "unrequited love affair with the city" (Gloria L. Cronin and Ben Siegel, eds., *Conversations with Saul Bellow* [Jackson: University Press of Mississippi, 1994], 104–6). Bellow is trying to explain here that Chicago is typically American, but he is also shoveling dirt on the grave of Algren's literary tradition. "What a good idea it seemed during the Depression to write about American life," he exclaims in an essay, "and to do with Chicago (or Manhattan or Minneapolis) what Arnold Bennett had done with Five Towns or H. G. Wells with London." Of course, he concludes, "Highly finished works of art were not produced by American and British writers like Dreiser in the Midwest, or Arnold Bennett and H. G. Wells in provincial England" (Bellow, *It All Adds Up: From the Dim Past to the Uncertain Future* [New York: Viking, 1994], 118). Enter Bellow, to provide the "highly finished" work; exit Algren, a tribal Chicagoan, a Chicago writer (with all the resonances of unpolished style and depression-era mustiness that Bellow seems to associate with the term) who had not managed to negotiate the transition to life after the urban village.

8. Algren, *City on the Make*, 55.

9. Algren, *Man with the Golden Arm*, 319–20.

10. Algren, *City on the Make*, 53–54.

11. See Drew, *Nelson Algren*, 101.

12. Brooks returned the favor by pushing the Illinois Arts Council to give Algren a $6,000 cash award. See Brooks, *Report from Part One* (Detroit: Broadside Press, 1972), 77–78, 109.

13. Algren, *City on the Make*, 105. The line appears in "People of These Parts."

14. Drake and Cayton, *Black Metropolis*, 2:755.

15. Gwendolyn Brooks, "Life for My Child Is Simple, and Is Good," in *Blacks* (Chicago: David Company, 1987), 120. This collection contains the books *A Street in Bronzeville* (1945) and *Annie Allen* (1949). All quotations from Brooks's poetry originally appeared in these books, but citations are to the 1987 collection *Blacks*.

16. Gwendolyn Brooks, "Kitchenette Building," in *Blacks*, 20.

17. Gwendolyn Brooks, "Of De Witt Williams on His Way to Lincoln Cemetery," in *Blacks*, 39.

18. Gwendolyn Brooks, "The Birth in a Narrow Room," in *Blacks*, 83.

19. Algren, *City on the Make*, 10.

20. Gwendolyn Brooks, "Men of Careful Turns, Haters of Forks in the Road," in *Blacks*, 139.

21. Ibid., 140.

22. Nelson Algren, "Ode to Lower Finksville," in *Chicago: City on the Make* (Oakland, Calif.: Angel Island Publications, 1961), 144–45.

23. Mike Royko, "Algren's Golden Pen," *Chicago Sun-Times*, 13 May 1981, reprinted in Mike Royko, *Sez Who? Sez Me* (New York: E. P. Dutton, 1982), 233–36.

24. Royko is known as a consummate newspaper writer, a maker of short sentences devoid of the purple touches to which other columnists are prone, but he offers formal nods to the considerably more ornate prose of Algren. Chapter 6 of *Boss*, for instance, begins with the line "The desk sergeant was drunk" (107). The chapter's opening anecdote frames an account of the astoundingly bald-faced corruption of Chicago's police force and Daley's efforts to contain police scandals, but it also gestures to the opening of Algren's *Golden Arm*, which begins with the line "The captain never drank." It may

seem an innocuous resonance, but for a writer who publicly places himself in Algren's debt, "The captain never drank" has the referential heft of "Call me Ishmael": one does not casually echo the opening. The corrupt captain provides the template for the corrupt sergeant, much as Algren provided a template of Chicago writing for Royko. (I am indebted to Sebastian Rotella, a reporter who knows how to slip literary references into the newspaper, for calling my attention to Royko's gesture of homage.)

25. Mike Royko, "San-Fran-York on the Lake," *Chicago Daily News* (no date available), reprinted in Mike Royko, *I May Be Wrong, but I Doubt It* (Chicago: Henry Regnery, 1968), 3–6.

26. Mike Royko, "Why I Moved to the Lakefront," *Chicago Sun-Times*, 22 November 1981, reprinted in Mike Royko, *Like I Was Sayin'* . . . (New York: Berkley, 1985 [1984]), 177–81.

27. Royko skewers Michael Novak, whose *Rise of the Unmeltable Ethnics* is an earnest, humid account of white-ethnic golden age and decline, in his column "The Sensuous Ethnic, by N.," *Chicago Daily News*, 2 September 1971.

28. Royko, *Boss*, 32. Royko's reading of the old neighborhood in *Boss*, now twenty-five years old, renews its ironic charge when read against a recent narrative of decline, Alan Ehrenhalt's *The Lost City: Discovering the Forgotten Virtues of Community in the Chicago of the 1950s* (New York: Basic Books, 1995). Ehrenhalt joins other contemporary observers, usually on the political right, who have taken to regarding the 1950s as the last period of healthy urbanism in America. Ehrenhalt treats Chicago's neighborhood order of the 1950s, still sustaining the momentum of the urban village but also buoyed by the same postwar prosperity that would help to break up industrial urbanism, as the site of an exemplary golden age that collapsed in a terrible fall during the 1960s.

29. Royko, *Boss*, 126.

30. Richard J. Daley, quoted in *Quotations from Mayor Daley*, ed. Peter Yessne (New York: Pocket Books, 1969), 124. Stuart Dybek uses a version of the line—"we shall rise to new platitudes"—in his story "Blight," discussed in this chapter.

31. "The Writer in Chicago: A Roundtable," *TriQuarterly* 60 (Spring/Summer 1984): 337.

32. The knife sharpener is in "Nighthawks," in Stuart Dybek, *The Coast of Chicago* (New York: Knopf, 1990), 85; the restaurant is in "Sauerkraut Soup," in Stuart Dybek, *Childhood and Other Neighborhoods* (New York: Viking, 1980), 122–38.

33. Stuart Dybek, "Blight," in *The Coast of Chicago*, 42–44.

34. Ibid., 49–50.

35. Ibid., 54.

36. James T. Fisher, "Clearing the Streets of the Catholic Lost Generation," *South Atlantic Quarterly* 93 (1994): 603–29.

37. Dybek, "Blight," 69–70.

38. Ibid., 69.

39. Ibid., 48.

40. The grandmother is in Isabel Allende's *The House of the Spirits*, but Dybek points out (in a letter to the author, 25 April 1996) that his own grandmother also did not observe much distinction between the living and the dead—both were liable to come visiting. He suggests that the "strong parallels" between the mysticisms of Old World

folklore and New World syncretism help explain his affinity for Latin American magical realism when he did encounter it.

41. Algren, *Golden Arm*, 62.

42. Ibid., 99.

43. Dybek, "Blight," 71.

44. Algren, *Golden Arm*, 97.

45. Algren, *City on the Make*, 74.

Chapter 5

1. I have borrowed the term "contact zone" from Mary Louise Pratt (see her *Imperial Eyes: Travel Writing and Transculturation* [New York: Routledge, 1992], 6–7), but I use it in a more limited sense than she does. I do not propose an analogy between South Street and the colonial frontiers she studies; I do wish to retain her emphasis on "co-presence, interaction, interlocking understandings and practices, often within radically asymmetrical relations of power"—conditions produced in encounters between neighborhoods as well as nations.

2. Philadelphia City Planning Commission, *The Plan for Center City Philadelphia* (Philadelphia: City Planning Commission, 1963), 26.

3. That body of work includes seminal urban research by Erving Goffman, John Szwed, Eli Anderson, Jonathan Rubinstein, and, to extend the line back to the era of the Chicago School, W. E. B. Du Bois.

4. See, for instance, Dennis Clark, "'Ramcat' and Rittenhouse Square: Related Communities," in *The Divided Metropolis: Social and Spatial Dimensions of Philadelphia, 1800–1975,* ed. William W. Cutler III and Howard Gilette Jr. (Westport, Conn.: Greenwood Press, 1980), 125–40.

5. I asked two of the three living South Street authors discussed in part 2 if they had read any of the other South Street novels. David Bradley said he did not read William Gardner Smith's *South Street* until after his own *South Street* had been published. Diane McKinney-Whetstone said she had read Bradley but not Smith and that Bradley left little impression on her. Neither had read or heard of Dunphy.

6. Two much-publicized incidents in Grays Ferry in early 1997 ushered in a new chapter in the continuing postwar history of racially inflected violence in the South Street milieu. In February, a group of white men leaving an Irish social club in Grays Ferry assaulted a black woman and her teenage son. Eight of them were charged with "ethnic intimidation." A month later, two black men shot and killed a sixteen-year-old white man during a drugstore robbery. Police decided that this was not a racially motivated crime, but many whites in the neighborhood assumed the killing was in retaliation for the earlier assault. Blacks and whites turned to the same cultural forms—editorials, rallies, phone calls to radio talk shows—to contest the meanings of the two assaults, and nearly identical charges of "hate crime" were made from all quarters. Mayor Ed Rendell and various national figures were eventually drawn into the continuing cultural engagement at close quarters of blacks and whites in the streets below South.

7. Philadelphia City Planning Commission, *Plan for Center City Philadelphia*, 7.

8. Philadelphia City Planning Commission, *Comprehensive Plan: The Physical*

Development Plan for the City of Philadelphia (Philadelphia: City Planning Commission, 1960), ix.

9. Ibid., 13.

10. The Philadelphia Standard Metropolitan Statistical Area includes Philadelphia, Delaware, Chester, Montgomery, and Bucks counties in Pennsylvania and Gloucester, Camden, and Burlington counties in New Jersey.

11. Philadelphia City Planning Commission, *Comprehensive Plan*, 13.

12. Philadelphia City Planning Commission, *Center City Plan*, 10.

13. Philadelphia City Planning Commission, *Comprehensive Plan*, 25.

14. Philadelphia City Planning Commission, *Center City Plan*, 7.

15. Urban renewal projects, a crucial glue binding together this Democratic alliance in the 1950s, also contributed to its dissolution in the 1960s. Battles over the distribution and execution of projects exacerbated internal conflicts among the alliance's constituent interests. The Crosstown Expressway plan set various blocs of business activists, planners, political and financial entrepreneurs, a largely black population of inner-city residents, and the heavily white-ethnic Democratic machine against one another in a microcosm of the postwar Democratic Party's fragmentation in the 1960s.

16. On Philadelphia's reform-planning complex, see Carolyn Adams et al., *Philadelphia: Neighborhoods, Division, and Conflict in a Postindustrial City* (Philadelphia: Temple University Press, 1991), 101–23; Carolyn Adams, "Philadelphia: The Private City in the Post-Industrial Era," in *Snowbelt Cities: Metropolitan Politics in the Northeast and Midwest since World War II*, ed. Richard M. Bernard (Bloomington: Indiana University Press, 1990), 209–26; John F. Bauman, *Public Housing, Race, and Renewal: Urban Planning in Philadelphia, 1920–1974* (Philadelphia: Temple University Press, 1987), 118–43. I am indebted to these three analyses in particular for my understanding of postindustrial South Philadelphia and the forces shaping its physical circumstances.

17. Adams, "Philadelphia," 213.

18. Adams et al., *Philadelphia*, 116.

19. Ibid., 81, and 39–40.

20. Mollenkopf, *Contested City*, 13.

21. Adams et al., *Philadelphia*, 79.

22. Gladstone Associates, *South Central Project Area; Philadelphia, Pennsylvania; Phase One Submission*, July 1972, 90–92. Gladstone Associates, a Washington, D.C., consulting firm, conducted interviews of merchants and residents in the vicinity of South Street as part of a study evaluating the Crosstown plan. The report is in the archives of Philadelphia's Department of City Planning.

23. Edmund Bacon, *Design of Cities* (New York: Viking, 1967), 243.

24. Among Philadelphia's main service industries are financial services, education, health, and real estate.

25. Philadelphia City Planning Commission, *Center City Plan*, 32.

26. In *Mermaids, Monasteries, Cherokees, and Custer: The Stories behind Philadelphia Street Names* (Chicago: Bonus Books, 1990), 211, Robert Alotta notes that South Street was originally named Cedar Street but that it was "commonly known as South as early as 1707" and officially renamed in 1853.

27. Gladstone Associates, *South Central Project Area*, 16–17.

28. Denise Scott Brown, *Urban Concepts* (New York: St. Martin's Press, 1990), 34.

29. Robert Venturi, Denise Scott Brown, and Steven Izenour, *Learning from Las Vegas* (Cambridge, Mass.: MIT Press, 1972), 126.

30. Gladstone Associates, *South Central Project Area*, 3–9.

31. I am indebted for my understanding of the long and intricate Crosstown dispute—sketched here in only the broadest terms—to Denise Scott Brown (interview with the author, 11 December 1992) and to Michelle Osborn's excellent, concise account of it in "The Crosstown Is Dead Long Live the Crosstown?" *Architectural Forum* 135, no. 3 (October 1971): 38–41.

32. Osborn ("Crosstown," 40) mentions the Kerner Commission's popularization of the term "institutional racism" and the growing vogue in planning circles for "community participation." For an early summation of the critique of urban renewal, see *Urban Renewal: The Record and the Controversy*, ed. James Q. Wilson (Cambridge, Mass.: MIT Press, 1966).

33. Mitchell and the 1970 consultants' study (conducted by Alan M. Voorhees and Associates), quoted in Osborn, "Crosstown," 40–41.

34. Brown, interview, 11 December 1992.

35. Venturi, Brown, and Izenour, *Learning from Las Vegas*, 126–33; Brown, interview, 11 December 1992.

36. Brown, *Urban Concepts*, 34.

37. Martin Meyerson, foreword to Kirk Petshek, *The Challenge of Urban Reform* (Philadelphia: Temple University Press, 1973), xi. For further treatments of Philadelphia as an example of urban reform and revitalization, see Jeanne R. Lowe, *Cities in a Race with Time: Progress and Poverty in America's Renewing Cities* (New York: Random House, 1967), 313–404; David B. Carlson, "Downtown's Dramatic Comeback," *Architectural Forum* 120, no. 2 (February 1964): 98–103; "Urban Renewal: Remaking the American City," *Time*, 6 November 1964, esp. 69–71; "A City's Future Takes Shape," *Life*, 24 December 1965, 168–74; "Does the American City Have a Future" (special issue), *Saturday Review*, 8 January 1966, esp. 48 and 98.

Chapter 6

1. For Smith on Wright's "wooden, Dreiser-esque" style, see LeRoy S. Hodges, *Portrait of an Expatriate: William Gardner Smith, Writer* (Westport, Conn.: Greenwood Press, 1985), 22.

2. Gerald Clarke, *Capote: A Biography* (New York: Simon and Schuster, 1988), 190.

3. Dunphy published five novels after *John Fury*, his first: *Friends and Vague Lovers* (New York: Farrar, Straus, 1952), *Nightmovers* (New York: Morrow, 1968), *An Honest Woman* (New York: Random House, 1971), *First Wine* (Baton Rouge: Louisiana State University Press, 1982), and *The Murderous McLaughlins* (New York: McGraw Hill, 1988). He also wrote *Dear Genius: A Memoir of My Life with Truman Capote* (New York: McGraw Hill, 1987).

4. William Gardner Smith, *Return to Black America* (Englewood Cliffs, N.J.: Prentice Hall, 1970), 6, 28–33.

5. For more on William Gardner Smith's biography, see Hodges, *Portrait of an Expatriate*. Smith's four novels are *Last of the Conquerors* (New York: Farrar, Straus, 1948), *Anger at Innocence* (New York: Farrar, Straus, 1950), *South Street* (New York: Farrar, Straus and Young, 1954), and *The Stone Face* (New York: Farrar, Straus, 1963).

6. The street name is spelled "Seigal" in *John Fury*, but the street in the novel closely resembles the western end of Sigal Street in South Philadelphia.

7. Jack Dunphy, *John Fury* (New York: Harper and Brothers, 1946), 269. Subsequent references in the text.

8. For historical material on Irish South Philadelphia, see Murray Dubin, *South Philadelphia: Mummers, Memories, and the Melrose Diner* (Philadelphia: Temple University Press, 1996), 15–37; and Clark, "'Ramcat' and Rittenhouse Square: Related Communities," 125–40.

9. Dunphy, *John Fury*, n.p., preceding p. 1.

10. For more on Irish industrial urbanism as a literary subject, on Farrell's domination of that literature, and on Farrell's central role in Irish-American literary history, see Charles Fanning, *The Irish Voice in America: Irish-American Fiction from the 1760s to the 1980s* (Lexington: University Press of Kentucky, 1990), esp. 257–357.

11. Dunphy acknowledges Stein's influence in a note on the jacket of *John Fury*.

12. James T. Farrell, "The Story of a Simple Man," review of *John Fury*, *Saturday Review*, 9 November 1946, 31.

13. Jack Conroy, "The American Irish Circa 1900," review of *John Fury*, *Chicago Sun Book Week*, 8 December 1946, 8.

14. Bauman, *Public Housing, Race, and Renewal*, gives a complete account of conflicts over race and housing in postwar Philadelphia.

15. Smith, *South Street*, 92. Subsequent references in the text.

16. For more on Smith's views of Wright, Himes, and the Negro writer's duty to avoid social detachment, especially during moments of social crisis, see William Gardner Smith, "The Negro Writer: Pitfalls and Compensations," *Phylon* 11 (1950): 297–303.

17. On the ethnic heterogeneity of this stretch of postwar South Street, see Gladstone Associates, *South Central Project Area*, 1–36, 68–104, Appendixes 1–4.

18. Smith, *Return to Black America*, 35; Sol Yurick, *The Warriors* (New York: Holt, Rhinehart and Winston, 1965).

19. Philadelphia City Planning Commission, *Comprehensive Plan*, v.

20. Philadelphia City Planning Commission, *Center City Plan*, 26.

21. As an educated, artistic, and interracial couple, they would, along with homosexuals, be typical "urban pioneers." For more on urban pioneers as a group, see John A. Jakle and David Wilson, *Derelict Landscapes: The Wasting of America's Built Environment* (Savage, Md.: Rowman and Littlefield, 1992), 228.

22. For an identical periodization of urban life, see Edward Hoagland, "Violence, Violence," in *Reading the Fights*, ed. Joyce Carol Oates and Daniel Halpern (New York: Prentice Hall, 1988), 61–63. Hoagland tells a story of American decline as a movement from the rigorous and controlled violence of boxing, "a very nineteenth century" practice "*from the era of cart horses in the street*," to the late 1960s' "crushing, befuddling climate of general violence" typified by the war in Vietnam, "*racial-college riots*," and urban crime (my italics).

23. Philadelphia City Planning Commission, *Center City Plan*, 32.

Chapter 7

1. For an argument as to the greater "maturity" of *The Chaneysville Incident* (which

won the 1982 Pen/Faulkner Prize), see Valerie Smith, "David Bradley," in *Afro-American Fiction Writers after 1955*, ed. Thadious M. Davis and Trudier Harris III (Detroit: Gale Research, 1984), 28–32.

2. Dexter has told the story of his beating and its relation to his writing many times over the years. For a concise version, see "Pete Dexter," in *Contemporary Authors*, v. 131, ed. Susan M. Trotsky (Detroit: Gale Research, 1991), 144, 146.

3. Diane McKinney-Whetstone supplied the details of her biography in an interview with the author, 11 July 1996.

4. Bradley says he did not read Smith's novel until after his own had been written and published (interview with the author, 11 December 1992).

5. David Bradley, *South Street* (New York: Viking, 1975), 5. Subsequent references in the text.

6. In at least one later edition of *South Street* (New York: Scribner, 1986), Bradley changed the cross street of the intersection of Grays Ferry and South from Twenty-second to Twenty-third (which is in fact the cross street of that three-way intersection in Philadelphia). I take this as a sign that the writer of socially observant urban literature, no matter how imaginative, acknowledges a responsibility to the city of fact to get things "right."

7. Valerie Smith, "David Bradley," 28.

8. William Gardner Smith, *South Street*, 21.

9. David Bradley, quoted in Valerie Smith, "David Bradley," 28.

10. Nelson Algren, quoted in W. J. Weatherby, "The Last Interview," in Nelson Algren, *The Devil's Stocking* (New York: Arbor House, 1983), 9. See my conclusion for more on this novel and Algren's writing of the black inner city.

11. Albert Murray, *The Omni-Americans* (New York: Outerbridge and Dienstfrey, 1970), esp. 97–112, 121–41. I discuss Murray's criticism at greater length in chapter 10.

12. Roger D. Abrahams, *Deep Down in the Jungle . . . : Negro Narrative Folklore from the Streets of Philadelphia* (Hatboro, Penn.: Folklore Associates, 1964).

13. Will Nixon, "David Bradley," *Poets and Writers*, July/August 1990, 30.

14. Bradley is unimpressed by the notion of a uniquely African American oral tradition derived from African roots. "Every fucking culture known to man, woman, and child has an oral tradition. To talk about the African oral tradition and ignore *Beowulf* is to pretend that Negroes are somehow doing something that Celts, Franks—wherever you lived—didn't, and that's ridiculous." Bradley, quoted in Nixon, "David Bradley," 31.

15. Bradley, interview, 11 December 1992.

16. Pete Dexter, *God's Pocket* (New York: Warner Books, 1983), 62 and 9. Subsequent references in the text.

17. The high-rise housing in the South Philadelphia of fact to which *God's Pocket* refers is called Southwark Plaza, not Southwark Homes.

18. Algren, *City on the Make*, 23.

19. Diane McKinney-Whetstone, *Tumbling* (New York: William Morrow, 1996), 340. Subsequent references in the text.

Chapter 8

1. Warren Miller, "One Score in Harlem," review of Claude Brown, *Manchild in the Promised Land, Saturday Review*, 28 August 1965, 49.

2. For a bibliographic listing of the vast literature about black Americans produced during the 1960s, see *The Negro in America: A Bibliography*, 2d ed., ed. Elizabeth W. Miller and Mary L. Fisher (Cambridge, Mass.: Harvard University Press, 1970).

3. "Death of an Author," *Newsweek*, 9 May 1966, 106–7.

4. Warren Miller, quoted in Jeanette Wakin, interview with Warren Miller, *Saturday Review*, 13 June 1959, 18.

5. Warren Miller, *The Cool World* (1959; reprint, Greenwich, Conn.: Fawcett Publications, 1960), 149–50.

6. Kenneth Clark's *Dark Ghetto: Dilemmas of Social Power* (New York: Harper and Row, 1965) and *Manchild* have often been cited in tandem, typically to set the stage for discussions of Harlem or ghettos in general. For examples of such linked citations, see John S. Adams, "The Geography of Riots and Civil Disorders," in *Black America: Geographic Perspectives*, ed. Robert T. Ernst and Lawrence Hugg (Garden City, N.Y.: Doubleday, 1976), 277–79; Michael N. Danielson and Jameson W. Doig, *New York: The Politics of Urban Regional Development* (Berkeley: University of California Press, 1982), 52–54; Thomas Vietorisz and Bennett Harrison, *The Economic Development of Harlem* (New York: Praeger, 1970), 3–9.

7. Frances Carol Locher, ed., *Contemporary Authors*, vols. 73–76 (Detroit: Gale Research, 1978), 88–89.

8. The description of urban blacks as "a misplaced people" is in Claude Brown, *Manchild in the Promised Land* (1965; reprint, New York: New American Library, 1966), vii.

9. Review of *Manchild in the Promised Land, Newsweek*, 27 December 1965, 73.

Chapter 9

1. Beauregard, *Voices of Decline*, 169.

2. Zukin, *Cultures of Cities*, 39. Zukin uses the phrase "institutionalization of fear" to describe a general tendency on the part of the state and corporate capital to abandon the War on Poverty, to choose fortification of social barriers over any effort to ameliorate poverty or otherwise manage thoroughgoing social change. I have extended the term here (an extension she might well not endorse) to also embrace those criticisms from the left that institutionalized in urban discourse the fear of the police felt by residents of the ghetto, explaining that fear as a logical effect of racial conflict between a white ruling class and a black underclass.

3. Beauregard, *Voices of Decline*, 172.

4. *Report of the National Advisory Commission on Civil Disorders* (New York: New York Times Company, 1968), 1.

5. Ibid., 10.

6. Kwame Ture [Stokely Carmichael] and Charles V. Hamilton, *Black Power: The Politics of Liberation in America* (1967; reprint, New York: Random House, 1992), 162.

7. James de Jongh, *Vicious Modernism: Black Harlem and the Literary Imagination* (Cambridge: Cambridge University Press, 1990), 145.

8. John Hull Mollenkopf, "The Postindustrial Transformation of the Political Order in New York City," in *Power, Culture, and Place: Essays on New York City*, ed. John Hull Mollenkopf (New York: Russell Sage Foundation, 1988), 223.

9. Norman I. Fainstein, Susan S. Fainstein, and Alex Schwartz, "Economic Shifts

and Land Use in the Global City: New York, 1940–1987," in *Atop the Urban Hierarchy*, ed. Robert Beauregard (Totowa, N.J.: Rowman and Littlefield, 1989), 51–53.

10. See, e.g., the summary account of Moses's reputation in *New York 1960: Architecture and Urbanism between the Second World War and the Bicentennial*, ed. Robert Λ. M. Stern, Thomas Mellin, and David Fishman (New York: Monacelli Press, 1995), 37–46; Robert Caro, *The Power Broker* (New York: Alfred A. Knopf, 1974); Marshall Berman, *All That Is Solid Melts into Air* (New York: Simon and Schuster, 1982); and Joel Schwartz, *The New York Approach: Robert Moses, Urban Liberals, and Redevelopment of the Inner City* (Columbus: Ohio State University Press, 1993).

11. Jason Epstein, "The Last Days of New York," in *The Fiscal Crisis of American Cities*, ed. Roger Alcaly and David Mermelstein (New York: Random House, 1976), 63.

12. Ibid., 60–61.

13. New York City Planning Commission, *Plan for New York City* (New York: New York City Planning Commission, 1969), 1:5.

14. Ibid.

15. The ethnographic literature dealing with the urban "white ethnics"—also lumped together during the postwar period as "Catholics," hardhats, white backlash, and Nixon's Silent Majority—is vast and various. One might begin with three books covering the three cities treated in this study: on Chicago, William Kornblum, *Blue Collar Community* (Chicago: University of Chicago Press, 1974); on Philadelphia, Peter Binzen, *Whitetown USA* (New York: Random House, 1970); on New York City, Jonathan Rieder, *Canarsie: The Jews and Italians of Brooklyn against Liberalism* (Cambridge, Mass.: Harvard University Press, 1985). See also William Kornblum and James Beshers, "White Ethnicity: Ecological Dimensions," in *Power, Culture, and Place*, 201–22.

16. Nick Buck and Norman Fainstein, "A Comparative History, 1880–1973," in *Divided Cities: New York and London in the Contemporary World*, ed. Susan S. Fainstein, Ian Gordon, and Michael Harloe (Cambridge, Mass.: Blackwell, 1992), 51–52.

17. New York City Planning Commission, *Plan for New York City*, 1:5.

18. Fainstein, Fainstein, and Schwartz, "Economic Shifts and Land Use in the Global City," 52.

19. New York City Planning Commission, *Plan for New York City*, 4:135, 140.

20. Ibid., 135–40.

21. Albert Murray questions Harlem's role in urban discourse as an exemplary ghetto in "Social Science Fiction in Harlem," a review of *Manchild in the Promised Land* and *Dark Ghetto, New Leader*, 17 January 1966, 20–23.

22. Charles N. Glaab and A. Theodore Brown, *A History of Urban America*, 3d ed. (New York: Macmillan, 1983), 337. Glaab and Brown support this assertion with quotations from Ralph Ellison and Claude Brown.

23. For more on Claude Brown's connection to the editors of *Dissent*, see chapter 12.

24. Ralph Ellison, "Harlem is Nowhere," in *Shadow and Act* (New York: Random House, 1964), 295–96, 298.

25. Wini Breines considers the emphasis of delinquency experts on delinquent boys, and the ways in which the study of delinquent youth "reproduced the male bias of work devoted to studying adults," in her essay "The 'Other' Fifties: Beats and Bad Girls," in *Not June Cleaver: Women and Gender in Postwar America, 1945–1960*, ed. Joanne Meyerowitz (Philadelphia: Temple University Press, 1994), 382–408.

26. See James Gilbert, *A Cycle of Outrage: America's Reaction to the Juvenile Delinquent in the 1950s* (New York: Oxford University Press, 1986), esp. chapter 7.

27. Gilbert, *Cycle of Outrage*, and Lewis Yablonsky, *The Violent Gang*, rev. ed. (Baltimore: Pelican Books, 1970), both trace connections between the delinquency panic of the 1950s and the "youth culture" crisis in the 1960s.

28. See Harrison Salisbury, *The Shook-Up Generation* (New York: Harper and Brothers, 1958).

29. Gilbert, *Cycle of Outrage*, 25.

30. Gilbert's *Cycle of Outrage*, esp. chapter 4, strenuously pursues this line of argument.

31. Jane Jacobs, *The Death and Life of Great American Cities* (New York: Random House, 1961), 47, 50.

32. Ibid., 30–31. Although Jacobs wrote before the urban crisis took mature shape, she presciently maps its generic social landscape. The staunchly Italian North End of Boston, an enclaved remnant of the industrial neighborhood order, serves as her ideal of the safe street. Her own block of Hudson Street in the West Village "works" because immigrant-ethnic small businessmen—recalling Majurcek, Sophie Majcinek's Division Street grocer-god, weighing virtue like sugar in the lost golden age—provide security for the negligent young office workers colonizing the block. Boston's black Roxbury section, the Morningside Heights area near Columbia University on the edge of Harlem, and various high-rise housing projects serve as her exemplary landscapes of fear. Despite her rejection of the categories of analysis that the urban crisis would elevate to canonical status, Jacobs's drawing of the distinction between safe streets and violent "slums" in her calculus of urban fear could be easily subsumed by the racial logic of urban crisis.

33. James Q. Wilson, *Thinking About Crime*, rev. ed. (New York: Random House, 1983), 14–15. The book was originally published in 1975.

34. Stuart Scheingold, *The Politics of Law and Order: Street Crime and Public Policy* (New York: Longman, 1984), xi.

35. Wilson, *Thinking About Crime*, 14.

36. See, e.g., Donald J. Mulvihill and Melvin M. Tumin, eds., *Crimes of Violence: A Staff Report Submitted to the National Commission on the Causes and Prevention of Violence* (Washington, D.C.: U.S. Government Printing Office, 1969). Other such efforts include Thomas Rose, ed., *Violence in America: A Historical and Contemporary Reader* (New York: Random House, 1969); Allen D. Grimshaw, ed., *Racial Violence in the United States* (Chicago: Aldine, 1969). For more on the Violence Commission in its historical moment, see Richard Slotkin, *Gunfighter Nation: The Myth of the Frontier in Twentieth-Century America* (New York: Atheneum, 1992), 555–60.

37. "Crime: Rising Tide," *Newsweek*, 16 August 1965, 20–21. For an extended reading of this issue of *Newsweek*, see my conclusion.

38. Ibid., 20.

39. For a useful discussion of the relation between violence in the streets and in political discourse since the mid-1960s, see Scheingold, *Politics of Law and Order*, and Stuart Scheingold, *The Politics of Street Crime: Criminal Process and Cultural Obsession* (Philadelphia: Temple University Press, 1991). See also Thomas E. Cronin, Tania Z. Cronin, and Michael Milakovich, *U.S. v. Crime in the Streets* (Bloomington: Indiana

University Press, 1981), esp. 5–10, on the "notoriously unreliable" UCR in the 1960s, and 15–18, on the role of representations in sustaining the notion of a crime wave.

40. Clark, *Dark Ghetto*, xiii–xiv.

41. *New York Herald-Tribune*, 25 January 1965, 6. The "New York City in Crisis" series was published later in 1965 in book form: Barry Gottehrer, *New York City in Crisis* (New York: David McKay, 1965).

42. For an account of Gottehrer's career, see Barry Gottehrer, *The Mayor's Man* (Garden City, N.Y.: Doubleday, 1975).

43. Richard Slotkin notes the parallels between press accounts of the fighting in Vietnam, especially during the struggle for the city of Hue during the Tet offensive of 1968, and the fighting in the streets of American cities during urban riots. See Slotkin, *Gunfighter Nation*, 549–54.

44. *New York Herald-Tribune*, 24 February 1965, 1, 10.

45. Ibid.

46. Warren Miller, "Teen-Ager in Trouble," review of Ira Henry Freeman, *Out of the Burning*, New York Times Book Review, 19 June 1960, 14.

47. *New York Herald-Tribune*, 25 January 1965, 6.

48. Ibid.

49. See, e.g., stories on rising crime (5, 10, 13, 16, and 18 February) and letters to the editor printed in the issues of 29 January and 5 February.

50. *New York Herald-Tribune*, 13 February 1965, 1.

51. *New York Herald-Tribune*, 5 February 1965, 7.

52. *New York Herald-Tribune*, 10 February 1965, 1, 11.

53. *New York Herald-Tribune*, 5 February 1965, 3.

54. Ralph Ellison, *Invisible Man* (New York: New American Library, 1952), 8.

55. Ibid., 7.

Chapter 10

1. "Death of an Author," 106–7.

2. Kefauver emphasizes this aspect of the Juvenile Delinquency Subcommittee's mission in his introduction to *Organized Crime in America*, ed. Gus Tyler (Ann Arbor: University of Michigan Press, 1962), xi–xii. Tyler confines his examination of delinquency to the street-corner society of inner-city gangs.

3. Salisbury, *Shook-Up Generation*, 73.

4. *Shook-Up Generation* constituted a departure for Salisbury, whose life's work was devoted to describing the world-historical encounter between East and West. The one book on delinquency stands out oddly among his many books on wars, revolutions, and the great powers, an anomaly that testifies to the seriousness with which many contemporary observers treated the subject. In *Cycle of Outrage*, Gilbert notes that a Roper opinion poll in 1959 "suggested that delinquency was viewed more seriously than open-air testing of atomic weapons or school segregation or political corruption" (63), although delinquency consistently ranked lower in similar Gallup polls during the 1950s.

5. Albert K. Cohen, *Delinquent Boys: The Culture of the Gang* (Glencoe, Ill.: Free Press, 1955), 32.

6. Richard Cloward and Lloyd E. Ohlin, *Delinquency and Opportunity: A Theory of Delinquent Gangs* (Glencoe, Ill.: Free Press, 1960).

7. By the early 1960s, both President Kennedy and his brother Robert, the attorney general, understood the problem of delinquency to have been subsumed by the problem of race. For the provenance of this change in the federal government's understanding of delinquency and response to it, see Nicholas Lemann, *The Promised Land: The Great Black Migration and How It Changed America* (New York: Alfred A. Knopf, 1991), 123–29. On the notorious Blackstone Rangers' role in poverty programs, see D. J. R. Bruckner, "Chicago Gang Inquiry Splits Daley, Negroes," *Los Angeles Times*, 15 July 1968, 1. See also Yablonsky, *Violent Gang*, 13–16.

8. See Fredric Wertham's classic assault on mass culture, *Seduction of the Innocent* (New York: Rinehart, 1954).

9. For more on the delinquent genres, see Wertham's *Seduction of the Innocent* and Gilbert's *Cycle of Outrage* (especially chapters 11 and 12). See also Miriam Linna, *Bad Seed* (Philadelphia: Running Press, 1992), a book of gorgeously sordid postcard reproductions of paperback delinquent novels' covers. A note appended to the introduction of *Bad Seed* (no page number) identifies Linna as editor of "a JD paperback collectors' publication" (also entitled *Bad Seed*) and owner of "the world's largest collection of juvenile delinquent paperbacks and related popular culture ephemera."

10. Gwendolyn Brooks, "We Real Cool" and "The Leaders," in *Blacks*, 331, 447–48.

11. Wakin, interview with Miller, 18.

12. Miller, *Cool World*, 150. Subsequent references in the text.

13. See, e.g., Richard Wright, *Native Son* (1940; reprint, New York: New American Library, 1950), 19 and 22, in which Bigger Thomas fantasizes about flying like a bird up and out of the social landscape defined by rail lines and streetcars. See also Farrell, *Studs Lonigan*, 86: Lonigan, having escaped his El-bounded neighborhood and entered Jackson Park, fantasizes about flying up and out of his Chicago to a place where he might live in a palace, have servants, and otherwise lead the kind of life that can exist only at some fantastic remove from the social landscape to which the novel brutally returns him.

14. Dan Wakefield, review of *Cool World*, *Nation*, 1 August 1959, 56.

15. James Baldwin, "War Lord of the Crocadiles," *New York Times Book Review*, 21 June 1959, 4.

16. Robert Gutwillig, "Keep Moving," *Commonweal*, 3 July 1959, 359.

17. Saul, "Deep Down, Out of the Sun," 18, 40.

18. See, e.g., ibid., 40, and James W. Byrd, review of *Cool World*, *Phylon* 21 (Winter 1960): 394–96.

19. "Jungle Book," *Time*, 15 June 1965, 94–95.

20. As late as 1964, a social scientist named Frank Reissman, author of *The Culturally Deprived Child*, argued in a speech to his academic colleagues at a conference on Urban Education and Cultural Deprivation that "providing teachers with sociological analyses of disadvantaged groups, while valuable, is not sufficient to develop deep interest and excitement. . . . Discussions around books like Warren Miller's *The Cool World*, and the movie made from it, are more helpful and stimulating than any anthropological text." Reissman's speech at the Syracuse University Conference on Urban Education and

Cultural Deprivation, July 15–16, 1964, quoted in Luther P. Jackson Jr., "Uncle Remus Again," *Negro History Bulletin* 28 (December 1964): 70–71.

21. For skeptical responses to Miller's rendering of Duke's voice, see, e.g., reviews of *Cool World* in *New Yorker*, 6 June 1959, 168, and in *New Statesman*, 31 October 1959, 596.

22. *New York Herald-Tribune*, 21 April 1966, 24.

23. Warren Miller, *The Siege of Harlem* (New York: McGraw-Hill, 1964), 15. Subsequent references in the text.

24. Grace Boggs and James Boggs, "The City Is the Black Man's Land," *Monthly Review* 17 (April 1966): 35–46; Eldridge Cleaver, "The Land Question," *Ramparts* 6 (May 1968): 51–53.

25. V. S. Pritchett, quoted in *New York 1960*, ed. Stern, Mellins, and Fishman, 864.

26. "Topical but Funny," *Time*, 14 August 1964, 68–69; Lindsay Patterson, "A New State Uptown," *Saturday Review*, 22 August 1964, 31–32; Joseph Epstein, "Topic Number One," *New Republic*, 5 September 1964, 26–29.

27. Wakin, interview with Miller, 18.

28. John O. Killens, "Remove Your Skin before Digging," *Book Week*, 23 August 1964, 8.

29. John O. Killens, "Explanation of the 'Black Psyche,'" *New York Times Magazine*, 7 June 1964, 37–38.

30. Killens, "Remove Your Skin before Digging," 5, 8.

31. Ibid.

32. Albert Murray, *The Omni-Americans: New Perspectives on Black Experience and American Culture* (New York: Outerbridge and Dienstfrey, 1970), 3.

33. Albert Murray, "Warren Miller and His Black Face Vaudeville," in *Omni-Americans*, 129. This review essay was originally published in 1964.

34. Ibid., 130.

35. Ibid., 132–33.

Chapter 11

1. Brown, *Manchild in the Promised Land*, 372. Subsequent references in the text.

2. Claude Brown told the story of his dealings with Macmillan in an interview with the author, 21 June 1993.

3. Piri Thomas traces his movement from delinquency through adult criminality to prison, conversion, reform, and social work in *Down These Mean Streets* (1967), *Savior, Savior, Hold My Hand* (1972), and *Seven Long Times* (1974).

4. Brown's and Dunmeyer's testimony, along with that of Ralph Ellison, is reproduced in its entirety in "Harlem's America," a special issue of *New Leader*, 26 September 1966.

5. *New Leader*, 26 September 1966, 4–21. Two years later, at the catastrophic Democratic national convention in Chicago, Ribicoff would have a famously acrimonious encounter with Mayor Richard J. Daley. In his speech nominating George McGovern for the party's presidential candidate, Ribicoff said, "If we had McGovern, we wouldn't have the Gestapo in the streets of Chicago." Daley, shouting from the convention floor, did not call Ribicoff "a beautiful cat"; at least one lip reader, having studied

footage of the episode, concluded that Daley said, "Fuck you, you Jew son of a bitch, you lousy motherfucker. Go home." Daley's apologists maintain he was saying "faker." See Royko, *Boss*, 188–89.

6. Claude Brown endeavors to explain the nuances of authentic "Colored English" in "The Language of Soul," *Esquire*, April 1968, 88.

7. Guy Daniels, "Claude Brown's World," *New Republic*, 25 September 1965, 26.

8. Norman Podhoretz, "Nobody Wants to Hear That Nonsense in Harlem," *New Republic*, 16 October 1965, 20.

9. Henry Louis Gates Jr., "Introduction: On Bearing Witness," in *Bearing Witness: Selections from African-American Autobiography in the Twentieth Century*, ed. Henry Louis Gates Jr. (New York: Random House, 1991), 3–5.

10. Clark, *Dark Ghetto*, xx–xxi, xv.

11. Lewis Killian and Charles Grigg, *Racial Crisis in America* (Englewood Cliffs, N.J.: Prentice Hall, 1964), 73, quoted in Ture [Carmichael] and Hamilton, *Black Power*, 61.

12. Brown, interview, 21 June 1993.

13. United States Commission on Civil Rights, *A Time to Listen . . . A Time to Act* (Washington, D.C.: U.S. Commission on Civil Rights, 1967), 1.

14. Brown discussed his rejection of the suggested glossary in interview, 21 June 1993.

15. Claude Brown has noted (interview, 21 June 1993) that during this period he also read Hal Ellson, one of the most popular writers of genre fiction about delinquents.

16. For a generic sample of contemporary and near-contemporary deghettoization narratives and conventional black success stories built around athletes, artists, political figures, professionals, and entrepreneurs, see Sammy Davis Jr. with Jane Boyar and Burt Boyar, *Yes I Can: The Story of Sammy Davis, Jr.* (New York: Farrar, Straus, Giroux, 1965); Arna Bontemps, *Famous Negro Athletes* (New York: Dodd, Mead, 1964); and a group of collections, appearing a few years later during the urban crisis, that gathered together widely circulated life stories: e.g., George R. Metcalfe, *Black Profiles* (New York: McGraw-Hill, 1968), Phillip T. Drotning and Wesley W. South, *Up from the Ghetto* (New York: Cowles, 1970), and James J. Flynn, *Negroes of Achievement in Modern America* (New York: Dodd, Mead, 1970).

17. Scenes very much like this one occur as well in the literature of juvenile delinquency. See, for instance, an almost identical incident in Ira Henry Freeman, *Out of the Burning* (1960; reprint, New York: Pocket Books, 1961), 20–21, in which the narrating protagonist's brother sends him back outside to fight the McClennon brothers.

18. See, for example, Peter Heller, "Floyd Patterson," "Archie Moore," and "Sugar Ray Robinson," in *"In This Corner . . . !": Forty World Champions Tell Their Stories* (New York: Simon and Schuster, 1973); Floyd Patterson with Milton Gross, *Victory over Myself* (New York: Random House, 1962); Archie Moore and Leonard B. Pearl, *Any Boy Can: The Archie Moore Story* (Englewood Cliffs, N.J.: Prentice Hall, 1971).

19. Black athletes in general and boxers in particular enjoyed a special representative status that gave their opinions of the urban crisis more weight than the opinions of professional athletes about social issues would ordinarily carry. Muhammad Ali regularly aired his views on the intertwined urban and racial crises and became a lightning rod for the views of others. Archie Moore wrote an open letter, reprinted and disseminated by the United States Information Agency, denouncing violence after the riots in

Detroit in 1967 (see Moore and Pearl, *Any Boy Can*, 2). Harlem's ruling clique in *Siege of Harlem* pokes fun at this elevation of black athletes and their coaches (typically white, especially in 1964) to the status of urban intellectual by pointing out that the inevitable panels convened to study the ghetto always include an ex-coach.

20. In 1984, Brown wrote a piece on Harlem's new generation of delinquents—"Manchild in Harlem," *New York Times Magazine*, 16 September 1984—in which he revealed that Turk was in fact Douglas Jones, a good heavyweight who reached a number two ranking, "was robbed of the decision" in a bout with the young Cassius Clay in 1963, and eventually retired from the ring and became "a liquor salesman who would like a different job" (36). (For a good account of the Jones-Clay bout, see A. J. Liebling, "Anti-Poetry Night," in *A Neutral Corner: Boxing Essays by A.J. Liebling*, ed. Fred Warner and James Barbour [San Francisco: North Point Press, 1990].) Having brought Turk's story up to date, Brown updates his own story: "I continue to write." A note accompanying the article states that Brown, "who teaches at City College, is finishing a book about the effects on urban America of a 30-odd-year heroin epidemic." At age forty-six, when fighters of his generation have their careers in the ring well behind them, the writer as firebrand plucked from out of the burning reminds us that he still has an inside story to tell about the second ghetto.

21. See, for example, Malcolm X, *Autobiography of Malcolm X* (New York: Grove, 1965); Kuwasi Balagoon, et al., *Look for Me in the Whirlwind: The Collective Autobiography of the New York Twenty-one* (New York: Random House, 1971); Eldridge Cleaver, *Soul on Ice* (New York: McGraw-Hill, 1968); Mwilini Abubadika, *The Education of Sonny Carson* (New York: Norton, 1972).

Chapter 12

1. Daniels, "Claude Brown's World," 26.

2. Mailer, Baldwin, and Schaap provided blurbs for the paperback edition; Howe apparently wrote a letter recommending the book to potential reviewers. Citations follow for those reviews of *Manchild* not cited elsewhere: Garry Wills, "In Defense of Uncle Toms," *Commonweal*, 12 November 1965, 178–80; Romulus Linney, "Growing Up the Hard Way," *New York Times Book Review*, 22 August 1965, 1; Daniel Aaron, "Out of the Closet," *New Statesman*, 5 August 1966, 204; Whitney Balliett, "Please, Mr. Goldberg," *New Yorker*, 13 November 1965, 242–44.

3. Warren Miller, "Teen-Ager in Trouble," *New York Times Book Review*, 19 June 1960, 14.

4. Miller, "One Score in Harlem," 49.

5. Miller, "Teen-Ager in Trouble," 14.

6. Raymond Schroth, "In the Promised Land," *America*, 28 August 1965, 213.

7. Ibid.

8. Tom Wolfe, "A Harlem Writer Who Makes James Baldwin Look Like a Tourist," *Sunday Herald-Tribune Magazine*, 18 July 1965, 4.

9. Ibid.

10. See, e.g., Sharon Malinowski, ed., *Black Writers: A Selection of Sketches from Contemporary Authors* (Detroit: Gale Research, 1994), 428–29; Elizabeth W. Miller and Mary L. Fisher, eds., *The Negro in America: A Bibliography,* 2d ed. (Cambridge, Mass.: Harvard University Press, 1970), 79–80.

11. President's Commission on Law Enforcement and Administration of Justice, *The Challenge of Crime in a Free Society* (Washington, D.C.: U.S. Government Printing Office, 1967), 60; Edward Banfield, *The Unheavenly City* (Boston: Little, Brown, 1970), 212.

12. Wolfe, "A Harlem Writer Who Makes James Baldwin Look Like a Tourist," 5; Brown, interview, 21 June 1993.

13. A prefatory note from "the Editors" on the inside front page (no page number) outlines the narrative of decline (*Dissent* 8 [Summer 1961]).

14. Herbert Slochower, "The Juvenile Delinquent and the Mythic Hero," *Dissent* 8 (Summer 1961): 417.

15. Michael Harrington, "Harlem Today," *Dissent* 8 (Summer 1961): 371.

16. Claude Brown, "Harlem, My Harlem," *Dissent* 8 (Summer 1961): 378.

17. Robert Nichols, "The City: A Poem," 219; Percival Goodman and Paul Goodman, "Banning Cars from Manhattan," 304; Daniel Bell, "The Three Faces of New York," 222; all in *Dissent* 8 (Summer 1961).

18. Brown, interview, 21 June 1993.

19. Miller, "One Score in Harlem," 49.

20. Nat Hentoff, "Sprung from the Alley, a Rare Cat," *Book Week*, 22 August 1965, 5.

21. Paul Goodman, "Growing Up Black," *New York Review of Books*, 26 August 1965, 8–10.

22. Brown, *Manchild in the Promised Land*, 87.

23. "Ghetto Graduate," *Economist*, 24 September 1966, 1259.

24. Miller, "One Score in Harlem," 49.

25. Warren Miller, "Author's Note," in *The Sleep of Reason* (Boston: Little, Brown, 1960), xiii. Miller explains that the manuscript was circulated to New York publishers while the Army-McCarthy hearings were being held, that no publisher would touch it, and that the novel was therefore first published in England.

26. Michael Stone's article "Three Lives" in *New York*, 30 January 1989, 35–42, casts Claude Brown in the role of founding father by featuring him as the oldest of three characters who together provide a generational portrait of New York's postwar ghettos. Brown (age fifty-one), Darryel Gordon (twenty-three, born the year of *Manchild*'s publication), and a baby named Lucy together "track the story of the city's slums" (35). For Brown, the elder statesman and prototypical "manchild," that story is a narrative of decline with which Nelson Algren (or Irving Howe, for that matter) would feel right at home: "During his childhood, Brown recalls, 'a lot of the older people used to say that the place was going to hell, but Harlem was in its innocence compared to today.' " Asked how he would "have fared growing up in the ghetto today," Brown readily responds (in the article's closing line), " ' I'd be dead' " (42).

27. Sapphire, *Push* (New York: Alfred A. Knopf, 1996), 3.

28. Brown, interview, 21 June 1993.

Conclusion

1. These credentials had great importance in the sense that they defined how Schulberg's authorial persona inhabited the city of feeling. Algren, for instance, recognized

Schulberg as a writer from Algren's literary neighborhood, with similar proclivities, expertise, and background, and Algren told his friends that he wanted to make money so he could back boxers as Schulberg had done and own race horses (see Shay, *Nelson Algren's Chicago*, xiv). (Schulberg had, in language highly derivative of Algren's, lauded *City on the Make* in the *New York Times Book Review*, 21 October 1951, 3.) But Schulberg was not some regular guy from the old neighborhood made good. His other set of credentials—a Deerfield and Dartmouth education, a Hollywood insider's childhood as the son of movie pioneer B. P. Schulberg—were of equal or greater importance in positioning him to become a published author and a successful writer of screenplays. This second set of credentials was on display in his Hollywood stories and in his first novel, *What Makes Sammy Run?* (1941).

2. Budd Schulberg, "Introduction," in *From the Ashes: Voices of Watts*, ed. Budd Schulberg (1967; reprint, Cleveland: World Publishing, 1969), 2.

3. Ibid., 2–3.

4. Ibid., 9.

5. Ibid., 2, 9.

6. "Crime: Rising Tide," 20.

7. Ibid., 21.

8. Ibid.

9. President's Commission on Law Enforcement and Administration of Justice, *Challenge of Crime in a Free Society*, 60.

10. "The Survivor," *Newsweek*, 16 August 1965, 81.

11. Nelson Algren, *Notes from a Sea-Diary: Hemingway All the Way* (New York: G. P. Putnam's Sons, 1965), 42. Subsequent references in the text.

12. "The Wildest Side," *Newsweek*, 16 August 1965, 81–82.

13. Algren, *Who Lost an American?* 285.

14. Algren's *Devil's Stocking* was first published as *Calhoun*, in Germany and in a German translation, in 1980.

15. Nelson Algren, "Hurricane Carter Awaits the Bell," *Los Angeles Times*, 28 July 1974, sec. CAL, 60.

16. For Algren on barroom murder, see "The Face on the Barroom Floor" in *Neon Wilderness*. Algren incorporated the short story into *Walk on the Wild Side*. For boxers, see *Never Come Morning*, as well as "Stickman's Laughter" in *Neon Wilderness*.

17. Rubin "Hurricane" Carter, *The Sixteenth Round: From Number One Contender to Number 45472* (New York: Viking, 1974), 131–32.

18. John Aldridge, "Two Realists from Chicago," *New York Times Book Review*, 9 October 1983, 9, 32–33.

19. Brown, interview, 21 June 1993.

20. *Manchild in the Promised Land* asserts that the Northern urban promised land has not delivered on its promise, but *Manchild* is not primarily a decline narrative. In it, Brown is more concerned with mapping a new, emergent order than with detailing the collapse of the old. In the 1980s and 1990s, though, Brown has developed the narrative of Harlem's decline from the knowable, if hard, world of his youth to a present state of incomprehensible chaos. See, for instance, "Manchild in Harlem," in which Brown describes his horror at seeing how a new generation of violent young men have transformed and been transformed by a Harlem he no longer knows. "Contrary to the

cliché," he is obliged to conclude, "the more things change in Harlem the worse they appear to get" (76). In 1989, Brown told an interviewer, "A lot of the older people used to say that the place was going to hell, but Harlem was in its innocence compared to today" (Stone, "Three Lives," 42). Brown recalls the Harlem of his youth as structured by a now-absent network of neighbors, teachers, and clergy. Asked how he would have fared growing up in today's Harlem, in the absence of that network, Brown says he would be dead. The decline narrative classically emphasizes such an absence of structure rather than the emergence of new ones, the passing of what was rather than the coming of what will be. In "Mean Streets," *New York Times Book Review*, 22 December 1996, 10–11, Brown's review of *Still Life in Harlem* by Eddy L. Harris, Brown explains that Harris "traces [Harlem's] decline" from "neighborhood" to "slum." There are, as I have asserted elsewhere in this study, more ways to say "There goes the neighborhood" than to say almost anything else about American urbanism in the second half of the twentieth century.

Index

Designer: Barbara Jellow
Compositor: David Peattie
Text: 10/12 Times Roman
Display: Helvetica
Printer and Binder: Haddon Craftsmen, Inc.